Microsoft®

Microsoft® Office Home and Student 2010

Step by Step

Joyce Cox
Joan Lambert
Curtis Frye

PUBLISHED BY
Microsoft Press
A Division of Microsoft Corporation
One Microsoft Way
Redmond, Washington 98052-6399

Copyright © 2010 by Online Training Solutions, Inc.

Library of Congress Control Number: 2010928519

ISBN: 978-0-7356-2721-5

3 4 5 6 7 8 9 10 11 12 QG 6 5 4 3 2 1

Printed and bound in the United States of America.

A CIP catalogue record for this book is available from the British Library.

Microsoft Press books are available through booksellers and distributors worldwide. For further information about international editions, contact your local Microsoft Corporation office or contact Microsoft Press International directly at fax (425) 936-7329. Visit our Web site at www.microsoft.com/mspress. Send comments to mspinput@microsoft.com.

Microsoft, Microsoft Press, Access, ActiveSync, ActiveX, Encarta, Excel, Georgia, InfoPath, Internet Explorer, OneNote, Outlook, PivotTable, PowerPoint, SharePoint, SkyDrive, SmartArt, Windows, Windows Live, Windows Media, Windows Mobile and Windows Vista are either registered trademarks or trademarks of the Microsoft group of companies. Other product and company names mentioned herein may be the trademarks of their respective owners.

The example companies, organizations, products, domain names, e-mail addresses, logos, people, places, and events depicted herein are fictitious. No association with any real company, organization, product, domain name, e-mail address, logo, person, place, or event is intended or should be inferred.

This book expresses the author's views and opinions. The information containe[d in this book is provided without] any express, statutory, or implied warranties. Neither the authors, Microsoft [Corporation, nor its resellers, or] distributors will be held liable for any damages caused or alleged to be cause[d either directly or indirectly by] this book.

Acquisitions Editor: Juliana Aldous
Developmental Editor: Devon Musgrave
Project Editor: Joel Panchot
Editorial Production: Online Training Solutions, Inc.
Cover: Girvin

Body Part No. X16-95577

Contents

Introducing Microsoft Office Home and Student 2010 xi

Modifying the Display of the Ribbon xiii

Features and Conventions of This Book xix

Using the Practice Files xxi

Your Companion eBook xxiv

Getting Help xxv

Part 1   Microsoft Office Home and Student 2010

1   Explore Office 2010   3

Working in the Program Environment 4

Changing Program Settings 17

Customizing the Ribbon 26

Customizing the Quick Access Toolbar 31

Key Points 35

2   Work with Files   37

Creating and Saving Files 38

    Sidebar: File Compatibility with Earlier Versions of Office Programs 44

Opening, Moving Around in, and Closing Files 46

Viewing Files in Different Ways 52

Key Points 60

What do you think of this book? We want to hear from you!

Microsoft is interested in hearing your feedback so we can continually improve our books and learning resources for you. To participate in a brief online survey, please visit:

microsoft.com/learning/booksurvey

Part 2   **Microsoft Word 2010**

3   Edit and Proofread Text   63

   Making Text Changes 64
      Sidebar: About the Clipboard 72
   Finding and Replacing Text 73
   Fine-Tuning Text 79
   Correcting Spelling and Grammatical Errors 87
      Sidebar: Viewing Document Statistics 93
   Inserting Saved Text 93
      Sidebar: Inserting One Document into Another. 97
   Key Points 97

4   Change the Look of Text   99

   Quickly Formatting Text. 100
   Changing a Document's Theme 106
   Manually Changing the Look of Characters 111
      Sidebar: Character Formatting and Case Considerations 119
   Manually Changing the Look of Paragraphs. 119
      Sidebar: Finding and Replacing Formatting 130
   Creating and Modifying Lists 130
      Sidebar: Formatting Text as You Type 136
   Key Points 137

5   Organize Information in Columns and Tables   139

   Presenting Information in Columns 140
   Creating Tabbed Lists 147
   Presenting Information in Tables 149
      Sidebar: Performing Calculations in Tables .158
      Sidebar: Other Layout Options 159
   Formatting Tables 160
      Sidebar: Quick Tables 164
   Key Points 165

6   Add Simple Graphic Elements   167

Inserting and Modifying Pictures 168

Sidebar: About Clip Art 174

Changing a Document's Background. 176

Inserting Building Blocks 183

Sidebar: Drawing Text Boxes 196

Adding WordArt Text 197

Sidebar: Formatting the First Letter of a Paragraph 202

Key Points 203

7   Preview, Print, and Distribute Documents   205

Previewing and Adjusting Page Layout. 206

Controlling What Appears on Each Page 212

Printing Documents 217

Preparing Documents for Electronic Distribution 219

Key Points 224

Part 3   Microsoft Excel 2010

8   Set Up a Workbook   227

Creating Workbooks. 228

Modifying Workbooks 233

Modifying Worksheets 237

Customizing the Excel 2010 Program Window 241

Zooming In on a Worksheet 242

Arranging Multiple Workbook Windows. 243

Adding Buttons to the Quick Access Toolbar .244

Customizing the Ribbon. 246

Maximizing Usable Space in the Program Window. 249

Key Points 253

9   Work with Data and Excel Tables   255

Entering and Revising Data 256

Moving Data Within a Workbook. 260

Finding and Replacing Data. 264

Correcting and Expanding Upon Worksheet Data .269

Defining Excel Tables 274

Key Points 279

10 Perform Calculations on Data   281

Naming Groups of Data 282
Creating Formulas to Calculate Values 286
Summarizing Data That Meets Specific Conditions 296
Finding and Correcting Errors in Calculations 300
Key Points 307

11 Change Workbook Appearance   309

Formatting Cells 310
Defining Styles 316
Applying Workbook Themes and Excel Table Styles 320
Making Numbers Easier to Read 327
Changing the Appearance of Data Based on Its Value .332
Adding Images to Worksheets 339
Key Points 345

12 Focus on Specific Data by Using Filters   347

Limiting Data That Appears on Your Screen 348
Manipulating Worksheet Data 354
    Selecting List Rows at Random 354
    Summarizing Worksheets with Hidden and Filtered Rows 355
    Finding Unique Values Within a Data Set 358
Defining Valid Sets of Values for Ranges of Cells 361
Key Points 367

Part 4 Microsoft PowerPoint 2010

13 Work with Slides   371

Adding and Deleting Slides 371
Adding Slides with Ready-Made Content 374
    Sidebar: Working with Slide Libraries 379
    Sidebar: Exporting Presentations as Outlines 380
Dividing Presentations into Sections 380
Rearranging Slides and Sections 384
Key Points 387

14   Work with Slide Text   389

Entering Text in Placeholders 390
Adding Text Boxes. 393
    Sidebar: Changing the Default Font for Text Boxes. 400
Editing Text. 400
    Sidebar: About the Clipboard 405
Correcting and Sizing Text While Typing. 406
Checking Spelling and Choosing the Best Words 412
    Sidebar: Researching Information and Translating Text 417
Finding and Replacing Text and Fonts. 418
Key Points 421

15   Format Slides   423

Applying Themes. 423
Using Different Color and Font Schemes 426
Changing the Slide Background 429
Changing the Look of Placeholders 433
Changing the Alignment, Spacing, Size, and Look of Text. 437
    Sidebar: Non–Color Scheme Colors. 444
Key Points 445

16   Add Simple Visual Enhancements   447

Inserting Pictures and Clip Art Images. 448
Inserting Diagrams 454
    Sidebar: Graphic Formats. 455
    Sidebar: Converting Existing Bullet Points into Diagrams. 462
Inserting Charts 462
Drawing Shapes. 470
    Sidebar: Connecting Shapes 478
Adding Transitions. 479
Key Points 483

17   Review and Deliver Presentations   **485**

Setting Up Presentations for Delivery 486

Previewing and Printing Presentations 491

Preparing Speaker Notes and Handouts 495

Sidebar: Enhanced Handouts 501

Finalizing Presentations 502

Sidebar: Setting Up Presenter View 508

Delivering Presentations 509

Key Points 512

Part 5   Microsoft OneNote 2010

18   Explore OneNote 2010   **515**

Navigating in the OneNote Program Window 516

Sidebar: Working with Multiple Notebooks 518

Working in the OneNote Program Window 519

Working from the Ribbon and Quick Access Toolbar 519

Working in the Backstage View 522

Exploring OneNote in the Default Notebook 526

Customizing OneNote 535

Key Points 537

19   Create and Configure Notebooks   **539**

Creating a Notebook for Use by One Person 540

Creating a Notebook for Use by Multiple People 543

Sharing a New or Existing Notebook 544

Managing a Shared Notebook 548

Creating Sections and Pages 550

Creating Pages and Subpages 551

Naming Sections and Pages 554

Creating Sections and Section Groups 555

Key Points 561

20 Create and Organize Notes

563

Working with Note Containers 564

Entering Content Directly onto a Page 565

Referencing External Files 565

Creating Handwritten Notes 567

Inserting Images 568

Formatting Notes, Pages, and Sections 569

Sidebar: Tagging Content. 578

Sending Content to OneNote 579

Collecting Screen Clippings 581

Collecting Web Notes. 583

Sidebar: Inserting the Date and Time. 584

Capturing Audio and Video Notes. 585

Sidebar: Missing the OneNote Icon? 590

Taking Notes on the Side. 591

Sidebar: Collecting Information Outside of OneNote. 593

Key Points 594

Glossary **595**

Index. **605**

About the Authors **640**

What do you think of this book? We want to hear from you!

Microsoft is interested in hearing your feedback so we can continually improve our books and learning resources for you. To participate in a brief online survey, please visit:

microsoft.com/learning/booksurvey

Introducing Microsoft Office Home and Student 2010

Microsoft Office 2010 is a comprehensive system of programs, servers, services, and solutions, including a dozen desktop productivity programs that you can install on your computer, and four new online program versions. To meet the varying needs of individuals and organizations, Microsoft offers five different Office 2010 software suites, each consisting of a different subset of programs. The following table identifies the programs available in each of the software suites.

	Office Home and Student 2010	Office Home and Business 2010	Office Standard 2010	Office Professional 2010	Office Professional Plus 2010
Access				Yes	Yes
Communicator					Yes
Excel	Yes	Yes	Yes	Yes	Yes
InfoPath					Yes
OneNote	Yes	Yes	Yes	Yes	Yes
Outlook		Yes	Yes	Yes	Outlook with Business Contact Manager
PowerPoint	Yes	Yes	Yes	Yes	Yes
Publisher			Yes	Yes	Yes
SharePoint Workspace					Yes
Word	Yes	Yes	Yes	Yes	Yes
Office Web Apps			Yes		Yes

Office Standard and Office Professional Plus are available only to volume licensing subscribers. The Office Web Apps, which are available with Office Standard and Office Professional Plus, and available to the general public through Windows Live, are online versions of Word, Excel, PowerPoint, and OneNote. You can store documents online and work with them from within any Web browser window by using the Office Web Apps.

This book provides instructional material for the following programs, which together form the Office Home and Student 2010 software suite:

- **Microsoft Word 2010** A word-processing program with which you can quickly and efficiently author and format documents.

- **Microsoft Excel 2010** A spreadsheet program with which you can analyze, communicate, and manage information.

- **Microsoft PowerPoint 2010** A program with which you can develop and present dynamic, professional-looking presentations.

- **Microsoft OneNote 2010** A digital notebook program in which you can collect and organize many types of electronic information, and quickly locate information when you need it.

The information in this book applies to these programs in all the software suites. If you have a software suite other than Office Home and Student, or if you installed one or more of these programs independently of a software suite, this is the right book for you.

Certification

Desktop computing proficiency is increasingly important in today's business world. When screening, hiring, and training employees, more employers are relying on the objectivity and consistency of technology certification to ensure the competence of their workforce. As an employee or job seeker, you can use technology certification to prove that you already have the skills you need to succeed. A Microsoft Office Specialist (MOS) is an individual who has demonstrated worldwide skill standards through a certification exam in one or more of the Office 2010 programs, including Microsoft Access, Excel, Outlook, PowerPoint, or Word. To learn more about the MOS program, visit the Microsoft Office Specialist Certification page at go.microsoft.com/fwlink/?LinkId=193884.

Let's Get Started!

Office 2010 includes new features, new functionality, and an easy-to-use interface intended to streamline your computing experience and make it easier to learn new programs. We're excited to bring you this glimpse into the inner workings of selected features in the core Office programs. We'll start with the basics and work into the most interesting and necessary features of each program. If you are an experienced Office user, you can skim Chapter 1, "Explore Office 2010," skip Chapter 2, "Work with Files," and jump right into the program-specific chapters.

Modifying the Display of the Ribbon

The goal of the Microsoft Office 2010 working environment is to make working with Office files—including Microsoft Word documents, Excel workbooks, PowerPoint presentations, Outlook e-mail messages, and Access databases—as intuitive as possible. You work with an Office file and its contents by giving commands to the program in which the document is open. All Office 2010 programs organize commands on a horizontal bar called the *ribbon*, which appears across the top of each program window whether or not there is an active document.

A typical program window ribbon.

Commands are organized on task-specific tabs of the ribbon and in feature-specific groups on each tab. Commands generally take the form of buttons and lists. Some appear in galleries in which you can choose from among multiple options. Some groups have related dialog boxes or task panes that contain additional commands.

Throughout this book, we discuss the commands and ribbon elements associated with the program feature being discussed. In this section, we discuss the general appearance of the ribbon, things that affect its appearance, and ways of locating commands that aren't visible on compact views of the ribbon.

See Also For detailed information about the ribbon, see "Working in the Program Environment" in Chapter 1, "Explore Office 2010."

Tip Some older commands no longer appear on the ribbon but are still available in the program. You can make these commands available by adding them to the Quick Access Toolbar. For more information, see "Customizing the Quick Access Toolbar" in Chapter 1, "Explore Office 2010."

Dynamic Ribbon Elements

The ribbon is dynamic, meaning that the appearance of commands on the ribbon changes as the width of the ribbon changes. A command might be displayed on the ribbon in the form of a large button, a small button, a small labeled button, or a list entry. As the width of the ribbon decreases, the size, shape, and presence of buttons on the ribbon adapt to the available space.

For example, when sufficient horizontal space is available, the buttons on the Review tab of the Word program window are spread out and you're able to see more of the commands available in each group.

The Review tab of the Word program window at 1024 pixels wide.

If you decrease the width of the ribbon, small button labels disappear and entire groups of buttons are hidden under one button that represents the group. Click the group button to display a list of the commands available in that group.

The Review tab of the Word program window at 675 pixels wide.

When the window becomes too narrow to display all the groups, a scroll arrow appears at its right end. Click the scroll arrow to display hidden groups.

The Review tab of the Word program window at 340 pixels wide.

Changing the Width of the Ribbon

The width of the ribbon is dependent on the horizontal space available to it, which depends on these three factors:

- **The width of the program window** Maximizing the program window provides the most space for ribbon elements. You can resize the program window by clicking the button in its upper-right corner or by dragging the border of a non-maximized window.

  On a computer running Windows 7, you can maximize the program window by dragging its title bar to the top of the screen.

- **Your screen resolution** Screen resolution is the amount of information your screen displays, expressed as *pixels wide by pixels high*. The greater the screen resolution, the greater the amount of information that will fit on one screen. Your screen resolution options are dependent on your monitor. At the time of writing, possible screen resolutions range from 800 × 600 to 2048 × 1152. In the case of the ribbon, the greater the number of pixels wide (the first number), the greater the number of buttons that can be shown on the ribbon, and the larger those buttons can be.

On a computer running Windows 7, you can change your screen resolution from the Screen Resolution window of Control Panel.

You set the resolution by dragging the pointer on the slider.

● **The density of your screen display** You might not be aware that you can change the magnification of everything that appears on your screen by changing the screen magnification setting in Windows. Setting your screen magnification to 125% makes text and user interface elements larger on screen. This increases the legibility of information, but it means that less information fits onto each screen.

On a computer running Windows 7, you can change the screen magnification from the Display window of Control Panel.

See Also For more information about display settings, refer to *Windows 7 Step by Step* (Microsoft Press, 2009), *Windows Vista Step by Step* (Microsoft Press, 2006), or *Windows XP Step by Step* (Microsoft Press, 2002) by Joan Lambert Preppernau and Joyce Cox.

You can choose one of the standard display magnification options or create another by setting a custom text size.

The screen magnification is directly related to the density of the text elements on screen, which is expressed in dots per inch (dpi) or points per inch (ppi). (The terms are interchangeable, and in fact are both used in the Windows dialog box in which you change the setting.) The greater the dpi, the larger the text and user interface elements appear on screen. By default, Windows displays text and screen elements at 96 dpi. Choosing the Medium - 125% display setting changes the dpi of text and screen elements to 120 dpi. You can choose a custom setting of up to 500 percent magnification, or 480 dpi, in the Custom DPI Setting dialog box.

You can choose a magnification of up to 200 percent from the lists or choose a greater magnification by dragging the ruler from left to right.

Adapting Exercise Steps

The screen images shown in the exercises in this book were captured at a screen resolution of 1024 × 768, at 100% magnification, and with the default text size (96 dpi). If any of your settings are different, the ribbon on your screen might not look the same as the one shown in the book. For example, you might see more or fewer buttons in each of the groups, the buttons you see might be represented by larger or smaller icons than those shown, or the group might be represented by a button that you click to display the group's commands.

When we instruct you to give a command from the ribbon in an exercise, we do it in this format:

● On the **Insert** tab, in the **Illustrations** group, click the **Chart** button.

If the command is in a list, we give the instruction in this format:

● On the **Page Layout** tab, in the **Page Setup** group, click the **Breaks** button and then, in the list, click **Page**.

The first time we instruct you to click a specific button in each exercise, we display an image of the button in the page margin to the left of the exercise step.

If differences between your display settings and ours cause a button on your screen to not appear as shown in the book, you can easily adapt the steps to locate the command. First, click the specified tab. Then locate the specified group. If a group has been collapsed into a group list or group button, click the list or button to display the group's commands. Finally, look for a button that features the same icon in a larger or smaller size than that shown in the book. If necessary, point to buttons in the group to display their names in ScreenTips.

If you prefer not to have to adapt the steps, set up your screen to match ours while you read and work through the exercises in the book.

Features and Conventions
of This Book

This book has been designed to lead you step by step through tasks you're likely to want to perform in Microsoft Word 2010, Excel 2010, PowerPoint 2010, and OneNote 2010. These four programs are available as part of the Microsoft Office Home and Student 2010 software suite.

See Also This book, *Microsoft Office Home and Student 2010 Step by Step*, includes a selection of instructional content for each program in the Office Home and Student 2010 software suite. For more complete coverage of the features of Word, Excel, or PowerPoint, refer to the corresponding program-specific *Step by Step* book.

Each chapter of this book includes self-contained topics that teach you about specific program features. Most topics conclude with a step-by-step exercise in which you practice using the program. The following features of this book will help you locate specific information:

- **Detailed table of contents** Scan the listing of the topics and sidebars within each chapter.

- **Chapter thumb tabs** Easily locate the beginning of each chapter by looking at the colored blocks on the odd-numbered pages.

- **Topic-specific running heads** Within a chapter, quickly locate a topic by looking at the running heads at the top of odd-numbered pages.

- **Glossary** Look up the meaning of a word or the definition of a concept.

- **Detailed index** Look up specific tasks and features in the index, which has been carefully crafted with the reader in mind.

You can save time when reading this book by understanding how the *Step by Step* series shows exercise instructions, keys to press, buttons to click, and other information. These conventions are listed in the table on the next page.

Convention	Meaning
SET UP	This paragraph preceding a step-by-step exercise indicates the practice files that you will use when working through the exercise. It also indicates any requirements you should attend to or actions you should take before beginning the exercise.
CLEAN UP	This paragraph following a step-by-step exercise provides instructions for saving and closing open files or programs before moving on to another topic. It also suggests ways to reverse any changes you made to your computer while working through the exercise.
1 2	Blue numbered steps guide you through hands-on exercises in each topic.
1 2	Black numbered steps guide you through procedures in sidebars and expository text.
See Also	This paragraph directs you to more information about a topic in this book or elsewhere.
Troubleshooting	This paragraph alerts you to a common problem and provides guidance for fixing it.
Tip	This paragraph provides a helpful hint or shortcut that makes working through a task easier.
Important	This paragraph points out information that you need to know to complete a procedure.
Keyboard Shortcut	This paragraph provides information about an available keyboard shortcut for the preceding task.
Key combinations	A plus sign (+) between two keys means that you must press those keys at the same time. For example, "Press Ctrl+B" means that you should hold down the Ctrl key while you press the B key.
🖫	Pictures of buttons appear in the margin the first time the button is used in an exercise.
Interface objects	In exercises that begin with SET UP information, the names of program elements, such as buttons, commands, windows, and dialog boxes, as well as files, folders, or text that you interact with in the steps, are shown in bold black type.
User input	In exercises that begin with SET UP information, text that you should type is shown in bold blue type.

Using the Practice Files

Before you can complete the exercises in this book, you need to copy the book's practice files to your computer. These practice files, and other information, can be downloaded from the book's detail page, located at:

http://go.microsoft.com/fwlink/?Linkid=192152

Display the detail page in your Web browser and follow the instructions for downloading the files.

Important The Office Home and Student 2010 software suite is not available from this Web page. You should purchase and install that software suite before using this book.

The following table lists the practice files for this book.

Chapter	File
Chapter 1: Explore Office 2010	None
Chapter 2: Work with Files	Prices_start.docx
	Procedures_start.docx
	Rules_start.docx
Chapter 3: Edit and Proofread Text	Bamboo_start.docx
	Brochure_start.docx
	Letter_start.docx
	Orientation_start.docx
	RulesRegulations_start.docx
Chapter 4: Change the Look of Text	AgendaA_start.docx
	AgendaB_start.docx
	Information_start.docx
	OrientationDraft_start.docx
	RulesDraft_start.docx
Chapter 5: Organize Information in Columns and Tables	ConsultationA_start.docx
	ConsultationB_start.docx
	RepairCosts_start.docx
	RoomPlanner_start.docx

Chapter	File
Chapter 6: Add Simple Graphic Elements	Announcement_start.docx
	Authors_start.docx
	Flyer_start.docx
	Joan.jpg
	Joyce.jpg
	MarbleFloor.jpg
	OTSI-Logo.png
Chapter 7: Preview, Print, and Distribute Documents	InfoSheetA_start.docx
	InfoSheetB_start.docx
	InfoSheetC_start.docx
	OfficeInfo_start.docx
Chapter 8: Set Up a Workbook	ExceptionSummary_start.xlsx
	ExceptionTracking_start.xlsx
	MisroutedPackages_start.xlsx
	PackageCounts_start.xlsx
	RouteVolume_start.xlsx
Chapter 9: Work with Data and Excel Tables	2010Q1ShipmentsByCategory_start.xlsx
	AverageDeliveries_start.xlsx
	DriverSortTimes_start.xlsx
	Series_start.xlsx
	ServiceLevels_start.xlsx
Chapter 10: Perform Calculations on Data	ConveyerBid_start.xlsx
	ITExpenses_start.xlsx
	PackagingCosts_start.xlsx
	VehicleMiles_start.xlsx
Chapter 11: Change Workbook Appearance	CallCenter_start.xlsx
	Dashboard_start.xlsx
	ExecutiveSearch_start.xlsx
	HourlyExceptions_start.xlsx
	HourlyTracking_start.xlsx
	Phone.jpg
	Texture.jpg
	VehicleMileSummary_start.xlsx

Chapter	File
Chapter 12: Focus on Specific Data by Using Filters	Credit_start.xlsx ForFollowUp_start.xlsx PackageExceptions_start.xlsx
Chapter 13: Work with Slides	Projects.pptx ServiceA_start.pptx ServiceB_start.pptx ServiceC_start.pptx ServiceD_start.pptx ServiceOrientation.docx
Chapter 14: Work with Slide Text	BuyingTripsB_start.pptx BuyingTripsC_start.pptx CommunityServiceA_start.pptx CommunityServiceB_start.pptx CommunityServiceC_start.pptx
Chapter 15: Format Slides	BusinessTravelA_start.pptx BusinessTravelB_start.pptx ColorDesign_start.pptx CompanyMeetingA_start.pptx CompanyMeetingB_start.pptx LandscapingA_start.pptx
Chapter 16: Add Simple Visual Enhancements	Agastache.jpg JournalingA_start.pptx JournalingB_start.pptx Penstemon.jpg WaterConsumption.xlsx WaterSavingA_start.pptx WaterSavingB_start.pptx WaterSavingC_start.pptx
Chapter 17: Review and Deliver Presentations	Harmony_start.pptx Meeting_start.pptx SavingWater_start.pptx ServiceOrientationA_start.pptx ServiceOrientationB_start.pptx YinYang.png

Chapter	File
Chapter 18: Explore OneNote 2010	None
Chapter 19: Create and Configure Notebooks	None
Chapter 20: Create and Organize Notes	SBS Content Entry folder ADatumLogo.png Cabo.jpg California_Poppy.jpg Desert.jpg Landscaping.pptx

Your Companion eBook

The eBook edition of this book allows you to:

- Search the full text
- Print
- Copy and paste

To download your eBook, please see the instruction page at the back of this book.

Getting Help

Every effort has been made to ensure the accuracy of this book. If you do experience problems, please consult the sources listed in the following sections.

Getting Help with This Book

If your question or issue concerns the content of this book or its practice files, please first consult the book's errata page, which can be accessed at:

http://go.microsoft.com/fwlink/?Linkid=192152

This page provides information about known errors and corrections to the book. If you do not find your answer on the errata page, send your question or comment to Microsoft Press Technical Support at:

mspinput@microsoft.com

Getting Help with Office 2010

If your question is about one of the programs in the Microsoft Office Home and Student 2010 software suite, and not about the content of this book, your first recourse is the Help system for the individual program. This system is a combination of tools and files stored on your computer when you installed the software suite or program and, if your computer is connected to the Internet, information available from the Microsoft Office Online Web site. You can find Help information in the following ways:

- To find out about an item on the screen, you can display a ScreenTip. For example, to display a ScreenTip for a button, point to the button without clicking it. The ScreenTip gives the button's name, the associated keyboard shortcut if there is one, and a description of what the button does when you click it.

- In the program window, you can click the Help button (a question mark in a blue circle) at the right end of the ribbon to display the program-specific Help window.

- After opening a dialog box, you can click the Help button (also a question mark) at the right end of the dialog box title bar to display the program-specific Help window. Sometimes, topics related to the functions of that dialog box are already identified in the window.

To practice getting help, you can work through the following exercise.

 SET UP You don't need any practice files to complete this exercise. Start Word, and then follow the steps.

1. At the right end of the ribbon, click the **Microsoft Word Help** button.

   The Word Help window opens.

You can change the size of the font in the window by clicking the Change Font Size button on the toolbar.

If you are connected to the Internet, clicking any of the buttons below the Microsoft Office banner (Products, Support, Images, and Templates) takes you to a corresponding page of the Office Web site.

2. Below the bulleted list under **Browse Word 2010 support**, click **see all**.

The window changes to display a list of Help topics.

3. In the list of topics, click **Activating Word**.

Word Help displays a list of topics related to activating Microsoft Office programs. You can click any topic to display the corresponding information.

4. On the toolbar, click the **Show Table of Contents** button.

The window expands to accommodate two panes. The Table Of Contents pane appears on the left. Like the table of contents in a book, it is organized in sections.

If you're connected to the Internet, Word displays sections, topics, and training available from the Office Online Web site as well as those stored on your computer.

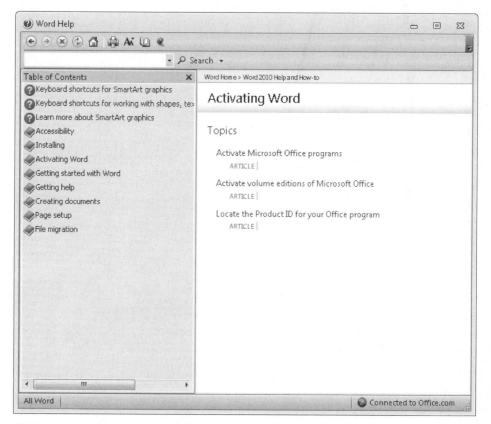

Clicking any section (represented by a book icon) displays that section's topics (represented by Help icons).

5. In the **Table of Contents** pane, click a few sections and topics. Then click the **Back** and **Forward** buttons to move among the topics you have already viewed.

6. At the right end of the **Table of Contents** title bar, click the **Close** button.

7. At the top of the **Word Help** window, click the **Type words to search for** box, type saving, and then press the Enter key.

The Word Help window displays topics related to the word you typed.

Next and Back buttons appear, making it easier to search for the topic you want.

8. In the results list, click the **Recover earlier versions of a file in Office 2010** topic.

   The selected topic appears in the Word Help window.

9. Below the title at the top of the topic, click **Show All**.

   Word displays any information that has been collapsed under a heading and changes the Show All button to Hide All. You can jump to related information by clicking hyperlinks identified by blue text.

   Tip You can click the Print button on the toolbar to print a topic. Only the displayed information is printed.

✖ CLEAN UP Click the Close button at the right end of the Word Help window.

More Information

If your question is about an Office 2010 program or another Microsoft software product and you cannot find the answer in the product's Help system, please search the appropriate product solution center or the Microsoft Knowledge Base at:

support.microsoft.com

In the United States, Microsoft software product support issues not covered by the Microsoft Knowledge Base are addressed by Microsoft Product Support Services. Location-specific software support options are available from:

support.microsoft.com/gp/selfoverview/

Part 1

Microsoft Office Home and Student 2010

1 Explore Office 2010. 3

2 Work with Files 37

Chapter at a Glance

Work in the program environment, **page 4**

Change program settings, **page 17**

Customize the ribbon, **page 26**

Customize the Quick Access Toolbar, **page 31**

1 Explore Office 2010

In this chapter, you will learn how to

- ✔ Work in the program environment.
- ✔ Change program settings.
- ✔ Customize the ribbon.
- ✔ Customize the Quick Access Toolbar.

Microsoft Office 2010 programs have a common user interface—the way the program looks and the way you interact with it—which means that skills and techniques you learn in one program are also useful in the others.

Certain information that you provide in one Office 2010 program is made available to other Office 2010 programs so that you don't have to provide it individually in each program. Other settings are specific to the program you're working in. The basic Office 2010 user interface includes a standard method of giving commands by using tools gathered on a dynamic toolbar, called the ribbon. Commands are represented by buttons, by lists or galleries from which you choose settings, or by fields in task panes and dialog boxes in which you specify settings. You can customize some of the content that is available from the ribbon by hiding sets of commands (tabs) or by creating custom tabs. You can also collect frequently used buttons, lists, and galleries on a separate toolbar, the Quick Access Toolbar, so that they are available to you from anywhere in the program.

Each program has standard settings based on the way that most people work with the program. However, you can customize the settings to meet your specific needs and to fit the way that you work.

In this chapter, you'll first familiarize yourself with the standard Office 2010 program working environment. Then you'll customize the working environment, ribbon, and Quick Access Toolbar in Microsoft Word 2010, using techniques that are common to working in any Office 2010 program.

> **Practice Files** You don't need any practice files to complete the exercises in this chapter. For more information about practice file requirements, see "Using the Practice Files" at the beginning of this book.

Working in the Program Environment

The most common way to start any Office 2010 program is from the Start menu, displayed when you click the Start button at the left end of the Windows Taskbar. On the Start menu, click All Programs, click the Microsoft Office folder, and then click the program you want to start.

When you start Microsoft Word, Excel, or PowerPoint without opening a specific file, the program window appears, displaying a new blank document, workbook, or presentation. When you start Microsoft OneNote without opening a specific notebook, the program window displays the notebook you opened most recently.

The Word 2010 program window.

See Also Windows 7 introduced many efficient new window-management techniques. For information about ways to work with a program window on a Windows 7 computer, refer to *Windows 7 Step by Step* by Joan Lambert Preppernau and Joyce Cox (Microsoft Press, 2009).

A typical Office 2010 program window contains the following elements:

● The title bar displays the name of the active document. At the left end of the title bar is the program icon, which you click to display commands to move, size, and close the program window. Three buttons at the right end of the title bar serve the same functions in all Windows programs: You can temporarily hide the program window by clicking the Minimize button, adjust the size of the window by clicking the Restore Down/Maximize button, and close the active document or exit the program by clicking the Close button.

Maximize

Minimize ——————— Close

The default buttons on the Quick Access Toolbar in the Excel program window.

● By default, the Quick Access Toolbar appears to the right of the program icon at the left end of the title bar. Each program has a default set of Quick Access Toolbar buttons; most commonly, the default Quick Access Toolbar displays the Save, Undo, and Redo buttons. You can change the location of the Quick Access Toolbar and customize it to include any command to which you want to have easy access.

The default buttons on the Quick Access Toolbar in the Excel program window.

● Below the title bar is the ribbon. All the commands for working with file content are available from this central location so that you can work efficiently with the program.

Dialog box launcher   Tabs   Groups

The ribbon in the PowerPoint program window.

See Also The appearance of buttons and groups on the ribbon changes depending on the width of the program window. For information about changing the appearance of the ribbon to match our images, see "Modifying the Display of the Ribbon" at the beginning of this book.

● Across the top of the ribbon is a set of tabs. Clicking a tab displays an associated set of commands.

Tip You might find it efficient to add all the commands you use frequently to the Quick Access Toolbar and display it below the ribbon, directly above the workspace. For information, see "Customizing the Quick Access Toolbar" later in this chapter.

● Commands related to managing the program and files (rather than file content) are gathered together in the Backstage view, which you display by clicking the colored File tab located at the left end of the ribbon. Commands available in the Backstage view are organized on named pages, which you display by clicking the page tabs located in the left pane.

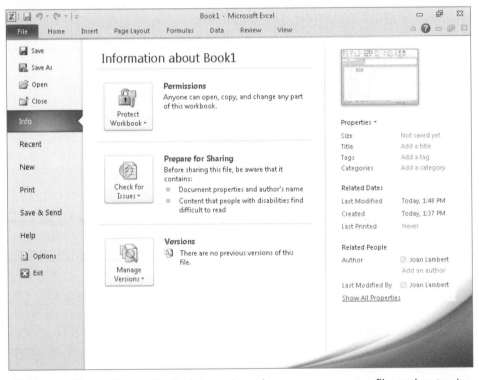

Clicking the File tab displays the Backstage view, where you can manage files and customize the program.

● Commands related to working with file content are represented as buttons on the remaining tabs. The Home tab is active by default.

Tip Don't be alarmed if your ribbon has tabs not shown in our screens. You might have installed programs that add their own tabs to the ribbon.

● On each tab, buttons are organized into named groups. Depending on your screen resolution and the size of the program window, the commands in a group might be displayed as labeled buttons, as unlabeled icons, or as one or more large buttons that you click to display the commands within the group. You might want to experiment with the screen resolution and width of the program window to understand their effect on the appearance of tab content.

● If a button label isn't visible, you can display the command, a description of its function, and its keyboard shortcut (if it has one) in a ScreenTip by pointing to the button.

ScreenTips can include the command name, description, and keyboard shortcut.

Tip You can control the display of ScreenTips and of feature descriptions in ScreenTips. Simply display the Backstage view, click Options to open the program's Options dialog box, and click the ScreenTip setting you want in the User Interface Options area of the General page. For more information, see "Changing Program Settings" later in this chapter.

● Related but less common commands might be available in a dialog box or task pane, which you display by clicking the dialog box launcher located in the lower-right corner of the group.

Tip You might find that less commonly used commands from earlier versions of a program are not available from the ribbon. However, these commands are still available. You can make missing commands accessible by adding them to the Quick Access Toolbar. For more information, see "Customizing the Quick Access Toolbar" later in this chapter.

- Some buttons include an integrated or separate arrow. To determine whether a button and arrow are integrated, point to the button or arrow to display its border. If a button and its arrow are integrated within one border, clicking the button will display options for refining the action of the button. If the button and arrow have separate borders, clicking the button will carry out the default action indicated by the button's current icon. You can change the default action of the button by clicking the arrow and then clicking the action you want.

The arrow of the Change Styles button is integrated, and the arrow of the Paste button is separate.

- Above the right end of the ribbon is the Minimize The Ribbon button. Clicking this button hides the commands but leaves the tab names visible. You can then click any tab name to temporarily display its commands. Clicking anywhere other than the ribbon hides the commands again. When the full ribbon is temporarily visible, you can click the button at its right end, shaped like a pushpin, to make the display permanent. When the full ribbon is hidden, you can click the Expand The Ribbon button to redisplay it.

  Keyboard Shortcut Press Ctrl+F1 to minimize or expand the ribbon.

- Clicking the Help button at the right end of the ribbon displays the program-specific Help window in which you can use standard techniques to find information.

  Keyboard Shortcut Press F1 to display the Help window for the active program.

  See Also For information about the Help system, see "Getting Help" at the beginning of this book.

- Across the bottom of the program window, the status bar displays information about the current file and provides access to certain program functions. You can control the contents of the status bar by right-clicking it to display the Customize Status Bar menu, on which you can click any item to display or hide it.

Customize Status Bar		
	Formatted Page Number	6
	Section	1
✓	Page Number	6 of 19
	Vertical Page Position	3.5"
	Line Number	11
	Column	45
✓	Word Count	6,351
✓	Number of Authors Editing	
✓	Spelling and Grammar Check	Errors
✓	Language	
✓	Signatures	Off
✓	Information Management Policy	Off
✓	Permissions	Off
	Track Changes	Off
	Caps Lock	Off
	Overtype	Insert
	Selection Mode	
✓	Macro Recording	Not Recording
✓	Upload Status	
✓	Document Updates Available	No
✓	View Shortcuts	
✓	Zoom	120%
✓	Zoom Slider	

You can specify which items you want to display on the status bar.

● At the right end of the status bar in the Word, Excel, and PowerPoint program windows are the View Shortcuts toolbar, the Zoom button, and the Zoom slider. These tools provide you with convenient methods for adjusting the display of file content.

View Shortcuts toolbar

Zoom button

Zoom slider

You can change the file content view by clicking buttons on the View Shortcuts toolbar and change the magnification by clicking the Zoom button or adjusting the Zoom slider.

See Also For information about changing the file content view, see "Viewing Files in Different Ways" in Chapter 2, "Work with Files."

The goal of all these features of the program environment is to make working in the program as intuitive as possible. Commands for tasks you perform often are readily available, and even those you might use infrequently are easy to find.

For example, when a formatting option has several choices available, they are often displayed in a gallery of thumbnails. These thumbnails display visual representations of each choice. If you point to a thumbnail in a gallery, the Live Preview feature shows you what that choice will look like if you apply it to the selected content.

Live Preview shows the effect on the selected content of clicking the option you are pointing to.

In this exercise, you'll start Word and explore the tabs and groups on the ribbon. Along the way, you'll work with galleries and the Live Preview feature.

SET UP You don't need any practice files to complete this exercise; just follow the steps.

1. On the **Start** menu, click **All Programs**, click **Microsoft Office**, and then click **Microsoft Word 2010**.

   Tip If this is the first time you've started an Office 2010 program, Office prompts you to enter your full name and initials. Office 2010 programs use this information when tracking changes, responding to messages, and so on. Next, Office prompts you to select the type of information you want to share over the Internet, and offers the option of signing up for automatic program updates from the Microsoft Update service. None of these options place you at risk, and all can be quite useful.

   The Word program window opens in Print Layout view, displaying a blank document. On the ribbon, the Home tab is active. Buttons related to working with document content are organized on this tab in five groups: Clipboard, Font, Paragraph, Styles, and Editing.

2. Point to each button on the **Home** tab.

   Word displays information about the button in a ScreenTip.

The ScreenTip for the Format Painter button displays the button's name, keyboard shortcut, and function.

Tip A button representing a command that cannot be performed on the selected file content is inactive (gray), but pointing to it still displays its ScreenTip.

3. Click the **Insert** tab, and then explore its buttons.

Buttons related to all the items you can insert into the document are organized on this tab in seven groups: Pages, Tables, Illustrations, Links, Header & Footer, Text, and Symbols.

The Insert tab of the ribbon.

4. Click the **Page Layout** tab, and then explore its buttons.

Buttons related to the appearance of the document are organized on this tab in five groups: Themes, Page Setup, Page Background, Paragraph, and Arrange.

The Page Layout tab of the ribbon.

5. In the **Page Setup** group, display the ScreenTip for the **Margins** button.

   The ScreenTip tells you how you can adjust the margins.

6. In the lower-right corner of the **Page Setup** group, click the **Page Setup** dialog box launcher.

   The Page Setup dialog box opens.

In the Page Setup dialog box, you can specify several page layout options in one location.

   Notice that you can preview the results of your changes before applying them.

7. Click **Cancel** to close the dialog box.

8. In the **Themes** group, click the **Themes** button.

   The group expands to display a gallery of the available themes.

The theme controls the color scheme, fonts, and special effects applied to file content.

9. Press the Esc key to close the gallery without making a selection.

10. In the **Page Background** group, click the **Page Color** button, and then in the top row of the **Theme Colors** palette, point to each box in turn.

    The blank document page shows a live preview of what it will look like if you click the color you are pointing to. You can see the effect of the selection without actually applying it.

11. Press Esc to close the palette without making a selection.

12. Click the **References** tab, and then explore its buttons.

    Buttons related to items you can add to documents are organized on this tab in six groups: Table Of Contents, Footnotes, Citations & Bibliography, Captions, Index, and Table Of Authorities. You will usually add these items to longer documents, such as reports.

The References tab of the ribbon.

13. Click the **Mailings** tab, and then explore its buttons.

    Buttons related to creating mass mailings are organized on this tab in five groups: Create, Start Mail Merge, Write & Insert Fields, Preview Results, and Finish.

The Mailings tab of the ribbon.

14. Click the **Review** tab, and then explore its buttons.

    Buttons related to proofreading documents, working in other languages, adding comments, tracking and resolving document changes, and protecting documents are organized on this tab in seven groups: Proofing, Language, Comments, Tracking, Changes, Compare, and Protect.

The Review tab of the ribbon.

15. Click the **View** tab, and then explore its buttons.

    Buttons related to changing the view and other aspects of the display are organized on this tab in five groups: Document Views, Show, Zoom, Window, and Macros.

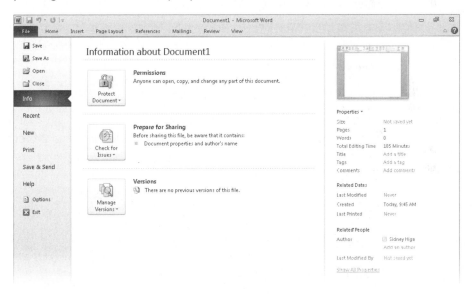

The View tab of the ribbon.

16. On the ribbon, click the **File** tab, which is color-coded to match the logo color of the Word program.

    The Backstage view of Word 2010 is displayed. Commands related to managing documents (such as creating, saving, and printing) are available in this view.

17. If the **Info** page is not already displayed in the Backstage view, click **Info** in the left pane.

    On the Info page of the Backstage view, the middle pane provides options to control who can work on the document, to remove properties (associated information), and to access versions of the document automatically saved by Word. The right pane displays the associated properties, as well as dates of modification, creation, and printing, and the names of people who created and edited the document.

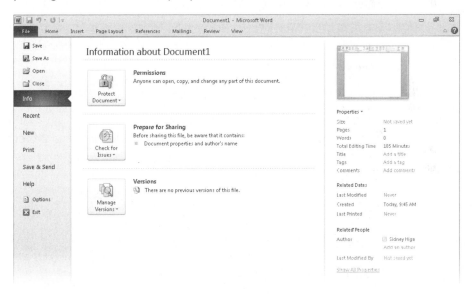

The Info page displays and provides commands for changing the information attached to a document.

See Also For information about working with properties, see "Preparing Documents for Electronic Distribution" in Chapter 7, "Preview, Print, and Distribute Documents."

18. In the left pane, click **Recent**.

    The Recent page displays the names of the documents you recently worked on. By default a maximum of 20 names is displayed. You can change this number on the Advanced page of the Word Options dialog box.

    See Also For information about the Options dialog box, see "Changing Program Settings" later in this chapter.

19. In the left pane, click **New**.

    The New page displays all the templates on which you can base a new document.

    See Also For information about creating documents, see "Creating and Saving Files" in Chapter 2, "Work with Files."

20. In the left pane, click **Print**.

    The Print page displays all print-related commands and provides a pane for previewing the current document as it will appear when printed.

    See Also For information about printing, see Chapter 7, "Preview, Print, and Distribute Documents."

21. In the left pane, click **Share**.

    The Share page displays all the commands related to making the current document available to other people.

    See Also For information about working with shared documents, refer to *Microsoft Word 2010 Step by Step* by Joyce Cox and Joan Lambert (Microsoft Press, 2010).

22. In the left pane, click **Help**.

    The Help page displays all the ways you can get help and support for Word.

The right pane of the Help page displays your Office edition, its version number, and your product ID, which you will need if you contact Microsoft Product Support.

23. On the **Help** page, under **Tools for Working With Office**, click **Options**.

    The Word Options dialog box opens. In this dialog box are program settings that control the way the program looks and performs.

Word Options	? ☒

General options for working with Word.

User Interface options

- ☑ Show Mini Toolbar on selection ⓘ
- ☑ Enable Live Preview ⓘ

Color scheme: Silver ▾

ScreenTip style: Show feature descriptions in ScreenTips ▾

Personalize your copy of Microsoft Office

User name: Sidney Higa

Initials: SH

Start up options

- ☐ Open e-mail attachments in Full Screen Reading view ⓘ

General | Display | Proofing | Save | Language | Advanced | Customize Ribbon | Quick Access Toolbar | Add-Ins | Trust Center

OK | Cancel

You can also display this dialog box by clicking Options in the left pane of the Backstage view.

See Also For information about the Options dialog box, see "Changing Program Settings" later in this chapter.

24. At the bottom of the **Word Options** dialog box, click **Cancel**.

    You return to the blank document with the Home tab active on the ribbon.

 CLEAN UP Leave the blank document open if you're continuing directly to the next exercise.

Changing Program Settings

Earlier in this chapter, we mentioned that you can change settings in the Options dialog box for each program to customize the program environment in various ways. After you work with a program for a while, you might want to refine more settings to tailor the program to the way you work. Knowing your way around the Options dialog box makes the customizing process more efficient.

In this exercise, you'll open the Word Options dialog box and explore several of the available pages.

→ **SET UP** You don't need any practice files to complete this exercise. Open a blank document if necessary, and then follow the steps.

1. On the **Home** tab, in the **Font** group, point to the **Bold** button.

   Word displays a ScreenTip that includes the button name, its keyboard shortcut, and a description of its purpose.

2. Display the Backstage view, and click **Options**.

   The Word Options dialog box opens, displaying the General page.

Word Options	? ✕
General	General options for working with Word.
Display	
Proofing	**User Interface options**
Save	☑ Show Mini Toolbar on selection ⓘ
Language	☑ Enable Live Preview ⓘ
Advanced	Color scheme: Silver ▾
Customize Ribbon	ScreenTip style: Show feature descriptions in ScreenTips ▾
Quick Access Toolbar	**Personalize your copy of Microsoft Office**
Add-Ins	User name: Joan Lambert
Trust Center	Initials: JL
	Start up options
	☐ Open e-mail attachments in Full Screen Reading view ⓘ

The General page of the Word Options dialog box.

If you prefer not to see the Mini Toolbar when you select text, you can disable that feature by clearing the Show Mini Toolbar On Selection check box. Similarly, you can disable the live preview of styles and formatting by clearing the Enable Live Preview check box.

3. Under **User Interface options**, display the **Color scheme** list, and click **Black**.

4. Display the **ScreenTip style** list, and click **Don't show feature descriptions in ScreenTips**.

5. Under **Personalize your copy of Microsoft Office**, verify that the **User Name** and **Initials** are correct, or change them to the way you want them to appear.

6. Click **OK** to close the **Word Options** dialog box.

   The program window elements are now black and shades of gray.

7. In the **Font** group, point to the **Bold** button.

   The ScreenTip now includes only the button name and its keyboard shortcut.

8. Open the **Word Options** dialog box, and in the left pane, click **Display**.

   On this page, you can adjust how documents look on the screen and when printed.

Word Options		? ✕
General	⌕ Change how document content is displayed on the screen and when printed.	
Display		
Proofing	**Page display options**	
Save	☐ Show white space between pages in Print Layout view ⓘ	
Language	☑ Show highlighter marks ⓘ	
Advanced	☑ Show document tooltips on hover	
	Always show these formatting marks on the screen	
Customize Ribbon	☐ Tab characters →	
Quick Access Toolbar	☐ Spaces ⋯	
Add-Ins	☐ Paragraph marks ¶	
Trust Center	☐ Hidden text ª͟b͟c͟	
	☐ Optional hyphens ¬	
	☐ Object anchors ⚓	
	☐ Show all formatting marks	
	Printing options	
	☑ Print drawings created in Word ⓘ	
	☐ Print background colors and images	
	☐ Print document properties	
	☐ Print hidden text	
	☐ Update fields before printing	
	☐ Update linked data before printing	

The Display page of the Word Options dialog box.

9. In the left pane, click **Proofing**.

   This page provides options for adjusting the AutoCorrect settings and for refining the spelling-checking and grammar-checking processes.

   See Also For information about AutoCorrect and checking spelling, see "Correcting Spelling and Grammatical Errors" in Chapter 3, "Edit and Proofread Text."

The Proofing page of the Word Options dialog box.

10. Display the **Save** page.

    On this page, you can change the default document format; the location and save frequency of the AutoRecover file (a backup file created by Word while you're working in the file); the default location to which Word saves files you create; and the default location for files you check out from document management servers (such as Microsoft SharePoint) and drafts of those files saved while you are working offline.

The Save page of the Word Options dialog box.

The Save page also has options for specifying whether you want the fonts used within the current document to be embedded in the document, in the event that someone who opens the document doesn't have those fonts on his or her computer.

11. Under **Save documents**, display the **Save files in this format** list.

Notice the many formats in which you can save files. One of these is the Word 97-2003 Document format that creates .doc files compatible with earlier versions of Word. If you upgraded to Word 2010 but your colleagues are still working in an earlier version of the program, you might want to select this option so that they will be able to view and work with any document you create.

Tip If you want to save just one document in a format that is compatible with earlier versions of the program, you can click Word 97-2003 in the Save As Type list of the Save As dialog box.

12. Click away from the list to close it, and then display the **Language** page.

If you create documents for international audiences, you can make additional editing languages available on this page. You can also specify the display, Help, and ScreenTip languages.

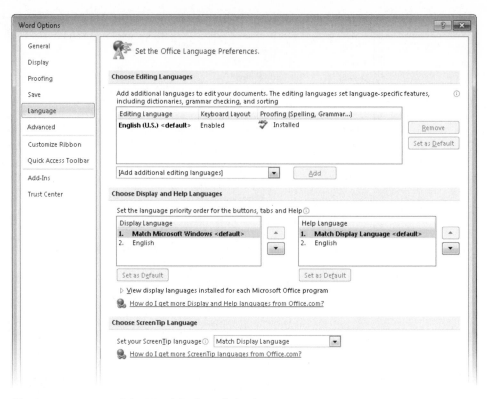

The Language page of the Word Options dialog box.

13. Display the **Advanced** page.

This page includes options related to editing document content; displaying documents on-screen; printing, saving, and sharing documents; and a variety of other options. Although these options are labeled *Advanced*, they are the ones you're most likely to want to adjust to suit the way you work.

See Also For information about advanced Word 2010 options that aren't discussed in this book, refer to *Microsoft Word 2010 Step by Step* by Joyce Cox and Joan Lambert (Microsoft Press, 2010).

The Advanced page of the Word Options dialog box.

14. Take a few minutes to explore all the options on this page.

    In the General area at the bottom of the page are two buttons:

    ○ **File Locations** You click this button to change the default locations of various types of files associated with Word and its documents.

    ○ **Web Options** You click this button to adjust settings for converting a document to a Web page.

15. Skipping over the Customize Ribbon and Quick Access Toolbar pages, which we discuss in later topics in this chapter, click **Add-Ins**.

    This page displays all the active and inactive add-ins and enables you to add and remove them. (Add-ins are utility programs that provide additional functionality to an Office program.)

The Add-Ins page of the Word Options dialog box.

16. Display the **Trust Center** page.

    This page provides links to information about privacy and security. It also provides access to the Trust Center settings that control the actions Word takes in response to documents that are provided by certain people or companies, that are saved in certain locations, or that contain potentially harmful elements such as ActiveX controls or macros.

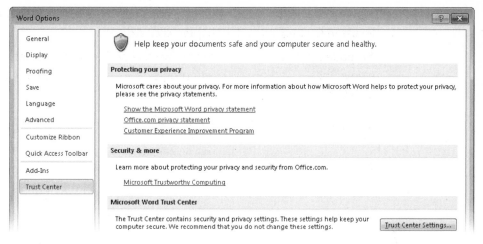

The Trust Center page of the Word Options dialog box.

17. Under **Microsoft Office Word Trust Center**, click **Trust Center Settings**, and then in the left pane of the **Trust Center** dialog box, click **Trusted Locations**.

On this page, you can specify the locations from which Word will not block content.

The Trusted Locations page of the Trust Center dialog box.

CLEAN UP Close the Trust Center dialog box. Reverse any changes you don't want to keep before moving on. Then close the Word Options dialog box. Leave the blank document open if you're continuing directly to the next exercise.

Customizing the Ribbon

The ribbon was designed to make all the commonly used commands visible so that people can more easily discover the full potential of an Office 2010 program. But many people use an Office program to perform the same set of tasks all the time, and for them, seeing buttons (or even entire groups of buttons) that they never use is just another form of clutter.

See Also For information about minimizing and expanding the ribbon, see "Customizing the Quick Access Toolbar" later in this chapter.

Would you prefer to see fewer commands than appear on the ribbon by default? Or would you prefer to see more specialized groups of commands? Well, you can. From the Customize Ribbon page of an Office 2010 program's Options dialog box, you can control the tabs that appear on the ribbon, and the groups that appear on the tabs.

The Customize Ribbon page of the Word Options dialog box.

On this page, you can customize the ribbon in the following ways:

● If you rarely use a tab, you can turn it off.

● If you use the commands in only a few groups on each tab, you can remove the groups you don't use. (The group is not removed from the program, just from its tab.)

● You can move a predefined group by removing it from one tab and then adding it to another.

● You can duplicate a predefined group by adding it to another tab.

● You can create a custom group on any tab and then add commands to it. (You cannot add commands to a predefined group.)

● You can create a custom tab on the ribbon. For example, you might want to do this if you use only a few commands from each tab and you find it inefficient to flip between them.

Don't be afraid to experiment with the ribbon to come up with the configuration that best suits the way you work. If at any point you find that your new ribbon is harder to work with rather than easier, you can always reset everything back to the default configuration.

Tip If you upgraded from Office 2007 or an earlier version of Office, you might find that some commands present in the earlier version are not available on the ribbon. A few old features have been abandoned, but others that people used only rarely have simply not been exposed in the user interface. If you want to use one of these hidden features, you can make it a part of your program environment by adding it to the ribbon or to the Quick Access Toolbar. You can find a list of all the commands that do not appear on the ribbon but are still available in a program by displaying the Customize Ribbon page of the program's Options dialog box and then clicking Commands Not In The Ribbon in the Choose Commands From list.

In this exercise, you'll customize the ribbon in the Word program window by using techniques that are common to all Office 2010 programs. You'll turn off tabs, remove groups, create a custom group, and add a command to the group. Then you'll create a tab and move groups of buttons to it. Finally, you'll reset the ribbon to its default state.

 SET UP You don't need any practice files to complete this exercise. Open a blank document if necessary, and then follow the steps.

1. Open the **Word Options** dialog box, and then click **Customize Ribbon**.

   The Customize Ribbon page is displayed.

2. In the list on the right, clear the check boxes of the **Insert**, **Page Layout**, **References**, **Mailings**, and **Review** tabs. Then click **OK**.

The ribbon now displays only the File, Home, and View tabs.

The only tab you can't customize is the File tab, which is your link to the Backstage view.

3. Redisplay the **Customize Ribbon** page of the **Word Options** dialog box, and in the right pane, select the **Page Layout** check box. Then click the plus sign to display the groups on this tab.

4. Above the left pane, click **Choose commands from** and then, in the list, click **Main Tabs**. In the **Main Tabs** list, click the plus sign adjacent to **Page Layout** to display the groups that are predefined for this tab.

5. In the right pane, click the **Paragraph** group, and then click **Remove**.

The group is removed from the Page Layout tab on the ribbon (the list on the right) but is still available in the list on the left. You can add it back to the Page Layout tab or add it to a different tab at any time.

6. In the right pane, click the plus sign adjacent to **Home** to display its groups, and then click the word **Home**.

7. Below the right pane, click **New Group**. When the **New Group (Custom)** group is added to the bottom of the Home group list, click **Rename**, type *Final* in the **Display name** box, and click **OK**. Then click the **Move Up** button until the **Final** group is at the top of the list.

Because of its location in the list, the new group will appear at the left end of the Home tab.

Main Tabs
☐ ✓ Home
        Final (Custom)
        ⊞ Clipboard
        ⊞ Font
        ⊞ Paragraph
        ⊞ Styles
        ⊞ Editing
⊞ ☐ Insert
☐ ✓ Page Layout
        ⊞ Themes
        ⊞ Page Setup
        ⊞ Page Background
        ⊞ Arrange
⊞ ☐ References
⊞ ☐ Mailings
⊞ ☐ Review
⊞ ✓ View
⊞ ☐ Developer

You have created a custom group on the Home tab.

8. In the **Choose commands from** list, click **File Tab**.

   The available commands list changes to include only the commands that are available in the Backstage view, which you display by clicking the File tab.

9. In the available commands list, click **Inspect Document**, and click **Add**. Then repeat this step to add **Mark as Final**.

   The two commands are added to the custom group.

Main Tabs
☐ ✓ Home
        ☐ Final (Custom)
                📄 Inspect Document
                🔖 Mark as Final
        ⊞ Clipboard
        ⊞ Font
        ⊞ Paragraph
        ⊞ Styles
        ⊞ Editing
⊞ ☐ Insert
☐ ✓ Page Layout
        ⊞ Themes
        ⊞ Page Setup
        ⊞ Page Background
        ⊞ Arrange
⊞ ☐ References
⊞ ☐ Mailings
⊞ ☐ Review

You can add commands to a custom group but not to a predefined group.

10. In the right pane, remove the **Font**, **Paragraph**, and **Styles** groups from the **Home** tab, and remove the **Page Background** group from the **Page Layout** tab.

11. Click the word **Home**, and then below the list, click **New Tab**.

    A new tab is added to the right pane and is selected for display on the ribbon. It has automatically been given one custom group.

12. Click **Remove** to remove the custom group.

13. Click **New Tab (Custom)**, and then click **Rename**. In the **Rename** dialog box, type **Formatting** in the **Display name** box, and click **OK**.

14. Display **Main Tabs** in the list on the left, and then expand the **Home** and **Page Layout** tabs.

15. With the **Formatting** tab selected in the right pane, add the **Font**, **Paragraph**, and **Styles** groups from **Home** in the left pane, and then add **Page Background** from **Page Layout**.

    The right pane shows the new configuration of the Home, Formatting, and Page Layout tabs.

You have moved groups from the Home and Page Layout tabs to a new Formatting tab.

16. In the **Word Options** dialog box, click **OK**.

    The Home tab displays the new Final group.

![Screenshot of the custom Home tab showing File, Home, Formatting, Page Layout, and View tabs, with Inspect Document, Mark as Final buttons in the Final group, Paste, Cut, Copy, Format Painter in the Clipboard group, and Find, Replace, Select in the Editing group.]

The custom Home tab.

17. Click the **Formatting** tab.

    The formatting commands are now collected on the Formatting tab.

![Screenshot of the custom Formatting tab in ProceduresEdited - Microsoft Word, showing Font, Paragraph, Styles, and Page Background groups with various formatting commands.]

The custom Formatting tab.

18. Display the **Customize Ribbon** page of the **Word Options** dialog box. In the lower-right corner, click **Reset**, and then click **Reset all customizations**. Then in the message box asking you to confirm that you want to delete all ribbon and Quick Access Toolbar customizations, click **Yes**.

19. Click **OK** to close the **Word Options** dialog box.

    The default ribbon configuration is restored.

 CLEAN UP Close the open document.

Customizing the Quick Access Toolbar

If you regularly use a few buttons that are scattered on various tabs of the ribbon and you don't want to switch between tabs to access the buttons or crowd your ribbon with a custom tab, you might want to add these frequently used buttons to the Quick Access Toolbar. They are then always visible in the upper-left corner of the program window.

Clicking Quick Access Toolbar in the left pane of a program's Options dialog box displays the page where you specify which commands you want to appear on the toolbar.

The Quick Access Toolbar page of the Word Options dialog box.

On this page, you can customize the ribbon in the following ways:

- You can define a custom Quick Access Toolbar for the program, or you can define a custom Quick Access Toolbar for a specific file.

- You can add any command from any group of any tab, including contextual tabs, to the toolbar.

- You can display a separator between different types of buttons.

- You can move buttons around on the toolbar until they are in the order you want.

- You can reset everything back to the default Quick Access Toolbar configuration.

If you never use more than a few buttons, you can add those buttons to the Quick Access Toolbar and then hide the ribbon by double-clicking the active tab or by clicking the Minimize The Ribbon button. Only the Quick Access Toolbar and tab names remain visible. You can temporarily redisplay the ribbon by clicking the tab you want to view.

You can permanently redisplay the ribbon by double-clicking any tab or by clicking the Expand The Ribbon button.

As you add buttons to the Quick Access Toolbar, it expands to accommodate them. If you add many buttons, it might become difficult to view the text in the title bar, or not all the buttons on the Quick Access Toolbar might be visible, defeating the purpose of adding them. To resolve this problem, you can move the Quick Access Toolbar below the ribbon by clicking the Customize Quick Access Toolbar button and then clicking Show Below The Ribbon.

In this exercise, you'll add a couple buttons to the Quick Access Toolbar for all documents, and then you'll test the buttons.

SET UP You don't need any practice files to complete this exercise. Open a blank document, and then follow the steps.

1. Open the **Word Options** dialog box, and then click **Quick Access Toolbar**.

   The Customize The Quick Access Toolbar page displays a list of available commands on the left side, and a list of the currently displayed commands on the right side.

   Tip If you want to create a Quick Access Toolbar that is specific to the active file, click the arrow at the right end of the box below Customize Quick Access Toolbar, and then click For <file name>. Then any command you select will be added to a toolbar specific to that file instead of the toolbar for the program.

2. At the top of the available commands list on the left, double-click **Separator**.

3. Scroll down the available commands list, click the **Quick Print** command, and then click **Add**.

4. Repeat step 3 to add the **Text Highlight Color** command.

   The Text Highlight Color command is added to the list of commands that will appear on the Quick Access Toolbar.

The arrow to the right of the command indicates that clicking this button on the Quick Access Toolbar will display a menu of options.

5. Click **OK** to close the **Word Options** dialog box.

   The Quick Access Toolbar now includes the default Save, Undo, and Repeat buttons and the custom Quick Print and Text Highlight Color buttons, separated by a line.

   You have added two buttons to the Quick Access Toolbar.

   To print a document with the default settings, you no longer have to click the File tab to display the Backstage view. Click Print in the left pane, and then click the Print button.

6. If you want to test printing from the Quick Access Toolbar, ensure that your printer is turned on, and then on the Quick Access Toolbar, click the **Quick Print** button.

   Now let's see how easy it is to highlight or remove highlighting from text when you are working primarily with the commands on a tab other than the Home tab.

7. Click the **Review** tab. Then select the first highlighted paragraph, **Proof of notice of meeting**.

8. On the Quick Access Toolbar, click the **Text Highlight Color** arrow, and then click **No Color**.

   The yellow highlight is removed from the selection. The No Color option becomes the default for the Text Highlight Color button.

9. Select the next highlighted paragraph, and on the Quick Access Toolbar, click the **Text Highlight Color** button.

   The yellow highlight is removed from the selection.

10. Display the **Quick Access Toolbar** page of the **Word Options** dialog box, click **Reset**, and then click **Reset only Quick Access Toolbar**.

11. In the **Reset Customizations** message box, click **Yes** to return the Quick Access Toolbar to its default contents. Then click **OK** to close the **Word Options** dialog box.

CLEAN UP Close the open document.

Key Points

- The Office 2010 program environment is flexible and can be customized to meet your needs.

- Most of the settings that control the working environment are gathered on the pages of the Options dialog box.

- You can customize the ribbon to make the development tools you need most often easily accessible.

- You can provide one-click access to any command by adding a button for it to the Quick Access Toolbar, either for the program or for one file.

Chapter at a Glance

Create and save files, **page 38**

Open, move around in, and close files, **page 46**

View files in different ways, **page 52**

2 Work with Files

In this chapter, you will learn how to

✔ Create and save files.

✔ Open, move around in, and close files.

✔ View files in different ways.

When working in Microsoft Word, Excel, or PowerPoint, you save content in individual files. In each program, you can save files as different types depending on each file's purpose. The standard files are Word documents, Excel workbooks, and PowerPoint presentations. Regardless of the program or file type, you use similar techniques for creating, saving, moving around in, and viewing files in each program.

When working in OneNote, content is saved in individual files representing pages that are part of a notebook structure. OneNote creates the files for you and saves your changes as you work, so you don't need to. However, you use some of the same techniques for moving around in and viewing files as you do in other Microsoft Office 2010 programs.

In this chapter, you'll practice working with files in Word, using techniques that are common to working in files created in Word, Excel, or PowerPoint. First you'll create and save a document and then save an existing document in a different location. Then you'll open an existing document, move around in it, and close it. Finally, you'll explore various ways of viewing file content.

> **Practice Files** Before you can complete the exercises in this chapter, you need to copy the book's practice files to your computer. The practice files you'll use to complete the exercises in this chapter are in the Chapter02 practice file folder. A complete list of practice files is provided in "Using the Practice Files" at the beginning of this book.

Creating and Saving Files

When you start Word, Excel, or PowerPoint without opening a specific file, the program displays a blank document, workbook, or presentation in which you can start entering content. A blinking cursor (in the form of a vertical line) in the text pane or worksheet cell shows where the next character you type will appear.

When an Office 2010 program is running, you can create a new file from the New page of the Backstage view, which you display by clicking the File tab on the ribbon.

From the New page, you can create a document based on a preformatted template.

Tip More documents may be added to those available from Microsoft Office Online, so the templates available on your New page might be different from those shown here.

The documents listed on the New page are based on templates, which are sets of formats that have been saved in such a way that you can use them as a pattern for new documents. For example, in Word 2010 the icons in the top section of the Available Templates gallery are:

● **Blank document** Clicking this icon opens a document formatted with the standard settings. The document contains no content.

  Tip The standard Word document settings are based on a template named Normal, which is installed on your computer as part of the Office installation. You can make changes to the Normal template but it is not customary or advisable to do so.

- **Blog post** Clicking this icon opens a document containing the basic elements of a blog post in a document window. The document window includes additional functionality enabling you to easily post directly to an existing blog site from within Word.

- **Recent templates** Clicking this icon displays a page on which you can select from the most recent templates you have used.

   Tip Clicking the Back button or the Home button takes you back to the New page.

- **Sample templates** Clicking this icon displays a page on which you can select from sample documents that come with Word.

- **My templates** Clicking this icon displays a dialog box in which you can select a template you have created as the basis for a new document.

- **New from existing** Clicking this icon displays a dialog box in which you can select an existing document as the basis for a new document.

The icons in the Office.com Templates section represent categories of common types of files for the program you're working in. Depending on how many templates are available in a category, the icon might be a folder. Regardless, clicking one of these icons displays more templates that are available for download from the Microsoft Office Online Web site. You can also search for specific file types by entering the type you want in the Search Office.com For Templates box and clicking the Start Searching button.

See Also For information about document templates, refer to *Microsoft Word 2010 Step by Step* by Joyce Cox and Joan Lambert (Microsoft Press, 2010).

When you find a template you might want to use as the basis for your new file, clicking its icon displays a preview of that file in the right pane. You can then click the Create button in the right pane to create the file.

Tip Double-clicking an icon creates that type of file without first displaying it in the preview pane.

Each file you create from the New page of the Backstage view is temporary until you save it. To save a document, workbook, or presentation for the first time, you click the Save button on the Quick Access Toolbar or click Save in the Backstage view. Either action displays the Save As dialog box, where you can assign a name and storage location to the file.

By default, the Save As dialog box displays the contents of your Documents library.

Troubleshooting This graphic shows the Save As dialog box as it appears when Word is running on Windows 7. If you are using a different version of the Windows operating system, your dialog box will look different but the way you work in it will be similar.

If you want to save the file in a folder other than the one shown in the Address bar at the top of the dialog box, you can click the arrow or chevrons in the Address bar or click locations in the Navigation pane on the left to display the folder you want. If you want to create a folder in which to store the file, you can click the New Folder button on the toolbar.

If you want to save a file in a format other than the one shown in the Save As Type box, click the Save As Type arrow and then, in the Save As Type list, click the file format you want.

After you save a file the first time, you can save subsequent changes by clicking the Save button. The new version of the file then overwrites the previous version.

Keyboard Shortcut Press Ctrl+S to save the current document.

Tip Windows 7 automatically retains previous file versions. To view previous versions of a file on a computer running Windows 7, right-click the file in Windows Explorer, and then click Restore Previous Versions.

If you want to keep both the new version and the previous version, click Save As in the Backstage view, and then save the new version with a different name in the same location or with the same name in a different location. (You can't store two files of the same type with the same name in the same folder.)

Tip By default, each program periodically saves the file you're working on in case the program stops responding or you lose electrical power. To adjust the frequency at which the program saves the file, display the Backstage view, click Options, click the Save tab in the left pane of the Options dialog box, and specify the period of time in the box to the right of the Save AutoRecover Information Every check box. Then click OK.

In this exercise, you'll work with files in Word by using techniques that are common to all Office 2010 programs. You'll create a blank document, enter text, and save the document in a folder that you create.

SET UP You don't need any practice files to complete this exercise. Start Word, and then follow the steps.

1. On the ribbon, click the **File** tab to display the Backstage view. Then in the left pane of the Backstage view, click **New**.

2. On the **New** page, double-click **Blank document**.

   Word creates a blank document temporarily called *Document2* and displays it in its own program window in Print Layout view. Document1 is still open, but its window is hidden by the Document2 window.

   Tip Word created Document1 when you started the program.

   See Also For information about switching between open windows, see "Viewing Files in Different Ways" later in this chapter.

3. With the cursor at the beginning of the new document, type **Parks Appreciation Day**, and then press the Enter key.

   The text appears in the new document.

4. Type the following sentence (including the period):

Help beautify our city by participating in the annual cleanup of Log Park, Swamp Creek Park, and Linkwood Park. This is a lot of fun! Volunteers receive a free T-shirt and barbeque lunch. Bring your own gardening tools and gloves.

Notice that you did not need to press Enter when the cursor reached the right margin because the text automatically continued on the next line.

Parks Appreciation Day

Help beautify our city by participating in the annual cleanup of Log Park, Swamp Creek Park, and Linkwood Park. This is a lot of fun! Volunteers receive a free T-shirt and barbecue lunch. Bring your own gardening tools and gloves.

You press Enter at the end of each paragraph; the Word Wrap feature takes care of wrapping each line.

Tip If a red or green wavy line appears under a word or phrase, Word is flagging a possible error in spelling or grammar. For now, ignore any errors.

5. Press Enter, and then type the following sentence (including the period):

The Service Committee is coordinating groups to participate in this event. If you are interested in spending time outdoors with your family and friends while improving the quality of our parks, contact Paul Shen at paul@treyresearch.net.

6. On the Quick Access Toolbar, click the **Save** button.

The Save As dialog box opens, displaying the contents of your Documents library. In the File Name box, Word suggests the first words in the document as a possible name.

7. Navigate to your **Chapter02** practice file folder.

New folder

8. On the dialog box's toolbar, click the **New folder** button, type **My New Documents** as the name of the new folder, and press Enter. Then double-click the **My New Documents** folder.

9. In the **File name** box, click anywhere in **Parks Appreciation Day** to select it, and then replace this name by typing **My Announcement**.

    Important Each type of file is identified by a specific file name extension. For example, the extension .docx identifies documents created in Word 2010 or Word 2007 that don't contain macros. Windows 7 does not display these extensions by default, and you don't need to type them in the Save As dialog box. When you save a file, Word automatically adds whatever extension is associated with the type of file selected in the Save As Type box.

10. Click **Save**.

    The Save As dialog box closes, Word saves the My Announcement document in the My New Documents folder, and the name of the document, My Announcement, appears on the program window's title bar.

11. Display the Backstage view, and then click **Save As**.

    The Save As dialog box opens, displaying the contents of the My New Documents folder, because that is the last folder you worked with.

12. In the **Address** bar of the **Save As** dialog box, to the left of **My New Documents**, click **Chapter02**.

    The dialog box now displays the contents of the Chapter02 practice file folder, which is the folder that contains the My New Documents folder.

    See Also For information about working with the file properties that appear at the bottom of the Save As dialog box, see "Preparing Documents for Electronic Distribution" in Chapter 7, "Preview, Print, and Distribute Documents."

13. Click **Save**.

    Word saves the My Announcement document in the Chapter02 practice file folder. You now have two versions of the document saved with the same name but in different folders.

✖ **CLEAN UP** At the right end of the title bar, click the Close button (the X) to close the My Announcement document. Leave Document1 open for use in the next exercise.

File Compatibility with Earlier Versions of Office Programs

The Office 2010 programs use file formats based on a programming language called extended markup language, or more commonly, XML. These file formats, called the *Microsoft Office Open XML Formats*, were introduced with Microsoft Office 2007.

The Office Open XML formats provide the following benefits:

- File size is smaller because files are compressed when saved, decreasing the amount of disk space needed to store the file, and the amount of bandwidth needed to send files in e-mail, over a network, or across the Internet.

- Recovering at least some of the content of damaged files is possible because XML files can be opened in a text program such as Notepad.

- Security is greater because the standard file formats cannot contain macros, and personal data can be detected and removed from the file. (Word 2010 and Word 2007 provide a different file format—.docm—for documents that contain macros.)

Each Office 2010 program offers a selection of file formats intended to provide specific benefits. The file formats and file name extensions for Word 2010 documents include the following:

- Word Document (.docx)
- Word Macro-Enabled Document (.docm)
- Word Template (.dotx)
- Word Macro-Enabled Template (.dotm)
- Word XML Document (.xml)

The file formats and file name extensions for Excel 2010 documents include the following:

- Excel Workbook (.xlsx)
- Excel Macro-Enabled Workbook (.xlsm)
- Excel Binary Workbook (.xlsb)
- Excel Template (.xltx)
- Excel Macro-Enabled Template (.xltm)
- Excel Add-In (.xlam)

The file formats and file name extensions for PowerPoint 2010 documents include the following:

- PowerPoint Presentation (.pptx)
- PowerPoint Macro-Enabled Presentation (.pptm)
- PowerPoint Template (.potx)
- PowerPoint Macro-Enabled Template (.potm)
- PowerPoint Show (.ppsx)
- PowerPoint Macro-Enabled Show (.ppsm)
- PowerPoint Add-In (.ppam)
- PowerPoint XML Presentation (.xml)
- PowerPoint Picture Presentation (.pptx)

Other non–program specific file types, such as text files, Web pages, PDF files, and XPS files, are available from the Save As dialog box of each program.

Tip OneNote notebooks are stored in folders. For information about the OneNote file formats, see "Navigating in the OneNote Program Window" in Chapter 18, "Explore OneNote 2010."

You can open a file created with Office 2003, Office XP, Office 2000, or Office 97 in an Office 2010 program, but new features will not be available. The file name appears in the title bar with *[Compatibility Mode]* to its right. You can work in Compatibility mode, or you can convert the document to the current file format by displaying the Info page of the Backstage view and clicking the Convert button in the Compatibility Mode section. You can also click Save As in the Backstage view to save a copy of the file in the current format.

If you work with people who are using Office 2003, Office XP, Office 2000, or Office 97, you can save your documents in a format that they will be able to open and use by choosing the corresponding *97-2003* file format in the Save As Type list, or they can download the Microsoft Office Compatibility Pack for Word, Excel, and PowerPoint File Formats from the Microsoft Download Center (located at download.microsoft.com) so that they can open current Office files in their version of Office.

Opening, Moving Around in, and Closing Files

If a program isn't already running, you can start the program and simultaneously open an existing file by double-clicking the file in Windows Explorer. While a program is running, you can open an existing document from the Backstage view. If you have recently worked on the document you want to open, you can display the Recent page and simply click the document you want in the list. If the document is not available on the Recent page, clicking Open in the left pane displays the Open dialog box.

The Open dialog box, displaying the contents of a recently used folder.

By default, the Open dialog box displays your Documents library, with a combined view of your My Documents folder and the Public Documents folder. If you display the dialog box again in the same Word session, it displays the contents of the folder from which you last opened a file. To display the contents of a different folder, you can use the standard Windows techniques described in "Creating and Saving Files" earlier in this chapter. After you locate the document you want to work with, you can open it by clicking its file name and then clicking Open in the lower-right corner of the dialog box, or by simply double-clicking the file name.

Tip Clicking a file name and then clicking the Open arrow (not the button) displays a list of alternative ways in which you can open the file. To look through the file without making any inadvertent changes, you can open it as read-only, or you can open a separate copy of the file. After a computer crash or similar incident, you can open the file and attempt to repair any damage. You can also display the file in other versions and formats.

If you open a document that is too long to fit entirely on the screen, you can bring off-screen content into view without changing the location of the cursor by using the vertical scroll bar in the following ways:

- Click the scroll arrows to move up or down by one line.

- Click above or below the scroll box to move up or down by the height of one window.

- Drag the scroll box on the scroll bar to display the part of the document corresponding to the location of the scroll box. For example, dragging the scroll box to the middle of the scroll bar displays the middle of the document.

If the document is too wide to fit on the screen, Word displays a horizontal scroll bar that you can use in similar ways to move from side to side.

You can also move around in a document by moving the cursor. To place the cursor in a specific location, you simply click there. To move the cursor one page backward or forward, you click the Previous Page and Next Page buttons below the vertical scroll bar. You can also press a keyboard key to move the cursor. For example, pressing the Home key moves the cursor to the left end of a line.

Tip The location of the cursor is displayed on the status bar. You can also display its location by page, section, line, and column, and in inches from the top of the page. SImply select the option you want from the status bar shortcut menu.

The following table lists ways to use your keyboard to move the cursor.

Cursor movement	Key or keyboard shortcut
Left one character	Left Arrow
Right one character	Right Arrow
Down one line	Down Arrow
Up one line	Up Arrow
Left one word	Ctrl+Left Arrow
Right one word	Ctrl+Right Arrow
To the beginning of the current line	Home
To the end of the current line	End
To the beginning of the document	Ctrl+Home
To the end of the document	Ctrl+End
To the beginning of the previous page	Ctrl+Page Up
To the beginning of the next page	Ctrl+Page Down
Up one screen	Page Up
Down one screen	Page Down

In a long document, you might want to move quickly among elements of a certain type; for example, from graphic to graphic. Clicking the Select Browse Object button at the bottom of the vertical scroll bar displays a gallery of browsing options, such as Browse By Page and Browse By Graphic. (These options are also available on the Go To tab of the Find And Replace dialog box, which you display by clicking the Find arrow in the Editing group of the Home tab and then clicking Go To.) You can also display the Navigation task pane and move from heading to heading or page to page.

Keyboard Shortcut Press Ctrl+G to display the Go To tab of the Find And Replace dialog box.

See Also For information about using the Navigation task pane to search for specific content in a document, see "Finding and Replacing Text" in Chapter 3, "Edit and Proofread Text."

If more than one document is open, you can close the active document without exiting Word by clicking the Close button at the right end of the title bar. If only one document is open, clicking the Close button closes the document and also exits Word. If you want to close that document but leave Word running, you must click Close in the Backstage view.

In this exercise, you'll work with files in Word by using techniques that are common to all Office 2010 programs. You'll open an existing document, save a copy of the document, and explore various ways of moving around in it. Then you'll close the document.

SET UP You need the Rules_start document located in your Chapter02 practice file folder to complete this exercise. Continue from the previous exercise or exit and restart Word so that Document1 is the only open document. Then follow the steps.

1. Click the **File** tab to display the Backstage view, and then click **Open**.

   The Open dialog box opens, showing the contents of the folder you used for your previous open or save action.

2. Navigate to the location in which you saved the practice files for this book, and open the **Chapter02** folder.

3. Click the **Rules_start** document, and then click **Open**.

   The Rules_start document opens in the Word program window.

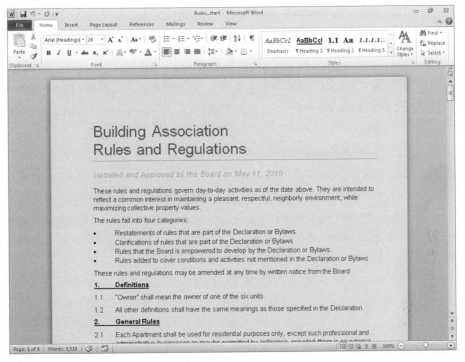

An existing document displayed in Print Layout view.

Troubleshooting The appearance of buttons and groups on the ribbon changes depending on the width of the program window. For information about changing the appearance of the ribbon to match our screen images, see "Modifying the Display of the Ribbon" at the beginning of this book.

4. Display the Backstage view, and in the left pane, click **Save As**. In the **Save As** dialog box, change the file name to **Rules**, and then click **Save**.

    Now you can experiment with the document without fear of overwriting the original.

5. In the second line of the document title, click at the end of the paragraph to position the cursor.

6. Press the Home key to move the cursor to the beginning of the line.

7. Press the Right Arrow key six times to move the cursor to the beginning of the word **and** in the heading.

8. Press the End key to move the cursor to the end of the line.

9. Press Ctrl+End to move the cursor to the end of the document.

10. Press Ctrl+Home to move the cursor to the beginning of the document.

11. At the bottom of the vertical scroll bar, click the **Next Page** button.

12. Click above the scroll box to change the view of the document by the height of one window.

13. Drag the scroll box to the top of the scroll bar.

    The beginning of the document comes into view. Note that the location of the cursor has not changed—just the view of the document.

14. Click to the left of the first row of the title to place the cursor at the top of the document, and then near the bottom of the vertical scroll bar, click the **Select Browse Object** button.

    A gallery of browsing choices opens.

The Select Browse Object gallery.

15. Move the pointer over the buttons representing the objects among which you can browse.

    As you point to each button, the name of the browsing option appears at the top of the gallery.

16. Click the **Browse by Page** button.

    The cursor moves from the beginning of page 1 to the beginning of page 2.

17. Click the **View** tab, and then in the **Show** group, select the **Navigation Pane** check box.

    The Navigation task pane opens on the left side of the screen, displaying an outline of the headings in the document. The heading of the section containing the cursor is highlighted.

From the Navigation task pane, you can move from heading to heading or from page to page.

18. In the **Navigation** task pane, click the **Landscaping** heading.

    Word scrolls the document and moves the cursor to the selected heading.

19. In the **Navigation** task pane, click the **Browse the pages in your document** tab (the one with the icon of four small pages). Then scroll through the thumbnails in the task pane, and click page **5**.

20. At the right end of the **Navigation** task pane title bar, click the **Close** button.

21. At the right end of the program window title bar, click the **Close** button.

    The Rules document closes, and Document1 becomes the active document.

22. Display the Backstage view, and then click **Close**.

    Document1 closes, leaving Word running.

    Troubleshooting In step 22, if you click the Close button at the right end of the title bar instead of clicking Close in the Backstage view, you'll close the open Word document and exit the Word program. To continue working, start Word again.

✖ **CLEAN UP** If you're continuing directly to the next exercise, leave Word running.

Viewing Files in Different Ways

In each program, you can display the content of a file in a variety of views, each suited to a specific purpose. You switch the view by clicking the buttons in the Document Views group on the View tab, or those on the View Shortcuts toolbar in the lower-right corner of the program window. The views in each program are specific to that program's files.

Word 2010 includes the following views:

- **Print Layout view**   This view displays a document on the screen the way it will look when printed. You can see page layout elements such as margins, page breaks, headers and footers, and watermarks.

- **Full Screen Reading view**   This view displays as much of the content of the document as will fit on the screen at a size that is appropriate for reading. In this view, the ribbon is replaced by one toolbar at the top of the screen with buttons for saving and printing the document, accessing references and other tools, highlighting text, and making comments. You can move from page to page and adjust the view by selecting options from the View Options menu. You can edit the document only if you turn on the Allow Typing option on this menu, and you can switch views only by clicking the Close button to return to the previous view.

- **Web Layout view**   This view displays the document the way it will look when viewed in a Web browser. You can see backgrounds and other effects. You can also see how text wraps to fit the window and how graphics are positioned.

- **Outline view**   This view displays the structure of a document as nested levels of headings and body text, and provides tools for viewing and changing its hierarchy.

- **Draft view**   This view displays the content of a document with a simplified layout so that you can type and edit quickly. You can't see page layout elements.

  See Also   For information about Web Layout view and Outline view, refer to *Microsoft Word 2010 Step by Step* by Joyce Cox and Joan Lambert (Microsoft Press, 2010).

Excel 2010 includes the following views:

- **Normal view**   This view displays the worksheet with column and row headers.

- **Page Layout view**   This view displays the worksheet on the screen the way it will look when printed, including page layout elements.

- **Page Break Preview view**   This view displays only the portion of the worksheet that contains content, and any page breaks. You can drag page breaks in this view to move them.

PowerPoint 2010 includes the following views:

- **Normal view** This view displays individual slides with active content objects such as text containers, and a separate pane into which you can enter notes.

- **Slide Sorter view** This view displays all the slides in a presentation. You can apply formatting to individual slides and to groups of slides, but you can't edit the slide content.

- **Notes Page view** This view displays each slide and its accompanying notes as they will look when printed in the Notes Page print layout.

- **Reading view** This view displays individual slides as they will appear on the screen, without active content objects. In this view, the ribbon is hidden. You can move from page to page and adjust the view by selecting options from a menu on the status bar. You can't edit slide content in this view.

See Also For information about OneNote 2010 notebook views, see Chapter 18, "Explore OneNote 2010."

When you want to focus on the layout of a document, worksheet, or slide, you can display rulers and gridlines to help you position and align elements. Simply select the corresponding check boxes in the Show group on the View tab. You can also adjust the magnification of the document by using the tools available in the Zoom group on the View tab, or the Zoom button or Zoom slider at the right end of the status bar. Clicking the Zoom button in either location displays a dialog box where you can select or type a percentage; or you can drag the Zoom slider to the left or right or click the Zoom Out or Zoom In button on either side of the slider to change the percentage incrementally.

You're not limited to working with one file at a time. You can easily switch between open files, and you can display more than one program window simultaneously. If you want to work with different parts of a document, you can open the document in a second window and display both, or you can split a window into two panes and scroll through each pane independently by using options in the Window group on the View tab.

Not represented on the View tab is a feature that can be invaluable when you are fine-tuning the layout of a document. Clicking the Show/Hide ¶ button in the Paragraph group on the Home tab turns the display of nonprinting and hidden characters on and off. Nonprinting characters, such as tabs and paragraph marks, control the layout of your document, and hidden characters provide the structure for behind-the-scenes processes, such as indexing. You can control the display of these characters for each window.

Tip You can hide any text by selecting it, clicking the Font dialog box launcher, selecting the Hidden check box, and clicking OK. When the Show/Hide ¶ button is turned on, hidden text is visible and is identified in the document by a dotted underline.

In this exercise, you'll work with files in Word by using techniques that are common to all Office 2010 programs. First you'll explore various ways that you can customize Print Layout view to make the work of developing documents more efficient. You'll turn white space on and off, zoom in and out, display the rulers and Navigation task pane, and view nonprinting characters and text. Then you'll switch to other views, noticing the differences so that you have an idea of which one is most appropriate for which task. Finally, you'll switch between open documents and view documents in more than one window at the same time.

SET UP You need the Procedures_start and Prices_start documents located in your Chapter02 practice file folder to complete this exercise. Open the Procedures_start document and save it as *Procedures*. Then follow the steps.

1. In **Print Layout** view, scroll through the document.

   As you can see, on all pages but the first, the printed document will have the title in the header at the top of the page, the page number in the right margin, and the date in the footer at the bottom of each page.

   See Also For information about headers and footers, refer to *Microsoft Word 2010 Step by Step* by Joyce Cox and Joan Lambert (Microsoft Press, 2010).

2. Point to the gap between any two pages, and when the pointer changes to two opposing arrows, double-click the mouse button. Then scroll through the document again.

   The white space at the top and bottom of each page and the gray space between pages are now hidden, as are the header and footer.

   Hiding white space between pages makes it quicker to scroll through a long document and easier to compare the content on two pages.

3. Restore the white space by pointing to the line that separates one page from the next and double-clicking the mouse button.

`100%`

4. Press Ctrl+Home to move to the top of the document, and then near the right end of the status bar, click the **Zoom** button.

The Zoom dialog box opens.

You can click a preset zoom percentage or specify your own.

5. Click **Many pages**. Then click the monitor button, click the second page thumbnail in the top row, and click **OK**.

The magnification changes so that you can see two pages side by side.

You can now scroll through the document two pages at a time.

6. At the bottom of the vertical scroll bar, click the **Next Page** button to display the third and fourth pages of the document.

7. On the **View** tab, click the **Zoom** button. Then in the **Zoom** dialog box, click **75%**, and click **OK**.

   Notice that the Zoom percentage and slider position are adjusted to reflect the new setting.

8. On the status bar, at the left end of the **Zoom** slider, click the **Zoom Out** button two times.

   As you click the button, the Zoom percentage decreases and the slider moves to the left.

9. At the right end of the **Zoom** slider, click the **Zoom In** button until the magnification is 100 percent.

10. On the **View** tab, in the **Show** group, select the **Ruler** check box.

    Horizontal and vertical rulers appear above and to the left of the page. On the rulers, the content area of the page is white and the margins are blue.

11. On the **Home** tab, in the **Paragraph** group, click the **Show/Hide ¶** button.

    Nonprinting characters such as spaces, tabs, and paragraph marks are now visible.

You can display the nonprinting characters that control the layout of the content.

12. On the **View Shortcuts** toolbar, click the **Full Screen Reading** button.

    Word displays the document in a format that's easy to read.

You can't edit content in Full Screen Reading view unless you set the view options to Allow Typing.

13. In the lower-right corner of the window, click the **Forward** button.

    You can now read the next two screens of information.

14. To the right of the screen indicator at the top of the window, click the **Previous Screen** button.

15. Point to each button on the toolbar at the top of the window to display its ScreenTip. Then in the upper-right corner, click the **Close** button to return to **Print Layout** view.

16. Press Ctrl+Home. Then on the **View Shortcuts** toolbar, click the **Web Layout** button, and scroll through the document.

    In a Web browser, the text column will fill the window and there will be no page breaks.

17. Press Ctrl+Home, and then on the **View Shortcuts** toolbar, click the **Outline** button.

    Word displays the document's hierarchical structure, and the Outlining tab appears on the ribbon.

18. On the **Outlining** tab, in the **Outline Tools** group, click the **Show Level** arrow, and in the list, click **Level 2**.

The document collapses to display only the Level 1 and Level 2 headings.

You can control the level of detail shown in the document's hierarchy.

19. On the **View Shortcuts** toolbar, click the **Draft** button, and then scroll through the document.

You can see the basic content of the document without any extraneous elements, such as margins and headers and footers. The active area on the ruler indicates the width of the text column, dotted lines indicate page breaks, and scrolling is quick and easy.

20. Display the Backstage view, click **Open**, and then in the **Open** dialog box displaying the contents of your **Chapter02** practice file folder, double-click **Prices_start**.

The Prices_start document opens in Print Layout view in its own window. Notice that the telephone number in the body of the memo has a dotted underline, which indicates that it is formatted as hidden.

21. Save the **Prices_start** document as **Prices** so that you can work with it without overwriting the original.

22. On the **Home** tab, in the **Paragraph** group, click the active **Show/Hide ¶** button to turn it off.

The telephone number is no longer visible.

23. On the **View** tab, in the **Window** group, click the **Switch Windows** button, and then in the list of open documents, click **Procedures**.

   The Procedures document is displayed in Draft view with nonprinting characters and hidden text turned on.

24. On the **View** tab, in the **Window** group, click the **Arrange All** button.

   The open windows are sized and stacked one above the other. Each window has a ribbon, so you can work with each document independently.

You can display more than one window at the same time.

> **Tip** The ribbons in each window take up a lot of screen space. To see more of each document, you can click the Minimize The Ribbon button to hide all but the tab names.

25. At the right end of the **Document1** window title bar, click the **Close** button. Then in either open window, click the **Arrange All** button again.

   Word resizes the open windows to occupy the available space.

26. At the right end of the **Prices** window title bar, click the **Maximize** button.

   The window expands to fill the screen.

27. On the **View** tab, in the **Show** group, clear the **Ruler** check box.

CLEAN UP Close the Procedures and Prices documents.

Key Points

- You create new documents, workbooks, presentations, and notebooks from the New page of the Backstage view. When creating documents, workbooks, and presentations, you can choose a blank template or a template that includes preset formatting and content placeholders.

- When you save a file, you specify its name, location, and file format in the Save As dialog box. Each program offers several file formats.

- The cursor indicates the location in which text will be inserted when you type. It's easy to move the cursor by clicking in the text or by pressing keys and keyboard shortcuts.

- You can view a file in a variety of ways, depending on your needs as you create the file and on the purpose for which you are creating it.

Part 2

Microsoft Word 2010

3 Edit and Proofread Text 63

4 Change the Look of Text 99

5 Organize Information in Columns and Tables. 139

6 Add Simple Graphic Elements 167

7 Preview, Print, and Distribute Documents. 205

Chapter at a Glance

Find and replace text, **page 73**

Make text changes, **page 64**

Navigation

parking

8 matches

campers, house trailers, buses, or trucks shall be stored in any **parking** space in any Common Area.

4.4 No Owner shall use his or her **parking** spaces in the common garage to store personal belongings

be stored in the front end of the assigned **parking** stall or in the Owner's unused assigned stall

6. **Parking** and Vehicles

6.3 Five **parking** spaces are reserved for guest parking for the entire complex. Commercial vehicles

File **Home** **Insert** **Page Layout**

Constantia (Boc   11

B *I* U   abc x₂ x²

Font

Paste Options:

Paste Special...

Set Default Paste...

Visit our showroom and purchase a Room Planner look around and see what really appeals to you. So designed around just one or two special pieces, so something   already what to cho   ur des is available   alking professiona

Bilingual Dictionary

wardrobe
for clothes armoire *féminin, (clothes)* garde-robe *féminin*

As an exam   r bedr new bed, a wardrobe, or perhaps a chair to sit in wh The Room Planner can be used countless times for

Fine-tune text, **page 79**

current economic and environmental conditions, as well as of political issues that co our ability to maintain a viable business. When we select our product sources, we str only to improve the local economy but to ensure the preservation of fragile ecolog complex balancing act, but we are commited to maximizing our positive impacts whi no correspondi

An exciting a to discuss any may contact S sidney@widew available May

In the meantim suppliers, a tr which outlines

Sincerely,

Spelling and Grammar: English (U.S.)

Repeated Word:

When we select our product sources, we strive to not only to improve the local economy but to to ensure the preservation of fragile ecologies.

Ignore Once
Ignore All
Add to Dictionary

Suggestions:

Delete
Delete All
AutoCorrect

☑ Check grammar

Undo   Cancel

Correct spelling and grammatical errors, **page 87**

Quick Parts ▾

General
Contact Block

Wide World Importers
Furniture and accessories for your world
(925) 555-0167
www.wideworldimporters.com

Insert saved text, **page 93**

▨ AutoText   ▸

▨ Document Property   ▸

▨ Field...

▨ Building Blocks Organizer...

▨ Save Selection to Quick Part Gallery...

3 Edit and Proofread Text

In this chapter, you will learn how to

- ✔ Make text changes.
- ✔ Find and replace text.
- ✔ Fine-tune text.
- ✔ Correct spelling and grammatical errors.
- ✔ Insert saved text.

As you learned in Chapter 1, "Explore Office 2010," entering text is a simple matter of typing. However, even the most accurate typists occasionally make mistakes, also known as *typos* (for *typographical errors*). Unless the documents you create are intended for no one's eyes but your own, you need to ensure that they are not only correct but also persuasive. Whether you are a novice or experienced writer, Microsoft Word 2010 has several tools that make creating professional documents easy and efficient.

- **Editing tools** These tools provide quick-selection techniques and drag-and-drop editing to make it easy to move and copy text anywhere you want it.

- **Search tools** These tools can be used to locate and replace words, phrases, and special characters, either one at a time or throughout a document.

    See Also For information about using the search tools to find and replace formatting, see the sidebar "Finding and Replacing Formatting" in Chapter 4, "Change the Look of Text."

- **Research tools** These tools make it easy to find synonyms, look up information, and translate words and phrases.

- **AutoCorrect and Spelling And Grammar** These features make it easy to correct typographical and grammatical errors before you share a document with others.

- **Quick Parts** These building blocks can be used to save and recall specialized terms or standard paragraphs.

  Tip Word also includes formatted building blocks for document elements such as cover pages, headers, and footers. For information, see "Inserting Building Blocks" in Chapter 6, "Add Simple Graphic Elements."

In this chapter, you'll edit the text in a document by inserting and deleting text, copying and pasting a phrase, and moving a paragraph. Then you'll replace one phrase with another throughout the entire document. Next, you'll replace a word with a synonym and translate another word. You'll also add misspelled words to the AutoCorrect list and check the spelling and grammar of a document. Finally, you'll save a couple of building blocks for insertion later in a document.

> **Practice Files** Before you can complete the exercises in this chapter, you need to copy the book's practice files to your computer. The practice files you'll use to complete the exercises in this chapter are in the Chapter03 practice file folder. A complete list of practice files is provided in "Using the Practice Files" at the beginning of this book.

Making Text Changes

You'll rarely write a perfect document that doesn't require any editing. You'll almost always want to add or remove a word or two, change a phrase, or move text from one place to another. You can edit a document as you create it, or you can write it first and then revise it. Or you might want to edit a document that you created for one purpose so that you can use it for a different purpose. For example, a letter might make an ideal starting point for a flyer, or a report might contain all the information you need for a Web document.

Inserting text is easy; you click to position the cursor and simply begin typing. Any existing text to the right of the cursor moves to make room for the new text.

Deleting text is equally easy. If you want to delete only one or a few characters, you can simply position the cursor and then press the Backspace or Delete key until the characters are all gone. Pressing Backspace deletes the character to the left of the cursor; pressing Delete deletes the character to the right of the cursor.

To delete more than a few characters efficiently, you need to know how to select the text. Selected text appears highlighted on the screen. You can drag through a section of text to select it, or you can select specific items as follows:

- **Word** Double-click anywhere in the word. The word and the space immediately following it are selected, but not any punctuation following the word.

- **Sentence** Click anywhere in the sentence while holding down the Ctrl key. Word selects all the characters in the sentence, from the first character through the space following the ending punctuation mark.

- **Paragraph** Triple-click anywhere in the paragraph. Word selects the text of the paragraph and the paragraph mark.

- **Adjacent words, lines, or paragraphs** Position the cursor at the beginning of the text you want to select, hold down the Shift key, and then press the Arrow keys to select one character or line at a time; hold down the Shift and Ctrl keys and press the Arrow keys to select one word at a time; or click at the end of the text that you want to select.

- **Non-adjacent words, lines, or paragraphs** Make the first selection, and then hold down the Ctrl key while selecting the next text block.

Tip When you select text, Word displays a box called the *Mini Toolbar* so that you can quickly format the selection. You can ignore this toolbar for now. For more information, see "Manually Changing the Look of Characters" in Chapter 4, "Change the Look of Text."

As an alternative way of selecting, you can use an invisible area in the document's left margin, called the *selection area*, to select items.

- **Line** Click in the selection area to the left of the line.

- **Paragraph** Double-click in the selection area to the left of the paragraph.

- **Entire document** Triple-click in the selection area.

  Keyboard Shortcut Press Ctrl+A to select all the content in the body of the document.

Selection area

In the selection area, the pointer becomes a right-pointing arrow.

After selecting the text you want to delete, press either Backspace or Delete.

Tip To release a selection, click anywhere in the window other than the selection area.

If you want to move or copy the selected text, you have three options:

- **Drag-and-drop editing** Use this feature, which is frequently referred to simply as *dragging*, when you need to move or copy text only a short distance—for example, within a paragraph. Start by using any of the methods described previously to select the text. Then point to the selection, hold down the mouse button, drag the text to its new location, and release the mouse button. To copy the selection, hold down the Ctrl key while you drag.

- **Cut, Copy, and Paste buttons** Use this method when you need to move or copy text between two locations that you cannot see at the same time—for example, between pages or between documents. Select the text, and click the Cut or Copy button in the Clipboard group on the Home tab. (The cut or copied item is stored in an area of your computer's memory called the *Microsoft Office Clipboard*, hence the name of the group.) Then reposition the cursor, and click the Paste button to insert the selection in its new location. If you click the Paste arrow instead of the button, Word displays a list of different ways to paste the selection.

Under Paste Options, buttons represent the ways in which you can paste the item.

Pointing to a button under Paste Options displays a preview of how the cut or copied item will look when pasted into the text in that format, so you can experiment with different ways of pasting until you find the one you want.

See Also For more information about the Clipboard, see the sidebar "About the Clipboard" later in this chapter.

● **Keyboard shortcuts** It can be more efficient to press key combinations to cut, copy, and paste selections than to click buttons on the ribbon. The main keyboard shortcuts for editing tasks are shown in the following table.

Task	Keyboard shortcut
Cut	Ctrl+X
Copy	Ctrl+C
Paste	Ctrl+V
Undo	Ctrl+Z
Repeat/Redo	Ctrl+Y

Using a keyboard shortcut to cut or copy a selection stores the item on the Clipboard, just as if you had clicked the corresponding button.

Tip No matter which method you use, when you cut text, Word removes it from its original location. When you copy text, Word leaves the text in the original location and repeats it in the new location.

If you make a change to a document and then realize that you made a mistake, you can easily reverse the change. You can undo your last editing action by clicking the Undo button on the Quick Access Toolbar. To undo an earlier action, click the Undo arrow and then click that action in the list.

Tip Selecting an action from the Undo list undoes that action and all the editing actions you performed after that one. You cannot undo only one action other than the last one you performed.

If you make a change to a document and want to repeat that change elsewhere, you can click the Repeat button on the Quick Access Toolbar. If the last task you performed was to undo an action, the Repeat button is replaced by the Redo button. So if you change your mind about whatever you undid, you can click the Redo button to return the text to its previous state. You can't redo multiple actions by clicking them in a list as you can with the Undo button, but you can click the Redo button repeatedly until the text is restored to what you want.

In this exercise, you'll edit the text in a document. You'll insert and delete text, undo the deletion, copy and paste a phrase, and move a paragraph.

SET UP You need the Orientation_start document located in your Chapter03 practice file folder to complete this exercise. Open the Orientation_start document, and save it as *Orientation*. Then follow the steps.

1. If formatting marks such as spaces and paragraph marks are not visible in the document, on the **Home** tab, in the **Paragraph** group, click the **Show/Hide ¶** button.

   Keyboard Shortcut Press Ctrl+* to turn formatting marks on or off. (You need to hold down the Shift key to activate the * key. So in effect, you are pressing Ctrl+Shift+8.)

2. In the second bullet point under **Project Goals**, double-click the word **natural** to select it, and then press Backspace.

3. In the third bullet point, click to the left of the **a** in the word **and**, hold down the Shift key, and then click to the right of the **e** in the word **motivate**.

   Word selects the text between the two clicks.

   Troubleshooting If Word selects the word *Engage* as well, you clicked before the space instead of after it. Click anywhere in the document to release the selection, and then repeat step 3, being sure to click after the space but before the word *and*.

Community·Service·Committee¶
Employee·Orientation¶

Proposal↵
Last·updated:·January· 25,· 2010¶

•**Project·Goals**¶
- •→ Familiarize·employees·with·the·concept·of·service.¶
- •→ Make·service·a·part·of·their·lives.¶
- •→ Engage·and·motivate·them.¶
- •→ Forge·a·sense·of·teamwork·among·all·employees·across·departments.¶
- •→ Provide·appropriate·skills·development·through·brainstorming,·planning,·and·leadership· opportunities.¶

You can use the Shift+click method to select as much text as you want.

4. Press Delete to delete the selection.

   Word also deletes the space after the selection.

5. In the fourth bullet point, double-click the word **Forge**, and then replace it by typing **Build**.

   Notice that you don't have to type a space after *Build*. Word inserts the space for you.

   Tip Word inserts and deletes spaces because the Use Smart Cut And Paste check box is selected on the Advanced page of the Word Options dialog box. If you want to be able to control the spacing yourself, click the Options button in the Backstage view, click Advanced, clear this check box (located in the Cut, Copy, And Paste area), and then click OK.

6. Scroll the page, and position the mouse pointer at the edge of the page to the left of the first bullet point under **Questions for Team Leaders**. Then with the pointer in the selection area, click to select the entire paragraph.

   Tip Clicking once selects this paragraph because it is only one line long. If the paragraph contained more than one line, you would need to double-click.

7. On the **Home** tab, in the **Clipboard** group, click the **Copy** button.

The selection is copied to the Clipboard.

8. If you can't see the bulleted list under **Questions for Department Reps**, click the **Next Page** button below the vertical scroll bar to move to the beginning of the next page. Then click to the left of **What** in the first bullet point under **Questions for Department Reps**, and in the **Clipboard** group, click the **Paste** arrow.

The Paste Options menu opens.

Paste Options:

Paste Special...
Set Default Paste...

The Paste Options menu includes buttons representing pasting options.

9. Point to the **Merge List** button, notice how the text will look with this paste option implemented, and then click the button.

The Paste Options button appears below and to the right of the inserted bullet point. You can click this button to display a list of paste options if you want to change the way the text has been pasted or the default way Word pastes. In this case, you can just ignore it.

10. In the **Set Up Team** section, triple-click anywhere in the paragraph that begins **The Committee will pursue** to select the entire paragraph.

11. In the **Clipboard** group, click the **Cut** button.

12. Press the Up Arrow key to move to the beginning of the preceding paragraph, and then in the **Clipboard** group, click the **Paste** button.

The two paragraphs switch places.

13. On the Quick Access Toolbar, click the **Undo** arrow, and then in the **Undo** list, click the third action (**Paste Merge List**).

Word undoes the previous cut-and-paste operation and the pasting of the copied text.

14. Press Ctrl+Home to move to the top of the document. Then position the pointer in the selection area adjacent to the third bullet point under **Project Goals**, and click to select the paragraph.

15. Point to the selection, hold down the mouse button, and then drag the paragraph up to the left of the word **Make** at the beginning of the preceding bullet point.

When you release the mouse, the bullet point moves to its new location.

16. With the text still selected, press the End key.

Word releases the selection and moves the cursor to the end of the paragraph.

17. Press the Spacebar, and then press Delete.

Word deletes the paragraph mark and merges the two bullet points.

Community·Service·Committee¶
Employee·Orientation¶

Proposal↵
Last·updated:·January· 25,·2010¶

•**Project·Goals**¶
 • → Familiarize·employees·with·the·concept·of·service.¶
 • → Engage·them.·Make·service·a·part·of·their·lives.¶
 • → Build·a·sense·of·teamwork·among·all·employees·across·departments.¶
 • → Provide·appropriate·skills·development·through·brainstorming,·planning,·and·leadership· opportunities.¶
 • → Meet·genuine·community·needs.¶

In the second bullet point, two bullets have now been combined into one.

✖ CLEAN UP If you prefer not to see formatting marks, turn them off. Then save and close the Orientation document.

About the Clipboard

You can view the items that have been cut or copied to the Clipboard in the Clipboard task pane, which you display by clicking the Clipboard dialog box launcher on the Home tab.

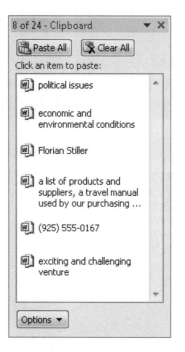

The Clipboard stores items that have been cut or copied from any Office program.

To paste an individual item at the cursor, you simply click the item in the Clipboard task pane. To paste all the items, click the Paste All button. You can point to an item, click the arrow that appears, and then click Delete to remove it from the Clipboard and the task pane, or you can remove all the items by clicking the Clear All button.

You can control the behavior of the Clipboard task pane by clicking Options at the bottom of the pane, and choosing the circumstances under which you want the task pane to appear.

To close the Clipboard task pane, click the Close button at the right end of its title bar.

Finding and Replacing Text

One way to ensure that the text in your documents is consistent and accurate is to use the Find feature to search for every occurrence of a particular word or phrase. For example, if you are responsible for advertising a trademarked product, you might want to search your marketing materials to check that every occurrence of the product's name is correctly identified as a trademark.

Clicking the Find button (not the arrow) in the Editing group on the Home tab displays the Navigation task pane with the Search tab active. As you type characters in the Search Document box at the top of the task pane, Word highlights all occurrences of those characters in the document and displays them in the search results list in the Navigation task pane.

Keyboard Shortcut Press Ctrl+F to display the Search tab of the Navigation task pane.

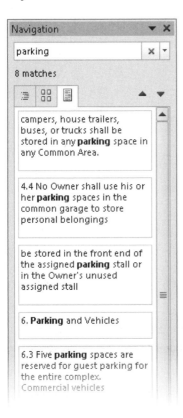

The Navigation task pane shows enough of the text surrounding the search term to identify its context.

When you point to a particular search result in the Navigation task pane, a ScreenTip displays the number of the page on which that result appears. You can click a search result to scroll the document to display the result's location.

Tip The beauty of the Navigation task pane is that you can continue editing your document as you normally would, without closing the pane.

If you want to be more specific about the text you are looking for—for example, if you want to look for occurrences that match the exact capitalization of your search term—click the arrow at the right end of the Search Document box in the Navigation task pane and then click Advanced Find to display the Find page of the Find And Replace dialog box. Clicking More in the lower-left corner expands the dialog box to make additional search options available.

You can make a search more specific by using the criteria in the Search Options area of the Find And Replace dialog box.

In the expanded dialog box, you can do the following:

- Guide the direction of the search by selecting Down, Up, or All from the Search list.

- Locate only text that matches the capitalization of the Find What text by selecting the Match Case check box.

- Exclude occurrences of the Find What text that appear within other words by selecting the Find Whole Words Only check box.

- Find two similar words, such as *effect* and *affect* by selecting the Use Wildcards check box and then entering a wildcard character in the Find What box. The two most common wildcard characters are:

    - ?, which represents any single character in this location in the Find What text.

    - *, which represents any number of characters in this location in the Find What text.

    Tip To see a list of the available wildcards, use Help to search for the term *wildcards*.

- Find occurrences of the search text that sound the same but are spelled differently, such as *there* and *their*, by selecting the Sounds Like check box.

- Find occurrences of a particular word in any form, such as *try*, *tries*, and *tried*, by selecting the Find All Word Forms check box. You can match a prefix or a suffix, and you can ignore punctuation and white space.

- Locate formatting, such as bold, or special characters, such as tabs, by selecting them from the Format or Special list.

    See Also For information about finding and replacing formatting, see the sidebar "Finding and Replacing Formatting" in Chapter 4, "Change the Look of Text."

If you want to substitute a specific word or phrase for another, you can use the Replace feature. Clicking the Replace button in the Editing group of the Home tab displays the Replace page of the Find And Replace dialog box.

Find and Replace	? ✕
Find **Re_p_lace** **Go To**	
Fi_n_d what: Susie	▼
Replace wi_t_h: Suzy	▼
[More >>]	[_R_eplace] [Replace _A_ll] [_F_ind Next] [Cancel]

Correcting errors and inconsistencies is easy with the Replace feature.

Keyboard Shortcut Press Ctrl+H to display the Replace page of the Find And Replace dialog box.

Tip If the Navigation task pane is open, you can click the arrow at the right end of the Search Document box and then click Replace. The Find And Replace dialog box opens with the search term from the Navigation task pane already in the Find What box.

On the Replace page, you can click the following:

- **Find Next** Finds the first occurrence or leaves the selected occurrence as it is and locates the next one

- **Replace** Replaces the selected occurrence with the text in the Replace With box and moves to the next occurrence

- **Replace All** Replaces all occurrences with the text in the Replace With box

   Tip Before clicking Replace All, ensure that the replacement is clearly defined. For example, if you want to change *trip* to *journey*, be sure to tell Word to find only the whole word *trip*; otherwise, *triple* could become *journeyle*.

As on the Find page, clicking More displays the options you can use to carry out more complicated replacements.

In this exercise, you'll find a phrase and make a correction to the text. Then you'll replace one phrase with another throughout the entire document.

  SET UP You need the RulesRegulations_start document located in your Chapter03 practice file folder to complete this exercise. Open the RulesRegulations_start document, and save it as *RulesRegulations*. Then follow the steps.

1. With the cursor at the beginning of the document, on the **Home** tab, in the **Editing** group, click the **Find** button (not its arrow).

   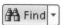

   The Navigation task pane opens, displaying the Search tab.

2. With the cursor in the **Search Document** box, type **Board**. (Don't type the period.)

The Navigation task pane displays 62 matches with the word *Board* and highlights every occurrence in the document.

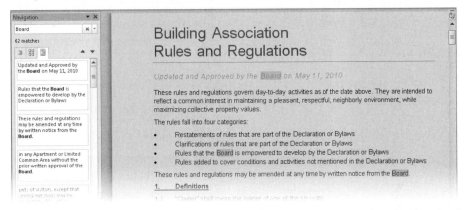

In the Navigation task pane, you can click each match to view its corresponding location in the document.

3. In the **Navigation** task pane, click the fifth match in the search results to jump to page **2**.

   Notice that under the heading *4. Storage*, Word has highlighted the *board* portion of *skateboards*. You need to restrict the search to the whole word *Board*.

4. In the **Navigation** task pane, click the arrow at the right end of the **Search Document** box.

   A menu of options for refining the search appears.

You can click options that allow you to find specific types of objects as well as text.

5. In the top part of the list, click **Advanced Find**.

   The Find And Replace dialog box opens with the Find page displayed. The Find What box already contains the search term from the Navigation task pane.

6. In the lower-left corner of the dialog box, click **More**.

   The dialog box expands to display options for refining the search.

7. In the **Search Options** area of the dialog box, select the **Match case** and **Find whole words only** check boxes. Then click **Reading Highlight**, click **Highlight All**, and click **Close**.

   Under the *4. Storage* heading, the word *skateboards* is no longer highlighted.

8. Press Ctrl+Home to move the cursor to the beginning of the document.

9. In the **Navigation** task pane, display the search options list again, and then click **Replace**.

   The Find And Replace dialog box opens with the Replace page active. The Find What box retains the entry from the previous search, and the Match Case and Find Whole Words Only check boxes are still selected.

10. Click **Less** to reduce the size of the box, and then drag the box by its title bar toward the top of the document.

11. Click the **Replace with** box, type **Association Board**, and then click **Find Next**.

    Word highlights the first occurrence of *Board*.

12. In the dialog box, click **Replace**.

    Word replaces the first occurrence of *Board* with *Association Board* and then finds the next occurrence.

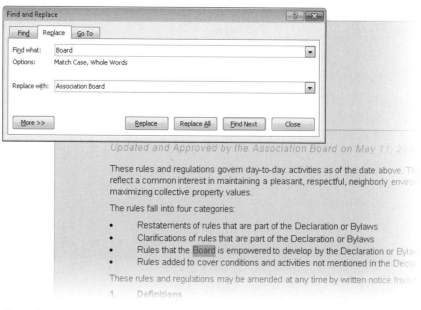

If you don't want to replace an occurrence, click Find Next to skip it.

13. Having tested the replacement, click **Replace All**.

14. When Word tells you how many replacements it made, click **OK** to close the message box. Then in the **Find and Replace** dialog box, click **Close**.

15. Press Ctrl+Home to move to the beginning of the document.

    In the *Updated and Approved* line of text, the word *Association* is now duplicated.

16. Use your new find and replace skills to replace any instances of **Association Association** in the document with **Association**.

 CLEAN UP Close the Navigation task pane. Then save and close the RulesRegulations document.

Fine-Tuning Text

Language is often contextual—you use different words and phrases in a marketing brochure than you would in a letter requesting immediate payment of an invoice or in an informal memo about a social gathering after work. To help you ensure that you're using the words that best convey your meaning in any given context, Word provides a thesaurus where you can look up alternative words, called *synonyms*, for a selected word. The Thesaurus is one of a set of research services provided by Word.

To look up alternatives for a word, you can right-click the word, and then click Synonyms to display a list from which you can choose the one you want. Alternatively, you can select the word and then click the Thesaurus button in the Proofing group on the Review tab. The Research task pane opens, displaying the selected word in the Search For box and synonyms for that word in the Thesaurus list.

Keyboard Shortcuts Press Shift+F7 to open the Research task pane and display Thesaurus entries for the active word, which is also displayed in the Search For box.

Research

Search for:

chips

Thesaurus: English (U.S.)

Back

▲ **Thesaurus: English (U.S.)**

  ▲ **fries (n.)**
    fries
    French-fried potatoes ...
    French fries (Dictionar...
    deep fried potatoes (Di...
    pommes frites (Diction...
  ▲ **marks (n.)**
    marks
    damages
    imperfections
    flaws
    blemishes
  ▲ **pieces (n.)**
    pieces
    bits
    crumbs
    flakes
    chunks
    morsels
  ▲ tokens (n.)

Get services on Office Marketplace

Research options...

You can click a synonym to display its synonyms and click again to repeat that process until you find exactly the word you want.

To replace the selected word with a synonym, point to your chosen synonym, click the arrow that appears, and then click Insert.

In addition to the Thesaurus, the Research task pane provides access to a variety of informational resources. You first open the Research task pane by clicking the Research button in the Proofing group and then enter a topic in the Search For box, specifying in the box below which resource Word should use to look for information about that topic.

Keyboard Shortcut Press the Alt key and click anywhere in the document to display the Research task pane.

You can choose a specific resource from the list or click All Reference Books or All Research Sites to widen the search.

Clicking Research Options at the bottom of the Research task pane displays the Research Options dialog box. In this dialog box, you can specify which of a predefined set of reference materials and other Internet resources will be available from the list.

You can click Add Services to include your favorite reference resources in the list.

Word also comes with three translation tools with which you can quickly translate words and phrases, or even entire documents.

● **Mini Translator**   You turn the Mini Translator on or off by clicking the Translate button in the Language group of the Review tab and then clicking Mini Translator. When the Mini Translator is turned on, you can point to a word or selected phrase to display a translation in the specified language. When the box containing the translation is displayed, you can click the Expand button to display the Research task pane, where you can change the translation language. You can also copy the translated word or phrase, or hear the word or phrase spoken for you.

Using the Mini Translator is the quickest way to obtain the translation of a selection.

● **Online bilingual dictionary** To obtain the translation of a word that does not appear in the text of a document, you can click Translate Selected Text in the Translate menu to display the Research task pane, type the word in the Search For box, specify the language you want, and then click Start Searching. Word consults the online bilingual dictionary for the language you chose and displays the result. You can then click Insert to enter a translated word in the document at the cursor.

Research	▼ ✕

Search for:

coffee	➡

Translation	▾

⊙Back ▾	⊙ ▾

◢ **Translation** ▲

Translate a word or sentence.
From

English (U.S.)	▾

To

Danish	▾

Translate the whole document.
➡
Translation options...

◢ **Microsoft® Translator**

kaffe

Insert ▾

Microsoft® Translator – Hc

Microsoft® Research ESL A

◢ **Can't find it?**

Try one of these alternatives
or see Help for hints on ▾

Get services on Office Marketplace

Research options...

You can use the bilingual dictionary to translate a selected word or the word you type in the Search For box.

- **Online machine translator** To translate an entire document, you can click Translate Document on the Translate menu. When Word displays a message that the document will be sent for translation by the Microsoft Translator service (which is free), click Send. The document and its translation then appear side by side in your Web browser. You can set the translation from and translation to languages in the boxes at the top of the Web page and click buttons to change the view.

The Microsoft Translator service translates complete documents into the language you select.

To change the default language used by the Mini Translator or the machine translator, you click Choose Translation Language on the Translate menu. Then in the Translation Language Options dialog box, you can select different language pairs for each type of translator.

You can translate from and to many languages, including Arabic, Chinese, Greek, Hebrew, Italian, Japanese, Korean, Polish, Portuguese, Russian, Spanish, and Swedish.

In this exercise, you'll use the Thesaurus to replace one word with another. Then you'll experiment with the Mini Translator.

SET UP You need the Brochure_start document located in your Chapter03 practice file folder to complete this exercise. Open the Brochure_start document, and save it as *Brochure*. Then follow the steps.

1. Double-click the word **acclaimed** in the second line of the first paragraph.

2. On the **Review** tab, in the **Proofing** group, click the **Thesaurus** button.

   The Research task pane opens, listing synonyms for the word *acclaimed*.

3. In the task pane, under **much-admired**, click **commended**.

   The word *commended* replaces *acclaimed* in the Search For box at the top of the task pane.

Synonyms for commended *are now listed in the task pane.*

4. Point to the word **celebrated**, click the arrow that appears to its right, and then click **Insert**.

   The word *celebrated* replaces *acclaimed* in the document.

5. Close the **Research** task pane.

   Tip You can open the Research task pane at any time by clicking the Research button in the Proofing group on the Review tab.

6. In the **Language** group, click the **Translate** button, and then click **Choose Translation Language**.

   The Translation Language Options dialog box opens.

7. Under **Choose Mini Translator language**, click the **Translate to** arrow, click **French (France)** in the list, and then click **OK**.

8. In the **Language** group, click the **Translate** button, and then click **Mini Translator [French (France)]**.

   The Mini Translator is now turned on.

9. In the last paragraph of the document, point to the word **wardrobe**, and then move the pointer over the shadow box that appears above the word.

   The Mini Translator appears, showing two French translations for the word *wardrobe*: *armoire* and *garde-robe*.

You can click the Play button to hear the translated word.

10. In the **Mini Translator** box, click the **Expand** button.

    The Research task pane opens, displaying the settings for translating from English into French.

11. Under **Bilingual Dictionary** in the **Research** task pane, double-click **armoire** to select it.

12. Right-click the selection, and click **Copy**.

13. In the document, double-click the word **wardrobe**.

14. Right-click the selection, and under **Paste Options** in the list, point to (don't click) the **Keep Text Only** button.

    Word displays a live preview of what the text will look like if you replace *wardrobe* with *armoire*.

15. Press the Esc key to close the shortcut menu and leave the word *wardrobe* in the text.

✖ CLEAN UP Close the Research task pane, and turn off the Mini Translator by clicking the Translate button in the Language group and clicking Mini Translator. Then save and close the Brochure document.

Correcting Spelling and Grammatical Errors

In the days of handwritten and typewritten documents, people might have tolerated a typographical or grammatical error or two because correcting such errors without creating a mess was difficult. Word-processing programs such as Word have built-in spelling and grammar checkers, so now documents that contain these types of errors are likely to reflect badly on their creators.

Tip Although Word can help you eliminate misspellings and grammatical errors, its tools are not infallible. You should always read through your document to catch any problems that the Word tools can't detect—for example, homonyms such as *their*, *there*, and *they're*.

Word provides these three tools to help you with the chore of eliminating spelling and grammar errors:

- **AutoCorrect** This feature corrects commonly misspelled words, such as *adn* to *and*, so that you don't have to correct them yourself. AutoCorrect comes with a long list of frequently misspelled words and their correct spellings. If you frequently misspell a word that AutoCorrect doesn't change, you can add it to the list in the AutoCorrect dialog box. If you deliberately mistype a word and don't want to accept the AutoCorrect change, you can reverse the correction by clicking the Undo button before you type anything else.

- **Error indicators** Word underlines potential spelling errors with red wavy under-lines and grammatical errors with green wavy underlines. You can right-click an underlined word or phrase to display suggested corrections in a shortcut menu.

- **Spelling and Grammar dialog box** If you want to check the spelling or grammar of the entire document, you can click the Spelling & Grammar button in the Proofing group on the Review tab. Word then works its way through the document and displays the Spelling And Grammar dialog box if it encounters a potential error.

The buttons in the Spelling And Grammar dialog box are dynamic and reflect the type of error found.

Keyboard Shortcut Press F7 to start checking the spelling and grammar from your current location in the document.

If the error is a misspelling, the Spelling And Grammar dialog box suggests correc-tions; if the error is a breach of grammar rules, the Spelling And Grammar dialog box tells you which rule you have broken and suggests corrections. You can implement a suggestion by double-clicking it in the Suggestions box.

In this exercise, you'll change an AutoCorrect setting and add a word to the AutoCorrect list. You'll check the spelling in the document and add terms to the custom dictionary, and then you'll find, review, and correct a grammatical error.

SET UP You need the Letter_start document located in your Chapter03 practice file folder to complete this exercise. Open the Letter_start document, and save it as *Letter*. Then follow the steps.

1. Click immediately to the left of **negative** in the last line of the first paragraph, and then type **coresponding**, followed by a space.

   As soon as you press the Spacebar, AutoCorrect changes *coresponding* to *corresponding*.

2. Click the **File** tab to display the Backstage view, and then click **Options**.

3. In the left pane of the **Word Options** dialog box, click **Proofing**, and then on the **Proofing** page, click **AutoCorrect Options**.

   The AutoCorrect dialog box opens, displaying the AutoCorrect page.

A selected check box indicates an error that AutoCorrect will automatically correct.

Tip You can clear the check box of any item you don't want corrected. For example, if you don't want AutoCorrect to capitalize the first letter that follows a period, clear the Capitalize First Letter Of Sentences check box.

4. In the **Replace** box, type **avalable**.

   Word scrolls the list below to show the entry that is closest to what you typed.

5. Press the Tab key to move the cursor to the **With** box, and then type **available**.

6. Click **Add** to add the entry to the correction list, and then click **OK**.

7. Click **OK** to close the **Word Options** dialog box.

8. Position the cursor at the end of the second paragraph, press the Spacebar, and then type **Sidney will not be avalable May 10-14** followed by a period.

   The word *avalable* changes to *available*.

9. In the first paragraph, right-click **sorces**, the first word with a red wavy underline.

   Word lists possible correct spellings for this word.

sources

sores

scores

source's

forces

Ignore

Ignore All

Add to Dictionary

AutoCorrect   ▶

Language   ▶

Spelling...

Look Up | ▶

Cut

Copy

Paste Options:

A

The shortcut menu also lists actions you might want to carry out, such as adding the word to the AutoCorrect list.

10. In the list, click **sources**.

    Word removes the red wavy underline and inserts the correction.

Tip Word's grammar checker helps identify phrases and clauses that don't follow traditional grammatical rules, but it's not always accurate. It's easy to get in the habit of ignoring green wavy underlines. However, it's wise to scrutinize them all to be sure that your documents don't contain any embarrassing mistakes.

11. Press Ctrl+Home to move to the beginning of the document, and then on the **Review** tab, in the **Proofing** group, click the **Spelling & Grammar** button.

    The Spelling And Grammar dialog box opens, with the duplicate word *to* in red in the Repeated Word box.

current economic and environmental conditions, as well as of political issues that could affect our ability to maintain a viable business. When we select our product sources, we strive to not only to improve the local economy but to to ensure the preservation of fragile ecologies. It is a complex balancing act, but we are committed to maximizing our positive impacts while causing no corresponding negative impacts.

An exciting a [ ] orate office to discuss any [ ] gents. You may contact S [ ] sidney@widev [ ] will not be available May [ ]

Spelling and Grammar: English (U.S.)

Repeated Word:

When we select our product sources, we strive to not only to improve the local economy but to to ensure the preservation of fragile ecologies.

Ignore Once
Ignore All
Add to Dictionary

Suggestions:

Delete
Delete All
AutoCorrect

☑ Check grammar

Options...   Undo   Cancel

In the meantime [ ] ducts and suppliers, a tra [ ] statement, which outlines

Sincerely,

Florian Stiller
President

Behind the dialog box, Word has highlighted the duplicate to *in the document.*

Troubleshooting If the errors we mention don't appear to be in the practice file, click Options at the bottom of the Spelling And Grammar dialog box. Then in the Word Options dialog box, under When Correcting Spelling And Grammar In Word, click Recheck Document. Click Yes to reset the spelling and grammar checkers, and then click OK.

12. Click **Delete**.

    Word deletes the second *to* and then displays the first word it does not recognize, *commited*, in red in the Not In Dictionary box.

13. With **committed** selected in the **Suggestions** box, click **AutoCorrect**.

    Word adds the misspelling and the selected correction to the AutoCorrect list, so that the next time you type *commited* by mistake, the spelling will be corrected for you as you type. The program then identifies a possible grammatical error.

This grammatical error is identified as an incorrect use of a comma.

You need to read the sentence and then decide whether and how to correct the error. In this case, the error is not related to the comma after *venture* but to the fact that there is no verb in the first half of the sentence.

14. In the **Comma Use** box, double-click the word **An** at the beginning of the sentence with the error, and type **The import business is an**. Then click **Change**.

    Word flags *Contoso* as a word it doesn't recognize.

    Troubleshooting If Word does not proceed to the next potential error after you click Change, click Resume to tell Word to continue with the spelling and grammar check.

    Contoso is a proper noun and is spelled correctly. You could click Ignore All to cause Word to skip over any other instances of this word in this document. However, if this name appears frequently in your documents, you can prevent Word from continuing to flag it by adding the word to the custom dictionary.

15. Click **Add to Dictionary**.

    Word displays a message indicating that it has finished checking the spelling and grammar of the document.

16. Click **OK** to close the message box.

    Tip The grammar checker doesn't always catch awkward phrasing. For example, note the error in the second sentence of the first paragraph of the Letter document. It's a good example of why you should always proofread your documents, to catch the things that Word doesn't.

CLEAN UP Save the Letter document, and then close it.

Viewing Document Statistics

As you type, Word keeps track of the number of pages and words in your document and displays this information at the left end of the status bar. To see the number of words in only part of the document, such as a few paragraphs, simply select that part. The status bar then displays the number of words in the selection, expressed as a fraction of the total, such as 250/800.

You can see more statistics in the Word Count dialog box, which you open by clicking the Word Count button in the Proofing group on the Review tab.

Word Count	?	X
Statistics:		
Pages	1	
Words	184	
Characters (no spaces)	979	
Characters (with spaces)	1,157	
Paragraphs	6	
Lines	22	

☑ Include textboxes, footnotes and endnotes

[Close]

In addition to counting pages and words, Word counts characters, paragraphs, and lines.

Word also gives you the option of including or excluding words in text boxes, footnotes, and endnotes.

Inserting Saved Text

Another way to ensure consistency in your documents while also saving time is to use building blocks. These are saved items that are available for use in any document. Word 2010 comes with many built-in building blocks for formatted items such as cover pages, headers and footers, tables, and text boxes. You can also save your own building blocks by using the Quick Parts feature.

See Also For information about the building blocks that come with Word, see "Inserting Building Blocks" in Chapter 6, "Add Simple Graphic Elements."

A custom building block can be a simple phrase or sentence that you type often, or it can include multiple paragraphs, formatting, graphics, and so on. The trick is to first ensure that the text is exactly the way you want it. Then you can save the building block and use it confidently wherever you need it.

To create a building block, you select the item you want to save, click Quick Parts in the Text group on the Insert tab, and save the selection in the Quick Parts gallery with an assigned name. You can then insert the building block at the cursor by clicking Quick Parts to display the gallery and clicking the thumbnail of the building block you want. Or you can insert it elsewhere by right-clicking the thumbnail in the gallery and then clicking one of the specified locations.

Quick Parts ▾

General

(925) 555-0167

(925) 555-0167

Insert at <u>C</u>urrent Document Position
Insert at Page <u>H</u>eader
Insert at Page <u>F</u>ooter
Insert at Be<u>g</u>inning of Section
Insert at E<u>n</u>d of Section
Insert at <u>B</u>eginning of Document
Insert at <u>E</u>nd of Document
Edit <u>P</u>roperties...
<u>O</u>rganize and Delete...
<u>A</u>dd Gallery to Quick Access Toolbar

You can insert a custom building block by selecting a location from a list.

Tip In a document, you can type the name of any building block and then press the F3 key to insert it at the cursor.

When you create a custom building block, Word saves it in a special file called the *Building Blocks template*. When you exit Word, you'll be asked whether you want to save this template. If you want to discard the building blocks you have created in this Word session, click Don't Save. If you want them to be available for future documents, click Save.

In this exercise, you'll save a company contact-information block and the Latin name of a plant as building blocks so that you can insert them elsewhere in a document.

SET UP You need the Bamboo_start document located in your Chapter03 practice file folder to complete this exercise. Open the Bamboo_start document, and save it as *Bamboo*. Then follow the steps.

1. At the top of the document, select the first four lines by using any of the selection techniques described earlier in this chapter.

2. On the **Insert** tab, in the **Text** group, click the **Quick Parts** button, and then click **Save Selection to Quick Part Gallery**.

    The Create New Building Block dialog box opens.

Word suggests the first few words of the selection as the name of the building block.

3. In the **Name** box, type **Contact Block**, and then click **OK**.

   Word saves the selection in the Quick Parts gallery.

4. In the third paragraph of the document, select **obatea acuminata aztectorum** (don't select the period). Then in the **Text** group, click the **Quick Parts** button.

   Notice that the company contact information now appears as a building block in the Quick Parts gallery.

The Quick Parts gallery displays only the building blocks you create. The built-in building blocks are available from other galleries, such as the Cover Page gallery.

5. Click **Save Selection to Quick Part Gallery**, type **oaa** in the **Name** box, and then click **OK**.

6. Press Ctrl+End to move the cursor to the end of the document, and then press the Spacebar.

7. Type **In particular, we recommend oaa** (don't type a period).

8. Press F3, and then type a period.

   Word replaces *oaa* with its building block, *obatea acuminata aztectorum*.

   Troubleshooting Pressing F3 substitutes the corresponding building block only if there is a space to the left of the building block name and the cursor is immediately to its right. If you want to enter a building block in existing text (rather than at the end of it), you need to ensure that there is a space after the cursor. Type two spaces, position the cursor between them, type the building block name, and then press F3.

9. Press Enter. Then in the **Text** group, click the **Quick Parts** button, and in the gallery, click the **Contact Block** entry.

   The company contact information appears at the cursor.

very adaptable, with some species deciduous and others evergreen. Although there isn't yet a complete knowledge about this plant, there are believed to be between 1100 and 1500 different species of bamboo. The color range is from light green leaves and culms (stems) to dark, rich shades of green or some combination thereof.

Because they are so easy to grow in such a variety of climates, there is a plant available for just about anyone who wishes to grow one in the backyard. Some dwarf species include chimonobambusa marmorea, indocalamus tessellatus, and pleioblastus chino vaginatus. Also suitable for the personal garden are those categorized as mid size. Examples of these types of plants are bambusa glaucophylla and otatea acuminata aztectorum. Plant starts and seeds are easier to find than ever, being available at nurseries and through mail order.

Choosing bamboo as part of home or garden design makes sense on many levels. Not only does it have an appealing look, but it supports the environment as well as the countries that produce it. In particular, we recommend otatea acuminata aztectorum.

Wide World Importers
Furniture and accessories for your world

(925) 555-0167
www.wideworldimporters.com

The two custom building blocks are inserted with just a few clicks.

CLEAN UP Save the Bamboo document, and then close it. When you exit Word, remember to click Don't Save when you are asked whether you want to save changes to the Building Blocks template.

Inserting One Document into Another

Sometimes you'll want to insert one saved document into another document. For example, you might want to compile four quarterly reports so that you can edit them to create an annual report. In this situation, it would be tedious to have to select and copy the text of each report and then paste it into the annual document. Instead, you can have Word insert the existing documents for you. Here's how:

1. Position the cursor where you want to insert the existing document, and then on the Insert tab, in the Text group, click the Object arrow.

2. In the list, click Text From File.

    The Insert File dialog box opens.

3. Locate the file you want, and double-click it to insert it at the cursor.

Key Points

- You can cut or copy text and paste it elsewhere in the same document or in a different document. Cut and copied text is stored on the Clipboard.

- Undo one action or the last several actions you performed by clicking the Undo button (or its arrow) on the Quick Access Toolbar. Click the Redo button if you change your mind again.

- You can find each occurrence of a word or phrase and replace it with another.

- Rely on AutoCorrect to correct common misspellings. Correct other spelling and grammatical errors individually as you type or by checking the entire document in one pass.

- You don't have to type and proof the same text over and over again. Instead, save the text as a building block and insert it with a few mouse clicks.

Chapter at a Glance

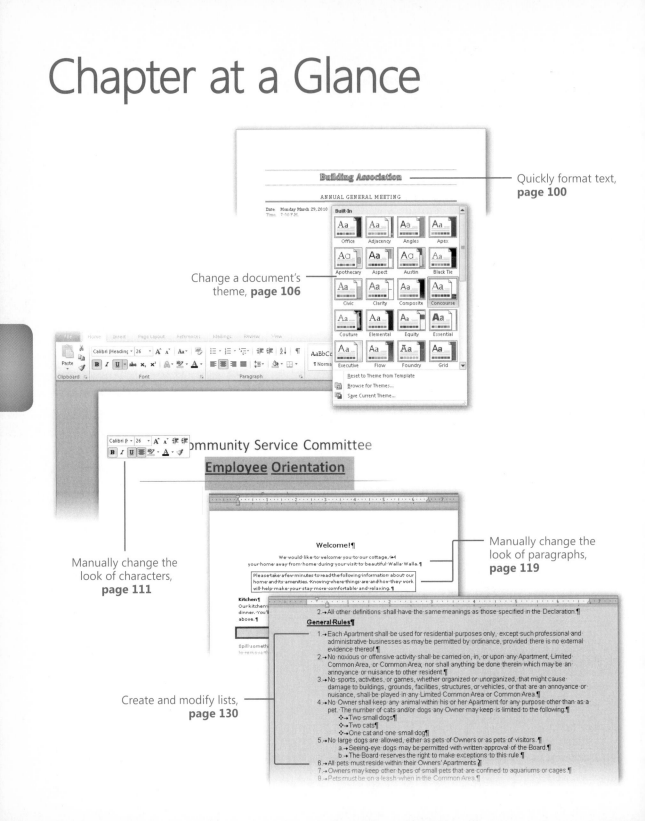

Quickly format text, **page 100**

Change a document's theme, **page 106**

Manually change the look of characters, **page 111**

Manually change the look of paragraphs, **page 119**

Create and modify lists, **page 130**

4 Change the Look of Text

In this chapter, you will learn how to

✔ Quickly format text.

✔ Change a document's theme.

✔ Manually change the look of characters.

✔ Manually change the look of paragraphs.

✔ Create and modify lists.

The appearance of your documents helps to convey their message. Microsoft Word 2010 can help you develop professional-looking documents whose appearance is appropriate to their contents. You can easily format the characters and paragraphs so that key points stand out and your arguments are easy to grasp. You can also change the look of major elements within a document by applying predefined sets of formatting called *Quick Styles*, and you can change the look of selected text by applying predefined combinations called *text effects*. In addition, you can change the fonts, colors, and effects throughout a document with one click by applying one of the built-in themes.

Tip A font consists of alphabetic characters, numbers, and symbols that share a common design.

In this chapter, you'll first experiment with built-in Quick Styles and text effects, and then you'll change the theme applied to a document. You'll change the look of individual words, and then you'll change the indentation, alignment, and spacing of individual paragraphs. You'll also add borders and shading to make paragraphs stand out. Finally, you'll create and format both bulleted and numbered lists.

> **Practice Files** Before you can complete the exercises in this chapter, you need to copy the book's practice files to your computer. The practice files you'll use to complete the exercises in this chapter are in the Chapter04 practice file folder. A complete list of practice files is provided in "Using the Practice Files" at the beginning of this book.

Quickly Formatting Text

You don't have to know much about character and paragraph formatting to be able to format your documents in ways that will make them easier to read and more professional looking. With a couple of mouse clicks, you can easily change the look of words, phrases, and paragraphs by using Quick Styles.

Word has several types of predefined Quick Styles, but the simplest are those you can apply to text.

- **Paragraph styles** You apply these to entire paragraphs, such as headings.
- **Character styles** You apply these to words.
- **Linked styles** You apply these to either paragraphs or words.

By default, Word makes just a few of the predefined Quick Styles available in the Quick Styles gallery in the Styles group on the Home tab. Quick Styles apply a combination of character formatting (such as font, size, and color) and paragraph formatting (such as line spacing).

AaBbCcDc	AaBbCcDc	**AaBbC**	AaB
¶ Normal	¶ No Spaci...	Heading 1	Title
AaBbCc.	*AaBbCcDc*	*AaBbCcDc*	**AaBbCcDc**
Subtitle	Subtle Em...	Emphasis	Intense E...
AaBbCcDc	*AaBbCcDc*	***AaBbCcDc***	AABBCCDC
Strong	Quote	Intense Q...	Subtle Ref...
AABBCCDC	**AABBCCDC**	AaBbCcDc	
Intense R...	Book Title	¶ List Para...	

Save Selection as a New Quick Style...
Clear Formatting
Apply Styles...

The Quick Styles gallery.

The styles displayed as thumbnails in the Quick Styles gallery have been designed to go well together, so applying styles from the gallery produces a harmonious effect. After you apply styles from the current set of styles, you can easily change the look of the entire document by switching to a different style set. The Quick Style names are the same; only their defined formatting changes. So if you have applied the Heading 1 style to a paragraph, you can change its formatting simply by changing the style set.

You display the list of available style sets by clicking the Change Styles button and then clicking Style Set.

Clicking one of these style sets displays thumbnails of its styles in the Quick Styles gallery.

You can point to any style set in the list to see a live preview of how the applied styles in a set will look, and you can click a style set to apply its definitions to the document.

See Also For information about creating custom styles, refer to *Microsoft Word 2010 Step by Step*, by Joyce Cox and Joan Lambert (Microsoft Press, 2010).

In addition to applying Quick Styles to quickly change the look of paragraphs and characters, you can apply predefined text effects to a selection to add more zing. Clicking the Text Effects button in the Font group on the Home tab displays a gallery of effects to choose from.

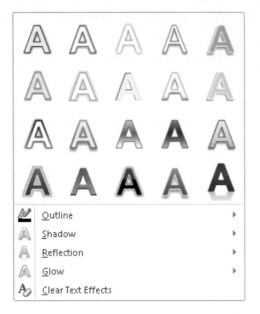

You can apply any predefined effect in the gallery to selected text, or you can click options at the bottom of the gallery and define a custom effect.

These effects are dramatic, so you'll probably want to restrict their use to document titles and similar elements to which you want to draw particular attention.

In this exercise, you'll experiment with Quick Styles and text effects.

SET UP You need the AgendaA_start document located in your Chapter04 practice file folder to complete this exercise. Open the AgendaA_start document, and save it as *AgendaA*. Then follow the steps.

1. In the lower-right corner of the program window, at the left end of the **Zoom Slider**, click the **Zoom Out** button until you can see all of the text.

   For example, if your current view is 100% and your resolution is 1024x768, you can click the Zoom Out button three times to set the zoom percentage to 70%.

2. Ensure that the cursor is located at the top of the document, at the beginning of the **Building Association** paragraph. Then on the **Home** tab, in the **Styles** group, point to each thumbnail in the displayed row of the **Quick Styles** gallery.

   The formatting of the first line changes to show you a live preview of how its text will look if you click the style you are pointing to. You don't have to actually apply the formatting to see its effect.

3. Without making a selection, click the **Down** arrow to the right of the gallery.

   The next row of the Quick Styles gallery appears.

4. Point to each thumbnail in this row of the **Quick Styles** gallery.

   Only the styles that are paragraph or linked styles affect the text. You cannot see a live preview of character styles unless the cursor is within a word or multiple words are selected.

5. To the right of the **Quick Styles** gallery, click the **More** button.

   Word displays the entire Quick Styles gallery. The style applied to the paragraph containing the cursor is surrounded by a border.

6. In the gallery, click the **Title** thumbnail.

   Word applies that style to the paragraph containing the cursor.

7. Click anywhere in the **ANNUAL GENERAL MEETING** line, and then in the gallery, click the **Heading 1** thumbnail.

8. Click anywhere in the **Agenda** line, and then in the gallery, click the **Heading 1** thumbnail.

   Notice that although you applied the same Heading 1 style to *ANNUAL GENERAL MEETING* and *Agenda*, the first heading looks bigger because of the use of all capital letters.

Building Association

ANNUAL GENERAL MEETING
Date: Monday March 29, 2010
Time: 7:00 P.M.

Agenda
Preliminaries

Call to order

Proof of notice of meeting

The styles make it easy to distinguish information.

Tip We have hidden formatting marks for this exercise.

9. Point in the selection area to the left of the **Preliminaries** line, and click to select the line. Then hold down the Ctrl key while clicking adjacent to the following lines:

   Approval of Minutes
   Board Reports
   Election of Board Members
   New Business
   Adjournment

10. Apply the **Heading 1** style to the selected lines. Then without moving the selection, click the **More** button and, in the gallery, click **Emphasis**.

    Applying the Emphasis character style on top of the Heading 1 paragraph style makes these headings italic, which looks lighter.

11. Select the **Date** and **Time** lines, and then in the **Quick Styles** gallery, click the **No Spacing** thumbnail.

12. Apply the **No Spacing** style to the three lines under **Preliminaries**, the two lines under **Board Reports**, and the two lines under **Election of Board Members**.

13. Press Ctrl+Home to release the selection and move the cursor to the top of the document.

    As you can see, the results look very professional.

> # Building Association
>
> **ANNUAL GENERAL MEETING**
> Date: Monday March 29, 2010
> Time: 7:00 P.M.
>
> ## Agenda
>
> ### *Preliminaries*
> Call to order
> Proof of notice of meeting
> Roll call to establish quorum
>
> ### *Approval of Minutes*
>
> ### *Board Reports*
> Financial report
> New rules and regulations

You have clearly defined the hierarchy of the agenda with just a few clicks.

14. In the **Styles** group, click the **Change Styles** button, point to **Style Set**, and then point to each style set in turn, watching the effect on the document.

15. When you finish exploring, click **Formal**.

    The formatting of the document changes and the headings and text take on the look assigned to this style set.

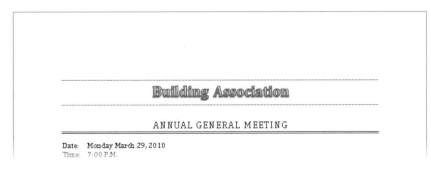

The Title, Heading 1, and Emphasis style definitions in the Formal style set produce a different look from those in the default set.

16. Select the document title. Then in the **Font** group, click the **Text Effects** button.

    Word displays the Text Effects gallery.

17. Point to each thumbnail in the gallery, observing the effect on the title behind the gallery.

18. Click the right-most thumbnail in the third row (**Fill - Red, Accent 2, Double Outline - Accent 2**). Then click away from the title to release the selection.

    The effect applied to the title makes it really stand out.

By using text effects, you can apply complex sets of formatting with a few clicks.

CLEAN UP Save the AgendaA document, and then close it.

Changing a Document's Theme

To enhance the look of a Word document whose components have been styled, you can apply a predefined theme. A theme is a combination of colors, fonts, and effects that project a certain feeling or tone. For example, the Flow theme uses a palette of blues and greens, the Calibri and Constantia fonts, and understated effects. You apply a theme to the entire document by clicking the Themes button in the Themes group on the Page Layout tab, and then making a selection from the Themes gallery.

The Themes gallery.

If you like the colors of one theme and the fonts of another, you can mix and match theme elements. First apply the theme that most closely resembles the look you want, and then in the Themes group, change the colors by clicking the Theme Colors button or the fonts by clicking the Theme Fonts button.

If you create a combination of colors and fonts that you would like to be able to use with other documents, you can save the combination as a new theme. By saving the theme in the default Document Themes folder, you make the theme available in the Themes gallery. However, you don't have to store custom themes in the Document Themes folder; you can store them anywhere on your hard disk, on removable media, or in a network location. To use a theme that is stored in a different location, you click the Themes button, and then click Browse For Themes at the bottom of the gallery. Locate the theme you want in the Choose Theme Or Themed Document dialog box, and then click Open to apply that theme to the current document.

Tip The bottom section of the Themes gallery displays themes downloaded from the Microsoft Office Online Web site. You can visit this Web site at office.microsoft.com to find additional themes and templates created by Microsoft and by other people.

In this exercise, you'll apply a theme to an existing document and change the colors and fonts. Then you'll save the new combination as a custom theme.

SET UP You need the AgendaB_start document located in your Chapter04 practice file folder to complete this exercise. Open the AgendaB_start document, and save it as *AgendaB*. Then follow the steps.

1. On the **Page Layout** tab, in the **Themes** group, click the **Themes** button.

   The Themes gallery appears.

2. Point to each thumbnail in turn to display a live preview of the theme. (Scroll through the gallery so that you can explore all the themes.)

3. In the **Themes** gallery, click **Trek**.

   The colors and fonts change to those defined for the selected theme.

4. In the **Themes** group, click the **Theme Colors** button.

   The Theme Colors gallery appears. (The currently selected color set, which is not shown in the graphic on the next page, is indicated by a border.)

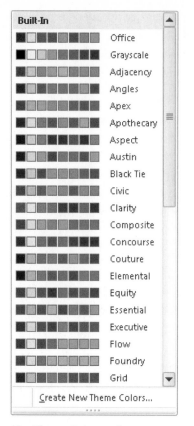

The Theme Colors gallery.

5. Preview any color set that interests you, and then in the gallery, click **Newsprint**.

   The Newsprint colors replace the Trek colors, but nothing else in the document changes.

6. In the **Themes** group, click the **Theme Fonts** button.

   The Theme Fonts gallery appears. The currently selected font set is highlighted. Each built-in option includes a set of two fonts—the first is used for headings and the second for body text.

The Theme Fonts gallery.

7. Preview any set of fonts that interests you, and then in the gallery, click **Apex**.

   The Apex fonts replace the Trek fonts, but the colors remain the same.

8. In the **Themes** group, click the **Themes** button, and then below the gallery, click **Save Current Theme**.

   The Save Current Theme dialog box opens and displays the contents of the Document Themes folder. (This dialog box resembles the Save As dialog box.) The Document Themes folder is the default location for saving any new themes you create.

9. In the **File name** box, replace the suggested name with **My Theme**, and then click **Save**.

10. In the **Themes** group, click the **Themes** button to display the gallery.

   Your new theme appears in the Custom section at the top of the gallery.

You can apply the custom theme to any document.

11. Click away from the gallery to close it without making a selection.

✖ **CLEAN UP** Save the AgendaB document, and then close it.

Tip If you want to delete the theme you created in this topic, open Windows Explorer and navigate to the C:\Users\<user name>\AppData\Roaming\Microsoft\Templates\Document Themes folder. (In Windows 7, you can click the Start button, type *Document Themes* in the Search box at the bottom of the Start menu, and then click the folder in the search results.) Then select My Theme, and press Delete.

Manually Changing the Look of Characters

As you have seen, Word 2010 makes changing the look of content in a styled document almost effortless. But styles can't do everything. To be able to precisely control the look of your text, you need to know how to manually change individual elements.

When you type text in a document, it is displayed in a particular font. By default the font used for text in a new Word document is Calibri, but you can change the font of any element at any time. The available fonts vary from one computer to another, depending on the programs installed. Common fonts include Arial, Verdana, and Times New Roman.

You can vary the look of a font by changing the following attributes:

● **Size** Almost every font comes in a range of sizes, which are measured in points from the top of letters that have parts that stick up (ascenders), such as *h*, to the bottom of letters that have parts that drop down (descenders), such as *p*. A point is approximately 1/72 of an inch (about 0.04 centimeters).

● **Style** Almost every font comes in a range of styles. The most common are regular (or plain), italic, bold, and bold italic.

● **Effect** Fonts can be enhanced by applying effects, such as underlining, small capital letters (small caps), or shadows.

● **Color** A palette of coordinated colors is available, and you can also specify custom colors.

● **Character spacing** You can alter the spacing between characters by pushing them apart or squeezing them together.

Although some attributes might cancel each other out, they are usually cumulative. For example, you might use a bold font in various sizes and various shades of green to make words stand out in a newsletter. Collectively, the font and its attributes are called *character formatting*.

You apply character formatting from one of three locations:

● **Mini Toolbar** Several common formatting buttons are available on the Mini Toolbar that appears when you point to selected text.

The Mini Toolbar is transparent until you point to it.

● **Font group on the Home tab** This group includes buttons for changing the font and most of the font attributes you are likely to use.

The Font group.

● **Font dialog box** If you are looking for an attribute, such as small caps, and don't see it in the Font group, click the Font dialog box launcher. All the attributes are gathered together on the Font page of the dialog box, except character spacing, which is on the Advanced page.

The Font page of the Font dialog box.

In this exercise, you'll format the text in a document by changing its font, style, size, color, and character spacing. You'll also highlight a few words. Then you'll return selected text to its original condition by clearing some formatting you no longer want.

SET UP You need the OrientationDraft_start document located in your Chapter04 practice file folder to complete this exercise. Open the OrientationDraft_start document, and save it as *OrientationDraft*. Then follow the steps.

1. In the **Employee Orientation** heading, click anywhere in the word **Orientation**.

2. On the **Home** tab, in the **Font** group, click the **Underline** button.

   Keyboard Shortcut Press Ctrl+U to underline the active word or selection.

   The word containing the cursor is now underlined. Notice that you did not have to select the entire word.

   Tip If you click the Underline arrow, you can choose an underline style and color from the Underline gallery.

3. In the same heading, click anywhere in the word **Employee**, and then on the Quick Access Toolbar, click the **Repeat** button.

   Keyboard Shortcut Press Ctrl+Y to repeat an action.

   Word repeats the previous formatting command. Again, although you did not select the entire word, it is now underlined.

4. In the selection area, click adjacent to **Employee Orientation** to select the entire heading.

   Word displays a transparent version of the Mini Toolbar. You can use the common commands on the Mini Toolbar to quickly change the look of the selection.

5. Point to the Mini Toolbar to make it fully visible. Then on the Mini Toolbar, click the **Bold** button.

   Keyboard Shortcut Press Ctrl+B to make the active word or selection bold.

The heading is now bold. The active buttons on the Mini Toolbar and in the Font group on the Home tab indicate the attributes you applied to the selection.

The ribbon reflects the settings in the Mini Toolbar.

Troubleshooting   The appearance of buttons and groups on the ribbon changes depending on the width of the program window. For information about changing the appearance of the ribbon to match our screen images, see "Modifying the Display of the Ribbon" at the beginning of this book.

6. On the Mini Toolbar, click the **Format Painter** button. Then move the pointer into the selection area to the left of the **Proposal** heading, and click the mouse button.

   Tip   The Format Painter button is also available in the Clipboard group on the Home tab.

   Word applies the formatting of *Employee Orientation* to *Proposal*.

7. Select **Employee Orientation**, and then on the **Home** tab, in the **Font** group, click the **Font** arrow.

   The Font gallery appears.

Word comes with many fonts.

8. Scroll through the gallery of available fonts, and then click **Impact**.

   Troubleshooting If Impact is not available, select any heavy font that catches your attention.

   The *Employee Orientation* heading now appears in the new font.

9. In the **Font** group, click the **Font Size** arrow, and then in the list, click **20**.

    The size of the heading text decreases to 20 points.

    Tip You can increase or decrease the font size in set increments by clicking the Grow Font and Shrink Font buttons in the Font group, or by clicking the same buttons on the Mini Toolbar that appears when you select text. You can also press Ctrl+> or Ctrl+<.

10. Click the **Font** dialog box launcher.

    Keyboard Shortcut Press Ctrl+Shift+F to display the Font dialog box.

    The Font dialog box opens.

11. Click the **Underline style** arrow, and then in the list, click **(none)**.

12. In the **Effects** area, select the **Small caps** check box.

13. Click the **Advanced** tab.

    Notice that the Spacing option is currently set to Expanded.

Font	? ✕

Font | **Advanced**

Character Spacing

Scale: 100%

Spacing: Expanded   By: 0.25 pt

Position: Normal   By:

☑ Kerning for fonts: 14   Points and above

OpenType Features

Ligatures: None

Number spacing: Default

Number forms: Default

Stylistic sets: Default

☐ Use Contextual Alternates

Preview

EMPLOYEE ORIENTATION

This font style is imitated for display. The closest matching style will be printed.

Set As Default   Text Effects...   OK   Cancel

The Advanced page of the Font dialog box.

14. To the right of the **Spacing** option, in the **By** box, select **0.25 pt**, type **10 pt** (the *pt* stands for *points*), and click **OK**. Then press Home to release the selection.

The manually formatted text appears in small capital letters with the spacing between the characters expanded by 10 points.

You can expand and contract the spacing between letters to create different effects.

15. Select **Employee Orientation** again. In the **Font** group, click the **Font Color** arrow, and then under **Theme Colors** in the palette, click the box at the right end of the top row (**Lime, Accent 6**).

The selected words are now lime green.

Tip To apply the Font Color button's current color, you can simply click the button (not its arrow). If you want to apply a color that is not shown under Theme Colors or Standard Colors, click More Colors at the bottom of the palette, and in the Colors dialog box, click the color you want in the color wheel.

16. In the first bullet point, select the phrase **concept of service**. Then in the **Font** group, click the **Text Highlight Color** arrow, and click the **Turquoise** box in the top row.

The selected phrase is now highlighted in turquoise, and the Text Highlight Color button shows turquoise as its active color.

Tip If you click the Text Color Highlight button without first making a selection, the shape of the mouse pointer changes to a highlighter that you can drag across text. Click the button again, or press Esc, to turn off the highlighter.

17. In the fifth bullet point, double-click the word **brainstorming**. Then hold down the Ctrl key while double-clicking **planning** and **leadership**.

18. In the **Font** group, click the **Change Case** button, and click **UPPERCASE**. Then click away from the bullet point to release the selection.

The selected words now appear in all capital letters.

Community Service Committee
EMPLOYEE ORIENTATION

Proposal

Updated: January 25, 2010

Project Goals
- Familiarize employees with the concept of service.
- Make service a natural part of their lives.
- Engage and motivate them.
- Forge a sense of teamwork among all employees across departments.
- Provide appropriate skills development through BRAINSTORMING, PLANNING, and LEADERSHIP opportunities.
- Meet genuine community needs.

Instead of retyping, you can have Word change the case of words.

19. Select the **Proposal** line. Then on the **Home** tab, in the **Font** group, click the **Clear Formatting** button.

Keyboard Shortcut Press Ctrl+Spacebar to clear manually applied formatting.

The formatting of the selected text is removed.

Tip You cannot click the Clear Formatting button to remove highlighting. If the highlight is the same color as that shown on the Text Highlight Color button, you can select the text and click the button to remove the highlighting. If the button shows a different color, select the text, click the Text Highlight Color arrow, and then click No Color.

✖ **CLEAN UP** Save the OrientationDraft document, and then close it.

Character Formatting and Case Considerations

The way you use case and character formatting in a document can influence its visual impact on your readers. Used judiciously, case and character formatting can make a plain document look attractive and professional, but excessive use can make it look amateurish and detract from the message. For example, using too many fonts in the same document is the mark of inexperience, so don't use more than two or three.

Bear in mind that lowercase letters tend to recede, so using all uppercase (capital) letters can be useful for titles and headings or for certain kinds of emphasis. However, large blocks of uppercase letters are tiring to the eye.

Tip Where do the terms *uppercase* and *lowercase* come from? Until the advent of computers, individual characters made of lead were assembled to form the words that would appear on a printed page. The characters were stored alphabetically in cases, with the capital letters in the upper case and the small letters in the lower case.

Manually Changing the Look of Paragraphs

As you know, you create a paragraph by typing text and then pressing the Enter key. The paragraph can consist of one word, one sentence, or multiple sentences. You can change the look of a paragraph by changing its indentation, alignment, and line spacing, as well as the space before and after it. You can also put borders around it and shade its background. Collectively, the settings you use to vary the look of a paragraph are called *paragraph formatting*.

In Word, you don't define the width of paragraphs and the length of pages by defining the area occupied by the text; instead you define the size of the white space—the left, right, top, and bottom margins—around the text. You click the Margins button in the Page Setup group on the Page Layout tab to define these margins, either for the whole document or for sections of the document.

See Also For information about setting margins, see "Previewing and Adjusting Page Layout" in Chapter 7, "Preview, Print, and Distribute Documents." For information about sections, see "Controlling What Appears on Each Page" in the same chapter.

Although the left and right margins are set for a whole document or section, you can vary the position of the paragraphs between the margins. The quickest way to indent a paragraph from the left is to click the Increase Indent button; clicking the Decrease Indent button has the opposite effect. You cannot increase or decrease the indent beyond the margins.

Another way to control the indentation of lines is by dragging markers on the horizontal ruler to indicate where each line of text starts and ends.

- **First Line Indent** Begins a paragraph's first line of text at this marker

- **Hanging Indent** Begins a paragraph's second and subsequent lines of text at this marker at the left end of the ruler

- **Left Indent** Indents the text to this marker

- **Right Indent** Wraps the text when it reaches this marker at the right end of the ruler

You display the ruler by clicking the Ruler check box in the Show group on the View tab, or by clicking the View Ruler button located at the top of the vertical scroll bar.

You can manually change a paragraph's indentation by moving markers on the horizontal ruler.

Setting a right indent indicates where the lines in a paragraph should end, but sometimes you might want to specify where only one line should end. For example, you might want to break a title after a particular word to make it look balanced on the page. You can end an individual line by inserting a text wrapping break (more commonly known as a *line break*). After positioning the cursor where you want the break to occur, you click the Breaks button in the Page Setup group on the Page Layout tab, and then click Text Wrapping. Word indicates the line break with a bent arrow. Inserting a line break does not start a new paragraph, so when you apply paragraph formatting to a line of text that ends with a line break, the formatting is applied to the entire paragraph, not just that line.

Keyboard Shortcut Press Shift+Enter to insert a line break.

You can also determine the positioning of a paragraph between the left and right margins by changing its alignment. You can click buttons in the Paragraph group on the Home tab to align paragraphs.

- **Align Left** Aligns each line of the paragraph at the left margin, with a ragged right edge

  Keyboard Shortcut Press Ctrl+L to left-align a paragraph.

- **Center** Aligns the center of each line in the paragraph between the left and right margins, with ragged left and right edges

  Keyboard Shortcut Press Ctrl+E to center-align a paragraph.

- **Align Right** Aligns each line of the paragraph at the right margin, with a ragged left edge

  Keyboard Shortcut Press Ctrl+R to right-align a paragraph.

- **Justify** Aligns each line between the margins, creating even left and right edges

  Keyboard Shortcut Press Ctrl+J to justify a paragraph.

Tip If you know that you want to create a centered paragraph, you don't have to type the text and then align the paragraph. You can use the Click And Type feature to create appropriately aligned text. Move the pointer to the center of a blank area of the page, and when the pointer's shape changes to an I-beam with centered text attached, double-click to insert the cursor in a centered paragraph. Similarly, you can double-click at the left edge of the page to enter left-aligned text and at the right edge to enter right-aligned text.

You can align lines of text in different locations across the page by using tab stops. The easiest way to set tab stops is to use the horizontal ruler. By default, Word sets left-aligned tab stops every half inch (1.27 centimeters), as indicated by gray marks below the ruler. To set a custom tab stop, you start by clicking the Tab button located at the left end of the ruler until the type of tab stop you want appears. You have the following options:

- **Left Tab** Aligns the left end of the text with the tab stop

- **Center Tab** Aligns the center of the text with the tab stop

- **Right Tab** Aligns the right end of the text with the tab stop

- **Decimal Tab** Aligns the decimal point in the text (usually a numeric value) with the tab stop

- **Bar Tab** Draws a vertical line at the position of the tab stop

After selecting the type of tab stop you want to set, you simply click the ruler where you want the tab stop to be. Word then removes any default tab stops to the left of the one you set.

This ruler has a custom left-aligned tab stop at the 1.5 inch mark and default tab stops every half inch to the right of the custom tab stop.

To change the position of an existing custom tab stop, you drag it to the left or right on the ruler. To delete a custom tab stop, you drag it away from the ruler.

To align the text to the right of the cursor with the next tab stop, you press the Tab key. The text is then aligned on the tab stop according to its type. For example, if you set a center tab stop, pressing Tab moves the text so that its center is aligned with the tab stop.

Tip To fine-tune the position of tab stops, click the Paragraph dialog box launcher on either the Home or Page Layout tab. In the Paragraph dialog box, click Tabs to display the Tabs dialog box. You might also open this dialog box if you want to use tab leaders—visible marks such as dots or dashes connecting the text before the tab with the text after it. For example, tab leaders are useful in a table of contents to carry the eye from the text to the page number.

To make it obvious where one paragraph ends and another begins, you can add space between them by adjusting the Spacing After and Spacing Before settings in the Paragraph group on the Page Layout tab. You can adjust the spacing between the lines in a paragraph by clicking the Line And Paragraph Spacing button in the Paragraph group on the Home tab.

The Line Spacing options.

When you want to make several adjustments to the alignment, indentation, and spacing of selected paragraphs, it is sometimes quicker to use the Paragraph dialog box than to click buttons and drag markers. Clicking the Paragraph dialog box launcher on either the Home tab or the Page Layout tab opens the Paragraph dialog box.

The Indents And Spacing page of the Paragraph dialog box.

You can do a lot with the options in the Paragraph dialog box, but to make a paragraph really stand out, you might want to put a border around it or shade its background. (For real drama, you can do both.) Clicking the Border arrow in the Paragraph group on the Home tab displays a gallery of border options.

	Bottom Border
	Top Border
	Left Border
	Right Border
	No Border
	All Borders
	Outside Borders
	Inside Borders
	Inside Horizontal Border
	Inside Vertical Border
	Diagonal Down Border
	Diagonal Up Border
	Horizontal Line
	Draw Table
	View Gridlines
	Borders and Shading...

The Borders gallery.

Clicking Borders And Shading at the bottom of the list displays the Borders And Shading dialog box, where you can select the style, color, width, and location of the border.

The Border page of the Borders And Shading dialog box.

In this exercise, you'll change text alignment and indentation, insert and modify tab stops, modify paragraph and line spacing, and add borders and shading to paragraphs.

SET UP You need the Information_start document located in your Chapter04 practice file folder to complete this exercise. Open the Information_start document, and save it as *Information*. Then click the Show/Hide ¶ button to turn on the display of formatting marks, and follow the steps.

1. Set the zoom percentage so that you can see almost all of the paragraphs in the document. Then on the **View** tab, in the **Show** group, select the **Ruler** check box.

   Tip In the following steps, we give measurements in inches. You can substitute approximate measurements in your own measuring system. If you want to change the measuring system Word uses, display the Backstage view, click Options, and in the Word Options dialog box, display the Advanced page. Then under Display, click the system you want in the Show Measurements In Units Of list, and click OK.

2. Select the first two paragraphs (**Welcome!** and the next paragraph). Then on the **Home** tab, in the **Paragraph** group, click the **Center** button.

   The lines are now centered between the margins.

   Tip When applying paragraph formatting, you don't have to select the entire paragraph.

3. After the comma in the second paragraph, click to the left of **your**. Then on the **Page Layout** tab, in the **Page Setup** group, click the **Breaks** button, and click **Text Wrapping**.

   Word inserts a line break character and moves the part of the paragraph that follows that character to the next line.

   The bent arrow after cottage indicates that you have inserted a line break.

   See Also For information about page and section breaks, see "Controlling What Appears on Each Page" in Chapter 7, "Preview, Print, and Distribute Documents."

4. Click anywhere in the next paragraph, and then on the **Home** tab, in the **Paragraph** group, click the **Justify** button.

   Word inserts space between the words in the lines of the paragraph so that the edges of the paragraph are flush against both the left and right margins.

5. Without moving the cursor, on the horizontal ruler, drag the **Left Indent** marker to the **0.5** inch mark.

   The First Line Indent and Hanging Indent markers move with the Left Indent marker.

6. At the right end of the ruler, drag the **Right Indent** marker to the **6** inch mark.

   The paragraph is now indented a half inch in from each of the side margins.

Left and right indents are often used to make paragraphs such as quotations stand out.

7. Click in the **Be careful** paragraph, and then in the **Paragraph** group, click the **Increase Indent** button.

8. Select the **Pillows**, **Blankets**, **Towels**, and **Dish towels** paragraphs, and with the **Left Tab** stop active at the left end of the ruler, click the ruler at the **2** mark.

   Word removes the default tab stops (indicated by gray lines below the ruler) up to the 2-inch mark and inserts a custom left-aligned tab at that location on the ruler.

9. Click to the left of **There** in the **Pillows** paragraph, and press the Tab key. Then insert tabs to the left of **You**, **These**, and **There** in the next three paragraphs.

   The part of each paragraph that follows the colon is now aligned at the 2-inch mark, producing more space than you need.

10. Select the four paragraphs containing tabs, and on the ruler, drag the **Left Tab** stop to the **1.25** mark.

11. Without changing the selection, on the ruler, drag the **Hanging Indent** marker to the **1.25** mark. Then press Home to release the selection.

    The Left Indent marker has moved as well, causing the second line of the second selected paragraph to start in the same location as the tab stop.

Hanging indents are often used to create table-like effects.

12. At the bottom of the document, select the three paragraphs containing dollar amounts. Where the horizontal and vertical rulers meet, click the **Tab** button until the **Decimal Tab** button is displayed and then click the ruler at the **3** mark.

13. Insert a tab to the left of each dollar amount.

    Word aligns the three paragraphs on the decimals.

14. Select the first paragraph containing tabs (**Pillows**), hold down the Ctrl key, and then select the paragraphs that begin with the following:

    Blankets
    Towels
    Limousine winery tour
    In-home massage

15. On the **Home** tab, in the **Paragraph** group, click the **Line Spacing** button, and click **Remove Space After Paragraph**. Then press the Home key.

    Now only the last paragraphs of the two lists have extra space after them.

Removing internal space from lists makes them easier to read.

16. Scroll up until the top of the document is in view, and click anywhere in the **Please take a few minutes** paragraph. On the **Home** tab, in the **Paragraph** group, click the **Border** arrow, and then click **Outside Borders**.

17. Click anywhere in the **Be careful** paragraph, click the **Border** arrow, and then at the bottom of the list, click **Borders and Shading**.

    The Borders And Shading dialog box opens, with the Borders page displayed.

18. Under **Setting**, click the **3-D** icon to select that border style. Scroll through the **Style** list and click the fourth style from the bottom. Then click the **Color** arrow, and under **Theme Colors** in the palette, click the **Red, Accent 2** box.

    Tip If you want only one, two, or three sides of the selected paragraphs to have a border, click the buttons surrounding the image in the Preview area.

19. Click the **Shading** tab.

    You can use the options on this page to format the background of the selected paragraph.

The Shading page of the Borders And Shading dialog box.

20. Click the **Fill** arrow, and under **Theme Colors**, click the lightest color in the red column (**Red, Accent 2, Lighter 80%**). Then click **OK** to close the **Borders and Shading** dialog box.

    A border surrounds the paragraph, and a light red color fills its background. The border stretches all the way to the right margin.

21. To achieve a more balanced look, in the **Paragraph** group, click the **Decrease Indent** button. Then click the **Center** button.

    The paragraph is now centered between the page margins and within its surrounding box.

A combination of a border and shading really makes text stand out. Don't overdo it!

✖ CLEAN UP Leave the rulers and formatting marks displayed for the next exercise, but change the zoom percentage back to 100%. Save the Information document, and then close it.

Finding and Replacing Formatting

In addition to searching for words and phrases in the Find And Replace dialog box, you can use the dialog box to search for a specific format and replace it with a different one.

See Also For information about finding and replacing text, see "Finding and Replacing Text" in Chapter 3, "Edit and Proofread Text."

To search for a specific format and replace it with a different format:

1. On the Home tab, in the Editing group, click the Replace button.

   Keyboard Shortcut Press Ctrl+H to display the Replace tab of the Find And Replace dialog box.

   The Find And Replace dialog box opens, displaying the Replace tab.

2. Click More to expand the dialog box. Then click Format, and on the Format menu, click either Font or Paragraph.

   Tip You can click Style to search for paragraph styles or character styles.

   The Find Font or Find Paragraph dialog box opens.

3. In the dialog box, click the format you want to find, and then click OK.

4. Click the Replace With text box, click Format, click Font or Paragraph, click the format you want to substitute for the Find What format, and then click OK.

5. Click Find Next to search for the first occurrence of the format, and then click Replace to replace that one occurrence or Replace All to replace every occurrence.

Creating and Modifying Lists

Lists are paragraphs that are usually formatted with a hanging indent so that the first line of each paragraph is longer than subsequent lines. Fortunately, Word takes care of the formatting of lists for you. You simply indicate the type of list you want to create. When the order of items is not important—for example, for a list of supplies needed to carry out a task—a bulleted list is the best choice. And when the order is important—for example, for the steps in a procedure—you will probably want to create a numbered list.

You can indicate the start of a list as follows:

- **Bulleted list** Type * (an asterisk) at the beginning of a paragraph, and then press the Spacebar or the Tab key before entering the list item text. Or click the Bullets button in the Paragraph group on the Home tab.

- **Numbered list** Type *1.* (the number 1 followed by a period) at the beginning of a paragraph, and then press the Spacebar or the Tab key before entering the list item text. Or click the Numbering button in the Paragraph group on the Home tab.

When you start a list in this fashion, Word automatically formats it as a bulleted or numbered list. When you press Enter to start a new item, Word continues the formatting to the new paragraph. Typing items and pressing Enter adds subsequent bulleted or numbered items. To end the list, press Enter twice; or click the Bullets arrow or Numbering arrow in the Paragraph group on the Home tab, and then in the library, click None.

Tip If you want to start a paragraph with an asterisk or number but don't want to format the paragraph as a bulleted or numbered list, click the AutoCorrect Options button that appears after Word changes the formatting, and then in the list, click the appropriate Undo option. You can also click the Undo button on the Quick Access Toolbar.

If you want to create a list that has multiple levels, you start off by creating the list in the usual way. Then when you want the next paragraph to be a level lower (indented more), you press the Tab key after pressing Enter and before you type the text of the item. If you want the next paragraph to be a level higher (indented less), you press Shift+Tab after pressing Enter. In the case of a bulleted list, Word changes the bullet character for each item level. In the case of a numbered list, Word changes the type of numbering used, based on a predefined numbering scheme.

Tip To create a multilevel numbered list with a scheme that is different from the default, you can click the Multilevel List button in the Paragraph group of the Home tab and then select a scheme from the List gallery. You can also define your own scheme.

If you type a set of paragraphs containing a series of items and then decide you want to turn the set into a list, you can select the paragraphs and then click the Bullets or Numbering button.

After you create a list, you can modify, format, and customize the list as follows:

- You can move items around in a list, insert new items, or delete unwanted items. If the list is numbered, Word automatically updates the numbers.

- You can sort items in a bulleted list into ascending or descending order by clicking the Sort button in the Paragraph group on the Home tab.

- For a bulleted list, you can change the bullet symbol by clicking the Bullets arrow in the Paragraph group and making a selection from the Bullets gallery. You can also define a custom bullet (even a picture bullet) by clicking Define New Bullet.

- For a numbered list, you can change the number style by clicking the Numbering arrow in the Paragraph group and making a selection from the Numbering gallery. You can also define a custom style by clicking Define New Number Format.

- You can modify the indentation of the list by dragging the indent markers on the horizontal ruler. You can change both the overall indentation of the list and the relationship of the first line to the other lines.

  See Also For information about paragraph indentation, see "Manually Changing the Look of Paragraphs" earlier in this chapter.

In this exercise, you'll create a bulleted list and a numbered list and then modify lists in various ways.

SET UP You need the RulesDraft_start document located in your Chapter04 practice file folder to complete this exercise. Open the RulesDraft_start document, and save it as *RulesDraft*. Then follow the steps.

1. With formatting marks and the rulers displayed, select the first four paragraphs under **The rules fall into four categories**, and then on the **Home** tab, in the **Paragraph** group, click the **Bullets** button.

   The selected paragraphs are reformatted as a bulleted list. Word indents the list and precedes each item with a bullet and a tab. The program also removes the space after all paragraphs except the last one.

2. With the paragraphs still selected, in the **Paragraph** group, click the **Bullets** arrow.

   The Bullets gallery appears.

The Bullets gallery offers several predefined bullet choices.

3. Under **Bullet Library**, point to each bullet character to display a live preview of its effect on the selected list items, and then click the bullet composed of four diamonds.

   The bullet character that begins each item in the selected list changes.

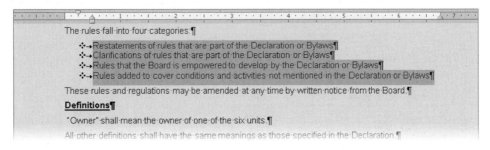

The·rules·fall·into·four·categories:¶
　　❖→Restatements·of·rules·that·are·part·of·the·Declaration·or·Bylaws¶
　　❖→Clarifications·of·rules·that·are·part·of·the·Declaration·or·Bylaws¶
　　❖→Rules·that·the·Board·is·empowered·to·develop·by·the·Declaration·or·Bylaws¶
　　❖→Rules·added·to·cover·conditions·and·activities·not·mentioned·in·the·Declaration·or·Bylaws¶
These·rules·and·regulations·may·be·amended·at·any·time·by·written·notice·from·the·Board.¶
Definitions¶
"Owner"·shall·mean·the·owner·of·one·of·the·six·units.¶
All·other·definitions·shall·have·the·same·meanings·as·those·specified·in·the·Declaration.¶

Different bullets are suited to different types of documents.

4. Select the two paragraphs below the **Definitions** heading, and then in the **Paragraph** group, click the **Numbering** button.

   Word numbers the two selected paragraphs sequentially.

5. Select the first four paragraphs below the **General Rules** heading, and then click the **Numbering** button.

   Word restarts the second numbered list from 1.

6. Select the next three paragraphs, and then in the **Paragraph** group, click the **Bullets** button.

   Word formats the paragraphs as a bulleted list, using the symbol you specified earlier. These three bullets are a second-level list of the preceding numbered item and should be indented.

7. With the three bulleted items still selected, in the **Paragraph** group, click the **Increase Indent** button.

   The bulleted paragraphs move to the right.

   Tip You can also adjust the indent level of a bulleted list by selecting its paragraphs, and on the horizontal ruler, dragging the Left Indent marker to the left or right. You can move just the Hanging Indent marker to adjust the space between the bullets and their text.

8. Select the remaining three paragraphs, and click the **Numbering** button.

   Word restarts this numbered list from 1, but you want it to continue the sequence of the previous numbered list.

9. Click anywhere in the **No large dogs** item, and then click the **Numbering** arrow.

   The Numbering gallery appears.

Recently Used Number Formats

1. ———
2. ———
3. ———

Numbering Library

None

1. ———
2. ———
3. ———

1) ———
2) ———
3) ———

I. ———
II. ———
III. ———

A. ———
B. ———
C. ———

a) ———
b) ———
c) ———

a. ———
b. ———
c. ———

i. ———
ii. ———
iii. ———

Document Number Formats

1. ———
2. ———
3. ———

⬅ Change List Level ▶
Define New Number Format...
Set Numbering Value...

The Numbering gallery offers several predefined number formats.

10. At the bottom of the gallery, click **Set Numbering Value**.

The Set Numbering Value dialog box opens.

Set Numbering Value [?] [X]

⦿ Start new list
◯ Continue from previous list
☐ Advance value (skip numbers)

Set value to:
[1] [▲▼]
Preview: 1.

[OK] [Cancel]

In this dialog box, you specify how this numbered list relates to the previous one.

11. Change the **Set value to** setting to **5**, and then click **OK**.

    Word renumbers the list after the bullet items so that it continues from the previous list.

12. In the **No large dogs** numbered item, click to the left of **Seeing**, press Enter, and then press Tab.

    Word first creates a new number 6 item and renumbers all subsequent items. However, when you press Tab to make the item second level, Word changes the 6 to a, indents the item, and restores the original numbers to the subsequent items.

13. Press the End key, and then press Enter. Then type **The Board reserves the right to make exceptions to this rule.** (type the period), and press Enter.

14. Click the **Numbering** arrow, click **Change List Level** at the bottom of the gallery, and click the first **1.** option. Then in the new first-level item, type **All pets must reside within their Owners' Apartments.**

    The lists are now organized hierarchically.

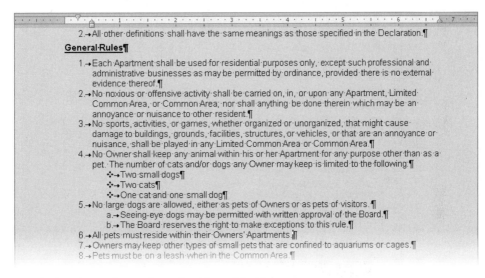

Word takes the work out of creating hierarchical lists.

15. Select the three bulleted paragraphs, and then in the **Paragraph** group, click the **Sort** button.

Formatting Text as You Type

The Word list capabilities are just one example of the program's ability to intuit how you want to format an element based on what you type. You can learn more about these and other AutoFormatting options by exploring the AutoCorrect dialog box. Display the Backstage view, click Options, click Proofing in the left pane of the Word Options dialog box, and then on the Proofing page, click AutoCorrect Options.

On the AutoFormat As You Type page, you can see the options Word implements by default, including bulleted and numbered lists. You can select and clear options to control AutoFormatting behavior.

The AutoFormat As You Type page of the AutoCorrect dialog box.

One interesting option is Border Lines. When this check box is selected, typing three consecutive hyphens (-) or three consecutive underscores (_) and pressing Enter draws a single line across the page. Three consecutive equal signs (=) draw a double line, and three consecutive tildes (~) draw a zigzag line.

The Sort Text dialog box opens.

You can sort text in lists in ascending or descending order.

16. With the **Ascending** option selected, click **OK**.

The order of the bulleted items changes to ascending alphabetical order.

✖ **CLEAN UP** If you want, turn off the rulers and formatting marks. Then save and close the RulesDraft document.

Key Points

- Quick Styles and style sets make it simple to apply combinations of character and paragraph formatting to give your documents a professional look.

- The same document can look very different depending on the theme applied to it. Colors, fonts, and effects can be combined to create just the look you want.

- You can format characters with an almost limitless number of combinations of font, size, style, and effect. For best results, resist the temptation to use more than a handful of combinations.

- You can change the look of paragraphs by varying their indentation, spacing, and alignment and by setting tab stops and applying borders and shading. Use these formatting options judiciously to create a balanced, uncluttered look.

- Bulleted and numbered lists are a great way to present information in an easy-to-read, easy-to-understand format. If the built-in bulleted and numbered formats don't provide what you need, you can define your own formats.

Chapter at a Glance

Present information in columns, **page 140**

Create tabbed lists, **page 147**

Present information in tables, **page 149**

Format tables, **page 160**

5 Organize Information in Columns and Tables

In this chapter, you will learn how to

✔ Present information in columns.

✔ Create tabbed lists.

✔ Present information in tables.

✔ Format tables.

Information in documents is most commonly presented as paragraphs of text. To make a text-heavy document more legible, you can flow the text in two or more columns, or you can display information in a table. For example, flowing text in multiple columns is a common practice in newsletters, flyers, and brochures; and presenting information in tables is common in reports.

When you need to present data in a document, using a table is often more efficient than describing the data in a paragraph, particularly when the data consists of numeric values. Tables make the data easier to read and understand. A small amount of data can be displayed in simple columns separated by tabs, which creates a tabbed list. A larger amount of data, or more complex data, is better presented in a table, which is a structure of rows and columns, frequently with row and column headings.

In this chapter, you'll first create and modify columns of text. Then you'll create a simple tabbed list. Finally, you'll create tables from scratch and from existing text, and format a table in various ways.

> **Practice Files** Before you can complete the exercises in this chapter, you need to copy the book's practice files to your computer. The practice files you'll use to complete the exercises in this chapter are in the Chapter05 practice file folder. A complete list of practice files is provided in "Using the Practice Files" at the beginning of this book.

Presenting Information in Columns

By default, Microsoft Word 2010 displays text in one column that spans the width of the page between the left and right margins. You can specify that text be displayed in two, three, or more columns to create layouts like those used in newspapers and magazines. When you format text to flow in columns, the text fills the first column on each page and then moves to the top of the next column. You can manually indicate where you want the text within each column to end.

The Columns gallery in the Page Setup group on the Page Layout tab displays several standard options for dividing text into columns. You can choose one, two, or three columns of equal width or two columns of unequal width. If the standard options don't suit your needs, you can specify the number and width of columns. The number of columns is limited by the width and margins of the page, and each column must be at least a half inch wide.

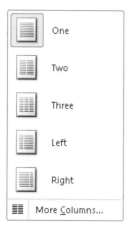

The Columns gallery displays the predefined column options.

No matter how you set up the columns initially, you can change the layout or column widths at any time.

You can format an entire document or a section of a document in columns. When you select a section of text and format it as columns, Word inserts section breaks at the beginning and end of the selected text to delineate the area in which the columnar formatting is applied. Within the columnar text, you can insert column breaks to specify where you want to end one column and start another. Section and column breaks are visible when you display formatting marks in the document.

Tip You can apply many types of formatting, including page orientation, to content within a specific section of a document without affecting the surrounding text. For information about sections, see "Controlling What Appears on Each Page" in Chapter 7, "Preview, Print, and Distribute Documents."

You can apply character and paragraph formatting to columnar text in the same way you would any text. Here are some formatting tips for columnar text:

● When presenting text in narrow columns, you can justify the paragraphs (align the text with the left and right edges) to achieve a neat and clean appearance. To justify the paragraphs, Word adjusts the spacing between words, essentially moving the empty space that would normally appear at the end of the line into the gaps between words.

● To more completely fill columns, you can have Word hyphenate the text to break words into syllables to fill up the gaps.

In this exercise, you'll flow the text in one section of a document into three columns. You'll justify the text in the columns, change the column spacing, and hyphenate the text. You'll then break a column at a specific location instead of allowing the text to flow naturally from one column to the next.

SET UP You need the RoomPlanner_start document located in your Chapter05 practice file folder to complete this exercise. Open the RoomPlanner_start document, and save it as *RoomPlanner*. Then display formatting marks and the rulers, and follow the steps.

1. Click at the beginning of the paragraph that begins **Take a look** (do not click in the selection area). Then scroll down until you can see the end of the document, hold down the Shift key, and click to the right of the paragraph mark after **credit cards**.

   Word selects the text from the *Take a look* paragraph through the end of the last paragraph (but not the empty paragraph).

   Tip If you want to format an entire document with the same number of columns, you can simply click anywhere in the document—you don't have to select the text.

2. On the **Page Layout** tab, in the **Page Setup** group, click the **Columns** button, and then in the **Columns** gallery, click **Three**.

   Word inserts a section break above the selected text and flows the text within the section into three columns.

3. Press Ctrl+Home to move to the top of the document.

The section break is visible above the columns.

Simple·Room·Design¶

With·the·Room·Planner,·you'll·never·make·a·design·mistake·again.·Created·by·acclaimed·interior· designers·to·simplify·the·redecorating·process,·this·planning·tool·incorporates·elements·of·color,· dimension,·and·style·to·guide·your·project.·It·includes·a·furniture·location·guide;·room·grid;·drawing· tools;·and·miniature·furniture,·rugs,·accessories,·and·color·swatches·that·match·our·large·in-store· selection.·Here's·how·to·use·the·planner·to·create·the·room·of·your·dreams!¶

¶⸻⸻⸻⸻Section Break (Continuous)⸻⸻⸻⸻

Take·a·look·at·how·your· home·is·decorated·and·note· the·things·you·like·and· dislike.·Pay·special·attention· to·the·color·scheme·and·to· how·each·room·"feels"·to· you.·Is·it·inviting?·Does·it· feel·comfortable?·Does·it· relax·you·or·does·it· invigorate·you?¶

Focus·on·the·room(s)·you·

love,·and·the·rest·will·fall· into·place.¶

Take·your·Room·Planner· home·and·get·to·work!· Adjust·the·planner·so·that·it· models·the·room· dimensions.·Don't·forget·to· place·the·windows·and· doors.·Arrange·the·furniture· placeholders·to·mirror·how· your·room·is·currently·set·

design·for·a·day·or·two.· Then·review·it·again.·Does·it· still·look·perfect,·or·is· something·not·quite·right?· You·might·need·to·"live"· with·the·new·plan·for·a·few· days,·especially·if·you've· made·big·changes.·When· everything·feels·just·right·to· you,·you're·ready·for·the· next·big·step!¶

A continuous section break changes the formatting of the subsequent text but keeps it on the same page.

4. On the **Home** tab, in the **Editing** group, click the **Select** button, and then click **Select All**.

Keyboard Shortcut Press Ctrl+A to select all the text in the document.

5. In the **Paragraph** group, click the **Justify** button.

Keyboard Shortcut Press Ctrl+J to justify paragraphs.

The spacing between the words changes to align all the paragraphs in the document with both the left and right margins. Because you applied the formatting to the entire document, the title is no longer centered. However, it is often quicker to apply formatting globally and then deal with the exceptions.

6. Press Ctrl+Home to move to the paragraph containing the document title. Then in the **Paragraph** group, click the **Center** button.

    Keyboard Shortcut Press Ctrl+E to center text.

    Word centers the document title between the left and right margins.

7. Adjust the zoom percentage until you can see about two-thirds of the first page of the document.

    See Also For information about adjusting the zoom percentage, see "Viewing Files in Different Ways" in Chapter 2, "Work with Files."

8. Click anywhere in the first column.

    On the horizontal ruler, Word indicates the margins of the columns.

On the ruler, the indent markers show the indentation of the active column.

Tip If your rulers aren't turned on, select the Ruler check box in the Show group of the View tab.

9. On the **Page Layout** tab, display the **Columns** gallery, and click **More Columns**.

    The Columns dialog box opens. The spacing between columns is set by default to a half inch.

Because the Equal Column Width check box is selected, you can adjust the width and spacing of only the first column.

Tip To separate the columns with vertical lines, select the Line Between check box.

10. In the **Width and spacing** area, in the **Spacing** box for column 1, type or select **0.2"**.

    Word changes the measurement in the Spacing box for column 2, and widens all the columns in the Preview area to reflect the new setting.

11. Click **OK**.

    Word reflows the columns to fit their new margins.

Simple·Room·Design¶

With·the·Room·Planner,·you'll·never·make·a·design·mistake·again.·Created·by·acclaimed·interior·designers·to·simplify·the·redecorating·process,·this·planning·tool·incorporates·elements·of·color,·dimension,·and·style·to·guide·your·project.·It·includes·a·furniture·location·guide;·room·grid;·drawing·tools;·and·miniature·furniture,·rugs,·accessories,·and·color·swatches·that·match·our·large·in-store·selection.·Here's·how·to·use·the·planner·to·create·the·room·of·your·dreams!¶

¶·············Section·Break·(Continuous)··············

Take·a·look·at·how·your·home·is· decorated· and· note· the· things·you·like·and·dislike.·Pay·special· attention· to·the·color·scheme·and·to·how·each·room·"feels"·to·you.· Is· it· inviting?· Does·it·feel·comfortable?·Does·it·relax·you·or·does·it·invigorate·you?¶

Focus· on· the· room(s)· you· would· most· like· to· change.· Brainstorm· all·the·things·you· would· change·in·that·room·if· you·could.·Don't·give·a·thought· to·any·financial·considerations.

Take·your·Room·Planner·home·and· get· to· work!· Adjust· the· planner·so·that·it·models·the·room·dimensions.·Don't·forget· to· place· the· windows· and· doors.· Arrange· the· furniture· placeholders· to· mirror· how· your·room·is·currently·set·up.· Add·the·current·colors,·too.¶

This· is·where·the·fun·begins!· Start·changing·things·around·a· bit.· Move· the· furniture,· add· different·colors,·and·watch·the· room· come· together!· Here's· where·you·can·tell·if·that·rich

changes.·When·everything·feels· just· right·to·you,·you're·ready· for·the·next·big·step!¶

Come· back·to·the·store.·Look· again· at·the·pieces·you·liked· during·your·last·visit·and·see·if· you·still·love·them.·If·you're·not· quite· sure,· go· back· to· your· planner· for· a· little· more· tweaking.·If·you·are·sure,·take·a· look·around·the·store·one·more· time· to· see· if· anything· else· catches· your· eye.· Then· make· your·purchases.·You're·almost· there!¶

Wider columns generally look neater on the page.

12. Click at the beginning of the **Take a look** paragraph. Then in the **Page Setup** group, click the **Hyphenation** button, and click **Automatic**.

Word hyphenates the text of the document, which fills in some of the large gaps between words.

13. Click anywhere in the **NOTE** paragraph in the third column.

14. On the horizontal ruler, at the left end of the third column, drag the **Hanging Indent** marker 0.25 inch (two marks) to the right.

All the lines in the *NOTE* paragraph except the first are now indented, offsetting the note from the paragraphs above and below it.

Take·a·look·at·how·your·home· is· decorated· and· note· the· things·you·like·and·dislike.·Pay· special·attention·to·the·color· scheme·and·to·how·each·room· "feels"· to· you.· Is· it· inviting?· Does·it·feel·comfortable?·Does· it·relax·you·or·does·it·invigorate· you?¶

Focus· on· the· room(s)· you· would· most· like· to· change.· Brainstorm· all·the·things·you· would· change·in·that·room·if· you·could.·Don't·give·a·thought· to·any·financial·considerations;· just· let· your· imagination· go· wild!· It· might· be· helpful· to· write· down· all· the· negatives· and·positives.·You·don't·need· to·come·up·with·solutions·all·at· once.·Just·be·clear·on·what·you· like· and· what· you· hate· about· that·room.¶

Visit· our· showroom· and· pur-chase·a·Room·Planner.·While·

planner·so·that·it·models·the· room·dimensions.·Don't·forget· to· place· the· windows· and· doors.· Arrange· the· furniture· placeholders· to· mirror· how· your·room·is·currently·set·up.· Add·the·current·colors,·too.¶

This· is· where·the·fun·begins!· Start·changing·things·around·a· bit.· Move· the· furniture,· add· different·colors,·and·watch·the· room· come· together!· Here's· where·you·can·tell·if·that·rich· red·rug·you·saw·in·the·show-room·enhances·or·overwhelms· your· room.· What· about· that· overstuffed· chair· that· caught· your· eye?· Place·a·furniture·or· accessory·shape,·and·then·color· it.·Does·it·look·great·or·is·it·too· jarring?· Change· the· color... does· that· help?· Don't· forget· about· the·walls.· Try·different· colors·to·see·the·effect·on·the· room·overall.¶

just· right·to·you,·you're·ready· for·the·next·big·step!¶

Come·back·to·the·store.·Look· again· at·the·pieces·you·liked· during·your·last·visit·and·see·if· you·still·love·them.·If·you're·not· quite· sure,· go· back· to· your· planner·for·a·little·more·tweak-ing.·If·you·are·sure,·take·a·look· around· the· store· one· more· time· to· see· if· anything· else· catches· your·eye.·Then· make· your·purchases.·You're·almost· there!¶

NOTE:· If·you·decided·to·paint· your·room,·do·that·before· your·new·pieces·are·deliv-ered.·You'll·want·to·start· enjoying·your·new·room·as· soon·as·your·purchases·ar-rive.¶

After·a·few·weeks,·ask·yourself· whether·the·room·is·as·great·as· you·thought·it·would·be.·Does· it·achieve·the·look·and·feel·you·

You can change the indentation of individual paragraphs within a column.

15. Display the bottom of page **1**. In the first column on page **1**, click at the beginning of the **Take your Room Planner home** paragraph. Then in the **Page Setup** group, click the **Breaks** button, and click **Column**.

Word inserts a column break. The text that follows the column break moves to the top of the second column.

16. At the bottom of the third column on page **1**, click at the beginning of the **If you're not sure** paragraph, and then on the Quick Access Toolbar, click the **Repeat Insertion** button to insert another column break.

Keyboard Shortcut Press Ctrl+Y to repeat the previous action.

Word inserts a column break. The text that follows the column break moves to the top of the first column on page 2.

✖ CLEAN UP Return the Zoom Level setting to 100%, and then save and close the RoomPlanner document.

Creating Tabbed Lists

If you have a relatively small amount of data to present, you might choose to display it in a tabbed list, which arranges text in simple columns separated by tabs. You can align the text within the columns by using left, right, centered, or decimal tab stops.

See Also For more information about setting tab stops, see "Manually Changing the Look of Paragraphs" in Chapter 4, "Change the Look of Text."

When entering text in a tabbed list, inexperienced Word users have a tendency to press the Tab key multiple times to align the columns of the list with the default tab stops. If you do this, you have no control over the column widths. To be able to fine-tune the columns, you need to set custom tab stops rather than relying on the default ones.

When setting up a tabbed list, you should press Tab only once between the items that you want to appear in separate columns. Next you apply any necessary formatting. And finally, you set the custom tab stops. Set left, right, centered, and decimal tabs to control the alignment of the column content, or set a bar tab to add a vertical line to visually separate list columns. By setting the tabs in order from left to right, you can check the alignment of the text within each column as you go.

In this exercise, you'll first enter text separated by tabs and format the text. Then you'll set custom tab stops to create a tabbed list.

 SET UP You need the ConsultationA_start document located in your Chapter05 practice file folder to complete this exercise. Open the ConsultationA_start document, and save it as *ConsultationA*. Then display formatting marks and the rulers, and follow the steps.

1. Set the zoom percentage to a level that is comfortable for you, and then press Ctrl+End to move the cursor to the blank line at the end of the document.

2. Type **Location**, press Tab, type **Discount Applies**, press Tab, type **Hourly Rate**, and then press Enter.

3. Add three more lines to the list by typing the following text, pressing the Tab and Enter keys where indicated.

In home Tab No Tab $50.00 Enter
Phone Tab Yes Tab $35.00 Enter
In store Tab Yes Tab $40.00 Enter

The tab characters push the items to the next default tab stop, but because some items are longer than others, they do not line up.

Available·Consultants·(check·your·consultant's·name)¶
Susan·Burk¶
Andy·Ruth¶
Carlos·Carvallo¶

Consultation·Fee·Schedule¶

Location   →   Discount·Applies   →   Hourly·Rate¶

In·home   →   No   → $50.00¶

Phone·Yes   → $35.00¶

In·store   →   Yes   → $40.00¶

¶

In a tabbed list, it's important to press the Tab key only once between items.

4. Select the first line of the tabbed list, and then on the Mini Toolbar that appears, click the **Bold** button.

Troubleshooting If the Mini Toolbar doesn't appear, click the Bold button in the Font group on the Home tab.

Keyboard Shortcut Press Ctrl+B to apply bold.

5. Select all four lines of the tabbed list, and then on the Mini Toolbar, click the **Increase Indent** button.

Tip It's more efficient to make all character and paragraph formatting changes to the text before setting tab stops. Otherwise, you might have to adjust the tab stops after applying the formatting.

6. With the tabbed list still selected, on the **Page Layout** tab, in the **Paragraph** group, under **Spacing**, change the **After** setting to **0 pt**.

7. Click the tab setting button at the junction of the horizontal and vertical rulers until the **Center Tab** button is active. (You will probably have to click only once.) Then click the **2.5** inch mark on the horizontal ruler.

On the ruler, Word sets a center-aligned tab stop that looks like the Center Tab icon. The items in the second column of the tabbed list center themselves at that position.

8. Click the tab setting button once.

   The Right Tab button is now active.

9. With the **Right Tab** button active, click the horizontal ruler at the **4.5** inch mark.

   On the ruler, Word sets a right-aligned tab stop that looks like the Right Tab icon. The items in the third column of the tabbed list right-align themselves at that position.

10. On the **Home** tab, in the **Paragraph** group, click the **Show/Hide ¶** button to hide the tabs, paragraph marks, and other formatting marks. Then click away from the tabbed list to see the results.

    The tabbed list resembles a simple table.

    Available Consultants (check your consultant's name)
    Susan Burk
    Andy Ruth
    Carlos Carvallo

    Consultation Fee Schedule

Location	Discount Applies	Hourly Rate
In home	No	$50.00
Phone	Yes	$35.00
In store	Yes	$40.00

You have created a simple table-like layout with just a few clicks.

CLEAN UP Save the ConsultationA document, and then close it.

Presenting Information in Tables

A table is a structure of vertical columns and horizontal rows. Each column and each row can be named with a heading, although some tables have only column headings or only row headings. At the junction of each column and row is a box called a *cell* in which data (text or numeric information) is stored.

You can create empty or predefined tables in a Word document in the following ways:

● The Insert Table gallery, which is available from the Tables group on the Insert tab, displays a simple grid.

You can create a simple table from the grid in the Insert Table gallery.

Clicking a cell in the grid inserts an empty table the width of the text column. The table has the number of rows and columns you indicated in the grid, with all the rows one line high and all the columns of an equal width.

● To insert a more customized empty table, you can click Insert Table on the menu at the bottom of the Insert Table gallery to open the Insert Table dialog box, in which you can specify the number of rows and columns and customize the column width.

You can create a custom-width table from the Insert Table dialog box.

● To insert a less clearly defined empty table, you can click Draw Table below the grid in the Insert Table gallery. This command displays a pencil with which you can draw cells directly in the Word document to create a table. The cells you draw connect by snapping to a grid, but you have some control over the size and spacing of the rows and columns.

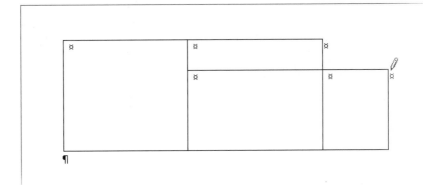

You can draw a table directly on the page.

See Also For information about drawing tables, refer to *Microsoft Word 2010 Step by Step*, by Joyce Cox and Joan Lambert (Microsoft Press, 2010).

● In addition to empty tables, you can insert any of the available Quick Tables, which are predefined tables of formatted data that you can replace with your own information. Built-in Quick Tables include a variety of calendars, simple tables, tables with subheadings, and tabbed lists. You can also save your own custom tables to the Quick Tables gallery so that you can easily insert a frequently used table structure and data into any document.

Enrollment in local colleges, 2010

College	New students	Graduating students	Change
Undergraduate			
Cedar University	110	103	+7
Elm College	223	214	+9
Maple Academy	197	120	+77
Pine College	134	121	+13
Oak Institute	202	210	-8
Graduate			
Cedar University	24	20	+4
Elm College	43	53	-10
Maple Academy	3	11	-8
Pine College	9	4	+5
Oak Institute	53	52	+1
Total	998	908	90

Source: Fictitious data, for illustration purposes only

The Quick Tables gallery includes a selection of predefined tables such as this one.

A new table appears in the document as a set of cells, usually bordered by gridlines. (In some Quick Tables, the gridlines are turned off.) Each cell contains an end-of-cell marker, and each row ends with an end-of-row marker. (The end-of-cell markers and end-of-row markers are identical in appearance, and are visible only when you display formatting marks in the document.) When you point to a table, a move handle appears in its upper-left corner and a size handle in its lower-right corner. When the cursor is in a table, two Table Tools contextual tabs—Design and Layout—appear on the ribbon.

Move handle   End-of-cell marker   Size handle   End-of-row marker

A table has its own controls and its own contextual ribbon tabs.

Tip The move handle and size handle appear only in Print Layout view and Web Layout view.

After you create a table, you can enter data (such as text, numbers, or graphics) into the table cells and press the Tab key to move the cursor from cell to cell. Pressing Tab when the cursor is in the last cell of a row moves the cursor to the first cell of the next row. Pressing Tab when the cursor is in the last cell of the last row adds a new row to the table and moves the cursor to the first cell of that row.

Tip You can move and position the cursor by pressing the Tab key or the Arrow keys, or by clicking in a table cell.

If the data you want to present in a table already exists in the document, either as regular text or as a tabbed list, you can convert the text to a table by selecting it and then clicking Convert Text To Table in the Insert Table gallery. Conversely, you can convert an active table to regular text by clicking the Convert To Text button in the Data group on the Layout tab.

You can modify a table's structure by changing the size of the table, changing the size of one or more columns or rows, or adding or removing rows, columns, or individual cells.

Tip To change a table's structure, you often need to select the entire table or a specific column or row. The simplest way to do this is to position the cursor in the table, column, or row, click the Select button in the Table group on the Layout tab, and then click the table element you want. Alternatively, you can point to the top edge of a column or left edge of a row and, when the pointer changes to an arrow, click to select the column or row.

The basic methods for manipulating a table or its contents are as follows:

- **Insert a row or column** Click anywhere in a row or column adjacent to where you want to make the insertion. Then on the Layout tab, in the Rows & Columns group, click the Insert Above, Insert Below, Insert Left, or Insert Right button.

The Rows & Columns group of the Layout tab.

  Selecting more than one row or column before you click an Insert button inserts that number of rows or columns in the table.

  Tip You can insert cells by clicking the Rows & Columns dialog box launcher and specifying in the Insert Cells dialog box how adjacent cells should be moved to accommodate the new cells.

- **Delete a row or column** Click anywhere in the row or column, and in the Rows & Columns group, click the Delete button. Then click Delete Cells, Delete Columns, Delete Rows, or Delete Table.

- **Resize an entire table** Drag the size handle.

- **Resize a single column or row** Without selecting the column, drag its right border to the left or right. Without selecting the row, drag its bottom border up or down. (If you select a column or row and then drag its border, only the selected column or row changes.)

- **Move a table** Point to the table, and then drag the move handle that appears in its upper-left corner to a new location. Or use the Cut and Paste commands in the Clipboard group on the Home tab to move the table.

- **Merge cells** Create cells that span multiple columns or rows by selecting the cells you want to merge and clicking the Merge Cells button in the Merge group on the Layout tab. For example, to center a title in the first row of a table, you can merge all the cells in the row to create one merged cell that spans the table's width.

- **Split cells** Divide one cell into multiple cells by clicking the Split Cells button in the Merge group on the Layout tab and then specifying the number of columns and rows you want.

- **Sort information** Click the Sort button in the Data group on the Layout tab to sort the rows in ascending or descending order by the data in any column. For example, in a table that has the column headings Name, Address, ZIP Code, and Phone Number, you can sort on any one of those columns to arrange the information in alphabetical or numerical order.

In this exercise, you'll work with two tables. First you'll create an empty table, enter and align text in the table cells, add rows to the table, and merge cells. Then you'll create a second table by converting an existing tabbed list, change the width of a column, and change the width of the entire table.

SET UP You need the ConsultationB_start document located in your Chapter05 practice file folder to complete this exercise. Open the ConsultationB_start document, and save it as *ConsultationB*. Then display formatting marks and the rulers, and follow the steps.

1. Click to the left of the second blank paragraph below **Please complete this form**.

2. On the **Insert** tab, in the **Tables** group, click the **Table** button. Then in the **Insert Table** gallery, point to (don't click) the cell that is five columns to the right and five rows down from the upper-left corner of the grid.

   Word highlights the cells that will be in the table, indicates the table dimensions in the gallery header, and creates a temporary table in the document.

You can preview the table with the number of columns and rows you have specified.

3. Click the cell.

    Word creates a blank table consisting of five columns and five rows. The cursor is located in the first cell. Because the table is active, Word displays the Design and Layout contextual tabs.

4. In the selection area to the left of the table, point to the first row of the table, and then click once to select it.

5. On the **Layout** contextual tab, in the **Merge** group, click the **Merge Cells** button.

    Word combines the five cells in the first row into one cell.

6. With the merged cell selected, in the **Alignment** group, click the **Align Center** button.

    The end-of-cell marker moves to the exact center of the merged cell to indicate that anything you type there will be centered both horizontally and vertically.

7. Type **Consultation Estimate**.

    The table now has content that looks like a table title.

Consultation Estimate				

Merged cells are often used for table titles and column headings.

8. Click the first cell in the second row, type **Type**, and then press Tab.

9. Type **Location**, **Consultant**, **Hourly Rate**, and **Total**, pressing Tab after each entry.

    Pressing Tab after the *Total* heading moves the cursor to the first cell of the third row. The table now has a row of column headings.

10. Select the column heading row, and then on the Mini Toolbar, click the **Bold** button.

11. In the third row, type **Window treatments**, **In home**, **Andy Ruth**, **$50.00**, and **$50.00**, pressing Tab after each entry.

    You have entered a complete row of data.

12. Select the last two rows, and then on the **Layout** tab, in the **Rows & Columns** group, click the **Insert Below** button.

    Word adds two new rows and selects them.

13. In the last row, click the first cell, hold down the Shift key, and then press the Right Arrow key four times to select the first four cells in the row.

14. In the **Merge** group, click the **Merge Cells** button.

    Word combines the selected cells into one cell.

15. In the **Alignment** group, click the **Align Center Right** button.

16. Type **Subtotal**, and then press Tab twice.

    Word adds a new row with the same structure to the bottom of the table.

Consultation· Estimate¤				
Type¤	**Location**¤	**Consultant**¤	**Hourly· Rate**¤	**Total**¤
Window· treatments¤	In·home¤	Andy· Ruth¤	$50.00¤	$50.00¤
¤	¤	¤	¤	¤
¤	¤	¤	¤	¤
¤	¤	¤	¤	¤
			Subtotal¤	¤
			¤	¤

When you add a new row, it has the same format as the one it is based on.

17. Type **Add trip fee**, press Tab twice to add a new row, and then type **Total**.

    Now you'll create a different table by converting existing text.

18. Scroll down to the bottom of the document, and select the rows of the tabbed list beginning with **Distance** and ending with **$20.00**.

19. On the **Insert** tab, in the **Tables** group, click the **Table** button, and then click **Convert Text to Table**.

    The Convert Text To Table dialog box opens.

You can separate text into columns based on the symbol you specify.

20. Verify that the **Number of columns** box displays **2**, and then click **OK**.

The selected text appears in a table with two columns and six rows.

21. Click anywhere in the table to release the selection, and then point to the right border of the table. When the pointer changes to two opposing arrows, double-click the border.

Word adjusts the width of the right column to accommodate its longest cell entry.

Tip You can also adjust the column width by changing the Table Column Width setting in the Cell Size group on the Layout tab.

22. Point to the **In-Home Trip Charge** table.

Word displays the move handle in the upper-left corner and the size handle in the lower-right corner.

23. Drag the size handle to the right, releasing the mouse button when the right edge of the table aligns approximately with the **4** inch mark on the horizontal ruler.

The width of the table expands.

Carlos·Carvallo¶

Consultation·Fee·Schedule¶

Location	→	Discount·Applies	→	Hourly·Rate¶
In·home	→	No	→	$50.00¶
Phone	→	Yes	→	$35.00¶
In·store	→	Yes	→	$40.00¶

In·Home·Trip·Charge¶

Distance¤	Fee¤	¤
0-5·miles¤	No·charge¤	¤
6-10·miles¤	$5.50¤	¤
11-20·miles¤	$7.00¤	¤
21-50·miles¤	$10.00¤	¤
Over·50·miles¤	$20.00¤	¤

¶

The table is now approximately as wide as the tabbed list above, creating a nice balance.

✖ **CLEAN UP** Save the ConsultationB document, and then close it.

Performing Calculations in Tables

When you want to perform calculations with the numbers in a Word table, you can create a formula that uses a built-in mathematical function. You construct a formula by using the tools in the Formula dialog box, which you display by clicking the Formula button in the Data group on the Layout contextual tab.

The Formula dialog box.

A formula consists of an equal sign (=), followed by a function name (such as SUM), followed by parentheses containing the location of the cells you want to use for the calculation. For example, the formula =SUM(Left) totals the cells to the left of the cell containing the formula.

To use a function other than SUM in the Formula dialog box, you click the function you want in the Paste Function list. You can use built-in functions to perform a number of calculations, including averaging (AVERAGE) a set of values, counting (COUNT) the number of values in a column or row, or finding the maximum (MAX) or minimum (MIN) value in a series of cells.

Although formulas commonly refer to the cells above or to the left of the active cell, you can also use the contents of specified cells or constant values in formulas. To use the contents of a cell, you type the cell address in the parentheses following the function name. The cell address is a combination of the column letter and the row number—for example, A1 is the cell at the intersection of the first column and the first row. A series of cells in a row can be addressed as a range consisting of the first cell and the last cell separated by a colon, such as A1:D1. For example, the formula =SUM(A1:D1) totals the values in row 1 of columns A through D. A series of cells in a column can be addressed in the same way. For example, the formula =SUM(A1:A4) totals the values in column A of rows 1 through 4.

Other Layout Options

You can control many aspects of a table in the Table Properties dialog box, which you display by clicking the Properties button in the Table group on the Layout tab. You can set the following options:

- On the Table page, you can specify the width of the entire table, as well as the way it interacts with the surrounding text.

- On the Row page, you can specify the height of each row, whether a row is allowed to break across pages, and whether a row of column headings should be repeated at the top of each page.

  Tip The Repeat As Header Row option is available only if the cursor is in the top row of the table.

- On the Column page, you can set the width of each column.

- On the Cell page, you can set the width of cells and the vertical alignment of text within them.

  Tip You can also control the widths of selected cells by changing the settings in the Cell Size group on the Layout tab.

- On either the Table page or Cell page, you can control the margins of cells (how close text comes to the cell border) by clicking Options and specifying top, bottom, left, and right settings.

  Tip You can also control the margins by clicking the Cell Margins button in the Alignment group on the Layout tab.

- On the Alt Text page, you can enter text that describes what the table is about.

Formatting Tables

Formatting a table to best convey its data can be a process of trial and error. With Word 2010, you can quickly get started by applying one of the table styles available in the Table Styles gallery on the Design contextual tab.

The table styles include a variety of borders, colors, and other attributes to give the table a professional look.

If you want to control the appearance of a table more precisely, you can use the commands on the Design and Layout tabs. You can also format the table content. As you saw in the previous exercise, you can apply character formatting to the text in tables just as you would to regular text, by clicking buttons on the Mini Toolbar. You can also click the buttons in the Font group on the Home tab. You can apply paragraph formatting, such as alignment and spacing, by clicking buttons in the Paragraph group on the Home tab. And you can apply both character and paragraph styles from the Quick Styles gallery.

In this exercise, you'll first apply a table style to a table. Then you'll format a table row and column. You'll also apply character and paragraph formatting to various cells so that the table's appearance helps the reader understand its data.

SET UP You need the RepairCosts_start document located in your Chapter05 practice file folder to complete this exercise. Open the RepairCosts_start document, and save it as *RepairCosts*. If formatting marks are displayed, hide them, and then follow the steps.

1. Click anywhere in the table, and then on the **Design** tab, point to each thumbnail in the first row of the **Table Styles** gallery to see its live preview.

2. In the **Table Style Options** group, clear the **Banded Rows** check box, and select the **Total Row** check box.

   The table style thumbnails no longer have banded rows, reflecting your changes.

3. In the **Table Styles** group, click the **More** button.

   The Table Styles gallery appears.

4. Preview all the styles in the gallery. When you finish exploring, click the second thumbnail in the fifth row (**Medium Shading 2 – Accent 1**).

   The style needs to be modified to suit the data, but it's a good starting point.

Building Association Estimated Repair Costs

Item	Repair Type	Quantity	Cost, $
Elastomeric Decks	Resurface	400 sq. ft.	1,600
Wood Decks	Replace	1,200 sq. ft.	6,500
Building Exterior	Repaint	9,000 sq. ft.	9,000
Roof	Reseal	5,000 sq. ft.	2,700
Entry Doors	Repaint	4	600
Carpet	Replace	150 sq. yds.	4,500
Intercom	Replace	1	2,500
Garage Door Opener	Replace	1	2,000
Steel Doors	Repaint	10	750
Exterior Trim	Repaint	800 ft.	4,500
Elevator Hydraulics	Replace	1	55,000
Fire Alarm System	Replace	1	3,000
TOTAL			110,550

This table style applies formatting to the header and total rows, the first column, and the text of the table.

5. Select all the cells in the last row by clicking in the selection area to its left. Then in the **Table Styles** group, click the **Borders** arrow, and click **Borders and Shading**.

   The Borders And Shading dialog box opens, displaying the borders applied to the selected cells.

6. On the **Borders** page of the dialog box, scroll to the top of the **Style** list, and click the thick black border.

7. In the **Preview** area, click the top border button once to remove the current border, and click again to apply the thick black border.

8. Click the **Shading** tab, and click the **Fill** arrow. Under **Theme Colors** in the palette, click the fifth box in the top row (**Blue, Accent 1**). Then click **OK**.

9. Without moving the selection, on the **Home** tab, in the **Font** group, click the **Font Color** arrow, and under **Theme Colors** in the palette, click the white box. Then press Home to release the selection.

   The table now has the same border at the top and bottom.

Building Association Estimated Repair Costs

Item	Repair Type	Quantity	Cost, $
Elastomeric Decks	Resurface	400 sq. ft.	1,600
Wood Decks	Replace	1,200 sq. ft.	6,500
Building Exterior	Repaint	9,000 sq. ft.	9,000
Roof	Reseal	5,000 sq. ft.	2,700
Entry Doors	Repaint	4	600
Carpet	Replace	150 sq. yds.	4,500
Intercom	Replace	1	2,500
Garage Door Opener	Replace	1	2,000
Steel Doors	Repaint	10	750
Exterior Trim	Repaint	800 ft.	4,500
Elevator Hydraulics	Replace	1	55,000
Fire Alarm System	Replace	1	3,000
TOTAL			110,550

You can customize a table style to meet your needs.

10. Point to the left side of the **Elastomeric Decks** cell, and when the pointer changes to a black right-pointing arrow, drag downward to select all the cells in the **Item** column *except* the **TOTAL** cell.

Shading ▾

11. On the **Design** tab, in the **Table Styles** group, click the **Shading** arrow, and under **Theme Colors**, click the third box in the blue column (**Blue, Accent 1, Lighter 40%**).

12. Select all the cells containing amounts in the **Cost, $** column, including the cell with the total. Then on the **Layout** tab, in the **Alignment** group, click the **Align Center Right** button.

> **Tip** If the first row of your table has several long headings that make it difficult to fit the table on one page, you can turn the headings sideways. Simply select the heading row and click the Text Direction button in the Alignment group on the Layout tab.

Now you can judge how well the table displays its data.

Building Association Estimated Repair Costs

Item	Repair Type	Quantity	Cost, $
Elastomeric Decks	Resurface	400 sq. ft.	1,600
Wood Decks	Replace	1,200 sq. ft.	6,500
Building Exterior	Repaint	9,000 sq. ft.	9,000
Roof	Reseal	5,000 sq. ft.	2,700
Entry Doors	Repaint	4	600
Carpet	Replace	150 sq. yds.	4,500
Intercom	Replace	1	2,500
Garage Door Opener	Replace	1	2,000
Steel Doors	Repaint	10	750
Exterior Trim	Repaint	800 ft.	4,500
Elevator Hydraulics	Replace	1	55,000
Fire Alarm System	Replace	1	3,000
TOTAL			110,550

The total now stands out better, and the amounts are easier to read.

> **Tip** If you will need to use this formatted table with different data in the future, you can save it as a Quick Table. For information about saving customized tables for future use, see the sidebar "Quick Tables" on the next page.

✖ CLEAN UP Save the RepairCosts document, and then close it.

Quick Tables

With Word 2010, you can create Quick Tables—preformatted tables with sample data that you can customize. To create a Quick Table:

1. On the Insert tab, in the Tables group, click the Table button, and then point to Quick Tables.

   The Quick Tables gallery appears.

The predefined Quick Tables meet several common needs.

2. Scroll through the gallery, noticing the types of tables that are available, and then click the one you want.

   For example, this is the Matrix Quick Table.

City·or·Town¤	Point·A¤	Point·B¤	Point·C¤	Point·D¤	Point·E¤	¤
Point·A¤	—¤	¤	¤	¤	¤	¤
Point·B¤	87¤	—¤	¤	¤	¤	¤
Point·C¤	64¤	56¤	—¤	¤	¤	¤
Point·D¤	37¤	32¤	91¤	—¤	¤	¤
Point·E¤	93¤	35¤	54¤	43¤	—¤	¤

The Matrix Quick Table includes row and column headings, placeholder data, and no summary data, such as totals.

3. On the Design tab, apply formatting to tailor the Quick Table to your needs.
   For example, here's the Matrix Quick Table after we formatted it.

City or Town	Point A	Point B	Point C	Point D	Point E
Point A	—				
Point B	87	—			
Point C	64	56	—		
Point D	37	32	91	—	
Point E	93	35	54	43	—

It is easy to customize a Quick Table for your own needs.

If you will use the table again, you can save it in the Quick Tables gallery. Select the table, display the Quick Tables gallery, and click Save Selection To Quick Tables Gallery. Then in the Create New Building Block dialog box, assign a name to the table, and click OK. Provided you save the Building Blocks template when Word prompts you to, the table will be available in the Quick Tables gallery for future use.

See Also For information about building blocks, see "Inserting Building Blocks" in Chapter 6, "Add Simple Graphic Elements."

Key Points

- To vary the layout of a document, you can divide text into columns. You can control the number of columns, the width of the columns, and the space between the columns.
- To clearly present a simple set of data, you can use tabs to create a tabbed list, with custom tab stops controlling the width and alignment of columns.
- You can create a table from scratch, or convert existing text to a table. You can control the size of the table and its individual structural elements.
- By using the built-in table styles, you can quickly apply professional-looking cell and character formatting to a table and its contents.
- You can enhance a table and its contents by applying text attributes, borders, and shading.

Chapter at a Glance

Insert and modify pictures, **page 168**

Change a document's background, **page 176**

Insert building blocks, **page 183**

Add WordArt text, **page 197**

6 Add Simple Graphic Elements

In this chapter, you will learn how to

- ✔ Insert and modify pictures.
- ✔ Change a document's background.
- ✔ Insert building blocks.
- ✔ Add WordArt text.

Some documents that you create in Microsoft Word 2010 are straightforward and require nothing more than words. Others might benefit from the addition of graphic elements to reinforce their concepts, to grab the reader's attention, or to make them more visually appealing. These graphic elements can include a wide variety of objects and effects, including:

- **Pictures** These objects are created outside of Word—photographs from digital cameras, clip art images, or files created on a computer with a graphics program. No matter what the origin of the picture, you can change its size and its position in relation to other content after you insert it in the Word document. For some types of pictures, you can make additional changes from within Word, such as cropping the picture or embellishing it by applying artistic effects.

- **Drawing objects** These objects are created within Word—text boxes, WordArt text, diagrams, charts, shapes, and other such objects. As with pictures, you can size, move, and format drawing objects from within Word.

   See Also For information about diagrams, charts, or shapes, refer to *Microsoft Word 2010 Step by Step*, by Joyce Cox and Joan Lambert (Microsoft Press, 2010).

- **Building blocks** You can draw attention to specific information and add graphic appeal by incorporating ready-made graphic building blocks (also called *Quick Parts*) into a document. These building blocks are combinations of drawing objects (and sometimes pictures) in a variety of formatting styles that you can select to insert elements such as cover pages, quotations pulled from the text (called *pull quotes*), and sidebars. You can also create your own building blocks, which then become available in the Quick Parts gallery.

- **Backgrounds** You can apply a variety of backgrounds to the pages of your document, including plain colors, gradients, textures, patterns, and pictures.

In this chapter, you'll first insert and modify pictures in a document. You'll experiment with page backgrounds, and then add three types of building blocks to a document. Finally, you'll have a bit of fun with WordArt.

> **Practice Files**   Before you can complete the exercises in this chapter, you need to copy the book's practice files to your computer. The practice files you'll use to complete the exercises in this chapter are in the Chapter06 practice file folder. A complete list of practice files is provided in "Using the Practice Files" at the beginning of this book.

Inserting and Modifying Pictures

You can insert digital photographs or pictures created in almost any program into a Word document. You specify the source of the picture you want to insert by clicking one of these two buttons, which are located in the Illustrations group on the Insert tab:

- **Picture** Click this button to insert a picture that is saved as a file on your computer, or on a device (such as an external hard drive or a digital camera) that is connected to your computer.

- **Clip Art** Click this button to insert one of hundreds of clip art images, such as photos and drawings of people, places, and things.

   See Also   For information about clip art, see the sidebar "About Clip Art" later in this chapter.

After you insert a picture in a document, you can modify the image by using commands on the Format contextual tab, which is displayed only when a picture or drawing object is selected. For example, you can click buttons in the Adjust group to change the picture's brightness and contrast, recolor it, apply artistic effects to it, and compress it to reduce the size of the document containing it. The Picture Styles group offers a wide range of picture styles that you can apply to a picture to change its shape and orientation, as well as add borders and picture effects. And finally, you can use the commands in the Size group for cropping and resizing pictures.

The Format contextual tab for pictures.

Troubleshooting The appearance of buttons and groups on the ribbon changes depending on the width of the program window. For information about changing the appearance of the ribbon to match our screen images, see "Modifying the Display of the Ribbon" at the beginning of this book.

See Also For information about using the commands in the Arrange group, refer to *Microsoft Word 2010 Step by Step*, by Joyce Cox and Joan Lambert (Microsoft Press, 2010).

In this exercise, you'll insert a couple of photographs and size and crop them. You'll modify one of them and then copy the modifications to the other one. Then you'll insert an illustration and apply an artistic effects to it.

SET UP You need the Authors_start document, the Joan and Joyce photographs, and the OTSI-Logo illustration located in your Chapter06 practice file folder to complete this exercise. Open the Authors_start document, and save it as *Authors*. Display the rulers and formatting marks, and then follow the steps.

1. Click to the left of the **Joyce has 30 years' experience** paragraph, press the Enter key, and press the Up Arrow key. Then on the **Insert** tab, in the **Illustrations** group, click the **Picture** button.

   The Insert Picture dialog box opens, displaying the contents of your Pictures library.

2. Navigate to the **Chapter06** practice file folder, and double-click the **Joyce** picture.

   Word inserts the picture at the cursor and displays the Format contextual tab on the ribbon.

   Troubleshooting If Word inserts a frame the size of the picture but displays only a sliver of the picture itself, Word cannot increase the line spacing to accommodate the picture because it is set to a specific amount. To correct this problem, click the Paragraph dialog box launcher, and in the Paragraph dialog box, change the Line Spacing setting to Single.

   Tip In this exercise, you insert pictures in blank paragraphs. By default, Word inserts the picture in-line with the text, meaning that Word increases the line spacing as necessary to accommodate the picture. If you were to type text adjacent to the picture, the bottom of the picture would align with the bottom of the text on the same line. After you insert a picture, you can change its position and the way text wraps around it.

   See Also For more information about positioning objects and wrapping text around them, see "Adding WordArt Text" later in this chapter. You can also refer to *Microsoft Word 2010 Step by Step*, by Joyce Cox and Joan Lambert (Microsoft Press, 2010).

3. In the lower-right corner of the picture, point to the handle (the circle). When the pointer changes to a double arrow, drag up and to the left until the right side of the picture's shadow frame is in line with the **1.75** inch mark on the horizontal ruler.

When you release the mouse button, the picture assumes its new size.

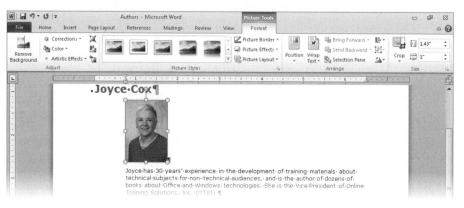

Because the ratio of the picture's height to its width (called the aspect ratio*) is locked, the height and width change proportionally.*

Tip You can fine-tune the size of a graphic by adjusting the Shape Height and Shape Width settings in the Size group on the Format tab.

4. On the **Format** contextual tab, in the **Size** group, click the **Crop** button.

Word surrounds the picture with crop handles.

5. Point to the bottom-middle handle, and when the pointer changes to a black T, drag upward until the picture is about 1 inch high.

Word grays out the part of the picture you have cropped away.

> .**Joyce·Cox**¶
>
> Joyce·has·30·years'·experience·in·the·development·of·training·materials·about· technical·subjects·for·non-technical·audiences,·and·is·the·author·of·dozens·of· books·about·Office·and·Windows·technologies.·She·is·the·Vice·President·of·Online· Training·Solutions,·Inc.·(OTSI).¶
>
> As·President·of·and·principal·author·for·Online·Press,·she·developed·the·*Quick· Course*·series·of·computer·training·books·for·beginning·and·intermediate·adult· learners.·She·was·also·the·first·managing·editor·of·Microsoft·Press,·an·editor·for· Sybex,·and·an·editor·for·the·University·of·California.¶

Word will not actually crop the picture until you turn off the crop button.

6. Click the **Crop** button to turn it off.

Word removes the crop handles and discards the gray part of the picture.

> **Tip** In addition to cropping a picture manually, you can click the Crop arrow and select from various options, including having Word crop a picture to fit a shape you select, cropping to a precise width:height ratio, filling an area with a picture, or fitting a picture to an area.

7. Click to the left of the **Joan has worked** paragraph, press Enter, and then press the Up Arrow key. Then repeat steps 1 through 6 to insert, size, and crop the **Joan** picture below the **Joan Lambert** heading.

8. With the **Joan** picture still selected, on the **Format** contextual tab, in the **Adjust** group, click the **Color** button.

   The Color gallery appears.

You can change the saturation and tone, as well as recolor the picture.

9. Under **Recolor** in the **Color** gallery, preview each option, and then click the second thumbnail in the first row (**Grayscale**).

   The picture is grayscaled—that is, each color is converted into a shade of gray.

10. In the **Adjust** group, click the **Corrections** button. Then in the **Corrections** gallery, under **Brightness and Contrast**, preview each option, and then click the fourth thumbnail in the top row (**Brightness: +20% Contrast: -40%**).

11. In the **Picture Styles** group, click the **More** button.

    The Picture Styles gallery appears.

You can apply frames, shadows, glows, and 3-D effects from the Picture Styles gallery.

Troubleshooting   The number of thumbnails per row in your galleries might be different than ours, depending on the screen resolution and the width of the program window. In the steps, look for the thumbnail with the name specified.

12. In the gallery, preview each thumbnail, and then click the first thumbnail in the fifth row (**Bevel Rectangle**). Click away from the picture to see the effect.

    The photograph now has a three-dimensional appearance.

> ·**Joan·Lambert**¶
>
> ¶
>
> Joan·has·worked·in·the·training·and·certification·industry·for·13·years.··As·
> President·of·OTSI,·Joan·is·responsible·for·guiding·the·translation·of·technical·
> information·and·requirements·into·useful,·relevant,·and·measurable·training·and·
> certification·tools.¶

This picture style gives the effect of a padded square button.

13. Click the **Joan** picture to select it, and then on the **Home** tab, in the **Clipboard** group, click the **Format Painter** button.

14. If necessary, scroll up in the document, and click the **Joyce** picture.

   Word copies the grayscale format, color corrections, and picture style from one picture to the other.

15. Scroll down until the **Online Training Solutions, Inc. (OTSI)** heading is visible, click to the left of the **OTSI specializes** paragraph, press Enter, and then press Up Arrow.

16. On the **Insert** tab, in the **Illustration** group, click the **Picture** button. Then in the **Chapter06** folder displayed in the **Insert Picture** dialog box, double-click the **OTSI-Logo** graphic.

17. With the logo selected, on the **Format** contextual tab, in the **Adjust** group, click the **Artistic Effects** button.

18. In the **Artistic Effects** gallery, preview each thumbnail, and then click the last thumbnail in the fifth row (**Glow Edges**). Click away from the picture to see the effect.

   The logo now has a black-and-white stylized effect.

·**Online·Training·Solutions,·Inc.·(OTSI)**¶

OTSI·specializes·in·the·design,·creation,·and·production·of·Office·and·Windows·training·products·for·office·and·home·computer·users.·For·more·information·about·OTSI,·visit·¶

www.otsi.com¶

You can use artistic effects to make pictures look like paintings, pencil sketches, cutouts and more.

Tip To move a picture, simply drag it to the desired location. To copy a graphic, hold down the Ctrl key while you drag, releasing first the mouse button and then the Ctrl key. (If you release Ctrl first, Word will move the image instead of copying it.)

CLEAN UP Save the Authors document, and then close it.

About Clip Art

If you want to dress up a document with a graphic but you don't have a suitable picture, you might want to search for a clip art image. Clip art comes in many different styles and formats, including illustrations, photographs, videos, and audio clips. The only thing the clips have in common is that they are free and available without any copyright restrictions.

Clicking the Clip Art button displays the Clip Art task pane, where you can enter a search term to look for an image on your computer or on the Office.com Web site. When clip art images matching your search term are displayed in the task pane, you can click an image to insert it in your document. If you don't want to insert an image at the cursor but want it to be available for use somewhere else, you can point to the image in the Clip Art task pane, click the arrow that appears, and then click Copy to store a copy of the image on the Microsoft Office Clipboard. If you find an image on Office.com and want to be able to insert it in documents when you are not online, you can point to the arrow, click Make Available Offline, and then store it in a clip art collection. You can also edit the keywords associated with an image and view its properties.

To find and insert a clip art image:

1. Position the cursor where you want the image to appear. Then on the Insert tab, in the Illustrations group, click the Clip Art button.

2. In the Clip Art task pane, select the current entry in the Search For box (or click in the box if there is no entry), and enter a keyword for the type of clip art you are looking for, such as *cats*. Then select the Include Office.com Content check box, and click Go.

   Tip You can restrict the search results to a particular type of clip art by selecting the type in the Results Should Be list.

   The task pane displays any clip art images that have your keyword associated with them.

Cat-related clip art images from your computer and Office.com.

3. In the task pane, click the image you want to insert into the document.

   You can then manipulate the clip art image the same way you would a picture.

Changing a Document's Background

Whether you're creating a document that will be printed, viewed on a computer, or published on the Internet and viewed in a Web browser, you can make your document stand out by adding a background color, texture, or picture to every page in a document. You can also add borders to every page.

See Also For information about creating documents for the Web, refer to *Microsoft Word 2010 Step by Step*, by Joyce Cox and Joan Lambert (Microsoft Press, 2010).

When it comes to backgrounds, the trick is to not overdo it. Your effects need to be subtle enough that they do not interfere with the text or other elements on the page.

In this exercise, you'll first apply a solid background color to every page. Then you'll create a two-color gradient across the pages. You'll fill the pages with one of the textures that come with Word and then fill them with a picture. Finally, you'll put a border around every page.

SET UP You need the MarbleFloor picture located in your Chapter06 practice file folder to complete this exercise. Open a blank document, turn off the rulers and formatting marks, and then follow the steps.

1. In the lower-right corner of the program window, click the **Zoom Level** button, and set the zoom percentage to display the whole page.

2. On the **Page Layout** tab, in the **Page Background** group, click the **Page Color** button, and then under **Theme Colors**, in the column of green boxes, click the second box from the top (**Olive Green, Accent 3, Lighter 60%**).

   The background of the document changes to the selected color.

3. In the **Page Background** group, click the **Page Color** button, and then click **Fill Effects**.

   The Fill Effects dialog box opens.

The Gradient page of the Fill Effects dialog box.

4. In the **Colors** area, click **Two colors**, and then leaving **Color 1** set to light green, click the **Color 2** arrow, and in the fifth column of boxes, select the top box (**Blue, Accent 1, Lighter 80%**).

   The Variants and Sample areas change to show graded combinations of the two colors.

5. In the **Shading styles** area, click each option in turn and observe the effects in the **Variants** and **Sample** areas. Then click **Diagonal Up**.

6. In the **Variants** area, click the option in the upper-left corner, and then click **OK**.

   The background of the document is now shaded from light green to light blue.

7. Display the **Fill Effects** dialog box again, and click the **Texture** tab.

On this page, you can select from a number of texture files that come with Word.

The Texture page of the Fill Effects dialog box.

8. Click the effect in the second column of the third row (**White Marble**), and then click **OK**.

The background changes to display the effect rather than the color.

The page with the White Marble texture applied to the background.

9. Display the **Fill Effects** dialog box again, and click the **Picture** tab. Then click **Select Picture**, and with the contents of your **Chapter06** practice file folder displayed in the **Select Picture** dialog box, double-click **MarbleFloor**. In the **Fill Effects** dialog box, click **OK**.

The background changes to display a blurred picture of a marble floor in the Doge's Palace in Venice.

The page with the MarbleFloor picture applied to the background.

Tip Word fills the page with as much of the picture as will fit. If one copy of the picture does not completely fill the page, Word inserts another copy, effectively "tiling" the image.

Page Borders

10. In the **Page Background** group, click the **Page Borders** button.

    The Borders And Shading dialog box opens with the Page Border page active.

The Page Border page is almost the same as the Borders page, except that an Art option is available at the bottom of the center pane.

11. In the **Setting** area of the **Borders and Shading** dialog box, click **Box**. Then in the **Color** list, click the third box in the blue column (**Blue, Accent 1, Lighter 40%**).

12. In the **Art** list, scroll down, clicking any art option you like to see it applied to the page in the **Preview** pane. When you find a style you like, click **OK**.

    We chose a classic double border near the bottom of the Art list.

The page with a double border applied on top of the picture background.

13. Press Ctrl+Enter to insert a page break, and then scroll to the second page.

    When you apply a background, it is reflected in all the pages of the document.

✖ **CLEAN UP** If you want, save the document as *PageBackground*, and then close it.

Inserting Building Blocks

To simplify the creation of professional-looking text elements, Word 2010 comes with ready-made visual representations of text, known as *building blocks*, which are available from various groups on the Insert tab. You can insert the following types of building blocks:

- **Cover page** You can quickly add a formatted cover page to a longer document such as a report by selecting a style from the Cover Page gallery. The cover page includes text placeholders for elements such as a title so that you can customize the page to reflect the content of the document.

  Tip You can also insert a blank page anywhere in a document—even in the middle of a paragraph—by positioning the cursor and then clicking the Blank Page button in the Pages group on the Insert tab.

- **Header and footer** You can display information on every page of a document in regions at the top and bottom of a page by selecting a style from the Header or Footer gallery. Word indicates the header and footer areas by displaying dotted borders and displays a Design contextual tab on the ribbon. You can enter information in the header and footer areas the same way you enter ordinary text. You can have a different header and footer on the first page of a document and different headers and footers on odd and even pages.

  Tip If your document contains section breaks, each successive section inherits the headers and footers of the preceding section unless you break the link between the two sections. You can then create a different header and footer for the current section. For information about sections, see "Controlling What Appears on Each Page" in Chapter 7, "Preview, Print, and Distribute Documents."

- **Page number** You can quickly add headers and footers that include only page numbers and require no customization by selecting the style you want from one of the Page Number galleries.

- **Text box** To reinforce key concepts and also alleviate the monotony of page after page of plain text, you can insert text boxes such as sidebars and quote boxes by selecting a style from the Text Box gallery. The formatted text box includes placeholder text that you replace with your own.

If you frequently use a specific element in your documents, such as a formatted title-subtitle-author arrangement at the beginning of reports, you can define it as a custom building block. It is then available from the Quick Parts gallery.

See Also For information about saving frequently used text as a custom building block, see "Inserting Saved Text" in Chapter 3, "Edit and Proofread Text."

You can see a list of all the available building blocks by clicking the Quick Parts button in the Text group on the Insert tab and then clicking Building Blocks Organizer.

The Building Blocks Organizer dialog box.

Initially the building blocks are organized by type, as reflected in the Gallery column. If you want to insert building blocks of the same design in a document, you might want to sort the list alphabetically by design name, by clicking the Name column heading. For example, a cover page, footer, header, quote box, and sidebar are all available with the Pinstripes design. Some elements, such as bibliographies, equations, tables of contents, tables, and watermarks, are not part of a design family and have their own unique names.

Tip You can see more information about each building block by dragging the horizontal scroll box to display the right side of the Building Blocks list.

At the bottom of the Building Blocks Organizer dialog box, you can click Edit Properties to display a dialog box where you can see the information about a selected building block in a more readable format. If you are viewing the properties associated with a custom building block, you can change them in this dialog box, but we don't recommend changing the properties assigned to a building block that came with Word.

Modify Building Block		
Name:	Pinstripes Sidebar	
Gallery:	Text Boxes	▼
Category:	Built-In	▼
Description:	Right-aligned sidebar with accent shadow	
Save in:	Building Blocks	▼
Options:	Insert content only	▼
	OK	Cancel

The Modify Building Block dialog box.

You can delete a selected custom building block from the list by clicking Delete at the bottom of the Building Blocks Organizer dialog box, and you can insert a selected building block into the document by clicking Insert.

In this exercise, you'll insert a cover page and add a header and footer to a document. You'll also insert two kinds of text boxes with the same design. Finally, you'll save a customized sidebar as a building block.

➡ **SET UP** You need the Flyer_start document located in your Chapter06 practice file folder to complete this exercise. Open the Flyer_start document, and save it as *Flyer*. Then follow the steps.

100%

1. Click the **Zoom Level** button in the lower-right corner of the program window. In the **Zoom** dialog box, click **Whole page**, and then click **OK**.

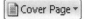

2. With the cursor at the top of the document, on the **Insert** tab, in the **Pages** group, click the **Cover Page** button.

The Cover Page gallery appears.

The thumbnails show the designs of the available cover pages.

3. Scroll through the **Cover Page** gallery to see the available options, and then click **Pinstripes**.

Word inserts the cover page at the beginning of the document and adds placeholders for the title, subtitle, date, company name, and author name.

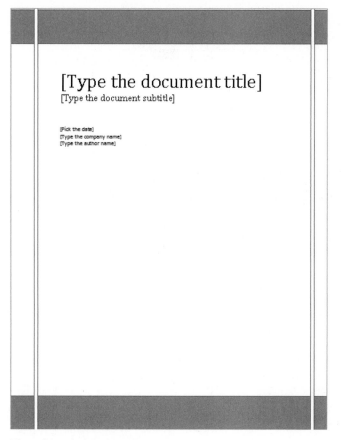

[Type the document title]

[Type the document subtitle]

[Pick the date]
[Type the company name]
[Type the author name]

The selected cover page.

Tip If any of the required information is attached to the document as properties, Word inserts the information instead of the placeholder.

4. Click anywhere in the title placeholder, and type **Simple Room Design** Then click the **Pick the date** placeholder, click the arrow that appears, and in the calendar, click today's date (indicated by a red box). Delete the remaining placeholder paragraphs.

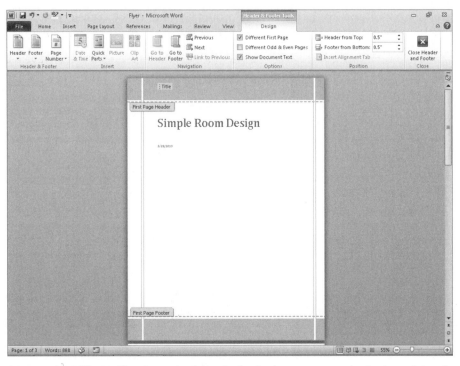

5. On the **Insert** tab, in the **Header & Footer** group, click the **Header** button. Scroll through the **Header** gallery, and then click **Pinstripes**.

Word displays the Design contextual tab, dims the text of the document, and indicates the header and footer areas with dotted lines.

Because the Different First Page check box in the Options group on the Design tab is selected, the header area is labeled First Page Header.

6. In the **Navigation** group, click the **Next** button.

Word moves to the next section of the document, which is the page after the cover page.

7. Type **Wide World Importers**. Then on the **Home** tab, in the **Paragraph** group, click the **Center** button.

8. On the **Design** tab, in the **Navigation** group, click the **Go to Footer** button.

   The cursor moves to the footer area at the bottom of the page.

9. In the **Header & Footer** group, click the **Page Number** button, point to **Current Position** in the list, and then in the gallery, click **Large Color**.

   Except for the first page of the document, the pages now have a header and footer.

Headers and footers can include any information you want repeated on each page in a section, including graphics.

Tip To use a numbering scheme other than Arabic numerals, to number pages by chapter, or to control the starting number, click the Page Number button in the Header & Footer group, and then click Format Page Numbers. In the Page Number Format dialog box, click the Number Format arrow, and then in the list, click the format you want.

10. In the **Close** group, click the **Close Header and Footer** button.

11. At the top of the second page, delete **Simple Room Design**. Then on the **Insert** tab, in the **Text** group, click the **Quick Parts** button, and click **Building Blocks Organizer**.

The Building Blocks Organizer shown at the beginning of this topic opens. The left pane displays a complete list of all the building blocks available on your computer. Clicking a building block in the left pane displays a preview in the right pane.

Tip The Building Blocks list you see on your computer includes AutoText entries for your user name and initials. To change either of these entries, display the Backstage view, click Options, and then on the General page of the Word Options dialog box, update your information and click OK.

12. Scroll through the **Building blocks** list, previewing a few of the building blocks. Then click the **Name** column heading, and scroll through the list again.

Notice that page elements of the same theme are coordinated.

The Building Blocks Organizer dialog box, after the Name column has been sorted.

13. In the **Building blocks** list, click **Pinstripes Quote** (the first of the **Pinstripes** text boxes), and then below the list, click **Insert**.

Word inserts the quote box halfway down the right side of the page.

Placeholder text in the quote box tells you how to insert your own text and format the block.

14. Click the **Zoom Out** button on the **Zoom Slider** until you can read the text of the document. Then select and copy the last sentence of the fourth paragraph (**Go with what you love...**).

15. Click the quote box to select the placeholder text. Then on the **Home** tab, in the **Clipboard** group, click the **Paste** arrow, and under **Paste Options**, click the **Keep Text Only** button.

The copied text replaces the placeholder, and because it was pasted as unformatted text, it retains the formatting of the placeholder text. The quote box automatically resizes to fit its new contents.

See Also For information about text boxes, see the sidebar "Drawing Text Boxes" later in this chapter.

16. Display the whole page again. Then scroll to the last page of the document, and click anywhere on the page.

17. On the **Insert** tab, in the **Text** group, click the **Text Box** button, scroll through the gallery, and click **Pinstripes Sidebar**.

Word inserts the sidebar down the right side of the page.

This sidebar consists of two overlapping, coordinated boxes.

18. If necessary, zoom out so that you can see the text well enough to edit it. Then at the beginning of the last paragraph of the document, delete **NOTE:** (including the colon and following space).

19. Select the last paragraph, and on the **Home** tab, in the **Clipboard** group, click the **Cut** button.

    Keyboard Shortcut Press Ctrl+X to cut the selected content to the Clipboard.

20. Click the sidebar to select the placeholder text. Then in the **Clipboard** group, click the **Paste** arrow, and under **Paste Options**, click the **Keep Text Only** button.

    The sidebar now contains the cut text.

The pasted text takes on the formatting assigned to the text box.

21. To widen the sidebar so that the Web site address fits on one line, click the sidebar text, and drag the blue handle on the dotted line at the left side of the white box to the left, until it sits slightly to the left of the frame of the white box.

    If the Web site address still doesn't fit, adjust the width of the sidebar again.

22. Click at the top of the sidebar's blue box. Then on the **Insert** tab, in the **Text** group, click the **Quick Parts** button, and click **Save Selection to Quick Part Gallery**.

   Troubleshooting If you click the text in the sidebar or elsewhere in the document after resizing the sidebar, the sidebar will no longer be selected and the Save Selection To Quick Part Gallery command will not be available.

   The Create New Building Block dialog box opens.

23. Replace the text in the **Name** box with **Order Sidebar**, and then click **OK**.

   You can now insert this custom sidebar from the Quick Parts gallery into other documents.

24. In the **Text** group, click the **Quick Parts** button.

   The Quick Parts gallery appears.

The Order Sidebar custom building block appears at the top of the gallery.

25. Click **Building Blocks Organizer**, and then in the **Building Blocks Organizer** dialog box, click the **Category** column heading to sort the **Building blocks** list by that column.

26. In the **Building blocks** list, scroll to the **General** category, and click **Order Sidebar** once.

The building block you just created appears in the preview pane.

The General category includes your custom building block and the user name and initials AutoText entries.

✖ **CLEAN UP** If you want, delete the building block you just created before you close the Building Blocks Organizer dialog box. Then save the Flyer document, and close it.

Important When you exit Word after saving a custom building block, you'll be asked whether you want to save changes to the template in which you stored the building block. If you want the building block to be available for future documents, click Save; otherwise, click Don't Save.

Drawing Text Boxes

If none of the predefined text-box building blocks meets your needs, you can draw your own text box. At the bottom of the Text Box gallery, click Draw Text Box, and then drag a box the size you want anywhere on the page. You can immediately start typing at the blinking cursor, and you can format the text the way you would any other text.

When a text box is surrounded by a dashed border, it's selected for text editing. To manipulate the text box itself, you need to click its frame.

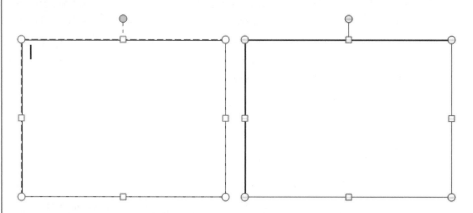

The text box on the left is selected for editing, and the one on the right is selected for manipulation.

When a text box has a solid border, you can reposition it by dragging it to another location, and you can change its size by dragging the size handles around its frame. You can change the outline and fill colors by using the commands in the Shape Styles group on the Format contextual tab.

You can link text boxes so that text flows from one to the next. To do so:

1. Click the first text box.

2. In the Text group on the Format contextual tab, click Create Link.

   The mouse pointer changes to a small pitcher.

3. Point to the second text box, and then when the mouse pointer changes to a pouring pitcher, click once.

   Note that the second text box must be empty.

Adding WordArt Text

If you're familiar with WordArt in earlier versions of Word, you're in for a surprise. WordArt has matured from the fun little tool you might have used in the past to create headings in molded shapes and gaudy colors. Its capabilities are now oriented toward creating more sophisticated display-text objects that you can position anywhere on the page. Although the WordArt object is attached to the paragraph that contained the cursor when you created it, you can move it independently from the text, even positioning it over the text if you want.

To insert a WordArt object, you click the WordArt button in the Text group on the Insert tab, and click a text style in the WordArt gallery. (The WordArt styles are the same as the text effects available in the Text Effects gallery in the Font group of the Home tab.) Then you enter your text in the text box that appears. You can edit the text, adjust the character formatting in the usual ways, and change the text style at any time.

Tip You can also select existing text before clicking the WordArt button to convert that text into a WordArt object.

See Also For information about character formatting, see "Manually Changing the Look of Characters" in Chapter 4, "Change the Look of Text." For information about text effects, see "Quickly Formatting Text" in the same chapter.

When a WordArt object is selected, the Format contextual tab appears on the ribbon. You can use the commands on this tab to format the WordArt object to meet your needs. For example, from the Format tab, you can add effects such as shadows and 3-D effects, change the fill and outline colors, and change the text direction and alignment. You can also position the WordArt object in any of several predefined locations on the page, as well as specify how the text should wrap around the object.

Tip Don't go too wild with WordArt formatting. Many WordArt Styles and Shape Styles take up space and can involve trial and error to produce a neat effect.

In this exercise, you'll insert a new WordArt object, modify it, and then position it on the page. Then you'll change the way it relates to the text on the page.

SET UP You need the Announcement_start document located in your Chapter06 practice file folder to complete this exercise. Open the Announcement_start document and save it as *Announcement*. Then with the rulers and formatting marks turned off, follow the steps.

1. On the **Insert** tab, in the **Text** group, click the **WordArt** button.

   The WordArt gallery appears, displaying the same formatted letters you see when you click the Text Effects button.

2. Click the third thumbnail in the fifth row (**Fill – Red, Accent 2, Warm Matte Bevel**).

   Word inserts a WordArt object with that text effect at the cursor. Because a graphic object is selected, the Format contextual tab appears on the ribbon.

The WordArt object contains placeholder text in the style you chose.

   Tip If formatting marks are displayed, you see an anchor icon adjacent to the first paragraph. You can ignore it for now.

   See Also For information about anchoring objects, refer to *Microsoft Word 2010 Step by Step*, by Joyce Cox and Joan Lambert (Microsoft Press, 2010).

3. With **Your Text Here** selected, type **The Room Planner**. (Don't type the period.)

   Tip WordArt objects can accommodate multiple lines. Simply press Enter if you want to start a new line.

4. Without moving the cursor, on the **Home** tab, in the **Paragraph** group, click the **Center** button.

5. Click the border of the text box to select the box, and then change the zoom percentage so that you can see the whole page.

6. On the **Format** contextual tab, in the **Arrange** group, click the **Position** button.

   The Position gallery appears.

You can position the WordArt object in one of 10 predefined positions.

7. Point to each thumbnail in turn to preview where each option will place the object. Then under **With Text Wrapping**, click the second thumbnail in the second row (**Position in Middle Center with Square Text Wrapping**).

The object moves to the middle of the page.

Don't worry if the word *Planner* is now truncated. Because of the interaction of the object with its surrounding text, sometimes not all the WordArt text fits in its box after you position it. You'll fix that in a minute.

8. In the **Arrange** group, click the **Wrap Text** button.

The Wrap Text gallery appears.

You can change the text wrapping without changing the position.

9. Point to each thumbnail in turn to preview their effects, and then click **Tight**.

10. In the **Arrange** group, click the **Wrap Text** button, and then click **More Layout Options**.

The Layout dialog box opens with the Text Wrapping page active.

If you know what kind of text wrapping you want, you can select it on this page of the dialog box, but you can't preview it.

11. In the **Distance from text** area, change the **Left** and **Right** settings to **0.3"**, and then click **OK**.

The text outside the box is no longer encroaching on the box.

If the word *Planner* was truncated in your box, the entire word should now be displayed. If it isn't, try increasing the Distance From Text settings to 0.4".

12. In the **WordArt Styles** group, display the **WordArt Quick Styles** gallery, and then click the fourth thumbnail in the third row (**Gradient Fill – Blue, Accent 1**).

Troubleshooting Depending on your screen resolution and program window size, you might have to click the Quick Styles button to display the gallery.

13. In the **Shape Styles** group, display the **Shape Styles** gallery, and then click the fourth thumbnail in the fourth row (**Subtle Effect – Olive Green, Accent 3**).

14. Press Ctrl+Home.

Now you can see the effect of the WordArt text.

This simple text banner is a stylish alternative to a traditional title.

15. If you want, experiment with combinations of the styles and formatting available on the **Format** tab.

For example, you might want to try some of the Text Effects options, such as the molding effects available in the Transform gallery.

CLEAN UP Save the Announcement document, and then close it.

Formatting the First Letter of a Paragraph

Many books, magazines, and reports begin the first paragraph of a section or chapter by using an enlarged, decorative capital letter. Called a *dropped capital*, or simply a *drop cap*, this effect can be an easy way to give a document a finished, professional look.

The Drop Cap gallery provides two basic drop-cap styles:

- **Dropped** Sits in the text column and displaces paragraph text
- **In margin** Hangs in the margin adjacent to the paragraph text

In either case, the drop cap is as tall as three lines of text and uses the same font as the rest of the paragraph.

To insert a drop cap:

1. Click anywhere in a paragraph of text, and then on the Insert tab, in the Text group, click the Drop Cap button.

2. Point to each thumbnail to display its live preview, and then click the one you want.

   Word inserts the first letter of the paragraph in a box. If you selected Dropped, Word rewraps the text to the right of the graphic.

For more options, click Drop Cap Options at the bottom of the Drop Cap gallery to open the Drop Cap dialog box. You can choose a font that is different from the paragraph and adjust the drop cap's height and distance from the text.

If you want to make the first word of the paragraph stand out, you can click to the right of the drop cap and type the rest of the word. If you do this, don't forget to delete the word from the beginning of the paragraph!

Key Points

- You can insert illustrations created with most graphics programs, as well as digital photos, into a Word document.

- A background color, texture, pattern, or picture can really give a document pizzazz, but be careful that it doesn't overwhelm the text.

- Word comes with predefined building blocks that quickly add graphic elements to a document.

- Using WordArt, you can easily add fancy text to a document and then format and position it for the best effect.

Chapter at a Glance

Preview and adjust page layout, **page 206**

Print documents, **page 217**

Control what appears on each page, **page 212**

Prepare documents for electronic distribution, **page 219**

7 Preview, Print, and Distribute Documents

In this chapter, you will learn how to

✔ Preview and adjust page layout.

✔ Control what appears on each page.

✔ Print documents.

✔ Prepare documents for electronic distribution.

When you finish developing a document, you'll often want to distribute either a printed version or an electronic version. Before committing the document to paper, you should check that the pages are efficiently laid out and that there are no glaring problems, such as headings that print on separate pages from their text. Microsoft Word 2010 provides several tools you can use to manipulate how much text appears on each page and to control page layout. It also provides tools for finalizing an electronic document and ensuring that the end product of all your hard work contains no traces of personal or confidential information. When you are ready to print, you can control precisely how many copies and what parts of your document appear on paper.

In this chapter, you'll first preview a document and make some adjustments to improve its presentation. Then you'll look at the options available for controlling page breaks. You'll print a document, and finally, you'll inspect and finalize it for electronic distribution.

> **Practice Files** Before you can complete the exercises in this chapter, you need to copy the book's practice files to your computer. The practice files you'll use to complete the exercises in this chapter are in the Chapter07 practice file folder. A complete list of practice files is provided in "Using the Practice Files" at the beginning of this book.

Previewing and Adjusting Page Layout

Usually while you're creating a document, you'll make decisions about the size of the margins and the direction of the page (called the *orientation*) to best suit your content. You can use the Margins and Orientation commands in the Page Setup group of the Page Layout tab to make any necessary adjustments to the document, and you can use the Size command to change the paper size.

You can also display the Page Setup dialog box, where you can make these basic layout changes all in one place.

You can adjust all the page layout settings in one place.

Working on your document in Print Layout view helps to ensure that the document looks tidy on the page. However, before you print the document, you'll almost always want to check how it will look on paper by previewing it. Previewing is essential for multipage documents but is helpful even for one-page documents. To preview a document, you display the Print page of the Backstage view and then page through the document displayed in the right pane. This view shows exactly how each page of the document will look when printed on the specified printer.

The Print page of the Backstage view.

If you don't like what you see in the preview pane of the Print page, you don't have to leave the Backstage view to make adjustments. The middle pane of the Print page provides tools for making the following changes:

- **Orientation** You can switch the direction in which a page is laid out on the paper. The default orientation is Portrait, in which the page is taller than it is wide. You can set the orientation to Landscape, in which the page is wider than it is tall.

- **Paper size** You can switch to one of the sizes available for the selected printer by making a selection from a list.

- **Margins** Changing the margins of a document changes where information can appear on each page. You can select one of Word's predefined sets of top, bottom, left, and right margins, or set custom margins.

    Tip All the pages of a document have the same orientation and margins unless you divide the document into sections. Then each section can have independent orientation and margin settings. For more information about sections, see "Controlling What Appears on Each Page" later in this chapter.

If your printer is capable of scaling the pages of your document, you'll also see an option to set the number of pages to print per sheet of paper, up to 16. You might use this option to print a booklet with two pages per sheet that will be folded in the middle. You might also be tempted to use this option to save paper, but bear in mind that the smaller the pages, the harder it is to read them.

You can also open the Page Setup dialog box from the Print page to make multiple adjustments in one place.

In this exercise, you'll preview a document, change the orientation, and adjust the margins.

SET UP You need the InfoSheetA_start document located in the Chapter07 practice file folder, and an active printer connection, to complete this exercise. Open the InfoSheetA_start document, and save it as *InfoSheetA*. Then follow the steps.

1. Display the Backstage view, and in the left pane, click **Print**.

    Keyboard Shortcut Press Ctrl+P to display the Print page of the Backstage view.

The Print page is displayed, with a preview of the document on the right. The shaded background of the document is not displayed because it will not be printed.

61%

2. In the lower-right corner of the preview pane, click the **Zoom** button, and then in the **Zoom** dialog box, click **Many pages**, click the monitor button, and click the second page icon in the top row of the grid (**1x2 Pages**). Then click **OK**.

Word displays the two pages of the document side by side.

You can preview multiple pages.

Tip If you want to preview a multipage document as it will look when printed on both sides of the page and bound, add a blank page to the beginning of the document before previewing it.

3. Under **Settings** in the middle pane, click **Custom Margins**.

The gallery of margin options appears.

Normal
Top: 1"   Bottom: 1"
Left: 1"   Right: 1"

Narrow
Top: 0.5"   Bottom: 0.5"
Left: 0.5"   Right: 0.5"

Moderate
Top: 1"   Bottom: 1"
Left: 0.75"   Right: 0.75"

Wide
Top: 1"   Bottom: 1"
Left: 2"   Right: 2"

Mirrored
Top: 1"   Bottom: 1"
Inside: 1.25"   Outside:1"

Office 2003 Default
Top: 1"   Bottom: 1"
Left: 1.25"   Right: 1.25"

Custom Margins

Custom Margins...

You can select predefined margins or set your own.

4. In the list, click **Wide**.

   The text rewraps within the new margins.

5. In the page range in the lower-left corner of the preview pane, click the **Next Page** button.

   The page range updates to show that the document now has three pages and that page 2 is the active page.

6. Click the **Next Page** button again to see the last page of the document.

7. At the bottom of the middle pane, click **Page Setup**.

   The Page Setup dialog box opens, displaying the Margins page. Notice that selecting Wide margins on the Print page set the left and right margins to 2 inches.

8. In the **Pages** area, display the **Multiple pages** list, and click **Mirror Margins**.

   The Preview area now displays two pages side by side, and in the Margins area, Left and Right have changed to Inside and Outside.

9. In the **Margins** area, change the value in the **Outside** box to **1"**.

Tip You can either type a new value or click the down arrow at the right end of the box.

In the pages in the Preview area, the width of the outside margins decreases.

You might use the Mirror Margins setting if you were planning on printing on both sides of the paper and then stapling the pages.

10. Return the **Multiple pages** setting to **Normal**, and in the **Margins** area, change the value in the **Left** box to **1"**.

11. If you want, in the **Page Setup** dialog box, click the **Paper** tab and then the **Layout** tab, and notice the available options on those pages. Then click **OK**.

On the Print page, the margins setting is now Normal Margins, and the page range indicator shows that the number of pages in the document has decreased to two.

✖ **CLEAN UP** Save the InfoSheetA document, and then close it.

Controlling What Appears on Each Page

When a document includes more content than will fit between its top and bottom margins, Word creates a new page by inserting a soft page break. If you want to break a page before Word would normally break it, you can insert a manual page break in one of three ways:

● Click Page Break in the Pages group on the Insert tab.

● Click Breaks in the Page Setup group on the Page Layout tab, and then click Page.

● Press Ctrl+Enter.

Tip As you edit the text in a document, Word changes the location of the soft page breaks, but the program cannot change the location of any manual page breaks you might have inserted.

If a paragraph breaks so that most of it appears on one page but its last line appears at the top of the next page, the line is called a *widow*. If a paragraph breaks so that its first line appears at the bottom of one page and the rest of the paragraph appears on the next page, the line is called an *orphan*. These single lines of text can make a document hard to read, so by default, Word specifies that a minimum of two lines should appear at the top and bottom of each page. However, on the Line And Page Breaks page of the Paragraph dialog box, you can change whether page breaks are allowed to create widows and orphans. You can also change the following options:

● **Keep with next** This option controls whether Word will break a page between the paragraph containing the cursor and the following paragraph.

● **Keep lines together** This option controls whether Word will break a page within a paragraph.

● **Page break before** This option controls whether Word will break a page before the paragraph containing the cursor.

The Line And Page Breaks page of the Paragraph dialog box.

Tip You can apply these options to individual paragraphs, or you can incorporate them into the styles you define for document elements such as headings. For information about styles, refer to *Microsoft Word 2010 Step by Step*, by Joyce Cox and Joan Lambert (Microsoft Press, 2010).

In addition to page breaks, you can insert section breaks in your documents. A section break identifies a part of the document that has page settings, such as orientation or margins, that are different from those of the rest of the document. For example, you might want to put a large table in its own section so that you can turn it sideways by changing its orientation to Landscape.

You insert a section break by clicking Breaks in the Page Setup group on the Page Layout tab and then selecting from the following section types:

- **Next Page** Starts the following section on the next page
- **Continuous** Starts a new section without affecting page breaks
- **Even Page** Starts the following section on the next even-numbered page
- **Odd Page** Starts the following section on the next odd-numbered page

If formatting marks are displayed, a section break appears in Print Layout view as a double-dotted line from the preceding paragraph mark to the margin, with the words *Section Break* and the type of section break in the middle of the line.

Tip To remove a page or section break, click at the left end of the break and then press the Delete key.

In this exercise, you'll insert page and section breaks, and ensure that the pages break in logical places.

➡ **SET UP** You need the OfficeInfo_start document located in the Chapter07 practice file folder to complete this exercise. Open the OfficeInfo_start document, and save it as *OfficeInfo*. Display formatting marks, and then follow the steps.

1. Scroll through the document, noticing any awkward page breaks, such as a topic or list that starts close to the bottom of a page.

2. On the **Home** tab, in the **Editing** group, click the **Select** button, and then click **Select All**.

3. Click the **Paragraph** dialog box launcher, and then in the **Paragraph** dialog box, click the **Line and Page Breaks** tab.

   Because different settings have been applied to different paragraphs in the document, all the check boxes have a solid filling.

When multiple paragraphs are selected, solid check boxes indicate that the paragraphs have different settings.

4. Double-click all the check boxes to clear them.

5. Select the **Keep lines together** check box (click more than once if necessary), and then click **OK**.

   This setting ensures that none of the paragraphs will be broken across two pages. Word alerts you to the presence of this formatting by displaying a square symbol to the left of each paragraph.

6. Press Ctrl+Home to release the selection, and then scroll through the document, again looking for untidy page breaks.

7. Click to the left of the **Facilities** heading.

8. On the **Insert** tab, in the **Pages** group, click the **Page Break** button.

   Keyboard Shortcut   Press Ctrl+Enter to insert a page break.

   Word breaks the page and moves the *Facilities* heading and the following text to the next page.

9. Scroll down to the bottom of page **3**, select the **Supplies** heading and the three lines that follow it (the third line is at the top of page **4**), and then display the **Line and Page Breaks** page of the **Paragraph** dialog box.

10. In the **Pagination** area, leave the **Keep lines together** check box selected, select the **Keep with next** check box, and then click **OK**.

    Word moves the selection to the next page.

11. Scroll down to page **9**, and click to the left of the **Shipping Quick Reference** heading.

    Tip If you drag the scroll box in the scroll bar, Word displays a ScreenTip with the number of the page that will be displayed if you release the mouse button.

12. On the **Page Layout** tab, in the **Page Setup** group, click the **Breaks** button, and then under **Section Breaks**, click **Next Page**.

    Word pushes the heading to the next page.

13. Scroll up until the text on page **9** is displayed.

    A double dotted line with the words *Section Break (Next Page)* appears at the right end of the paragraph preceding the section break.

> ▪ 2.→ Send·the·invoice·to·the·customer.¶
>
> ▪ 3.→ Enter·Tentative·in·the·customer's·Access·account·until·you·receive·the·check·and·the·check·
>   has·cleared·the·bank.¶...Section Break (Next Page)..

The section break indicator.

14. Scroll down to page **10**, and with the cursor in the **Shipping Quick Reference** heading, on the **Page Layout** tab, in the **Page Setup** group, click the **Margins** button. Then in the **Margins** gallery, click **Wide**.

    The table in the new section shrinks in width to fit between the wider margins.

15. On the **Insert** tab, in the **Header & Footer** group, click the **Header** button, and then click **Edit Header**.

    In the Navigation group of the Design contextual tab, the Link To Previous button is selected, meaning that the header of the new section has inherited the settings of the preceding section. Because the preceding section has no header on its first page, this one doesn't have one either.

16. On the **Design** contextual tab, in the **Options** group, clear the **Different First Page** check box. Then click the **Close Header and Footer** button.

Now the header from pages 2 through 9 of the preceding section is repeated on page 10 in this section.

Office·Procedures¶

Page·10¶

. **Shipping·Quick·Reference¶**

·	**Package·for·shipment¤**	¤
·	Customer·information,·existing·account?¤	¤
·	PO·for·payment·with·existing·account?¤	¤
·	Shipping·company/method·of·shipment?¤	¤
·	Delivery·when?¤	¤
·	Invoice·and·tracking·slip¤	¤
·	Process·order¤	¤
·	Paperwork·to·customer¤	¤

You might have to adjust the header settings after creating a new section.

✖ **CLEAN UP** Save the OfficeInfo document, and then close it.

Printing Documents

When you are ready to print a document, you display the Print page of the Backstage view, and then, to print one copy on the current printer with the settings shown, you simply click the Print button.

If you need to use settings other than the defaults, you can change the following:

- **Number of copies** Click the arrows or type the number you need.

- **Printer** Switch to a different printer, or click Printer Properties to change the printer options.

- **Print range** Print the entire document, the selected text, the current page, or a custom range of pages. (Point to the information icon to the right of the Pages box to see the format in which to enter a custom range.)

- **Sides of the paper** Print on one side or both sides, either manually or, if your printer has duplex capability, automatically.

- **Collation** For multiple copies of a multipage document, print all the pages in the document as a set or print all the copies of each page as a set.

If your printer has multiple paper trays or a manual paper feeder, you can select the paper source you want to use, on the Paper page of the Page Setup dialog box.

In this exercise, you'll see how to select a different printer before sending two copies of the current page of a document to be printed.

 SET UP You need the InfoSheetB_start document located in the Chapter07 practice file folder, and multiple active printer connections, to complete this exercise. Open the InfoSheetB_start document, and save it as *InfoSheetB*. Then follow the steps.

1. Display the Backstage view, and in the left pane, click **Print**.

   If you don't need to change any settings, you can simply click the Print button at the top of the middle pane of the Print page.

2. If you have more than one printer available and you want to switch printers, under **Printer** in the middle pane, click the option displaying the name of the default printer, and in the list, click the printer you want.

3. Point to the information icon to the right of the **Printer** area heading.

   Tip You can also point to the selected printer.

   Information about your printer's status is displayed.

You can check your printer's status without leaving the Print page.

4. In the **Copies** box next to the **Print** button, change the number of copies to **2**.

5. Under **Settings**, click the arrow to the right of the first box to expand the list of print options, and then in the list, click **Print Current Page**.

6. Leaving the other settings as they are, click the **Print** button at the top of the middle pane.

   Word prints two copies of the document's first page on the designated printer, and returns you to the document.

 CLEAN UP Close the InfoSheetB document.

Preparing Documents for Electronic Distribution

When a document is complete, you can distribute it in two basic ways: on paper or electronically. If you distribute it electronically, you need to ensure that no private or inappropriate information is attached to the file and that it can be viewed by the people to whom you are sending it.

Many documents go through several revisions, and some are scrutinized by multiple reviewers. During this development process, documents can accumulate information that you might not want in the final version, such as the names of people who worked on the document, comments that reviewers have added to the file, or hidden text about status and assumptions. This extraneous information is not a concern if the final version is to be delivered as a printout. However, these days, more and more files are delivered electronically, making this information available to anyone who wants to read it.

To examine some of the attached information, you can display the document's properties on the Info page of the Backstage view. You can change or remove the information in either the Document Panel or the Properties dialog box. However, Word provides a tool called the *Document Inspector* to automate the process of finding and removing all extraneous and potentially confidential information. After you run the Document Inspector, you see a summary of its search results, and you have the option of removing all the items found in each category.

Word also includes two other finalizing tools:

- **Check Accessibility** Checks for document elements and formatting that might be difficult for people with certain kinds of disabilities to read.

- **Check Compatibility** Checks for the use of features not supported in earlier versions of Word.

After you have handled extraneous information and accessibility and compatibility issues, you can mark a document as final and make it a read-only file, so that other people know that they should not make changes to this released document.

In this exercise, you'll inspect a document for inappropriate information and mark it as final.

SET UP You need the InfoSheetC_start document located in the Chapter07 practice file folder to complete this exercise. Open the InfoSheetC_start document, and save it as *InfoSheetC*. Then follow the steps.

1. Display the Backstage view, and in the left pane, click **Info**.

   In the right pane you see the properties that have been saved with the file. Some of the information, including the name of the author, was attached to the file by Word. Other information, such as the title, was added by a user.

The properties attached to this document.

Properties ▾

2. In the right pane, click the **Properties** button, and then in the list, click **Advanced Properties**.

   The Properties dialog box for this document opens. On the General page of the dialog box are properties maintained by Word.

3. Click the **Summary** tab.

   Notice that additional identifying information is displayed on this page.

These properties were entered by the people who worked on the document.

Tip To make a document easier to find in Windows Explorer, you can add tags in the Properties area of the Info page or keywords in the Properties dialog box.

4. Click **Cancel** to close the **Properties** dialog box.

5. In the **Prepare for Sharing** area of the **Info** page, click **Check for Issues**, and then click **Inspect Document**.

   Troubleshooting If Word asks whether you want to save changes to the file, click Yes.

   The Document Inspector dialog box opens, listing the items that will be checked.

6. Without changing the default selections in the **Document Inspector** dialog box, click **Inspect**.

   The Document Inspector reports the presence of the properties you viewed earlier, as well as some custom XML data.

The results of the inspection.

7. To the right of **Document Properties and Personal Information**, click **Remove All**.

8. To the right of **Custom XML Data**, click **Remove All**.

9. Click **Reinspect**, and then click **Inspect**.

   Word has removed the properties and XML data.

10. In the **Document Inspector** dialog box, click **Close**.

   The right pane of the Info page now shows that there are no custom properties attached to the document.

11. In the **Permissions** area of the **Info** page, click **Protect Document**, and then click **Mark As Final**.

    A message tells you that the document will be marked as final and then saved.

12. Click **OK**.

    A message tells you that the document has been marked as final and that typing, editing commands, and proofing marks are turned off.

13. Click **OK**.

    The Permissions area now indicates that the file is final.

The Info page reminds people that the file is final.

14. Click the **Insert** tab.

    An orange bar appears, notifying you that the document has been marked as final.

15. Click the **Insert** tab again.

    The tab's groups and buttons are displayed, but all of the buttons are inactive.

    Tip If you really want to make changes to the document, you can click a tab to display the orange bar and then click the Edit Anyway button to unmark the file.

✖ CLEAN UP Save the InfoSheetC document, and then close it.

Tip If you need to distribute a document electronically but you don't want to share the actual file, you can "print" the document to a new file in XML Paper Specification (XPS) format. For information, refer to *Microsoft Word 2010 Step by Step*, by Joyce Cox and Joan Lambert (Microsoft Press, 2010).

Key Points

- You should always preview a document before printing it.

- You can use page and section breaks and page break options to ensure that pages break in logical places.

- All the printing options are now gathered together on the Print page of the Backstage view.

- Before distributing a document, you can use the Document Inspector to remove private or inappropriate information.

Part 3
Microsoft Excel 2010

8   Set Up a Workbook. 227

9   Work with Data and Excel Tables 255

10 Perform Calculations on Data 281

11 Change Workbook Appearance 309

12 Focus on Specific Data by Using Filters 347

225

Chapter at a Glance

Create workbooks, **page 228**

Modify workbooks, **page 233**

Modify worksheets, **page 237**

Customize the Excel 2010 program window, **page 241**

8 Set Up a Workbook

In this chapter, you will learn how to

✔ Create workbooks.

✔ Modify workbooks.

✔ Modify worksheets.

✔ Customize the Excel 2010 program window.

When you start Microsoft Excel 2010, the program presents a blank workbook that contains three worksheets. You can add or delete worksheets, hide worksheets within the workbook without deleting them, and change the order of your worksheets within the workbook. You can also copy a worksheet to another workbook or move the worksheet without leaving a copy of the worksheet in the first workbook. If you and your colleagues work with a large number of documents, you can define property values to make your workbooks easier to find when you and your colleagues attempt to locate them by using the Windows search facility.

Another way to make Excel easier to use is by customizing the Excel program window to fit your work style. If you have several workbooks open at the same time, you can move between the workbook windows quickly. However, if you switch between workbooks frequently, you might find it easier to resize the workbooks so they don't take up the entire Excel window. If you do this, you just need to click the title bar of the workbook you want to modify to switch to it.

The Microsoft Office User Experience team has enhanced your ability to customize the Excel user interface. If you find that you use a command frequently, you can add it to the Quick Access Toolbar so it's never more than one click away. If you use a set of commands frequently, you can create a custom ribbon tab so they appear in one place. You can also hide, display, or change the order of the tabs on the ribbon.

In this chapter, you'll learn how to create and modify workbooks, create and modify worksheets, make your workbooks easier to find, and customize the Excel 2010 program window.

> **Practice Files** Before you can complete the exercises in this chapter, you need to copy the book's practice files to your computer. The practice files you'll use to complete the exercises in this chapter are in the Chapter08 practice file folder. A complete list of practice files is provided in "Using the Practice Files" at the beginning of this book.

Creating Workbooks

Every time you want to gather and store data that isn't closely related to any of your other existing data, you should create a new workbook. The default new workbook in Excel has three worksheets, although you can add more worksheets or delete existing worksheets if you want. Creating a new workbook is a straightforward process—you just click the File tab, click New, identify the type of workbook you want, and click the Create button.

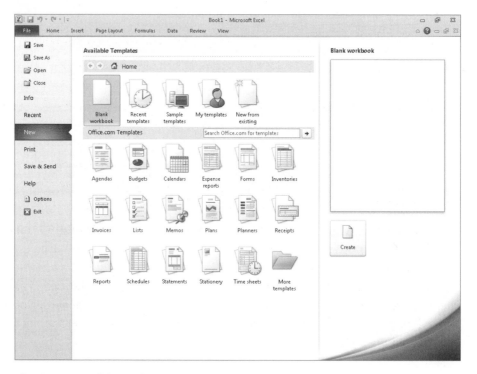

The New page of the Backstage view.

When you start Excel, the program displays a new, blank workbook; you can begin to type data into the worksheet's cells or open an existing workbook. In this book's exercises, you'll work with workbooks created for Consolidated Messenger, a fictional global shipping company. After you make changes to a workbook, you should save it to preserve your work.

Tip Readers frequently ask, "How often should I save my files?" It is good practice to save your changes every half hour or even every five minutes, but the best time to save a file is whenever you make a change that you would hate to have to make again.

When you save a file, you overwrite the previous copy of the file. If you have made changes that you want to save, but you also want to keep a copy of the file as it was when you saved it previously, you can use the Save As command to specify a name for the new file.

You also can use the controls in the Save As dialog box to specify a different format for the new file and a different location in which to save the new version of the file. For example, Lori Penor, the chief operating officer of Consolidated Messenger, might want to save an Excel file that tracks consulting expenses as an Excel 2003 file if she needs to share the file with a consulting firm that uses Excel 2003.

After you create a file, you can add information to make the file easier to find when you use the Windows search facility to search for it. Each category of information, or property, stores specific information about your file. In Windows, you can search for files based on the file's author or title, or by keywords associated with the file. A file tracking the postal code destinations of all packages sent from a vendor might have the keywords *postal*, *destination*, and *origin* associated with it.

To set values for your workbook's built-in properties, you can click the File tab, click Info, click Properties, and then click Show Document Panel to display the Document Properties panel just below the ribbon. The standard version of the Document Properties panel has fields for the file's author, title, subject, keywords, category, and status, and any comments about the file. You can also create custom properties by clicking the arrow located just to the right of the Document Properties label, and clicking Advanced Properties to display the Properties dialog box.

General workbook properties are based on the file and cannot be edited.

On the Custom page of the Properties dialog box, you can click one of the existing custom categories or create your own by typing a new property name in the Name field, clicking the Type arrow and selecting a data type (for example, Text, Date, Number, or Yes/No), selecting or typing a value in the Value field, and then clicking Add. If you want to delete an existing custom property, point to the Properties list, click the property you want to get rid of, and click Delete. After you finish making your changes, click the OK button. To hide the Document Properties panel, click the Close button in the upper-right corner of the panel.

In this exercise, you'll create a new workbook, save the workbook with a new name, assign values to the workbook's standard properties, and create a custom property.

SET UP You need the ExceptionSummary_start workbook located in your Chapter08 practice file folder to complete this exercise. Start Excel, and open the ExceptionSummary_start workbook. Then follow the steps.

1. Click the **File** tab, and then click **Close**.

   The ExceptionSummary_start workbook closes.

2. Click the **File** tab, and then click **New**.

   The New Workbook page of the Backstage view appears.

3. Click **Blank Workbook**, and then click **Create**.

   A new, blank workbook opens.

4. Click the **File** tab, and then click **Save As**.

   The Save As dialog box opens.

By default, the Save As dialog box displays the contents of your Documents library or the last folder you accessed from the dialog box.

5. Navigate to your **Chapter08** practice file folder. In the **File name** field, type **Exceptions 2010**.

6. Click the **Save** button.

   Excel 2010 saves your work, and the Save As dialog box closes.

7. Click the **File** tab, click **Info**, click **Properties**, and then click **Show Document Panel**.

   The Document Properties panel opens.

8. In the **Keywords** field, type exceptions, regional, percentage.

9. In the **Category** field, type performance.

10. Click the arrow at the right end of the Document Properties button, and then click **Advanced Properties**.

    The Exceptions 2010 Properties dialog box opens.

11. Click the **Custom** tab.

    The Custom page is displayed.

12. In the **Name** field, type **Performance**.

13. In the **Value** field, type **Exceptions**.

You can specify custom properties for a workbook.

14. Click the **Add** button, and then click **OK**.

    The Exceptions 2010 Properties dialog box closes.

15. On the Quick Access Toolbar, click the **Save** button to save your work.

    Keyboard Shortcut Press Ctrl+S to save a workbook.

CLEAN UP Close the Exceptions 2010 workbook.

Modifying Workbooks

Most of the time, you create a workbook to record information about a particular activity, such as the number of packages that a regional distribution center handles or the average time a driver takes to complete all deliveries on a route. Each worksheet within that workbook should represent a subdivision of that activity. To display a particular worksheet, just click the worksheet's tab on the tab bar (just below the grid of cells).

In the case of Consolidated Messenger, the workbook used to track daily package volumes could have a separate worksheet for each regional distribution center. New Excel workbooks contain three worksheets; because Consolidated Messenger uses nine regional distribution centers, you would need to create six new ones. To create a new worksheet, click the Insert Worksheet button at the right edge of the tab bar.

Insert Worksheet

When you create a worksheet, Excel assigns it a generic name such as Sheet4.

After you decide what type of data you want to store on a worksheet, you should change the default worksheet name to something more descriptive. For example, you could change the name of Sheet1 in the regional distribution center tracking workbook to *Northeast*. When you want to change a worksheet's name, double-click the worksheet's tab on the tab bar to highlight the worksheet name, type the new name, and press Enter.

Another way to work with more than one worksheet is to copy a worksheet from another workbook to the current workbook. One circumstance in which you might consider copying worksheets to the current workbook is if you have a list of your current employees in another workbook. You can copy worksheets from another workbook by right-clicking the tab of the sheet you want to copy and, on the shortcut menu, clicking Move Or Copy to display the Move Or Copy dialog box.

Selecting the Create A Copy check box leaves the copied worksheet in its original workbook, whereas clearing the check box causes Excel to delete the worksheet from its original workbook.

After the worksheet is in the target workbook, you can change the worksheets' order to make the data easier to locate within the workbook. To change a worksheet's location in the workbook, you drag its sheet tab to the desired location on the tab bar. If you want to remove a worksheet from the tab bar without deleting the worksheet, you can do so by right-clicking the worksheet's tab on the tab bar and clicking Hide on the context menu. When you want Excel to redisplay the worksheet, right-click any visible sheet tab and then click Unhide. In the Unhide dialog box, click the name of the sheet you want to display, and click OK.

To differentiate a worksheet from others, or to visually indicate groups or categories of worksheets in a multiple-worksheet workbook, you can easily change the color of a worksheet tab. To do so, right-click the tab, point to Tab Color, and then click the color you want.

Tip If you copy a worksheet to another workbook, and the destination workbook has the same Office Theme applied as the active workbook, the worksheet retains its tab color. If the destination workbook has another theme applied, the worksheet's tab color changes to reflect that theme. For more information on Office themes, see Chapter 11, "Change Workbook Appearance."

If you determine that you no longer need a particular worksheet, such as one you created to store some figures temporarily, you can delete the worksheet quickly. To do so, right-click its sheet tab, and then click Delete.

In this exercise, you'll insert and rename a worksheet, change a worksheet's position in a workbook, hide and unhide a worksheet, copy a worksheet to another workbook, change a worksheet's tab color, and delete a worksheet.

SET UP You need the ExceptionTracking_start workbook located in your Chapter08 practice file folder to complete this exercise. Open the ExceptionTracking_start file, and save it as *ExceptionTracking*. Then follow the steps.

1. On the tab bar, click the **Insert Worksheet** button.

   A new worksheet is displayed.

2. Right-click the new worksheet's sheet tab, and then click **Rename**.

   Excel highlights the new worksheet's name.

3. Type **2010**, and then press Enter.

4. On the tab bar, double-click the **Sheet1** sheet tab.

   Excel highlights the worksheet's name.

5. Type **2009**, and then press Enter.

6. Right-click the **2009** sheet tab, point to **Tab Color**, and then, in the **Standard Colors** area of the color palette, click the green square.

   Excel changes the 2009 sheet tab to green.

7. On the tab bar, drag the **2010** sheet tab to the left of the **Scratch Pad** sheet tab.

8. Right-click the **2010** sheet tab, and then click **Hide**.

   Excel hides the 2010 worksheet.

9. Right-click the **2009** sheet tab, and then click **Move or Copy**.

   The Move Or Copy dialog box opens.

You must specify the destination of the moved or copied worksheet.

10. Click the **To book** arrow, and then in the list, click **(new book)**.

11. Select the **Create a copy** check box.

12. Click **OK**.

    A new workbook opens, containing only the worksheet you copied into it.

13. On the Quick Access Toolbar, click **Save**.

    The Save As dialog box opens.

14. In the **File name** field, type *2009 Archive*, and then press Enter.

    Excel saves the workbook, and the Save As dialog box closes.

15. On the **View** tab, click the **Switch Windows** button, and then click **ExceptionTracking**.

    The ExceptionTracking workbook is displayed.

16. On the tab bar, right-click the **Scratch Pad** sheet tab, and then click **Delete**. In the dialog box that opens, click **Delete** to confirm the operation.

    The Scratch Pad worksheet is deleted.

17. Right-click the **2009** sheet tab, and then click **Unhide**.

    The Unhide dialog box opens.

The Unhide dialog box lists all hidden worksheets.

18. Click **2010,** and then click **OK**.

    The Unhide dialog box closes, and the 2010 worksheet is displayed in the workbook.

CLEAN UP Save and close the ExceptionTracking workbook and the 2009 Archive workbook.

Modifying Worksheets

After you put up the signposts that make your data easy to find, you can take other steps to make the data in your workbooks easier to work with. For example, you can change the width of a column or the height of a row in a worksheet by dragging the column's right border or the row's bottom border to the desired position. Increasing a column's width or a row's height increases the space between cell contents, making your data easier to read and work with.

Tip You can apply the same change to more than one row or column by selecting the rows or columns you want to change and then dragging the border of one of the selected rows or columns to the desired location. When you release the mouse button, all the selected rows or columns change to the new height or width.

Modifying column width and row height can make a workbook's contents easier to work with, but you can also insert a row or column between cells that contain data to make your data easier to read. Adding space between the edge of a worksheet and cells that contain data, or perhaps between a label and the data to which it refers, makes the workbook's contents less crowded. You insert rows by clicking a cell and clicking the Home tab on the ribbon. Then, in the Cells group, in the Insert list, click Insert Sheet Rows. Excel inserts a row above the row that contains the active cell. You insert a column in much the same way, by choosing Insert Sheet Columns from the Insert list. When you do this, Excel inserts a column to the left of the active cell.

When you insert a row, column, or cell in a worksheet that has had formatting applied, the Insert Options button appears. Clicking the Insert Options button displays a list of choices you can make about how the inserted row or column should be formatted. The following table summarizes your options.

Option	Action
Format Same As Above	Applies the formatting of the row above the inserted row to the new row
Format Same As Below	Applies the formatting of the row below the inserted row to the new row
Format Same As Left	Applies the formatting of the column to the left of the inserted column to the new column
Format Same As Right	Applies the formatting of the column to the right of the inserted column to the new column
Clear Formatting	Applies the default format to the new row or column

If you want to delete a row or column, right-click the row or column head and then, on the shortcut menu that appears, click Delete. You can temporarily hide rows or columns by selecting those rows or columns and then, on the Home tab, in the Cells group, clicking the Format button, pointing to Hide & Unhide, and then clicking either Hide Rows or Hide Columns. The rows or columns you selected disappear, but they aren't gone for good, as they would be if you'd used Delete. Instead, they have just been removed from the display until you call them back. To return the hidden rows to the display, select the row or column headers on either side of the hidden rows or columns. Then, on the Home tab, in the Cells group, click the Format button, point to Hide & Unhide, and then click either Unhide Rows or Unhide Columns.

Important If you hide the first row or column in a worksheet, you must click the Select All button in the upper-left corner of the worksheet (above the first row header and to the left of the first column header) or press Ctrl+A to select the entire worksheet. Then, on the Home tab, in the Cells group, click Format, point to Hide & Unhide, and then click either Unhide Rows or Unhide Columns to make the hidden data visible again.

Just as you can insert rows or columns, you can insert individual cells into a worksheet. To insert a cell, click the cell that is currently in the position where you want the new cell to appear. On the Home tab, in the Cells group, in the Insert list, click Insert Cells to display the Insert dialog box. In the Insert dialog box, you can choose whether to shift the cells surrounding the inserted cell down (if your data is arranged as a column) or to the right (if your data is arranged as a row). When you click OK, the new cell appears, and the contents of affected cells shift down or to the right, as appropriate. In a similar vein, if you want to delete a block of cells, select the cells, and on the Home tab, in the Cells group, in the Delete list, click Delete Cells to display the Delete dialog box—complete with options that enable you to choose how to shift the position of the cells around the deleted cells.

Tip The Insert dialog box also includes options you can click to insert a new row or column; the Delete dialog box has similar options for deleting an entire row or column.

If you want to move the data in a group of cells to another location in your worksheet, select the cells you want to move and use the mouse pointer to point to the selection's border. When the pointer changes to a four-pointed arrow, you can drag the selected cells to the desired location on the worksheet. If the destination cells contain data, Excel displays a dialog box asking whether you want to overwrite the destination cells' contents. If you want to replace the existing values, click OK. If you don't want to overwrite the existing values, click Cancel and insert the required number of cells to accommodate the data you want to move.

In this exercise, you'll insert a column and row into a worksheet, specify insert options, hide a column, insert a cell into a worksheet, delete a cell from a worksheet, and move a group of cells within the worksheet.

SET UP You need the RouteVolume_start workbook located in your Chapter08 practice file folder to complete this exercise. Open the RouteVolume_start workbook, and save it as *RouteVolume*. Then follow the steps.

1. On the **May 12** worksheet, select cell **A1**.

2. On the **Home** tab, in the **Cells** group, click the **Insert** arrow, and then in the list, click **Insert Sheet Columns**.

   A new column A appears.

3. In the **Insert** list, click **Insert Sheet Rows**.

   A new row 1 appears.

4. Click the **Insert Options** button that appears below the lower-right corner of the selected cell, and then click **Clear Formatting**.

   Excel removes the formatting from the new row 1.

5. Right-click the column header of column E, and then click **Hide**.

   Column E disappears.

	A	B	C	D	F	G	H	I	J
1									
2		Route	Volume						
3		1	6413						
4		2	2208						
5		3	7052						
6		4	9229						
7		5	1425						
8		6	4329						
9		7	8410						
10		8	8785						
11		9	5812						
12		10	1112						
13									
14									
15									
16									
17									
18									

Hiding a row or column also hides the accompanying row or column header.

6. On the tab bar, click the **May 13** sheet tab.

   The worksheet named *May 13* appears.

7. Click cell **B6**.

⊞✕ Delete ▾

8. On the **Home** tab, in the **Cells** group, click the **Delete** arrow, and then in the list, click **Delete Cells**.

   The Delete dialog box opens.

```
┌─────────────────────────────────┐
│ Delete              [ ? ] [ X ]  │
├─────────────────────────────────┤
│ Delete                           │
│   ○ Shift cells left             │
│   ◉ Shift cells up               │
│   ○ Entire row                   │
│   ○ Entire column                │
│                                  │
│   [   OK   ]      [  Cancel  ]   │
└─────────────────────────────────┘
```

   When deleting cells, you can specify whether to affect the column or row.

9. If necessary, click **Shift cells up**, and then click **OK**.

   The Delete dialog box closes and Excel deletes cell B6, moving the cells below it up to fill in the gap.

10. Click cell **C6**.

11. In the **Cells** group, in the **Insert** list, click **Insert Cells**.

   The Insert dialog box opens.

12. If necessary, click **Shift cells down**, and then click **OK**.

   The Insert dialog box closes, and Excel creates a new cell C6, moving cells C6:C11 down to accommodate the inserted cell.

13. In cell **C6**, type **4499**, and then press Enter.

14. Select cells **E13:F13**.

15. Point to the border of the selected cells. When your mouse pointer changes to a four-pointed arrow, drag the selected cells to cells **B13:C13**.

   The dragged cells replace cells B13:C13.

You can drag cell content to another location.

✖ **CLEAN UP** Save the RouteVolume workbook, and then close it.

Customizing the Excel 2010 Program Window

How you use Excel 2010 depends on your personal working style and the type of data collections you manage. The Excel product team interviews customers, observes how differing organizations use the program, and sets up the user interface so that many users won't need to change it to work effectively. If you do want to change the Excel program window, including the user interface, you can. You can change how Excel displays your worksheets; zoom in on worksheet data; add frequently used commands to the Quick Access Toolbar; hide, display, and reorder ribbon tabs; and create custom tabs to make groups of commands readily accessible.

Zooming In on a Worksheet

One way to make Excel easier to work with is to change the program's zoom level. Just as you can "zoom in" with a camera to increase the size of an object in the camera's viewer, you can use the zoom setting to change the size of objects within the Excel 2010 program window. For example, if Peter Villadsen, the Consolidated Messenger European Distribution Center Manager, displayed a worksheet that summarized his distribution center's package volume by month, he could click the View tab and then, in the Zoom group, click the Zoom button to display the Zoom dialog box. The Zoom dialog box contains controls that he can use to select a preset magnification level or to type in a custom magnification level. He could also use the Zoom control in the lower-right corner of the Excel 2010 window.

You can zoom in or out incrementally or set a specific magnification level.

Clicking the Zoom In control increases the size of items in the program window by 10 percent, whereas clicking the Zoom Out control decreases the size of items in the program window by 10 percent. If you want more fine-grained control of your zoom level, you can use the slider control to select a specific zoom level or click the magnification level indicator, which indicates the zoom percentage, and use the Zoom dialog box to set a custom magnification level.

The Zoom group on the View tab also contains the Zoom To Selection button, which fills the program window with the contents of any selected cells, up to the program's maximum zoom level of 400 percent.

Tip The minimum zoom level in Excel 2010 is 10 percent.

Arranging Multiple Workbook Windows

As you work with Excel, you will probably need to have more than one workbook open at a time. For example, you could open a workbook that contains customer contact information and copy it into another workbook to be used as the source data for a mass mailing you create in Microsoft Word 2010. When you have multiple workbooks open simultaneously, you can switch between them by clicking the View tab and then, in the Window group, clicking the Switch Windows button and clicking the name of the workbook you want to view.

You can arrange your workbooks within the Excel window so that most of the active workbook is shown but the others are easily accessible. To do so, click the View tab and then, in the Window group, click the Arrange All button. Then, in the Arrange Windows dialog box, click Cascade.

The best arrangement depends on the number and content of the open windows.

Many Excel 2010 workbooks contain formulas on one worksheet that derive their value from data on another worksheet, which means you need to change between two worksheets every time you want to see how modifying your data changes the formula's result. However, an easier way to approach this is to display two copies of the same workbook simultaneously, displaying the worksheet that contains the data in the original window and displaying the worksheet with the formula in the new window. When you change the data in either copy of the workbook, Excel updates the other copy. To display two copies of the same workbook, open the desired workbook and then, in the View tab's Window group, click New Window. Excel opens a second copy of the workbook. To display the workbooks side by side, on the View tab, in the Window group, click Arrange All. Then, in the Arrange Windows dialog box, click Vertical and then click OK.

If the original workbook's name is *Exception Summary*, Excel 2010 displays the name *Exception Summary:1* on the original workbook's title bar and *Exception Summary:2* on the second workbook's title bar.

Arranging windows vertically.

Troubleshooting The appearance of buttons and groups on the ribbon changes depending on the width of the program window. For information about changing the appearance of the ribbon to match our images, see "Modifying the Display of the Ribbon" at the beginning of this book.

Adding Buttons to the Quick Access Toolbar

As you continue to work with Excel 2010, you might discover that you use certain commands much more frequently than others. If your workbooks draw data from external sources, for example, you might find yourself using the Refresh All button on the Data tab quite often than the program's designers might have expected. You can make any button accessible with one click by adding the button to the Quick Access Toolbar, located just above the ribbon.

To add a button to the Quick Access Toolbar, display the Customize The Quick Access Toolbar page of the Excel Options dialog box. This page contains two panes. The pane on the left lists all of the controls that are available within a given category, and the pane on the right lists the controls currently displayed on the Quick Access Toolbar. In the Choose Commands From list, click the category that contains the control you want to add. Excel 2010 displays the available commands in the box below the Choose Commands From field. Click the control you want, and then click the Add button.

You can change a button's position on the Quick Access Toolbar by clicking its name in the right pane and then clicking either the Move Up or Move Down button at the right edge of the dialog box.

To remove a button from the Quick Access Toolbar, click the button's name in the right pane, and then click the Remove button. When you're done making your changes, click the OK button. If you prefer not to save your changes, click the Cancel button. If you saved your changes but want to return the Quick Access Toolbar to its original state, click the Reset button and then click either Reset Only Quick Access Toolbar, which removes any changes you made to the Quick Access Toolbar, or Reset All Customizations, which returns the entire ribbon interface to its original state.

You can also choose whether your Quick Access Toolbar changes affect all your workbooks or just the active workbook. To control how Excel applies your change, in the Customize Quick Access Toolbar list, click either For All Documents to apply the change to all of your workbooks or For Workbook to apply the change to the active workbook only.

If you'd like to export your Quick Access Toolbar customizations to a file that can be used to apply those changes to another Excel 2010 installation, click the Import/Export button and then click Export All Customizations. Use the controls in the dialog box that opens to save your file. When you're ready to apply saved customizations to Excel, click the Import/Export button, click Import Customization File, select the file in the File Open dialog box, and click Open.

Customizing the Ribbon

Excel 2010 enhances your ability to customize the entire ribbon by enabling you to hide and display ribbon tabs, reorder tabs displayed on the ribbon, customize existing tabs (including tool tabs, which appear when specific items are selected), and to create custom tabs.

To begin customizing the ribbon, click the File tab and then click Options. In the Excel Options dialog box, click Customize Ribbon to display the Customize The Ribbon page.

The Customize The Ribbon page of the Excel Options dialog box.

To select which tabs appear in the tabs pane on the right side of the screen, click the Customize The Ribbon field's arrow and then click either Main Tabs, which displays the tabs that can appear on the standard ribbon; Tool Tabs, which displays the tabs that appear when you click an item such as a drawing object or PivotTable; or All Tabs.

Tip The procedures taught in this section apply to both the main tabs and the tool tabs.

Each ribbon tab's name has a check box next to it. If a tab's box is selected, then that tab appears on the ribbon. You can hide a tab by clearing the check box and bring it back by selecting the check box. You can also change the order in which the tabs are displayed on the ribbon. To do so, click the name of the tab you want to move and then click the Move Up or Move Down arrows to reposition the selected tab.

Just as you can change the order of the tabs on the ribbon, you can change the order of groups on a tab. For example, the Page Layout tab contains five groups: Themes, Page Setup, Scale To Fit, Sheet Options, and Arrange. If you use the Themes group infrequently, you could move the group to the right end of the tab by clicking the group's name and then clicking the Move Down button until the group appears in the desired position.

You can add, remove, and change the order of groups on a tab.

To remove a group from a built-in ribbon tab, click the name of the group in the right pane and click the Remove button. If you remove a group from a built-in tab and later decide you want to put it back on the tab, display the tab in the right pane. Then, click the Choose Commands From field's arrow and click Main Tabs. With the tab displayed, in the left pane, click the expand control (which looks like a plus sign) next to the name of the tab that contains the group you want to add back. You can now click the name of the group in the left pane and click the Add button to put the group back on the selected ribbon tab.

The built-in ribbon tabs are designed efficiently, so adding new command groups might crowd the other items on the tab and make those controls harder to find. Rather than adding controls to an existing ribbon tab, you can create a custom tab and then add groups and commands to it. To create a custom ribbon tab, click the New Tab button on the Customize The Ribbon page of the Excel Options dialog box. When you do, a new tab named New Tab (Custom), which contains a group named New Group (Custom), appears in the tab list.

You can add an existing group to your new ribbon tab by clicking the Choose Commands From field's arrow, selecting a collection of commands, clicking the group you want to add, and then clicking the Add button. You can also add individual commands to your ribbon tab by clicking a command in the command list and clicking the Add button. To add a command to your tab's custom group, click the new group in the right tab list, click the command in the left list, and then click the Add button. If you want to add another custom group to your new tab, click the new tab, or any of the groups within that tab, and then click New Group.

The New Tab (Custom) name doesn't tell you anything about the commands on your new ribbon tab, so you can rename it to reflect its contents. To rename any tab on the ribbon, display the Customize The Ribbon page of the Excel Options dialog box, click the tab you want to modify, and then click the Rename button. Type the tab's new name in the Rename dialog box, and click OK. To rename any group on the ribbon, click the name of the group, and then click Rename. When you do, a different version of the Rename dialog box appears. Click the symbol that you want to use to represent the group on the ribbon, type a new name for the group in the Display Name box, and click OK.

You can select a symbol to represent a group of commands on the ribbon.

If you'd like to export your ribbon customizations to a file that can be used to apply those changes to another Excel 2010 installation, click the Import/Export button and then click Export All Customizations. Use the controls in the dialog box that opens to save your file. When you're ready to apply saved customizations to Excel, click the Import/Export button, click Import Customization File, select the file in the File Open dialog box, and click Open.

When you're done customizing the ribbon, click the OK button to save your changes or click Cancel to keep the user interface as it was before you started this round of changes. You can also change a ribbon tab, or the entire ribbon, back to the state it was in when you installed Excel. To restore a single ribbon tab, click the tab you want to restore, click the Reset button, and then click Reset Only Selected Ribbon Tab. To restore the entire ribbon, including the Quick Access Toolbar, click the Reset button and then click Reset All Customizations.

Maximizing Usable Space in the Program Window

You can increase the amount of space available inside the program window by hiding the ribbon, the formula bar, or the row and column labels.

To hide the ribbon, double-click the active tab label. The tab labels remain visible at the top of the program window, but the tab content is hidden. To temporarily redisplay the ribbon, click the tab label you want. Then click any button on the tab, or click away from the tab, to rehide it. To permanently redisplay the ribbon, double-click any tab label.

Keyboard Shortcut Press Ctrl+F1 to hide and unhide the ribbon.

To hide the formula bar, clear the Formula Bar check box in the Show/Hide group on the View tab. To hide the row and column labels, clear the Headings check box in the Show/Hide group on the View tab.

In this exercise, you'll change your worksheet's zoom level, zoom in to emphasize a selected cell range, switch between multiple open workbooks, cascade multiple open workbooks within the Excel program window, add a button to the Quick Access Toolbar, and customize the ribbon.

SET UP You need the PackageCounts_start and MisroutedPackages_start workbooks located in your Chapter08 practice file folder to complete this exercise. Open the PackageCounts_start and MisroutedPackages_start workbooks, and save them as *PackageCounts* and *MisroutedPackages*, respectively. Then follow the steps.

1. In the **MisroutedPackages** workbook, in the lower-right corner of the Excel 2010 window, click the **Zoom In** control five times.

   The worksheet's zoom level changes to 150%.

2. Select cells **B2:C11**.

3. On the **View** tab, in the **Zoom** group, click the **Zoom to Selection** button.

   Excel displays the selected cells so they fill the program window.

Zoom to Selection

Magnifying selected cells.

4. On the **View** tab, in the **Zoom** group, click the **Zoom** button.

   The Zoom dialog box opens.

You can select a preset magnification level or enter a custom magnification level.

5. Click **100%**, and then click **OK**.

   The worksheet returns to its default zoom level.

6. On the **View** tab, in the **Window** group, click the **Switch Windows** button, and then click **PackageCounts**.

The PackageCounts workbook opens.

7. On the **View** tab, in the **Window** group, click the **Arrange All** button.

The Arrange Windows dialog box opens.

8. Click **Cascade**, and then click **OK**.

Excel cascades the open workbook windows within the program window.

Switch among cascaded windows by clicking the visible part of a window frame.

9. Click the **File** tab, and then click **Options**.

The Excel Options dialog box opens.

10. Click **Quick Access Toolbar**.

The Customize The Quick Access Toolbar page opens.

11. Click the **Choose commands from** arrow, and then in the list, click **Review Tab**.

The commands in the Review Tab category appear in the command list.

12. Click the **Spelling** command, and then click **Add**.

Excel adds the Spelling command to the Quick Access Toolbar.

Adding commands to the Quick Access Toolbar.

13. Click **Customize Ribbon**.

    The Customize The Ribbon page of the Excel Options dialog box appears.

14. If necessary, click the **Customize the Ribbon** box's arrow and click **Main Tabs**. In the right tab list, click the **Review** tab and then click the **Move Up** button three times.

    Excel moves the Review tab between the Insert and Page Layout tabs.

15. Click the **New Tab** button.

    A tab named New Tab (Custom) appears below the most recently active tab in the Main Tabs list.

16. Click the **New Tab (Custom)** tab name, click the **Rename** button, type My Commands in the **Display Name** box, and click **OK**.

    The new tab's name changes to My Commands.

17. Click the **New Group (Custom)** group and then click **Rename**. In the **Rename** dialog box, click the icon that looks like a paint palette (second row, fourth from the right). Then type Formatting in the **Display name** box, and click **OK**.

    The new group's name changes to Formatting.

18. In the right tab list, click the **My Commands** tab name. Then, on the left side of the dialog box, click the **Choose Commands From** box's arrow and click **Main Tabs**.

    The Main Tabs group of ribbon tabs appears in the left tab list.

19. In the left tab list, click the **Home** tab's expand control, click the **Styles** group's name, and then click the **Add** button.

    The Styles group is added to the My Commands tab.

20. In the left tab list, under the **Home** tab, click the **Number** group's expand control.

    The commands in the Number group appear.

21. In the right tab list, click the **Formatting** group you created earlier. Then, in the left tab list, click the **Number Format** item and click the **Add** button.

    Excel 2010 adds the Number Format item to the Formatting custom group.

22. Click **OK** to save your ribbon customizations, and then click the **My Commands** tab on the ribbon.

Your custom tab.

Important The remaining exercises in this book assume you are using Excel 2010 as it was installed on your computer.

✖ **CLEAN UP** Reset the ribbon to its original configuration, and then save and close all open workbooks. If you are not continuing directly to the next chapter, exit Excel.

Key Points

- Save your work whenever you do something you'd hate to have to do again.
- Assigning values to a workbook's properties makes it easier to find your workbook using the Windows search facility.
- Be sure to give your worksheets descriptive names.
- If you want to use a worksheet's data in another workbook, you can send a copy of the worksheet to that other workbook without deleting the original worksheet.
- You can delete a worksheet you no longer need, but you can also hide a worksheet in the workbook. When you need the data on the worksheet, you can unhide it.
- You can save yourself a lot of bothersome cutting and pasting by inserting and deleting worksheet cells, columns, and rows.
- Customize your Excel 2010 program window by changing how it displays your workbooks, zooming in on data, adding frequently used buttons to the Quick Access Toolbar, and rearranging or customizing the ribbon to meet your needs.

Chapter at a Glance

Move data within
a workbook,
page 260

Enter and
revise data,
page 256

Find and replace
data, **page 264**

Define Excel
tables, **page 274**

Correct and expand
upon worksheet
data, **page 269**

9 Work with Data and Excel Tables

In this chapter, you will learn how to

- ✔ Enter and revise data.
- ✔ Move data within a workbook.
- ✔ Find and replace data.
- ✔ Correct and expand upon worksheet data.
- ✔ Define Excel tables.

With Microsoft Excel 2010, you can visualize and present information effectively by using charts, graphics, and formatting, but the data is the most important part of any workbook. By learning to enter data efficiently, you will make fewer data entry errors and give yourself more time to analyze your data so you can make decisions about your organization's performance and direction.

Excel provides a wide variety of tools you can use to enter and manage worksheet data effectively. For example, you can organize your data into Excel tables, which enables you to store and analyze your data quickly and efficiently. Also, you can enter a data series quickly, repeat one or more values, and control how Excel formats cells, columns, and rows moved from one part of a worksheet to another with a minimum of effort. With Excel, you can check the spelling of worksheet text, look up alternative words by using the Thesaurus, and translate words to foreign languages.

In this chapter, you'll learn how to enter and revise Excel data, move data within a workbook, find and replace existing data, use proofing and reference tools to enhance your data, and organize your data by using Excel tables.

> **Practice Files** Before you can complete the exercises in this chapter, you need to copy the book's practice files to your computer. The practice files you'll use to complete the exercises in this chapter are in the Chapter09 practice file folder. A complete list of practice files is provided in "Using the Practice Files" at the beginning of this book.

Entering and Revising Data

After you create a workbook, you can begin entering data. The simplest way to enter data is to click a cell and type a value. This method works very well when you're entering a few pieces of data, but it is less than ideal when you're entering long sequences or series of values. For example, Craig Dewar, the Vice President of Marketing for Consolidated Messenger, might want to create a worksheet listing the monthly program savings that large customers can realize if they sign exclusive delivery contracts with Consolidated Messenger. To record those numbers, he would need to create a worksheet tracking each customer's monthly program savings.

Customer	Month	Program Savings
Contoso	January	$ 172,631
Contoso	February	$ 137,738
Contoso	March	$ 26,786
Fabrikam	January	$ 216,816
Fabrikam	February	$ 113,351
Fabrikam	March	$ 44,312
Lucerne Publishing	January	$ 145,891
Lucerne Publishing	February	$ 245,951
Lucerne Publishing	March	$ 132,776
Wide World Importers	January	$ 197,070
Wide World Importers	February	$ 128,051
Wide World Importers	March	$ 245,695

The process of entering repeated content can be simplified by using the AutoFill option.

Repeatedly entering the sequence January, February, March, and so on can be handled by copying and pasting the first occurrence of the sequence, but there's an easier way to do it: use AutoFill. With AutoFill, you enter the first element in a recognized series, click and hold the mouse button down on the fill handle at the lower-right corner of the cell, and drag the fill handle until the series extends far enough to accommodate your data. Using a similar tool, FillSeries, you can enter two values in a series and use the fill handle to extend the series in your worksheet. For example, if you want to create a series starting at 2 and increasing by 2, you can put 2 in the first cell and 4 in the second cell, select both cells, and then use the fill handle to extend the series to your desired end value.

You do have some control over how Excel extends the values in a series when you drag the fill handle. For example, if you drag the fill handle up (or to the left), Excel extends the series to include previous values. If you type *January* in a cell and then drag that cell's fill handle up (or to the left), Excel places *December* in the first cell, *November* in the second cell, and so on.

Another way to control how Excel extends a data series is by holding down the Ctrl key while you drag the fill handle. For example, if you select a cell that contains the value *January* and then drag the fill handle down, Excel extends the series by placing *February* in the next cell, *March* in the cell after that, and so on. If you hold down the Ctrl key while you drag the fill handle, however, Excel repeats the value *January* in each cell you add to the series.

Tip Be sure to experiment with how the fill handle extends your series and how pressing the Ctrl key changes that behavior. Using the fill handle can save you a lot of time entering data.

Other data entry techniques you'll use in this section are AutoComplete, which detects when a value you're entering is similar to previously entered values; Pick From Drop-Down List, from which you can choose a value from among the existing values in a column; and Ctrl+Enter, which you can use to enter a value in multiple cells simultaneously.

Troubleshooting If an AutoComplete suggestion doesn't appear as you begin typing a cell value, the option might be turned off. To turn on AutoComplete, click the File tab, and then click Options. In the Excel Options dialog box, display the Advanced page. In the Editing Options area of the page, select the Enable AutoComplete For Cell Values check box, and then click OK.

The following table summarizes these data entry techniques.

Method	Action
AutoFill	Enter the first value in a recognized series and use the fill handle to extend the series.
FillSeries	Enter the first two values in a series and use the fill handle to extend the series.
AutoComplete	Type the first few letters in a cell, and if a similar value exists in the same column, Excel suggests the existing value.
Pick From Drop-Down List	Right-click a cell, and then click Pick From Drop-Down List. A list of existing values in the cell's column is displayed. Click the value you want to enter into the cell.
Ctrl+Enter	Select a range of cells, each of which you want to contain the same data, type the data in the active cell, and press Ctrl+Enter.

Another handy feature in Excel is the AutoFill Options button that appears next to data you add to a worksheet by using the fill handle.

The AutoFill options allow you to specify the manner in which Excel fills a range of cells.

Clicking the AutoFill Options button displays a list of actions Excel can take regarding the cells affected by your fill operation. The options in the list are summarized in the following table.

Option	Action
Copy Cells	This copies the contents of the selected cells to the cells indicated by the fill operation.
Fill Series	This action fills the cells indicated by the fill operation with the next items in the series.
Fill Formatting Only	This copies the format of the selected cell to the cells indicated by the fill operation, but does not place any values in the target cells.
Fill Without Formatting	This action fills the cells indicated by the fill operation with the next items in the series, but ignores any formatting applied to the source cells.
Fill Days, Weekdays, and so on	The appearance of this option changes according to the series you extend. For example, if you extend the values *Wed*, *Thu*, and *Fri*, Excel presents two options, Fill Days and Fill Weekdays, and you can select the one you want. If you do not use a recognized sequence, this option does not appear.

In this exercise, you'll enter data by using multiple methods and control how Excel formats an extended data series.

 SET UP You need the Series_start workbook located in your Chapter09 practice file folder to complete this exercise. Start Excel, open the Series_start workbook, and save it as *Series*. Then follow the steps.

1. On the **Monthly** worksheet, select cell **B3**, and then drag the fill handle down until it covers cells **B3:B7**.

   Excel repeats the value *Fabrikam* in cells B4:B7.

2. Select cell **C3**, hold down the Ctrl key, and drag the fill handle down until it covers cells **C3:C7**.

   Excel repeats the value *January* in cells C4:C7.

3. Select cell **B8**, and then type the letter **F**.

   Excel displays the characters *abrikam* in reverse colors.

	A	B	C	D	E	F	G	H
1								
2		**Customer**	Month	Category	Amount			
3		Fabrikam	January	Ground	$ 14,501.98			
4		Fabrikam	January	3Day	$ 3,501.75			
5		Fabrikam	January	2Day	$ 5,599.10			
6		Fabrikam	January	Overnight	$ 35,907.82			
7		Fabrikam	January	Priority Overnight	$ 17,333.25			
8		Fabrikam						
9								
10								
11								
12								

Excel suggests completed words based on those already present in the worksheet.

4. Press Tab to accept the value *Fabrikam* for the cell.

5. In cell **C8**, type **February**.

6. Right-click cell **D8**, and then click **Pick From Drop-down List**.

   A list of values in column D appears below cell D8.

You can restrict cell entries by defining them in a drop-down list.

7. From the list, click **2Day**.

8. In cell **E8**, type **11802.14**, and then press Tab or Enter.

9. Select cell **B2**, and then drag the fill handle so that it covers cells **C2:E2**.

   Excel replaces the values in cells C2:E2 with the value *Customer.*

10. Click the **AutoFill Options** button, and then click **Fill Formatting Only**.

    Excel restores the original values in cells C2:E2 but applies the formatting of cell B2 to those cells.

✖ **CLEAN UP** Save the Series workbook, and then close it.

Moving Data Within a Workbook

You can move to a specific cell in lots of ways, but the most direct method is to click the desired cell. The cell you click will be outlined in black, and its contents, if any, will appear in the formula bar. When a cell is outlined, it is the active cell, meaning that you can modify its contents. You use a similar method to select multiple cells (referred to as a cell range)—just click the first cell in the range, hold down the left mouse button, and drag the mouse pointer over the remaining cells you want to select. After you select the cell or cells you want to work with, you can cut, copy, delete, or change the format of the contents of the cell or cells. For instance, Gregory Weber, the Northwest Distribution

Center Manager for Consolidated Messenger, might want to copy the cells that contain a set of column labels to a new page that summarizes similar data.

Important If you select a group of cells, the first cell you click is designated as the active cell.

You're not limited to selecting cells individually or as part of a range. For example, you might need to move a column of price data one column to the right to make room for a column of headings that indicate to which service category (ground, three-day express, two-day express, overnight, or priority overnight) a set of numbers belongs. To move an entire column (or entire columns) of data at a time, you click the column's header, located at the top of the worksheet. Clicking a column header highlights every cell in that column and enables you to copy or cut the column and paste it elsewhere in the workbook. Similarly, clicking a row's header highlights every cell in that row, enabling you to copy or cut the row and paste it elsewhere in the workbook.

When you copy a cell, cell range, row, or column, Excel copies the cells' contents and formatting. In previous versions of Excel, you would paste the cut or copied items and then click the Paste Options button to select which aspects of the cut or copied cells to paste into the target cells. The problem with using the Paste Options button was that there was no way to tell what your pasted data would look like until you completed the paste operation. If you didn't like the way the pasted data looked, you had to click the Paste Options button again and try another option.

With the new Paste Live Preview capability in Excel, you can see what your pasted data will look like without committing to the paste operation. To preview your data using Paste Live Preview, cut or copy worksheet data and then, on the Home tab of the ribbon, in the Clipboard group, click the Paste button's arrow to display the Paste gallery, and point to one of the icons. When you do,

Excel displays a preview of how your data will appear if you click the paste option you're pointing to.

If you position your mouse pointer over one icon in the Paste gallery and then move it over another icon without clicking, Excel will update the preview to reflect the new option. Depending on the cells' contents, two or more of the paste options might lead to the same result.

Troubleshooting If pointing to an icon in the Paste gallery doesn't result in a live preview, that option might be turned off. To turn Paste Live Preview on, click the File tab and click Options to display the Excel Options dialog box. Click General, select the Enable Live Preview check box, and click OK.

After you click an icon to complete the paste operation, Excel displays the Paste Options button next to the pasted cells. Clicking the Paste Options button displays the Paste Options palette as well, but pointing to one of those icons doesn't generate a preview. If you want to display Paste Live Preview again, you will need to press Ctrl+Z to undo the paste operation and, if necessary, cut or copy the data again to use the icons in the Home tab's Clipboard group.

Troubleshooting If the Paste Options button doesn't appear, you can turn the feature on by clicking the File tab and then clicking Options to display the Excel Options dialog box. In the Excel Options dialog box, display the Advanced page and then, in the Cut, Copy, And Paste area, select the Show Paste Options Buttons When Content Is Pasted check box. Click OK to close the dialog box and save your setting.

After cutting or copying data to the Clipboard, you can access additional paste options from the Paste gallery and from the Paste Special dialog box, which you display by clicking Paste Special at the bottom of the Paste gallery.

You can conduct mathematical operations on cut or copied content when you paste it into another location.

In the Paste Special dialog box, you can specify the aspect of the Clipboard contents you want to paste, restricting the pasted data to values, formats, comments, or one of several other options. You can perform mathematical operations involving the cut or copied data and the existing data in the cells you paste the content into. You can transpose data—change rows to columns and columns to rows—when you paste it, by clicking Transpose in the Paste gallery or by selecting the Transpose check box in the Paste Special dialog box.

In this exercise, you'll copy a set of data headers to another worksheet, move a column of data within a worksheet, and use Paste Live Preview to control the appearance of copied data.

SET UP You need the 2010Q1ShipmentsByCategory_start workbook located in your Chapter09 practice file folder to complete this exercise. Open the 2010Q1ShipmentsByCategory_start workbook, and save it as *2010Q1ShipmentsByCategory*. Then follow the steps.

1. On the **Count** worksheet, select cells **B2:D2**.

2. On the **Home** tab, in the **Clipboard** group, click the **Copy** button.

   Excel copies the contents of cells B2:D2 to the Clipboard.

   Keyboard Shortcut Press Ctrl+C to copy worksheet contents to the Clipboard.

3. On the tab bar, click the **Sales** tab to display that worksheet.

4. Select cell **B2**.

5. On the **Home** tab, in the **Clipboard** group, click the **Paste** button's arrow, point to the first icon in the **Paste** group, and then click the **Keep Source Formatting** icon (the final icon in the first row of the **Paste** gallery.)

   Excel displays how the data would look if you pasted the copied values without formatting, and then pastes the header values into cells B2:D2, retaining the original cells' formatting.

6. Right-click the column header of column **I**, and then click **Cut**.

   Excel outlines column I with a marquee.

7. Right-click the header of column **E**, and then, under **Paste Options**, click **Paste**.

Excel pastes the contents of column I into column E.

Keyboard Shortcut Press Ctrl+V to paste worksheet contents exactly as they appear in the original cell.

Cutting and pasting a column removes the column from its original location.

Troubleshooting The appearance of buttons and groups on the ribbon changes depending on the width of the program window. For information about changing the appearance of the ribbon to match our screen images, see "Modifying the Display of the Ribbon" at the beginning of this book.

✖ **CLEAN UP** Save the 2010Q1ShipmentsByCategory workbook, and then close it.

Finding and Replacing Data

Excel worksheets can hold more than one million rows of data, so in large data collections it's unlikely that you would have the time to move through a worksheet one row at a time to locate the data you want to find. You can locate specific data in an Excel worksheet by using the Find And Replace dialog box, which has two pages (one named *Find*, the other named *Replace*) that you can use to search for cells that contain particular values. Using the controls on the Find page identifies cells that contain the data you specify; using the controls on the Replace page, you can substitute one value for another. For example, if one of Consolidated Messenger's customers changes its company name, you can change every instance of the old name to the new name by using the Replace functionality.

When you need more control over the data that you find and replace, for instance, if you want to find cells in which the entire cell value matches the value you're searching for, you can click the Options button to expand the Find And Replace dialog box.

You can limit your search to the current worksheet or expand it to include all worksheets in the workbook.

One way you can use the extra options in the Find And Replace dialog box is to use a specific format to identify data that requires review. As an example, Consolidated Messenger's Vice President of Marketing, Craig Dewar, could make corporate sales plans based on a projected budget for the next year and mark his trial figures using a specific format. After the executive board finalizes the numbers, he could use the Find Format capability in the Find And Replace dialog box to locate the old values and change them by hand.

The following table summarizes the Find And Replace dialog box controls' functions.

Control	Function
Find What field	Contains the value you want to find or replace
Find All button	Selects every cell that contains the value in the Find What field
Find Next button	Selects the next cell that contains the value in the Find What field
Replace With field	Contains the value to overwrite the value in the Find What field
Replace All button	Replaces every instance of the value in the Find What field with the value in the Replace With field
Replace button	Replaces the highlighted occurrence of the value in the Find What field and highlights the next cell that contains that value
Options button	Expands the Find And Replace dialog box to display additional capabilities

(continued)

Control	Function
Format button	Displays the Find Format dialog box, which you can use to specify the format of values to be found or values to be replaced
Within box	Enables you to select whether to search the active worksheet or the entire workbook
Search box	Enables you to select whether to search by rows or by columns
Look In box	Enables you to select whether to search cell formulas or values
Match Case check box	When checked, requires that all matches have the same capitalization as the text in the Find What field (for example, *cat* doesn't match *Cat*)
Match Entire Cell Contents check box	Requires that the cell contain exactly the same value as in the Find What field (for example, *Cat* doesn't match *Catherine*)
Close button	Closes the Find And Replace dialog box

To change a value by hand, select the cell, and then either type a new value in the cell or, in the formula bar, select the value you want to replace and type the new value. You can also double-click a cell and edit its contents within the cell.

In this exercise, you'll find a specific value in a worksheet, replace every occurrence of a company name in a worksheet, and find a cell with a particular formatting.

SET UP You need the AverageDeliveries_start workbook located in your Chapter09 practice file folder to complete this exercise. Open the AverageDeliveries_start workbook, and save it as *AverageDeliveries*. Then follow the steps.

1. If necessary, click the **Time Summary** sheet tab.

   The Time Summary worksheet is displayed.

2. On the **Home** tab, in the **Editing** group, click **Find & Select**, and then click **Find**.

   The Find And Replace dialog box opens with the Find tab displayed.

   Keyboard Shortcut Press Ctrl+F to display the Find tab of the Find And Replace dialog box.

3. In the **Find what** field, type **114**.

4. Click **Find Next**.

Excel highlights cell B16, which contains the value *114*.

You can conduct a simple text search, or expand the dialog box and select other options.

5. Delete the value in the **Find what** field, and then click the **Options** button.

   The Find And Replace dialog box expands to display additional search options.

6. Click **Format**.

   The Find Format dialog box opens.

7. Click the **Font** tab.

   The Font page is displayed.

The Font list displays the fonts that are installed on your computer.

8. In the **Font style** list, click **Italic**.

9. Click **OK**.

   The Find Format dialog box closes.

10. Click **Find Next**.

    Excel highlights cell D25.

11. Click **Close**.

    The Find And Replace dialog box closes.

12. On the tab bar, click the **Customer Summary** sheet tab.

    The Customer Summary worksheet is displayed.

13. On the **Home** tab, in the **Editing** group, click **Find & Select**, and then click **Replace**.

    The Find And Replace dialog box opens with the Replace tab displayed.

    Keyboard Shortcut Press Ctrl+H to display the Replace tab of the Find And Replace dialog box.

You can replace text, formatting, and formula elements.

14. Click the **Format** arrow to the right of the **Find what** field, and then in the list, click **Clear Find Format**.

The format displayed next to the Find What field disappears.

15. In the **Find what** field, type **Contoso**.

16. In the **Replace with** field, type **Northwind Traders**.

17. Click **Replace All**.

A message box appears, indicating that Excel made three replacements.

18. Click **OK** to close the message box.

19. Click **Close**.

The Find And Replace dialog box closes.

✖ **CLEAN UP** Save the AverageDeliveries workbook, and then close it.

Correcting and Expanding Upon Worksheet Data

After you enter your data, you should take the time to check and correct it. You do need to verify visually that each piece of numeric data is correct, but you can make sure that your worksheet's text is spelled correctly by using the Excel spelling checker. When the spelling checker encounters a word it doesn't recognize, it highlights the word and offers suggestions representing its best guess of the correct word. You can then edit the word directly, pick the proper word from the list of suggestions, or have the spelling checker ignore the misspelling. You can also use the spelling checker to add new words to a custom dictionary so that Excel will recognize them later, saving you time by not requiring you to identify the words as correct every time they occur in your worksheets.

Tip After you make a change in a workbook, you can usually remove the change as long as you haven't closed the workbook. To undo a change, click the Undo button on the Quick Access Toolbar. If you decide you want to keep a change, you can use the Redo command to restore it.

If you're not sure of your word choice, or if you use a word that is almost but not quite right for your intended meaning, you can check for alternative words by using the Thesaurus. Several other research tools are also available, such as the Bing decision engine and the Microsoft Encarta dictionary, to which you can refer as you create your workbooks. To display those tools, on the Review tab, in the Proofing group, click Research to display the Research task pane.

You can choose a research resource from the list in the top section of the Research task pane.

Finally, if you want to translate a word from one language to another, you can do so by selecting the cell that contains the value you want to translate, displaying the Review tab, and then, in the Language group, clicking Translate. The Research task pane opens (or changes if it's already open) and displays controls you can use to select the original and destination languages.

You can translate words and phrases into many different languages.

Important Excel translates a sentence by using word substitutions, which means that the translation routine doesn't always pick the best word for a given context. The translated sentence might not capture your exact meaning.

In this exercise, you'll check a worksheet's spelling, add terms to a dictionary, search the Thesaurus for an alternative word, and translate a word from English into French.

SET UP You need the ServiceLevels_start workbook located in your Chapter09 practice file folder to complete this exercise. Open the ServiceLevels_start workbook, and save it as *ServiceLevels*. Then follow the steps.

ABC
✓
Spelling

1. On the **Review** tab, in the **Proofing** group, click **Spelling**.

   The Spelling dialog box opens.

Spelling: English (U.S.)	? ✕
Not in Dictionary:	
shiped	Ignore Once
	Ignore All
	Add to Dictionary
Suggestions:	
shipped	Change
shaped	
shied	Change All
sniped	
shined	AutoCorrect
swiped	
Dictionary language: English (U.S.)	
Options...	Undo Last	Cancel

   The first misspelled word in the worksheet is displayed in the Not In Dictionary field.

2. Verify that the word *shipped* is highlighted in the **Suggestions** pane, and then click **Change**.

   Excel corrects the word and displays the next questioned word: *withn*.

3. Click **Change**.

   Excel corrects the word and displays the next questioned word: *TwoDay*.

4. Click **Add to Dictionary**.

   Excel adds the word to the dictionary and displays the next questioned word: *ThreeDay*.

5. Click **Add to Dictionary**.

   Excel adds the word to the dictionary.

6. In the **Spelling** dialog box, click **Close**.

   A message box indicates that the spelling check is complete.

7. Click **OK** to close the message box.

8. Click cell **B6**.

Thesaurus

9. On the **Review** tab, in the **Proofing** group, click **Thesaurus**.

The Research task pane opens.

Research   ▼ ✕
Search for:
Overnight   →
Thesaurus: English (U.S.)   ▼
⊕ Back ▼   ⊙ ▼
◢ **Thesaurus: English (U.S.)**   ▲
◢ **Instant (adj.)**
Instant
Immediate
Instantaneous
Sudden
Rapid
Dramatic
Meteoric
Abrupt
Gradual (Antonym)
Eventual (Antonym)
◢ **During the night (adv.)**
During the night
While sleeping (Diction...
All night (Dictionary Fo...
For the night (Dictionar...
◢ **Suddenly (adv.)**
Suddenly   ▼
🔲 Get services on Office Marketplace
🔍 Research options...

The Thesaurus displays synonyms for the word Overnight.

Translate

10. On the **Review** tab, in the **Language** group, click **Translate**.

The Research task pane displays the translation tools.

11. If necessary, in the **From** list, click **English (U.S.).**

12. In the **To** list, click **French (France).**

The Research task pane displays French words that mean *overnight*.

You can translate the same word into another language by choosing one from the To list.

✖ CLEAN UP Save the ServiceLevels workbook, and then close it.

Defining Excel Tables

With Excel, you've always been able to manage lists of data effectively, enabling you to sort your worksheet data based on the values in one or more columns, limit the data displayed by using criteria (for example, show only those routes with fewer than 100 stops), and create formulas that summarize the values in visible (that is, unfiltered) cells. In Excel 2007, the Excel product team extended your ability to manage your data by introducing Excel tables. Excel 2010 offers you the same capability.

Customer ▼	Month ▼	Program Savings ▼
Contoso	January	$ 172,631
Contoso	February	$ 137,738
Contoso	March	$ 26,786
Fabrikam	January	$ 216,816
Fabrikam	February	$ 113,351
Fabrikam	March	$ 44,312
Lucerne Publishing	January	$ 145,891
Lucerne Publishing	February	$ 245,951
Lucerne Publishing	March	$ 132,776
Wide World Importers	January	$ 197,070
Wide World Importers	February	$ 128,051
Wide World Importers	March	$ 245,695

Converting a data range to an Excel table provides many data-management capabilities.

To create an Excel table, type a series of column headers in adjacent cells, and then type a row of data below the headers. Click any header or data cell into which you just typed, and then, on the Home tab, in the Styles group, click Format As Table. In the gallery that opens, click the table style you want to apply. In the Format As Table dialog box, verify that the cells in the Where Is The Data For Your Table? field reflect your current selection and that the My Table Has Headers check box is selected, and then click OK.

Excel can also create an Excel table from an existing cell range as long as the range has no blank rows or columns within the data and there is no extraneous data in cells immediately below or next to the list. To create the Excel table, click any cell in the range and then, on the Home tab, in the Styles group, click the Format As Table button and select a table style. If your existing data has formatting applied to it, that formatting remains applied to those cells when you create the Excel table. If you want Excel to replace the existing formatting with the Excel table's formatting, right-click the table style you want to apply and then click Apply And Clear Formatting.

When you want to add data to an Excel table, click the rightmost cell in the bottom row of the Excel table and press the Tab key to create a new row. You can also select a cell in the row immediately below the last row in the table or a cell in the column immediately to the right of the table and type a value into the cell. After you enter the value and move out of the cell, the AutoCorrect Options action button appears. If you didn't mean to include the data in the Excel table, you can click Undo Table AutoExpansion to exclude the cells from the Excel table. If you never want Excel to include adjacent data in an Excel table again, click Stop Automatically Expanding Tables.

Tip To stop Table AutoExpansion before it starts, click the File tab, and then click Options. In the Excel Options dialog box, click Proofing, and then click the AutoCorrect Options button to display the AutoCorrect dialog box. Click the AutoFormat As You Type tab, clear the Include New Rows And Columns In Table check box, and then click OK twice.

You can add rows and columns to an Excel table, or remove them from an Excel table without deleting the cells' contents, by dragging the resize handle at the Excel table's lower-right corner. If your Excel table's headers contain a recognizable series of values (such as *Region1*, *Region2*, and *Region3*), and you drag the resize handle to create a fourth column, Excel creates the column with the label *Region4*—the next value in the series.

Excel tables often contain data you can summarize by calculating a sum or average, or by finding the maximum or minimum value in a column. To summarize one or more columns of data, you can add a Total row to your Excel table.

Customer ▼	Month ▼	Program Savings ▼
Contoso	January	$ 172,631
Contoso	February	$ 137,738
Contoso	March	$ 26,786
Fabrikam	January	$ 216,816
Fabrikam	February	$ 113,351
Fabrikam	March	$ 44,312
Lucerne Publishing	January	$ 145,891
Lucerne Publishing	February	$ 245,951
Lucerne Publishing	March	$ 132,776
Wide World Importers	January	$ 197,070
Wide World Importers	February	$ 128,051
Wide World Importers	March	$ 245,695
Total		$ **1,807,068**

The Total row automatically calculates the total of the preceding values.

When you add the Total row, Excel creates a formula that summarizes the values in the rightmost Excel table column. To change that summary operation, or to add a summary operation to any other cell in the Total row, click the cell, click the arrow that appears, and then click the summary operation you want to apply. Clicking the More Functions menu item displays the Insert Function dialog box, from which you can select any of the functions available in Excel.

Much as it does when you create a new worksheet, Excel gives your Excel tables generic names such as *Table1* and *Table2*. You can change an Excel table's name to something easier to recognize by clicking any cell in the table, clicking the Design contextual tab, and then, in the Properties group, editing the value in the Table Name box. Changing an Excel table name might not seem important, but it helps make formulas that summarize Excel table data much easier to understand. You should make a habit of renaming your Excel tables so you can recognize the data they contain.

See Also For more information about using the Insert Function dialog box and about referring to tables in formulas, see "Creating Formulas to Calculate Values" in Chapter 10, "Perform Calculations on Data."

If for any reason you want to convert your Excel table back to a normal range of cells, click any cell in the Excel table and then, on the Design contextual tab, in the Tools group, click Convert To Range. When Excel displays a message box asking if you're sure you want to convert the table to a range, click OK.

In this exercise, you'll create an Excel table from existing data, add data to an Excel table, add a Total row, change the Total row's summary operation, and rename the Excel table.

SET UP You need the DriverSortTimes_start workbook located in your Chapter09 practice file folder to complete this exercise. Open the DriverSortTimes_start workbook, and save it as *DriverSortTimes*. Then follow the steps.

1. Select cell **B2**.

Format as Table ▾

2. On the **Home** tab, in the **Styles** group, click **Format as Table**, and then select a table style.

   The Format As Table dialog box opens.

Format As Table	? ✕
Where is the data for your table?	
=$B$2:$C$17	📊
☑ My table has headers	
OK	Cancel

   The dialog box automatically displays the data range that includes the selected cell.

3. Verify that the range *=$B$2:$C$17* is displayed in the **Where is the data for your table?** field and that the **My table has headers** check box is selected, and then click **OK**.

   Excel creates an Excel table from your data and displays the Design contextual tab.

4. In cell **B18**, type **D116**, press Tab, type **100** in cell **C18**, and then press Enter.

   Excel includes the data in your Excel table.

5. Select a cell in the table. Then on the **Design** contextual tab, in the **Table Style Options** group, select the **Total Row** check box.

   A Total row appears at the bottom of your Excel table.

6. Select cell **C19**, click the arrow that appears at the right edge of the cell, and then click **Average**.

   Excel changes the summary operation to Average.

Drive ▼	Sorting Minutes ▼
D101	102
D102	162
D103	165
D104	91
D105	103
D106	127
D107	112
D108	137
D109	102
D110	147
D111	163
D112	109
D113	91
D114	107
D115	93
D116	100
Total	**119.4375**

You can change the summary operation performed in a table.

7. On the **Design** contextual tab, in the **Properties** group, type the value **SortTimes** in the **Table Name** field, and then press Enter.

   Excel renames your Excel table.

8. On the Quick Access Toolbar, click the **Save** button to save your work.

CLEAN UP Close the DriverSortTimes workbook. If you are not continuing directly to the next chapter, exit Excel.

Key Points

- You can enter a series of data quickly by typing one or more values in adjacent cells, selecting the cells, and then dragging the fill handle. To change how dragging the fill handle extends a data series, hold down the Ctrl key.

- Dragging a fill handle displays the Auto Fill Options button, which you can use to specify whether to copy the selected cells' values, extend a recognized series, or apply the selected cells' formatting to the new cells.

- With Excel, you can enter data by using a list, AutoComplete, or Ctrl+Enter. You should experiment with these techniques and use the one that best fits your circumstances.

- When you copy (or cut) and paste cells, columns, or rows, you can use the new Paste Live Preview capability to preview how your data will appear before you commit to the paste operation.

- After you paste cells, rows, or columns into your worksheet, Excel displays the Paste Options action button. You can use its controls to change which aspects of the cut or copied elements Excel applies to the pasted elements.

- By using the options in the Paste Special dialog box, you can paste only specific aspects of cut or copied data, perform mathematical operations, transpose data, or delete blank cells when pasting.

- You can find and replace data within a worksheet by searching for specific values or by searching for cells that have a particular format applied.

- Excel provides a variety of powerful proofing and research tools, enabling you to check your workbook's spelling, find alternative words by using the Thesaurus, and translate words between languages.

- With Excel tables, you can organize and summarize your data effectively.

Chapter at a Glance

Name groups of data, **page 282**

Create formulas to calculate values, **page 286**

Summarize data that meets specific conditions, **page 296**

Find and correct errors in calculations, **page 300**

10 Perform Calculations on Data

In this chapter, you will learn how to

✔ Name groups of data.

✔ Create formulas to calculate values.

✔ Summarize data that meets specific conditions.

✔ Find and correct errors in calculations.

Microsoft Excel 2010 workbooks give you a handy place to store and organize your data, but you can also do a lot more with your data in Excel. One important task you can perform is to calculate totals for the values in a series of related cells. You can also use Excel to discover other information about the data you select, such as the maximum or minimum value in a group of cells. By finding the maximum or minimum value in a group, you can identify your best salesperson, product categories you might need to pay more attention to, or suppliers that consistently give you the best deal. Regardless of your bookkeeping needs, Excel gives you the ability to find the information you want. And if you make an error, you can find the cause and correct it quickly.

Many times, you can't access the information you want without referencing more than one cell, and it's also often true that you'll use the data in the same group of cells for more than one calculation. Excel makes it easy to reference a number of cells at once, enabling you to define your calculations quickly.

In this chapter, you'll learn how to streamline references to groups of data on your worksheets and how to create and correct formulas

> **Practice Files** Before you can complete the exercises in this chapter, you need to copy the book's practice files to your computer. The practice files you'll use to complete the exercises in this chapter are in the Chapter10 practice file folder. A complete list of practice files is provided in "Using the Practice Files" at the beginning of this book.

Naming Groups of Data

When you work with large amounts of data, it's often useful to identify groups of cells that contain related data. For example, you can create a worksheet in which cells C4:I4 hold the number of packages Consolidated Messenger's Northeast processing facility handled from 5:00 P.M. to 12:00 A.M. on the previous day.

	5:00 PM	6:00 PM	7:00 PM	8:00 PM	9:00 PM	10:00 PM	11:00 PM
Northeast	10,208	13,889	17,570	21,251	24,932	28,613	32,294
Atlantic	8,472	9,013	9,554	10,095	10,636	11,177	11,718
Southeast	7,328	8,108	8,888	9,668	10,448	11,228	12,008
North Central	6,974	8,160	9,346	10,532	11,718	12,904	14,090
Midwest	9,558	10,902	12,246	13,590	14,934	16,278	17,622
Southwest	7,436	8,223	9,010	9,797	10,584	11,371	12,158
Mountain West	4,631	5,230	5,829	6,428	7,027	7,626	8,225
Northwest	9,105	10,346	11,587	12,828	14,069	15,310	16,551
Central	5,704	6,300	6,896	7,492	8,088	8,684	9,280

You can name a range of data and reference the entire range by using only the name.

Instead of specifying the cells individually every time you want to use the data they contain, you can define those cells as a range (also called a *named range*). For example, you can group the items from the cells described in the preceding paragraph into a range named *NortheastPreviousDay*. Whenever you want to use the contents of that range in a calculation, you can simply use the name of the range instead of specifying each cell individually.

Tip Yes, you could just name the range *Northeast*, but if you use the range's values in a formula in another worksheet, the more descriptive range name tells you and your colleagues exactly what data is used in the calculation.

To create a named range, select the cells you want to include in your range, click the Formulas tab, and then, in the Defined Names group, click Define Name to display the New Name dialog box. In the New Name dialog box, type a name in the Name field, verify that the cells you selected appear in the Refers To field, and then click OK. You can also add a comment about the range in the Comment field and select whether you want to make the name available for formulas in the entire workbook or just on an individual worksheet.

If the cells you want to define as a named range have labels in a row or column that's part of the cell group, you can use those labels as the names of the named ranges. For example, if your data appears in worksheet cells B4:I12 and the values in column B are the row labels, you can make each row its own named range. To create a series of named ranges from a group of cells, select all of the data cells, including the labels, display the Formulas tab and then, in the Defined Names group, click Create From Selection to display the Create Names From Selection dialog box. In the Create Names From Selection dialog box, select the check box that represents the labels' position in the selected range, and then click OK.

You can name ranges by their row or column labels.

A final way to create a named range is to select the cells you want in the range, click in the Name box next to the formula box, and then type the name for the range.

You can display the ranges available in a workbook by clicking the Name arrow.

To manage the named ranges in a workbook, display the Formulas tab, and then, in the Defined Names group, click Name Manager to display the Name Manager dialog box.

When you click a named range, Excel displays the cells it encompasses in the Refers To field.

Clicking the Edit button displays the Edit Name dialog box, which is a version of the New Name dialog box, enabling you to change a named range's definition; for example, by adding a column. You can also use the controls in the Name Manager dialog box to delete a named range (the range, not the data) by clicking it, clicking the Delete button, and then clicking OK in the confirmation dialog box that opens.

Tip If your workbook contains a lot of named ranges, you can click the Filter button in the Name Manager dialog box and select a criterion to limit the names displayed in the Name Manager dialog box.

In this exercise, you'll create named ranges to streamline references to groups of cells.

SET UP You need the VehicleMiles_start workbook located in your Chapter10 practice file folder to complete this exercise. Start Excel, open the VehicleMiles_start workbook, and save it as *VehicleMiles*. Then follow the steps.

1. Select cells **C4:G4**.

   You are intentionally leaving cell H4 out of this selection. You will edit the named range later in this exercise.

2. In the **Name** box at the left end of the formula bar, type **V101LastWeek**, and then press Enter.

   Excel creates a named range named *V101LastWeek*.

3. On the **Formulas** tab, in the **Defined Names** group, click **Name Manager**.

   The Name Manager dialog box opens.

4. Click the **V101LastWeek** name.

   The cell range to which the V101LastWeek name refers appears in the Refers To box at the bottom of the Name Manager dialog box.

5. Edit the cell range in the **Refers to** box to **=MilesLastWeek!$C$4:$H$4** (change the *G* to an *H*), and then click the check mark button to the left of the box.

   Excel changes the named range's definition.

![Name Manager dialog box showing V101LastWeek name with value {"159","144","124",...}, Refers To =MilesLastWeek!$C..., Scope Workbook. The Refers to box at the bottom contains =MilesLastWeek!$C$4:$H$4.]

You can make changes to a named range in the Name Manager dialog box.

6. Click **Close**.

   The Name Manager dialog box closes.

7. Select the cell range **C5:H5**.

8. On the **Formulas** tab, in the **Defined Names** group, click **Define Name**.

   The New Name dialog box opens.

9. In the **Name** field, type **V102LastWeek**.

10. Verify that the definition in the **Refers to** field is **=MilesLastWeek!$C$5:$H$5**.

11. Click **OK**.

    Excel creates the name and closes the New Name dialog box.

✖ CLEAN UP Save the VehicleMiles workbook, and then close it.

Creating Formulas to Calculate Values

After you add your data to a worksheet and define ranges to simplify data references, you can create a formula, which is an expression that performs calculations on your data. For example, you can calculate the total cost of a customer's shipments, figure the average number of packages for all Wednesdays in the month of January, or find the highest and lowest daily package volumes for a week, month, or year.

To write an Excel formula, you begin the cell's contents with an equal (=) sign; when Excel sees it, it knows that the expression following it should be interpreted as a calculation, not text. After the equal sign, type the formula. For example, you can find the sum of the numbers in cells C2 and C3 by using the formula =C2+C3. After you have entered a formula into a cell, you can revise it by clicking the cell and then editing the formula in the formula box. For example, you can change the preceding formula to =C3-C2, which calculates the difference between the contents of cells C2 and C3.

Troubleshooting If Excel treats your formula as text, make sure that you haven't accidentally put a space before the equal sign. Remember, the equal sign must be the first character!

Typing the cell references for 15 or 20 cells in a calculation would be tedious, but Excel makes it easy to enter complex calculations. To create a new calculation, click the Formulas tab, and then in the Function Library group, click Insert Function. The Insert Function dialog box opens, with a list of functions, or predefined formulas, from which you can choose.

You can locate a function, if you don't know its name, by entering key descriptors in the Search For A Function box and then clicking Go.

The following table describes some of the most useful functions in the list.

Function	Description
SUM	Finds the sum of the numbers in the specified cells
AVERAGE	Finds the average of the numbers in the specified cells
COUNT	Finds the number of entries in the specified cells
MAX	Finds the largest value in the specified cells
MIN	Finds the smallest value in the specified cells

Two other functions you might use are the *NOW* and *PMT* functions. The *NOW* function displays the time Excel updated the workbook's formulas, so the value will change every time the workbook recalculates. The proper form for this function is *=NOW()*. To update the value to the current date and time, just press the F9 key or display the Formulas tab and then, in the Calculation group, click the Calculate Now button. You could, for example, use the *NOW* function to calculate the elapsed time from when you started a process to the present time.

The *PMT* function is a bit more complex. It calculates payments due on a loan, assuming a constant interest rate and constant payments. To perform its calculations, the *PMT* function requires an interest rate, the number of payments, and the starting balance. The elements to be entered into the function are called *arguments* and must be entered in a certain order. That order is written as *PMT(rate, nper, pv, fv, type)*. The following table summarizes the arguments in the *PMT* function.

Argument	Description
rate	The interest rate, to be divided by 12 for a loan with monthly payments, by 4 for quarterly payments, and so on
nper	The total number of payments for the loan
pv	The amount loaned (*pv* is short for *present value*, or principal)
fv	The amount to be left over at the end of the payment cycle (usually left blank, which indicates 0)
type	0 or 1, indicating whether payments are made at the beginning or at the end of the month (usually left blank, which indicates 0, or the end of the month)

If Consolidated Messenger wanted to borrow $2,000,000 at a 6 percent interest rate and pay the loan back over 24 months, you could use the *PMT* function to figure out the monthly payments. In this case, the function would be written =*PMT(6%/12, 24, 2000000)*, which calculates a monthly payment of $88,641.22.

You can also use the names of any ranges you defined to supply values for a formula. For example, if the named range NortheastPreviousDay refers to cells C4:I4, you can calculate the average of cells C4:I4 with the formula =*AVERAGE(NortheastPreviousDay)*. With Excel, you can add functions, named ranges, and table references to your formulas more efficiently by using the Formula AutoComplete capability. Just as AutoComplete offers to fill in a cell's text value when Excel recognizes that the value you're typing matches a previous entry, Formula AutoComplete offers to help you fill in a function, named range, or table reference while you create a formula.

As an example, consider a worksheet that contains a two-column Excel table named *Exceptions*. The first column is labeled *Route*; the second is labeled *Count*.

Route	Count
101	7
102	0
103	4
104	6
105	18
106	12
107	3
108	3
109	8
110	9
111	8
112	18
113	12
114	16
115	12
116	9
117	10
118	6
119	10
120	4

You can reference and entire column in a formula by using the column name.

You refer to a table by typing the table name, followed by the column or row name in square brackets. For example, the table reference *Exceptions[Count]* would refer to the Count column in the Exceptions table.

To create a formula that finds the total number of exceptions by using the *SUM* function, you begin by typing =*SU*. When you type the letter *S*, Formula AutoComplete lists functions that begin with the letter *S*; when you type the letter *U*, Excel narrows the list down to the functions that start with the letters *SU*.

The AutoComplete list suggests functions that begin with the letters you type.

To add the *SUM* function (followed by an opening parenthesis) to the formula, click *SUM* and then press Tab. To begin adding the table reference, type the letter *E*. Excel displays a list of available functions, tables, and named ranges that start with the letter *E*. Click Exceptions, and press Tab to add the table reference to the formula. Then, because you want to summarize the values in the table's Count column, type a left square bracket and then, in the list of available table items, click Count. To finish creating the formula, type a right square bracket followed by a right parenthesis to create the formula *=SUM(Exceptions[Count])*.

If you want to include a series of contiguous cells in a formula, but you haven't defined the cells as a named range, you can click the first cell in the range and drag to the last cell. If the cells aren't contiguous, hold down the Ctrl key and select all of the cells to be included. In both cases, when you release the mouse button, the references of the cells you selected appear in the formula.

You can enter cells and cell ranges in a formula by selecting the cells while creating the formula.

Troubleshooting The appearance of buttons and groups on the ribbon changes depending on the width of the program window. For information about changing the appearance of the ribbon to match our screen images, see "Modifying the Display of the Ribbon" at the beginning of this book.

After you create a formula, you can copy it and paste it into another cell. When you do, Excel tries to change the formula so that it works in the new cells. For instance, suppose you have a worksheet where cell D8 contains the formula *=SUM(C2:C6)*. Clicking cell D8, copying the cell's contents, and then pasting the result into cell D16 writes *=SUM(C10:C14)* into cell D16. Excel has reinterpreted the formula so that it fits the surrounding cells! Excel knows it can reinterpret the cells used in the formula because the formula uses a relative reference, or a reference that can change if the formula is copied to another cell. Relative references are written with just the cell row and column (for example, *C14*).

Relative references are useful when you summarize rows of data and want to use the same formula for each row. As an example, suppose you have a worksheet with two columns of data, labeled *SalePrice* and *Rate*, and you want to calculate your sales representative's commission by multiplying the two values in a row. To calculate the commission for the first sale, you would type the formula *=B4*C4* in cell D4.

The formula is displayed in the formula bar, and its result is displayed in the cell.

Selecting cell D4 and dragging the fill handle until it covers cells D4:D9 copies the formula from cell D4 into each of the other cells. Because you created the formula using relative references, Excel updates each cell's formula to reflect its position relative to the starting cell (in this case, cell D4.) The formula in cell D9, for example, is *=B9*C9*.

Copying a formula to other cells automatically updates cell references to reflect the new location.

You can use a similar technique when you add a formula to an Excel table column. If the sale price and rate data were in an Excel table and you created the formula *=B4*C4* in cell D4, Excel would apply the formula to every other cell in the column. Because you used relative references in the formula, the formulas would change to reflect each cell's distance from the original cell.

In an Excel table, changing a formula in one cell automatically changes it in related cells.

If you want a cell reference to remain constant when the formula using it is copied to another cell, you can use an absolute reference. To write a cell reference as an absolute reference, type $ before the row letter and the column number. For example, if you want the formula in cell D16 to show the sum of values in cells C10 through C14 regardless of the cell into which it is pasted, you can write the formula as =SUM($C$10:$C$14).

Tip Another way to ensure your cell references don't change when you copy the formula to another cell is to click the cell that contains the formula, copy the formula's text in the formula bar, press the Esc key to exit cut-and-copy mode, click the cell where you want to paste the formula, and press Ctrl+V. Excel doesn't change the cell references when you copy your formula to another cell in this manner.

One quick way to change a cell reference from relative to absolute is to select the cell reference in the formula box and then press F4. Pressing F4 cycles a cell reference through the four possible types of references:

- Relative columns and rows (for example, C4)
- Absolute columns and rows (for example, $C$4)
- Relative columns and absolute rows (for example, C$4)
- Absolute columns and relative rows (for example, $C4)

In this exercise, you'll create a formula manually, revise it to include additional cells, create a formula that contains an Excel table reference, create a formula with relative references, and change the formula so it contains absolute references.

SET UP You need the ITExpenses_start workbook located in your Chapter10 practice file folder to complete this exercise. Open the ITExpenses_start workbook, and save it as *ITExpenses*. Then follow the steps.

1. If necessary, display the **Summary** worksheet. Then, in cell **F9**, type =C4, and press Enter.

   The value *$385,671.00* appears in cell F9.

2. Select cell **F9** and type =SU.

   Excel erases the existing formula, and Formula AutoComplete displays a list of possible functions to use in the formula.

3. In the **Formula AutoComplete** list, click **SUM**, and then press Tab.

   Excel changes the contents of the formula bar to *=SUM(*.

4. Select the cell range **C3:C8**, type a right parenthesis ( )) to make the formula bar's contents *=SUM(C3:C8)*, and then press Enter.

   The value *$2,562,966.00* appears in cell F9.

5. In cell **F10**, type =SUM(C4:C5), and then press Enter.

6. Select cell **F10**, and then in the formula box, select the cell reference **C4**, and press F4.

   Excel changes the cell reference to *$C$4*.

7. In the formula box, select the cell reference **C5**, press F4, and then press Enter.

   Excel changes the cell reference to *$C$5*.

8. On the tab bar, click the **JuneLabor** sheet tab.

   The JuneLabor worksheet opens.

9. In cell **F13**, type =SUM(J.

   Excel displays JuneSummary, the name of the table in the JuneLabor worksheet.

10. Press Tab.

    Excel extends the formula to read *=SUM(JuneSummary*.

11. Type **[**, and then in the **Formula AutoComplete** list, click **Labor Expense**, and press Tab.

Excel extends the formula to read *=SUM(JuneSummary[Labor Expense*.

The Formula AutoComplete list suggests suitable formula elements.

12. Type **])** to complete the formula, and then press Enter.

The value *$637,051.00* appears in cell F13.

✖ CLEAN UP Save the ITExpenses workbook, and then close it.

Summarizing Data That Meets Specific Conditions

Another use for formulas is to display messages when certain conditions are met. For instance, Consolidated Messenger's Vice President of Marketing, Craig Dewar, might have agreed to examine the rates charged to corporate customers who were billed for more than $100,000 during a calendar year. This kind of formula is called a *conditional formula*; one way to create a conditional formula in Excel is to use the *IF* function. To create a conditional formula, you click the cell to hold the formula and open the Insert Function dialog box. From within the dialog box, click *IF* in the list of available functions, and then click OK. When you do, the Function Arguments dialog box opens.

The IF function returns one value if a specified condition is true, and another if it is false.

When you work with an *IF* function, the Function Arguments dialog box has three boxes: Logical_test, Value_if_true, and Value_if_false. The Logical_test box holds the condition you want to check. If the customer's year-to-date shipping bill appears in cell G8, the expression would be *G8>100000*.

Now you need to have Excel display messages that indicate whether Craig Dewar should evaluate the account for a possible rate adjustment. To have Excel print a message from an *IF* function, you enclose the message in quotes in the Value_if_true or Value_if_false box. In this case, you would type *"High-volume shipper—evaluate for rate decrease."* in the Value_if_true box and *"Does not qualify at this time."* in the Value_if_false box.

Excel also includes several other conditional functions you can use to summarize your data, shown in the following table.

Function	Description
AVERAGEIF	Finds the average of values within a cell range that meet a given criterion
AVERAGEIFS	Finds the average of values within a cell range that meet multiple criteria
COUNT	Counts the number of cells in a range that contain a numerical value
COUNTA	Counts the number of cells in a range that are not empty
COUNTBLANK	Counts the number of cells in a range that are empty
COUNTIF	Counts the number of cells in a range that meet a given criterion
COUNTIFS	Counts the number of cells in a range that meet multiple criteria
IFERROR	Displays one value if a formula results in an error and another if it doesn't
SUMIF	Finds the sum of values in a range that meet a single criterion
SUMIFS	Finds the sum of values in a range that meet multiple criteria

You can use the *IFERROR* function to display a custom error message, instead of relying on the default Excel error messages to explain what happened. For example, you could use an *IFERROR* formula when looking up the CustomerID value from cell G8 in the Customers table by using the *VLOOKUP* function. One way to create such a formula is =*IFERROR(VLOOKUP(G8,Customers,2,false),"Customer not found")*. If the function finds a match for the CustomerID in cell G8, it displays the customer's name; if it doesn't find a match, it displays the text *Customer not found*.

See Also For more information about the VLOOKUP function, refer to *Microsoft Excel 2010 Step by Step*, by Curtis Frye (Microsoft Press, 2010).

Just as the *COUNTIF* function counts the number of cells that meet a criterion and the *SUMIF* function finds the total of values in cells that meet a criterion, the *AVERAGEIF* function finds the average of values in cells that meet a criterion. To create a formula using the *AVERAGEIF* function, you define the range to be examined for the criterion, the criterion, and, if required, the range from which to draw the values. As an example, consider a worksheet that lists each customer's ID number, name, state, and total monthly shipping bill.

A sample worksheet containing values necessary to create a formula.

If you want to find the average order of customers from the state of Washington (abbreviated in the worksheet as WA), you can create the formula =*AVERAGEIF(D3:D6, "WA", E3:E6)*.

The *AVERAGEIFS*, *SUMIFS*, and *COUNTIFS* functions extend the capabilities of the *AVERAGEIF*, *SUMIF*, and *COUNTIF* functions to allow for multiple criteria. If you want to find the sum of all orders of at least $100,000 placed by companies in Washington, you can create the formula =*SUMIFS(E3:E6, D3:D6, "=WA", E3:E6, ">=100000")*.

The *AVERAGEIFS* and *SUMIFS* functions start with a data range that contains values that the formula summarizes; you then list the data ranges and the criteria to apply to that range. In generic terms, the syntax runs =*AVERAGEIFS(data_range, criteria_range1, criteria1[,criteria_range2, criteria2...])*. The part of the syntax in square brackets (which aren't used when you create the formula) is optional, so an *AVERAGEIFS* or *SUMIFS* formula that contains a single criterion will work. The *COUNTIFS* function, which doesn't perform any calculations, doesn't need a data range—you just provide the criteria ranges and criteria. For example, you could find the number of customers from Washington who were billed at least $100,000 by using the formula =*COUNTIFS(D3:D6, "=WA", E3:E6, ">=100000")*.

In this exercise, you'll create a conditional formula that displays a message if a condition is true, find the average of worksheet values that meet one criterion, and find the sum of worksheet values that meet two criteria.

→ **SET UP** You need the PackagingCosts_start workbook located in your Chapter10 practice file folder to complete this exercise. Open the PackagingCosts_start workbook, and save it as *PackagingCosts*. Then follow the steps.

1. In cell **G3**, type the formula =**IF(F3>=35000, "Request discount", "No discount available")**, and press Enter.

   Excel accepts the formula, which displays *Request discount* if the value in cell F3 is at least 35,000 and displays *No discount available* if not. The value *Request discount* appears in cell G3.

2. Click cell **G3**, and drag the fill handle down until it covers cell **G14**.

   Excel copies the formula in cell G3 to cells G4:G14, adjusting the formula to reflect the cells' addresses. The results of the copied formulas appear in cells G4:G14.

3. In cell **I3**, type the formula =**AVERAGEIF(C3:C14, "=Box", F3:F14)**, and press Enter.

   The value *$46,102.50*, which represents the average cost per category of boxes, appears in cell I3.

4. In cell **I6**, type =**SUMIFS(F3:F14, C3:C14, "=Envelope", E3:E14, "=International")**.

   The value *$45,753.00*, which represents the total cost of all envelopes used for international shipments, appears in cell I6.

You can create a formula anywhere on a worksheet.

✖ CLEAN UP Save the PackagingCosts workbook, and then close it.

Finding and Correcting Errors in Calculations

Including calculations in a worksheet gives you valuable answers to questions about your data. As is always true, however, it is possible for errors to creep into your formulas. With Excel, you can find the source of errors in your formulas by identifying the cells used in a given calculation and describing any errors that have occurred. The process of examining a worksheet for errors is referred to as *auditing*.

Excel identifies errors in several ways. The first way is to display an error code in the cell holding the formula generating the error.

Error codes begin with a number sign (#).

When a cell with an erroneous formula is the active cell, an Error button is displayed next to it. Pointing to the Error button displays an arrow. Clicking the arrow displays a menu with options that provide information about the error and offer to help you fix it.

The following table lists the most common error codes and what they mean.

Error code	Description
#####	The column isn't wide enough to display the value.
#VALUE!	The formula has the wrong type of argument (such as text in a cell where a numerical value is required).
#NAME?	The formula contains text that Excel doesn't recognize (such as an unknown named range).
#REF!	The formula refers to a cell that doesn't exist (which can happen whenever cells are deleted).
#DIV/0!	The formula attempts to divide by zero.

Another technique you can use to find the source of formula errors is to ensure that the appropriate cells are providing values for the formula. For example, you might want to calculate the total number of deliveries for a service level, but you could accidentally create a formula referring to the service levels' names instead of their package quantities. You can identify the source of an error by having Excel trace a cell's *precedents*, which are the cells with values used in the active cell's formula. To do so, click the Formulas tab, and then in the Formula Auditing group, click Trace Precedents. When you do, Excel identifies those cells by drawing a blue tracer arrow from the precedents to the active cell.

You can also audit your worksheet by identifying cells with formulas that use a value from a given cell. For example, you might use one region's daily package total in a formula that calculates the average number of packages delivered for all regions on a given day. Cells that use another cell's value in their calculations are known as *dependents*, meaning that they depend on the value in the other cell to derive their own value. As with tracing precedents, you can click the Formulas tab, and then in the Formula Auditing group, click Trace Dependents.

Excel draws blue arrows from the active cell to those cells that have calculations based on that value.

If the cells identified by the tracer arrows aren't the correct cells, you can hide the arrows and correct the formula. To hide the tracer arrows on a worksheet, display the Formulas tab, and then in the Formula Auditing group, click Remove Arrows.

If you prefer to have the elements of a formula error presented as text in a dialog box, you can use the Error Checking dialog box to view the error and the formula in the cell in which the error occurs. To display the Error Checking dialog box, display the Formulas tab, and then in the Formula Auditing group, click the Error Checking button. You can use the controls in the Error Checking dialog box to move through the formula one step at a time, to choose to ignore the error, or to move to the next or the previous error. If you click the Options button in the dialog box, you can also use the controls in the Excel Options dialog box to change how Excel determines what is an error and what isn't.

You can have the Error Checking tool ignore formulas that don't use every cell in a region (such as a row or column).

Tip If you clear the Formulas That Omit Cells In A Region check box, you can create formulas that don't add up every value in a row, column, or range without Excel displaying an error.

For times when you just want to display the results of each step of a formula and don't need the full power of the Error Checking tool, you can use the Evaluate Formula dialog box to move through each element of the formula. To display the Evaluate Formula dialog box, you display the Formulas tab and then, in the Formula Auditing group, click the Evaluate Formula button. The Evaluate Formula dialog box is much more useful for examining formulas that don't produce an error but aren't generating the result you expect.

Finally, you can monitor the value in a cell regardless of where in your workbook you are by opening a Watch Window that displays the value in the cell. For example, if one of your formulas uses values from cells in other worksheets or even other workbooks, you can set a watch on the cell that contains the formula and then change the values in the other cells. To set a watch, click the cell you want to monitor, and then on the Formulas tab, in the Formula Auditing group, click Watch Window. Click Add Watch to have Excel monitor the selected cell.

As soon as you type in the new value, the Watch Window displays the new result of the formula. When you're done watching the formula, select the watch, click Delete Watch, and close the Watch Window.

In this exercise, you'll use the formula-auditing capabilities in Excel to identify and correct errors in a formula.

SET UP You need the ConveyerBid_start workbook located in your Chapter10 practice file folder to complete this exercise. Open the ConveyerBid_start workbook, and save it as *ConveyerBid*. Then follow the steps.

1. Click cell **D20**.

2. On the **Formulas** tab, in the **Formula Auditing** group, click **Watch Window**.

   The Watch Window opens.

Watch Window

In the Watch Window, you can monitor the results of selected formulas.

3. Click **Add Watch**, and then in the **Add Watch** dialog box, click **Add**.

   Cell D20 appears in the Watch Window.

4. Click cell **D8**.

   =SUM(C3:C7) appears in the formula bar.

5. In the **Formula Auditing** group, click the **Trace Precedents** button.

   A blue arrow begins at the cell range C3:C7 and points to cell D8.

The auditing arrow indicates that the cells in the range C3:C7 provide the value for the formula in cell D8.

6. In the **Formula Auditing** group, click the **Remove Arrows** button.

The arrow disappears.

7. Click cell **A1**.

8. In the **Formula Auditing** group, click the **Error Checking** button.

The Error Checking dialog box opens.

The dialog box displays the error found in cell D1.

9. Click **Next**.

   Excel displays a message box indicating that there are no more errors in the worksheet.

10. Click **OK**.

    The message box and the Error Checking dialog box close.

11. In the **Formula Auditing** group, click the **Error Checking** arrow, and then in the list, click **Trace Error**.

    Blue arrows appear, pointing to cell D21 from cells C12 and D19. These arrows indicate that using the values (or lack of values, in this case) in the indicated cells generates the error in cell D21.

12. In the **Formula Auditing** group, click **Remove Arrows**.

    The arrows disappear.

13. In the formula box, delete the existing formula, type =**C12/D20**, and press Enter.

    The value *14%* appears in cell D21.

14. Click cell **D21**.

15. In the **Formula Auditing** group, click the **Evaluate Formula** button.

    The Evaluate Formula dialog box opens.

The dialog box displays the formula from cell D21.

16. Click **Evaluate** three times to step through the formula's elements, and then click **Close**.

    The Evaluate Formula dialog box closes.

17. In the **Watch Window**, click the watch in the list.

18. Click **Delete Watch**.

   The watch disappears.

19. On the **Formulas** tab, in the **Formula Auditing** group, click **Watch Window**.

   The Watch Window closes.

 CLEAN UP Save the ConveyerBid workbook, and then close it. If you are not continuing directly to the next chapter, exit Excel.

Key Points

- You can add a group of cells to a formula by typing the formula, and then at the spot in the formula in which you want to name the cells, selecting the cells by using the mouse.

- By creating named ranges, you can refer to entire blocks of cells with a single term, saving you lots of time and effort. You can use a similar technique with table data, referring to an entire table or one or more table columns.

- When you write a formula, be sure you use absolute referencing ($A$1) if you want the formula to remain the same when it's copied from one cell to another, or use relative referencing (A1) if you want the formula to change to reflect its new position in the worksheet.

- Instead of typing a formula from scratch, you can use the Insert Function dialog box to help you on your way.

- You can monitor how the value in a cell changes by adding a watch to the Watch Window.

- To see which formulas refer to the values in the selected cell, use Trace Dependents; if you want to see which cells provide values for the formula in the active cell, use Trace Precedents.

- You can step through the calculations of a formula in the Evaluate Formula dialog box or go through a more rigorous error-checking procedure by using the Error Checking tool.

Chapter at a Glance

Define styles,
page 316

Format cells,
page 310

Apply workbook
themes and
Excel table styles,
page 320

Make numbers
easier to read,
page 327

Change the
appearance of
data based on
its value,
page 332

Add images to
worksheets, **page 339**

11 Change Workbook Appearance

In this chapter, you will learn how to

✔ Format cells.

✔ Define styles.

✔ Apply workbook themes and Excel table styles.

✔ Make numbers easier to read.

✔ Change the appearance of data based on its value.

✔ Add images to worksheets.

Entering data into a workbook efficiently saves you time, but you must also ensure that your data is easy to read. Microsoft Excel 2010 gives you a wide variety of ways to make your data easier to understand; for example, you can change the font, character size, or color used to present a cell's contents. Changing how data appears on a worksheet helps set the contents of a cell apart from the contents of surrounding cells. The simplest example of that concept is a data label. If a column on your worksheet contains a list of days, you can easily set apart a label (for example, *Day*) by presenting it in bold type that's noticeably larger than the type used to present the data to which it refers. To save time, you can define a number of custom formats and then apply them quickly to the desired cells.

You might also want to specially format a cell's contents to reflect the value in that cell. For example, Lori Penor, the chief operating officer of Consolidated Messenger, might want to create a worksheet that displays the percentage of improperly delivered packages from each regional distribution center. If that percentage exceeds a threshold, she could have Excel display a red traffic light icon, indicating that the center's performance is out of tolerance and requires attention.

In this chapter, you'll learn how to change the appearance of data, apply existing formats to data, make numbers easier to read, change data's appearance based on its value, and add images to worksheets.

> **Practice Files** Before you can complete the exercises in this chapter, you need to copy the book's practice files to your computer. The practice files you'll use to complete the exercises in this chapter are in the Chapter11 practice file folder. A complete list of practice files is provided in "Using the Practice Files" at the beginning of this book.

Formatting Cells

Excel spreadsheets can hold and process lots of data, but when you manage numerous spreadsheets it can be hard to remember from a worksheet's title exactly what data is kept in that worksheet. Data labels give you and your colleagues information about data in a worksheet, but it's important to format the labels so that they stand out visually. To make your data labels or any other data stand out, you can change the format of the cells that hold your data.

▲	A	B	C	D	E	F
1						
2						
3						
4		**Call Volume**				
5		Northeast	13,769			
6		Atlantic	19,511			
7		Southeast	11,111			
8		North Central	24,972			
9		Midwest	11,809			
10		Southwest	20,339			
11		Mountain West	20,127			
12		Northwest	12,137			
13		Central	20,047			
14						
15						
16						
17						

Include data labels to identify the data in a worksheet.

Most of the tools you need to change a cell's format can be found on the Home tab. You can apply the formatting represented on a button by selecting the cells you want to apply the style to and then clicking that button. If you want to set your data labels apart by making them appear bold, click the Bold button. If you have already made a cell's contents bold, selecting the cell and clicking the Bold button will remove the formatting.

Tip Deleting a cell's contents doesn't delete the cell's formatting. To delete a selected cell's formatting, on the Home tab, in the Editing group, click the Clear button (which looks like an eraser), and then click Clear Formats. Clicking Clear All from the same list will remove the cell's contents and formatting.

Buttons in the Home tab's Font group that give you choices, such as the Font Color button, have an arrow at the right edge of the button. Clicking the arrow displays a list of options accessible for that button, such as the fonts available on your system or the colors you can assign to a cell.

The Font Color gallery.

Another way you can make a cell stand apart from its neighbors is to add a border around the cell. To place a border around one or more cells, select the cells, and then choose the border type you want by selecting from the Border list in the Font group. Excel does provide more options: To display the full range of border types and styles, in the Border list, click More Borders. The Format Cells dialog box opens, displaying the Border page.

The Border page of the Format Cells dialog box contains the full range of tools you can use to define your cells' borders.

You can also make a group of cells stand apart from its neighbors by changing its shading, which is the color that fills the cells. On a worksheet that tracks total package volume for the past month, Lori Penor could change the fill color of the cells holding her data labels to make the labels stand out even more than by changing the labels' text formatting.

Tip You can display the most commonly used formatting controls by right-clicking a selected range. When you do, a Mini Toolbar containing a subset of the Home tab formatting tools appears above the shortcut menu.

If you want to change the attributes of every cell in a row or column, you can click the header of the row or column you want to modify and then select your desired format.

One task you can't perform by using the tools on the Home tab is to change the standard font for a workbook, which is used in the Name box and on the formula bar. The standard font when you install Excel is Calibri, a simple font that is easy to read on a computer screen and on the printed page. If you want to choose another font, click the File tab, and then click Options. On the General page of the Excel Options dialog box, set the values in the Use This Font and Font Size list boxes to pick your new display font.

Important The new standard font doesn't take effect until you exit Excel and restart the program.

In this exercise, you'll emphasize a worksheet's title by changing the format of cell data, adding a border to a cell range, and then changing a cell range's fill color. After those tasks are complete, you'll change the default font for the workbook.

SET UP You need the VehicleMileSummary_start workbook located in your Chapter11 practice file folder to complete this exercise. Start Excel, open the VehicleMileSummary_start workbook, and save it as *VehicleMileSummary*. Then follow the steps.

1. Click cell **D2**.

2. On the **Home** tab, in the **Font** group, click the **Bold** button.

   Excel displays the cell's contents in bold type.

3. In the **Font** group, click the **Font Size** arrow, and then in the list, click **18**.

   Excel increases the size of the text in cell D2.

	A	B	C	D	E	F	G	H	I	J	K
1											
2				Vehicle Mile Summary							
3											
4			Day								
5		VehicleID	Monday	Tuesday	Wednesday	Thursday	Friday	Saturday			
6		V101	159	144	124	108	125	165			
7		V102	113	106	111	116	119	97			
8		V103	87	154	124	128	111	100			
9		V104	137	100	158	96	127	158			
10		V105	86	132	154	97	154	165			
11		V106	159	163	155	101	89	160			
12		V107	111	165	155	92	91	94			
13		V108	101	162	123	87	93	140			
14		V109	164	159	116	97	149	120			
15		V110	100	107	143	144	152	132			
16											
17											
18											

Larger text simulates a page header.

4. Click cell **B5**, hold down the Ctrl key, and click cell **C4** to select the non-contiguous cells.

5. On the **Home** tab, in the **Font** group, click the **Bold** button.

   Excel displays the cells' contents in bold type.

6. Select the cell ranges **B6:B15** and **C5:H5**.

7. In the **Font** group, click the **Italic** button.

   Excel displays the cells' contents in italic type.

⊿	A	B	C	D	E	F	G	H	I
1									
2					Vehicle Mile Summary				
3									
4			Day						
5		VehicleID	Monday	Tuesday	Wednesday	Thursday	Friday	Saturday	
6		V101	159	144	124	108	125	165	
7		V102	113	106	111	116	119	97	
8		V103	87	154	124	128	111	100	
9		V104	137	100	158	96	127	158	
10		V105	86	132	154	97	154	165	
11		V106	159	163	155	101	89	160	
12		V107	111	165	155	92	91	94	
13		V108	101	162	123	87	93	140	
14		V109	164	159	116	97	149	120	
15		V110	100	107	143	144	152	132	
16									
17									
18									

Local formatting such as bold and italic emphasizes cell content.

8. Select the cell range **C6:H15**.

9. In the **Font** group, click the **Border** arrow, and then in the list, click **Outside Borders**.

   Excel places a border around the outside edge of the selected cells.

10. Select the cell range **B4:H15**.

11. In the **Border** list, click **Thick Box Border**.

   Excel places a thick border around the outside edge of the selected cells.

12. Select the cell ranges **B4:B15** and **C4:H5**.

13. In the **Font** group, click the **Fill Color** arrow, and then in the **Standard Colors** area of the color palette, click the yellow button.

   Excel changes the selected cells' background color to yellow.

You can distinguish header cells from other cells by applying a background color.

> **Troubleshooting** The appearance of buttons and groups on the ribbon changes depending on the width of the program window. For information about changing the appearance of the ribbon to match our screen images, see "Modifying the Display of the Ribbon" at the beginning of this book.

14. Click the **File** tab, and then click **Options**.

    The Excel Options dialog box opens.

15. If necessary, click **General** to display the **General** page.

16. In the **When creating new workbooks** area, in the **Use this font** list, click **Verdana**.

    Verdana appears in the Use This Font field.

17. Click **Cancel**.

    The Excel Options dialog box closes without saving your change.

✖ **CLEAN UP** Save the VehicleMileSummary workbook, and then close it.

Defining Styles

As you work with Excel, you will probably develop preferred formats for data labels, titles, and other worksheet elements. Instead of adding a format's characteristics one element at a time to the target cells, you can have Excel store the format and recall it as needed. You can find the predefined formats by displaying the Home tab, and then in the Styles group, clicking Cell Styles.

You can choose a style from the Cell Styles gallery, or create a custom style.

Clicking a style from the Cell Styles gallery applies the style to the selected cells, but Excel also displays a live preview of a format when you point to it. If none of the existing styles is what you want, you can create your own style by clicking New Cell Style at the bottom of the gallery to display the Style dialog box. In the Style dialog box, type the name of your new style in the Style Name field, and then click Format. The Format Cells dialog box opens.

A custom style can include number, alignment, font, and border formatting.

After you set the characteristics of your new style, click OK to make your style available in the Cell Styles gallery. If you ever want to delete a custom style, display the Cell Styles gallery, right-click the style, and then click Delete.

If all you want to do is apply formatting from one cell to the contents of another cell, use the Format Painter tool in the Clipboard group on the Home tab. Just click the cell that has the format you want to copy, click the Format Painter button, and then click the cells to which you want to apply the copied format. To apply the same formatting to multiple cells, double-click the Format Painter button and then click the target cells. When you're done applying the formatting, press the Esc key.

In this exercise, you'll create a style and apply the new style to a data label.

SET UP You need the HourlyExceptions_start workbook located in your Chapter11 practice file folder to complete this exercise. Open the HourlyExceptions_start workbook, and save it as *HourlyExceptions*. Then follow the steps.

Cell
Styles ▾

1. On the **Home** tab, in the **Styles** group, click **Cell Styles**, and then click **New Cell Style**.

   The Style dialog box opens.

The elements of the current style are described in the Cell Style dialog box.

2. In the **Style name** field, type **Crosstab Column Heading**.

3. Click the **Format** button. In the **Format Cells** dialog box, click the **Alignment** tab.

You can specify the alignment and direction of text.

4. In the **Horizontal** list, click **Center**.

5. Click the **Font** tab.

6. In the **Font style** list, click **Italic**.

   The text in the Preview pane appears in italicized text.

You can make changes on multiple pages of the Format Cells dialog box before closing it.

7. Click the **Number** tab.

   The Number page of the Format Cells dialog box is displayed.

8. In the **Category** list, click **Time**.

   The available time formats appear.

9. In the **Type** pane, click **1:30 PM**.

10. Click **OK** to save your changes.

    The Format Cells dialog box closes, and your new style's definition appears in the Style dialog box.

11. Click **OK**.

    The Style dialog box closes.

12. Select cells **C4:N4**.

13. On the **Home** tab, in the **Styles** group, click **Cell Styles**.

The Cell Styles gallery opens.

Custom					
Crosstab Col...					
Good, Bad and Neutral					
Normal	Crosstab Column Heading	Good	Neutral		
Data and Model					
Calculation	Check Cell	Explanatory ...	Input	Linked Cell	Note
Output	Warning Text				
Titles and Headings					
Heading 1	Heading 2	Heading 3	Heading 4	Title	Total
Themed Cell Styles					
20% - Accent1	20% - Accent2	20% - Accent3	20% - Accent4	20% - Accent5	20% - Accent6
40% - Accent1	40% - Accent2	40% - Accent3	40% - Accent4	40% - Accent5	40% - Accent6
60% - Accent1	60% - Accent2	60% - Accent3	60% - Accent4	60% - Accent5	60% - Accent6
Accent1	Accent2	Accent3	Accent4	Accent5	Accent6
Number Format					
Comma	Comma [0]	Currency	Currency [0]	Percent	

New Cell Style...
Merge Styles...

Your new style appears at the top of the gallery, in the Custom group.

14. Click the **Crosstab Column Heading** style.

Excel applies your new style to the selected cells.

✖ **CLEAN UP** Save the HourlyExceptions workbook, and then close it.

Applying Workbook Themes and Excel Table Styles

Microsoft Office 2010 includes powerful design tools that enable you to create attractive, professional documents quickly. The Excel product team implemented the new design capabilities by defining workbook themes and Excel table styles. A theme is a way to specify the fonts, colors, and graphic effects that appear in a workbook. Excel comes with many themes installed.

To apply an existing workbook theme, display the Page Layout tab. Then, in the Themes group, click Themes, and click the theme you want to apply to your workbook. By default, Excel applies the Office theme to your workbooks.

You can choose from among dozens of preformatted visual themes.

When you want to format a workbook element, Excel displays colors that are available within the active theme. For example, selecting a worksheet cell and then clicking the Font Color arrow displays a palette of colors. The theme colors appear at the top of the color palette—the standard colors and the More Colors link, which displays the Colors dialog box, appear at the bottom of the palette.

If you format workbook elements by using colors from the Theme Colors area, applying a different theme changes that object's colors.

You can change a theme's colors, fonts, and graphic effects by displaying the Page Layout tab and then, in the Themes group, selecting new values from the Colors, Fonts, and Effects lists. To save your changes as a new theme, display the Page Layout tab, and in the Themes group, click Themes, and then click Save Current Theme. Use the controls in the Save Current Theme dialog box that opens to record your theme for later use. Later, when you click the Themes button, your custom theme will appear at the top of the gallery.

Tip When you save a theme, you save it as an Office Theme file. You can apply the theme to other Office 2010 documents as well.

Just as you can define and apply themes to entire workbooks, you can apply and define Excel table styles. You select an Excel table's initial style when you create it; to create a new style, display the Home tab, and in the Styles group, click Format As Table. In the Format As Table gallery, click New Table Style to display the New Table Quick Style dialog box.

You can apply a standard Excel table style or create a custom table style.

Type a name for the new style, select the first table element you want to format, and then click Format to display the Format Cells dialog box. Define the element's formatting, and then click OK. When the New Table Quick Style dialog box reopens, its Preview pane displays the overall table style and the Element Formatting area describes the selected element's appearance. Also, in the Table Element list, Excel displays the element's name in bold to indicate it has been changed. To make the new style the default for new Excel tables created in the current workbook, select the Set As Default Table Quick Style For This Document check box. When you click OK, Excel saves the new table style.

Tip To remove formatting from a table element, click the name of the table element and then click the Clear button.

In this exercise, you'll create a new workbook theme, change a workbook's theme, create a new table style, and apply the new style to an Excel table.

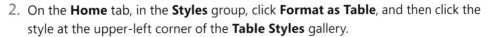

SET UP You need the HourlyTracking_start workbook located in your Chapter11 practice file folder to complete this exercise. Open the HourlyTracking_start workbook, and save it as *HourlyTracking*. Then follow the steps.

Format as Table ▾

1. If necessary, click any cell in the Excel table.

2. On the **Home** tab, in the **Styles** group, click **Format as Table**, and then click the style at the upper-left corner of the **Table Styles** gallery.

   Excel applies the style to the table.

3. On the **Home** tab, in the **Styles** group, click **Format as Table**, and then click **New Table Style**.

   The New Table Quick Style dialog box opens.

4. In the **Name** field, type **Exception Default**.

5. In the **Table Element** list, click **Header Row**.

6. Click **Format**.

   The Format Cells dialog box opens.

7. Click the **Fill** tab.

   The Fill page is displayed.

The fill colors shown in the palette are specific to the currently applied theme.

8. In the first row of color squares, just below the **No Color** button, click the third square from the left.

   The new background color appears in the Sample pane of the dialog box.

9. Click **OK**.

The Format Cells dialog box closes. When the New Table Quick Style dialog box reopens, the Header Row table element appears in bold, and the Preview pane's header row is shaded.

10. In the **Table Element** list, click **Second Row Stripe**, and then click **Format**.

    The Format Cells dialog box opens.

11. Just below the **No Color** button, click the third square from the left again.

    The new background color appears in the Sample pane of the dialog box.

12. Click **OK**.

    The Format Cells dialog box closes. When the New Table Quick Style dialog box reopens, the Second Row Stripe table element appears in bold, and every second row is shaded in the Preview pane.

The effect of your changes is shown in the Preview area.

13. Click **OK**.

The New Table Quick Style dialog box closes.

14. On the **Home** tab, in the **Styles** group, click **Format as Table**. In the gallery, in the **Custom** area, click the new format.

Excel applies the new format.

15. On the **Page Layout** tab, in the **Themes** group, click the **Fonts** arrow, and then in the list, click **Verdana**.

Excel changes the theme's font to Verdana (which is part of the Aspect font set).

	A	B	C	D	E	F	G	H	I
1									
2		Day	Region	Hour	Exceptions				
3		7/29/2010	Northeast	5:00 PM	104				
4		7/29/2010	Atlantic	5:00 PM	37				
5		7/29/2010	Southeast	5:00 PM	22				
6		7/29/2010	North Central	5:00 PM	19				
7		7/29/2010	Midwest	5:00 PM	37				
8		7/29/2010	Southwest	5:00 PM	72				
9		7/29/2010	Mountain West	5:00 PM	8				
10		7/29/2010	Northwest	5:00 PM	35				
11		7/29/2010	Central	5:00 PM	14				
12		7/29/2010	Northeast	6:00 PM	119				
13		7/29/2010	Atlantic	6:00 PM	44				
14		7/29/2010	Southeast	6:00 PM	37				
15		7/29/2010	North Central	6:00 PM	28				
16		7/29/2010	Midwest	6:00 PM	45				
17		7/29/2010	Southwest	6:00 PM	75				
18		7/29/2010	Mountain West	6:00 PM	10				
19		7/29/2010	Northwest	6:00 PM	44				
20		7/29/2010	Central	6:00 PM	17				

After changing a theme's colors, fonts, or effects, you can save the theme for reuse as a custom theme.

16. In the **Themes** group, click the **Themes** button, and then click **Save Current Theme**.

The Save Current Theme dialog box opens.

Custom themes are stored with other Office templates.

17. In the **File name** field, type **Verdana Office**, and then click **Save**.

    Excel saves your theme.

18. In the **Themes** group, click the **Themes** button, and then click **Origin**.

    Excel applies the new theme to your workbook.

✖ **CLEAN UP** Save the HourlyTracking workbook, and then close it.

Making Numbers Easier to Read

Changing the format of the cells in your worksheet can make your data much easier to read, both by setting data labels apart from the actual data and by adding borders to define the boundaries between labels and data even more clearly. Of course, using formatting options to change the font and appearance of a cell's contents doesn't help with idiosyncratic data types such as dates, phone numbers, or currency values.

As an example, consider U.S. phone numbers. These numbers are 10 digits long and have a 3-digit area code, a 3-digit exchange, and a 4-digit line number written in the form (###) ###-####. Although it's certainly possible to type a phone number with the expected formatting in a cell, it's much simpler to type a sequence of 10 digits and have Excel change the data's appearance.

You can tell Excel to expect a phone number in a cell by opening the Format Cells dialog box to the Number page and displaying the formats available for the Special category.

The Type list displays special formats that are specific to the location selected in the Locale list.

Clicking Phone Number in the Type list tells Excel to format 10-digit numbers in the standard phone number format. You can see this in operation if you compare the contents of the active cell and the contents of the formula box for a cell with the Phone Number formatting.

Troubleshooting If you type a 9-digit number in a field that expects a phone number, you won't see an error message; instead, you'll see a 2-digit area code. For example, the number 425550012 would be displayed as (42) 555-0012. An 11-digit number would be displayed with a 4-digit area code. If the phone number doesn't look right, you probably left out a digit or included an extra one, so you should make sure your entry is correct.

The Phone Number format applied to the number shown in the formula box.

Just as you can instruct Excel to expect a phone number in a cell, you can also have it expect a date or a currency amount. You can make those changes from the Format Cells dialog box by choosing either the Date category or the Currency category. The Date category enables you to pick the format for the date (and determine whether the date's appearance changes due to the Locale setting of the operating system on the computer viewing the workbook). In a similar vein, selecting the Currency category displays controls to set the number of places after the decimal point, the currency symbol to use, and the way in which Excel should display negative numbers.

Tip The Excel user interface enables you to make the most common format changes by displaying the Home tab of the ribbon and then, in the Number group, either clicking a button representing a built-in format or selecting a format from the Number Format list.

You can also create a custom numeric format to add a word or phrase to a number in a cell. For example, you can add the phrase *per month* to a cell with a formula that calculates average monthly sales for a year to ensure that you and your colleagues will recognize the figure as a monthly average. To create a custom number format, click the Home tab, and then click the Number dialog box launcher (found at the bottom right corner of the Number group on the ribbon) to display the Format Cells dialog box. Then, if necessary, click the Number tab.

In the Category list, click Custom to display the available custom number formats in the Type list. You can then click the base format you want and modify it in the Type box. For example, clicking the 0.00 format causes Excel to format any number in a cell with two digits to the right of the decimal point.

Tip The zeros in the format indicate that the position in the format can accept any number as a valid value.

To customize the format, click in the Type box and add any symbols or text you want to the format. For example, typing a dollar ($) sign to the left of the existing format and then typing *"per month"* (including quote marks) to the right of the existing format causes the number 1500 to be displayed as *$1500.00 per month*.

Important You need to enclose any text to be displayed as part of the format in quotes so that Excel recognizes the text as a string to be displayed in the cell.

In this exercise, you'll assign date, phone number, and currency formats to ranges of cells.

SET UP You need the ExecutiveSearch_start workbook located in your Chapter11 practice file folder to complete this exercise. Open the ExecutiveSearch_start workbook, and save it as *ExecutiveSearch*. Then follow the steps.

1. Click cell **A3**.

2. On the **Home** tab, click the **Font** dialog box launcher.

   The Format Cells dialog box opens.

3. If necessary, click the **Number** tab.

4. In the **Category** list, click **Date**.

   The Type list appears with a list of date formats.

The Type list displays date formats that are specific to the location selected in the Locale list.

5. In the **Type** list, click **3/14/01**.

6. Click **OK** to assign the chosen format to the cell.

   Excel displays the contents of cell A3 to reflect the new format.

7. Click cell **G3**.

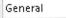

8. On the **Home** tab, in the **Number** group, click the **Number Format** button's down arrow and then click **More Number Formats**.

9. If necessary, click the **Number** tab in the **Format Cells** dialog box.

10. In the **Category** list, click **Special**.

    The Type list appears with a list of special formats.

11. In the **Type** list, click **Phone Number**, and then click **OK**.

    Excel displays the contents of the cell as (425) 555-0102, matching the format you selected, and the Format Cells dialog box closes.

12. Click cell **H3**.

13. Click the **Font** dialog box launcher.

14. In the **Format Cells** dialog box that opens, click the **Number** tab.

15. In the **Category** list, click **Custom**.

    The contents of the Type list are updated to reflect your choice.

The Sample area displays a preview of the currently selected number format.

16. In the **Type** list, click the **#,##0** item.

17. In the **Type** box, click to the left of the existing format, and type $. Then click to the right of the format, and type " **before bonuses**" (note the space after the opening quote).

18. Click **OK**.

The Format Cells dialog box closes.

The custom number formatting is applied to the value in the active cell.

✖ **CLEAN UP** Save the ExecutiveSearch workbook, and then close it.

Changing the Appearance of Data Based on Its Value

Recording package volumes, vehicle miles, and other business data in a worksheet enables you to make important decisions about your operations. And as you saw earlier in this chapter, you can change the appearance of data labels and the worksheet itself to make interpreting your data easier.

Another way you can make your data easier to interpret is to have Excel change the appearance of your data based on its value. These formats are called conditional formats because the data must meet certain conditions, defined in conditional formatting rules, to have a format applied to it. For example, if chief operating officer Lori Penor wanted to highlight any Thursdays with higher-than-average weekday package volumes, she could define a conditional format that tests the value in the cell recording total sales and changes the format of the cell's contents when the condition is met.

To create a conditional format, you select the cells to which you want to apply the format, display the Home tab, and then in the Styles group, click Conditional Formatting to display a menu of possible conditional formats. In Excel, you can define conditional formats that change how the program displays data in cells that contain values above or below the average values of the related cells, that contain values near the top or bottom of the value range, or that contain values duplicated elsewhere in the selected range.

When you select which kind of condition to create, Excel displays a dialog box that contains fields and controls you can use to define your rule. To display all of the rules for the selected cells, display the Home tab, and then in the Styles group, click Conditional Formatting. On the menu, click Manage Rules to display the Conditional Formatting Rules Manager.

The Conditional Formatting Rules Manager.

The Conditional Formatting Rules Manager enables you to control your conditional formats in the following ways:

- Create a new rule by clicking the New Rule button.

- Change a rule by clicking the rule and then clicking the Edit Rule button.

- Remove a rule by clicking the rule and then clicking the Delete Rule button.

- Move a rule up or down in the order by clicking the rule and then clicking the Move Up button or Move Down button.

- Control whether Excel continues evaluating conditional formats after it finds a rule to apply by selecting or clearing a rule's Stop If True check box.

- Save any new rules and close the Conditional Formatting Rules Manager by clicking OK.

- Save any new rules without closing the Conditional Formatting Rules Manager by clicking Apply.

- Discard any unsaved changes by clicking Cancel.

Tip Clicking the New Rule button in the Conditional Formatting Rules Manager opens the New Formatting Rule dialog box. The commands in the New Formatting Rule dialog box duplicate the options displayed when you click the Conditional Formatting button in the Styles group on the Home tab.

After you create a rule, you can change the format applied if the rule is true by clicking the rule and then clicking the Edit Rule button to display the Edit Formatting Rule dialog box. In that dialog box, click the Format button to display the Format Cells dialog box. After you define your format, click OK to display the rule.

A basic conditional formatting rule. Rules can include multiple criteria.

Important Excel doesn't check to make sure that your conditions are logically consistent, so you need to be sure that you plan and enter your conditions correctly.

Excel also enables you to create three other types of conditional formats: data bars, color scales, and icon sets.

Data bars summarize the relative magnitude of values in a cell range by extending a band of color across the cell.

When data bars were introduced in Excel 2007, they filled cells with a color band that decreased in intensity as it moved across the cell. This gradient fill pattern made it a bit difficult to determine the relative length of two data bars because the end points weren't as distinct as they would have been if the bars were a solid color. Excel 2010 enables you to choose between a solid fill pattern, which makes the right edge of the bars easier to discern, and a gradient fill, which you can use if you share your workbook with colleagues who use Excel 2007.

Excel also draws data bars differently than was done in Excel 2007. Excel 2007 drew a very short data bar for the lowest value in a range and a very long data bar for the highest value. The problem was that similar values could be represented by data bars of very different lengths if there wasn't much variance among the values in the conditionally formatted range. In Excel 2010, data bars compare values based on their distance from zero, so similar values are summarized using data bars of similar lengths.

Tip Excel 2010 data bars summarize negative values by using bars that extend to the left of a baseline that the program draws in a cell. You can control how your data bars summarize negative values by clicking the Negative Value And Axis button, which can be accessed from either the New Formatting Rule dialog box or the Edit Formatting Rule dialog box.

Color scales compare the relative magnitude of values in a cell range by applying colors from a two-color or three-color set to your cells.

Distribution Capacity	
Northeast	47%
Atlantic	75%
Southeast	39%
North Central	54%
Midwest	40%
Southwest	73%
Mountain West	51%
Northwest	69%
Central	41%

The intensity of a cell's color reflects the value's tendency toward the top or bottom of the values in the range.

Icon sets are collections of images that Excel displays when certain rules are met.

Distribution Capacity		
Northeast		47%
Atlantic		75%
Southeast		39%
North Central		54%
Midwest		40%
Southwest		73%
Mountain West		51%
Northwest		69%
Central		41%

An icon set can consist of three, four, or five images.

When icon sets were introduced in Excel 2007, you could apply an icon set as a whole, but you couldn't create custom icon sets or choose to have Excel 2007 display no icon if the value in a cell met a criterion. In Excel 2010, you can display any icon from any set for any criterion or display no icon.

When you click a color scale or icon set in the Conditional Formatting Rules Manager and then click the Edit Rule button, you can control when Excel applies a color or icon to your data.

Important Be sure to not include cells that contain summary formulas in your conditionally formatted ranges. The values, which could be much higher or lower than your regular cell data, could throw off your comparisons.

In this exercise, you'll create a series of conditional formats to change the appearance of data in worksheet cells displaying the package volume and delivery exception rates of a regional distribution center.

SET UP You need the Dashboard_start workbook located in your Chapter11 practice file folder to complete this exercise. Open the Dashboard_start workbook, and save it as *Dashboard*. Then follow the steps.

1. Select cells **C4:C12**.

2. On the **Home** tab, in the **Styles** group, click **Conditional Formatting**. On the menu, point to **Color Scales**, and then in the top row of the palette, click the second pattern from the left.

   Excel formats the selected range.

Color Scales conditional formatting applied to the first data range.

3. Select cells **F4:F12**.

4. On the **Home** tab, in the **Styles** group, click **Conditional Formatting**. On the menu, point to **Data Bars**, and then, in the **Solid Fill** group, click the orange data bar format.

   Excel formats the selected range.

5. Select cells **I4:I12**.

6. On the **Home** tab, in the **Styles** group, click **Conditional Formatting**. On the menu, point to **Icon Sets**, and then in the left column of the list of formats, click the three traffic lights with black borders.

   Excel formats the selected cells.

Three types of conditional formatting applied to the same data range.

7. With the range **I4:I12** still selected, on the **Home** tab, in the **Styles** group, click **Conditional Formatting**, and then click **Manage Rules**.

   The Conditional Formatting Rules Manager opens.

8. Click the **Icon Set** rule, and then click **Edit Rule**.

   The Edit Formatting Rule dialog box opens.

In the Edit Formatting Rule dialog box, you can customize conditional formatting.

9. Click the **Reverse Icon Order** button.

   Excel reconfigures the rules so the red light icon is at the top and the green light icon is at the bottom.

10. In the red light icon's row, in the **Type** list, click **Number**.

11. In the red light icon's **Value** field, type **0.7**.

12. In the yellow light icon's row, in the **Type** list, click **Number**.

13. In the yellow light icon **Value** field, type **0.5**.

14. Click **OK** twice to close the **Edit Formatting Rule** dialog box and the **Conditional Formatting Rules Manager**.

    Excel formats the selected cell range.

15. Click cell **C15**.

16. On the **Home** tab, in the **Styles** group, click **Conditional Formatting**. On the menu, point to **Highlight Cells Rules**, and then click **Less Than**.

    The Less Than dialog box opens.

17. In the left field, type **96%**.

18. In the **With** list, click **Red text**.

19. Click **OK**.

The Less Than dialog box closes, and Excel displays the text in cell C15 in red.

Custom conditional formatting includes cell and text colors.

✖ **CLEAN UP** Save the Dashboard workbook, and then close it.

Adding Images to Worksheets

Establishing a strong corporate identity helps customers remember your organization as well as the products and services you offer. Setting aside the obvious need for sound management, two important physical attributes of a strong retail business are a well-conceived shop space and an eye-catching, easy-to-remember logo. After you or your graphic artist has created a logo, you should add the logo to all your documents, especially any that might be seen by your customers. Not only does the logo mark the documents as coming from your company but it also serves as an advertisement, encouraging anyone who sees your worksheets to call or visit your company.

One way to add a picture to a worksheet is to display the Insert tab, and then in the Illustrations group, click Picture. Clicking Picture displays the Insert Picture dialog box, from which you can locate the picture you want to add from your hard disk. When you insert a picture, the Picture Tools Format contextual tab appears on the ribbon. You can use the tools on the Format contextual tab to change the picture's contrast, brightness, and other attributes. With the controls in the Picture Styles group, you can place a border around the picture, change the picture's shape, or change a picture's effects (such as shadow, reflection, or three-dimensional effects). Other tools, found in the Arrange and Size groups, enable you to rotate, reposition, and resize the picture.

You can place an image anywhere on a worksheet.

You can also resize a picture by clicking it and then dragging one of the handles that appears on the graphic. If you accidentally resize a graphic by dragging a handle, just click the Undo button to remove your change.

Excel 2010 includes a new built-in capability that you can use to remove the background of an image you insert into a workbook. To do so, click the image and then, on the Format contextual tab of the ribbon, in the Adjust group, click Remove Background. When you do, Excel attempts to identify the foreground and background of the image.

You can display only the image subject by removing the image background.

You can drag the handles on the inner square of the background removal tool to change how the tool analyzes the image. When you have adjusted the outline to identify the elements of the image you want to keep, click the Keep Changes button on the Background Removal contextual tab of the ribbon to complete the operation.

If you want to generate a repeating image in the background of a worksheet to form a tiled pattern behind your worksheet's data, you can display the Page Layout tab, and then in the Page Setup group, click Background. In the Sheet Background dialog box, click the image that you want to serve as the background pattern for your worksheet, and click OK.

Tip To remove a background image from a worksheet, display the Page Layout tab, and then in the Page Setup group, click Delete Background.

To achieve a watermark-type effect with words displayed behind the worksheet data, save the watermark information as an image, and then use the image as the sheet background; you could also insert the image in the header or footer, and then resize or scale it to position the watermark information where you want it.

In this exercise, you'll add an image to an existing worksheet, change its location on the worksheet, reduce the size of the image, and then set another image as a repeating background for the worksheet.

SET UP You need the CallCenter_start workbook and the Phone and Texture images located in your Chapter11 practice file folder to complete this exercise. Open the CallCenter_start workbook, and save it as *CallCenter*. Then follow the steps.

1. On the **Insert** tab, in the **Illustrations** group, click **Picture**.

   The Insert Picture dialog box opens.

2. Navigate to the **Chapter11** practice file folder, and then double-click the **Phone** image file.

   The image appears on your worksheet.

3. On the **Format** contextual tab, in the **Adjust** group, click **Remove Background**.

   Excel attempts to separate the image's foreground from its background.

4. Drag the handles at the upper-left and bottom-right corners of the outline until the entire phone, including the cord, is within the frame.

You resize an image on a worksheet by using the same techniques you do in a document.

5. On the **Background Removal** tab, click **Keep Changes**.

   Excel removes the highlighted image elements.

6. Move the image to the upper-left corner of the worksheet, click and hold the handle at the lower-right corner of the image, and drag it up and to the left until the image no longer obscures the **Call Volume** label.

	A	B	C	D	E
4		Call Volume			
5	Northeast	13,769			
6	Atlantic	19,511			
7	Southeast	11,111			
8	North Central	24,972			
9	Midwest	11,809			
10	Southwest	20,339			
11	Mountain West	20,127			
12	Northwest	12,137			
13	Central	20,047			

Images on worksheets are independent of worksheet cells.

7. On the **Page Layout** tab, in the **Page Setup** group, click **Background**.

    The Sheet Background dialog box opens.

8. Navigate to the **Chapter11** practice file folder, and then double-click the **Texture** image file.

    Excel repeats the image to form a background pattern.

You can use an image file to create a worksheet background.

9. On the **Page Layout** tab, in the **Page Setup** group, click **Delete Background**.

   Excel removes the background image.

   CLEAN UP Save the CallCenter workbook, and then close it. If you are not continuing directly to the next chapter, exit Excel.

Key Points

- If you don't like the default font in which Excel displays your data, you can change it.

- You can use cell formatting, including borders, alignment, and fill colors, to emphasize certain cells in your worksheets. This emphasis is particularly useful for making column and row labels stand out from the data.

- Excel comes with a number of existing styles that enable you to change the appearance of individual cells. You can also create new styles to make formatting your workbooks easier.

- If you want to apply the formatting from one cell to another cell, use the Format Painter to copy the format quickly.

- There are quite a few built-in document themes and Excel table formats you can apply to groups of cells. If you see one you like, use it and save yourself lots of formatting time.

- Conditional formats enable you to set rules so that Excel changes the appearance of a cell's contents based on its value.

- Adding images can make your worksheets more visually appealing and make your data easier to understand. Excel 2010 greatly enhances your ability to manage your images without leaving Excel.

Chapter at a Glance

Limit data that appears on your screen, **page 348**

Manipulate worksheet data, **page 354**

Define valid sets of values for ranges of cells, **page 361**

12 Focus on Specific Data by Using Filters

In this chapter, you will learn how to

✔ Limit data that appears on your screen.

✔ Manipulate worksheet data.

✔ Define valid sets of values for ranges of cells.

With Microsoft Excel 2010, you can manage huge data collections, but storing more than 1 million rows of data doesn't help you make business decisions unless you have the ability to focus on the most important data in a worksheet. Focusing on the most relevant data in a worksheet facilitates decision making, whether that data represents the 10 busiest days in a month or revenue streams that you might need to reevaluate. Excel offers a number of powerful and flexible tools with which you can limit the data displayed in your worksheet. When your worksheet displays the subset of data you need to make a decision, you can perform calculations on that data. You can discover what percentage of monthly revenue was earned in the 10 best days in the month, find your total revenue for particular days of the week, or locate the slowest business day of the month.

Just as you can limit the data displayed by your worksheets, you can create validation rules that limit the data entered into them as well. Setting rules for data entered into cells enables you to catch many of the most common data entry errors, such as entering values that are too small or too large, or attempting to enter a word in a cell that requires a number. If you add a validation rule to worksheet cells after data has been entered into them, you can circle any invalid data so that you know what to correct.

In this chapter, you'll learn how to limit the data that appears on your screen, manipulate list data, and create validation rules that limit data entry to appropriate values.

> **Practice Files** Before you can complete the exercises in this chapter, you need to copy the book's practice files to your computer. The practice files you'll use to complete the exercises in this chapter are in the Chapter12 practice file folder. A complete list of practice files is provided in "Using the Practice Files" at the beginning of this book.

Limiting Data That Appears on Your Screen

Excel spreadsheets can hold as much data as you need them to, but you might not want to work with all the data in a worksheet at the same time. For example, you might want to see the revenue figures for your company during the first third, second third, and final third of a month. You can limit the data shown on a worksheet by creating a filter, which is a rule that selects rows to be shown in a worksheet.

To create a filter, you click the cell in the data you want to filter and then, on the Home tab, in the Editing group, click Sort & Filter and then click Filter. When you do, Excel displays a filter arrow at the right edge of the top cell in each column of the data. The arrow indicates that the Excel AutoFilter capability is active.

Clicking the filter arrow displays a menu of filtering options and a list of the unique values in the column. The first few commands in the list are sorting commands, followed by the Clear Filter command and then the Filter By Color command. The next command that appears on the list depends on the type of data in the column. For example, if the column contains a set of dates, the command will be Date Filters. If the column contains several types of data, the command will be Number Filters. Clicking the command displays a list of commands specific to that data type.

Excel displays only commands relevant to the type of data you're filtering.

Important When you turn on filtering, Excel treats the cells in the active cell's column as a range. To ensure that the filtering works properly, you should always have a label at the top of the column you want to filter. If you don't, Excel treats the first value in the list as the label and doesn't include it in the list of values by which you can filter the data.

After you click a filtering option, you define the filter's criteria. For example, you can create a filter that displays only dates after 3/31/2010.

You can filter an Excel table to display only very specific information.

Troubleshooting The appearance of buttons and groups on the ribbon changes depending on the width of the program window. For information about changing the appearance of the ribbon to match our screen images, see "Modifying the Display of the Ribbon" at the beginning of this book.

If you want to see the highest or lowest values in a data column, you can create a Top 10 filter. Choosing the Top 10 command from the menu doesn't just limit the display to the top 10 values. Instead, it opens the Top 10 AutoFilter dialog box. From within this dialog box, you can choose whether to show values from the top or bottom of the list, define the number of items you want to see, and choose whether the number in the middle box indicates the number of items or the percentage of items to be shown when the filter is applied. Using the Top 10 AutoFilter dialog box, you can find your top 10 salespeople or identify the top 5 percent of your customers.

Excel 2010 includes a new capability called the *search filter*, which you can use to type a search string that Excel uses to identify which items to display in an Excel table or a data list. To use a search filter, click a column's filter arrow and start typing a character string in the Search box. As you type the character string, Excel limits the items displayed at the bottom of the filter panel to those that contain the character or characters you've entered. When the filter list's items represent the values you want to display, click OK.

You can enter partial or entire words in the Text Filters box.

When you point to Text Filters and then click Custom Filter, you can define a rule that Excel uses to decide which rows to show after the filter is applied. For instance, you can create a rule that determines that only days with package volumes of less than 100,000 should be shown in your worksheet. With those results in front of you, you might be able to determine whether the weather or another factor resulted in slower business on those days.

Excel indicates that a column has a filter applied by changing the appearance of the column's filter arrow to include an icon that looks like a funnel. After you finish examining your data by using a filter, you can remove the filter by clicking the column's filter arrow and then clicking Clear Filter. To turn off filtering entirely and remove the filter arrows, display the Home tab and then, in the Editing group, click Sort & Filter and then click Filter.

In this exercise, you'll filter worksheet data by using a series of AutoFilter commands, create a filter showing the five days with the highest delivery exception counts in a month, create a search filter, and create a custom filter.

SET UP You need the PackageExceptions_start workbook located in your Chapter12 practice file folder to complete this exercise. Start Excel, open the PackageExceptions_start workbook, and save it as *PackageExceptions*. Then follow the steps.

1. On the **ByRoute** worksheet, click any cell in the cell range **B2:F27**.

2. On the **Home** tab, in the **Editing** group, click **Sort & Filter**, and then click **Filter**.

   A filter arrow appears in each column's header cell.

3. Click the **Date** column filter arrow and then, from the menu that appears, clear the **March** check box.

   Excel changes the state of the Select All and 2010 check boxes to indicate that some items within those categories have been filtered.

A gray check box indicates that the option is valid for some, but not all, items.

4. Click **OK**.

   Excel hides all rows that contain a date from the month of March.

5. Click the **Center** column filter arrow and then, from the menu that appears, clear the **Select All** check box.

   Excel clears all the check boxes in the list.

6. Select the **Midwest** check box, and then click **OK**.

   Excel filters the table.

Excel displays only those exceptions that occurred in the Midwest distribution center during the month of April.

7. On the **Home** tab, in the **Editing** group, click **Sort & Filter**, and then click **Clear**.

    Excel clears all active filters but leaves the filter arrows in place.

8. Click the **Route** column header's filter arrow, and then type **RT9** in the **Search** box.

    The filter list displays only routes with identifiers that include the characters *RT9*.

9. Click **OK**.

    Excel applies the filter, displaying exceptions that occurred on routes with identifiers that contain the string *RT9*.

10. Click the **MarchDailyCount** sheet tab.

    The MarchDailyCount worksheet appears.

11. Click any cell in the Excel table.

12. Click the **Exceptions** filter arrow, click **Number Filters**, and then click **Top 10**.

    The Top 10 AutoFilter dialog box opens.

You can specify the rank, number, and type of items displayed by the Top 10 AutoFilter.

13. In the middle field, type **5**.

14. Click **OK**.

    Excel filters the table.

Excel displays the table rows that contain the five highest values in the column.

15. Click the **Exceptions** column filter arrow, and then click **Clear Filter from "Exceptions"**. Excel removes the filter.

16. Click the **Date** column filter arrow, click **Date Filters**, and then click **Custom Filter**. The Custom AutoFilter dialog box opens.

17. In the upper-left list, click **is after or equal to**. In the upper-right list, click **3/8/2010**. In the lower-left list, click **is before or equal to**. In the lower-right list, click **3/14/2010**.

18. Click **OK**.

    Excel filters the table.

Because you left the AND option selected, Excel displays all table rows that contain a date from 3/8/2010 to 3/14/2010, inclusive.

19. On the Quick Access Toolbar, click the **Undo** button to remove your filter.

CLEAN UP Save the PackageExceptions workbook, and then close it.

Manipulating Worksheet Data

Excel offers a wide range of tools you can use to summarize worksheet data. This section shows you how to select rows at random using the *RAND* and *RANDBETWEEN* functions, how to summarize worksheet data using the *SUBTOTAL* and *AGGREGATE* functions, and how to display a list of unique values within a data set.

Selecting List Rows at Random

In addition to filtering the data that is stored in your Excel worksheets, you can choose rows at random from a list. Selecting rows randomly is useful for choosing which customers will receive a special offer, deciding which days of the month to audit, or picking prize winners at an employee party.

To choose rows randomly, you can use the *RAND* function, which generates a random value between 0 and 1, and compare the value it returns with a test value included in the formula. As an example, suppose Consolidated Messenger wanted to offer approximately 30 percent of its customers a discount on their next shipment. A formula that returns a *TRUE* value 30 percent of the time would be *RAND<=0.3*; that is, whenever the random value was between 0 and 0.3, the result would be *TRUE*. You could use this formula to select each row in a list with a probability of 30 percent. A formula that displayed *TRUE* when the value was equal to or less than 30 percent, and *FALSE* otherwise, would be *=IF(RAND()<=0.3,"True","False")*.

If you recalculate this formula 10 times, it's very unlikely that you would see exactly three *TRUE* results and seven *FALSE* results. Just as flipping a coin can result in the same result 10 times in a row by chance, so can the *RAND* function's results appear to be off if you only recalculate it a few times. However, if you were to recalculate the function 10 thousand times, it is extremely likely that the number of *TRUE* results would be very close to 30 percent.

Tip Because the *RAND* function is a volatile function (it recalculates its results every time you update the worksheet), you should copy the cells that contain the *RAND* function in a formula and paste the formulas' values back into their original cells. To do so, select the cells that contain the *RAND* formulas and press Ctrl+C to copy the cell's contents. Then, on the Home tab, in the Clipboard group, in the Paste list, click Paste Values to replace the formula with its current result. If you don't replace the formulas with their results, you will never have a permanent record of which rows were selected.

The *RANDBETWEEN* function generates a random whole number within a defined range. For example, the formula *=RANDBETWEEN(1,100)* would generate a random integer value from 1 to 100, inclusive. The *RANDBETWEEN* function is very useful for creating sample data collections for presentations. Before the *RANDBETWEEN* function was introduced, you had to create formulas that added, subtracted, multiplied, and divided the results of the *RAND* function, which are always decimal values between 0 and 1, to create your data.

Summarizing Worksheets with Hidden and Filtered Rows

The ability to analyze the data that's most vital to your current needs is important, but there are some limitations to how you can summarize your filtered data by using functions such as *SUM* and *AVERAGE*. One limitation is that any formulas you create that include the *SUM* and *AVERAGE* functions don't change their calculations if some of the rows used in the formula are hidden by the filter.

Excel provides two ways to summarize just the visible cells in a filtered data list. The first method is to use AutoCalculate. To use AutoCalculate, you select the cells you want to summarize. When you do, Excel displays the average of values in the cells, the sum of the values in the cells, and the number of visible cells (the count) in the selection.

The AutoCalculate results are displayed on the status bar at the bottom of the Excel window.

To display the other functions you can use, right-click the status bar and select the function you want from the shortcut menu. If a check mark appears next to a function's name, that function's result appears on the status bar. Clicking a checked function name removes that function from the status bar.

AutoCalculate is great for finding a quick total or average for filtered cells, but it doesn't make the result available in the worksheet. Formulas such as =*SUM(C3:C26)* always consider every cell in the range, regardless of whether you hide a cell's row by right-clicking the row's header and then clicking Hide, so you need to create a formula by using either the *SUBTOTAL* function or the *AGGREGATE* function (which is new in Excel 2010) to summarize just those values that are visible in your worksheet. The *SUBTOTAL* function enables you to summarize every value in a range or summarize only those values in rows you haven't manually hidden. The *SUBTOTAL* function has this syntax: *SUBTOTAL(function_num, ref1, ref2, ...)*. The *function_num* argument holds the number of the operation you want to use to summarize your data. (The operation numbers are summarized in a table later in this section.) The *ref1, ref2,* and further arguments represent up to 29 ranges to include in the calculation.

As an example, assume you have a worksheet where you hid rows 20-26 manually. In this case, the formula =*SUBTOTAL(9, C3:C26, E3:E26, G3:G26)* would find the sum of all values in the ranges C3:C26, E3:E26, and G3:G26, regardless of whether that range contained any hidden rows. The formula =*SUBTOTAL(109, C3:C26, E3:E26, G3:G26)* would find the sum of all values in cells C3:C19, E3:E19, and G3:G19, ignoring the values in the manually hidden rows.

Important Be sure to place your *SUBTOTAL* formula in a row that is even with or above the headers in the range you're filtering. If you don't, your filter might hide the formula's result!

The following table lists the summary operations available for the *SUBTOTAL* formula. Excel displays the available summary operations as part of the Formula AutoComplete functionality, so you don't need to remember the operation numbers or look them up in the Help system.

Operation number (includes hidden values)	Operation number (ignores values in manually hidden rows)	Function	Description
1	101	AVERAGE	Returns the average of the values in the range
2	102	COUNT	Counts the cells in the range that contain a number
3	103	COUNTA	Counts the nonblank cells in the range
4	104	MAX	Returns the largest (maximum) value in the range
5	105	MIN	Returns the smallest (minimum) value in the range
6	106	PRODUCT	Returns the result of multiplying all numbers in the range
7	107	STDEV.S	Calculates the standard deviation of values in the range by examining a sample of the values
8	108	STDEV.P	Calculates the standard deviation of the values in the range by using all the values
9	109	SUM	Returns the result of adding all numbers in the range together
10	110	VAR.S	Calculates the variance of values in the range by examining a sample of the values
11	111	VAR.P	Calculates the variance of the values in the range by using all of the values

As the previous table shows, the *SUBTOTAL* function has two sets of operations. The first set (operations 1-11) represents operations that include hidden values in their summary, and the second set (operations 101-111) represents operations that summarize only values visible in the worksheet. Operations 1-11 summarize all cells in a range, regardless of whether the range contains any manually hidden rows. By contrast, the operations 101-111 ignore any values in manually hidden rows. What the *SUBTOTAL* function doesn't do, however, is change its result to reflect rows hidden by using a filter.

The new *AGGREGATE* function extends the capabilities of the *SUBTOTAL* function. With it, you can select from a broader range of functions and use another argument to determine which, if any, values to ignore in the calculation. *AGGREGATE* has two possible syntaxes, depending on the summary operation you select. The first syntax is *=AGGREGATE(function_num, options, ref1…)*, which is similar to the syntax of the *SUBTOTAL* function. The other possible syntax, *=AGGREGATE(function_num, options, array, [k])*, is used to create *AGGREGATE* functions that use the *LARGE, SMALL, PERCENTILE.INC, QUARTILE.INC, PERCENTILE.EXC,* and *QUARTILE.EXC* operations.

The following table summarizes the summary operations available for use in the *AGGREGATE* function.

Number	Function	Description
1	AVERAGE	Returns the average of the values in the range.
2	COUNT	Counts the cells in the range that contain a number.
3	COUNTA	Counts the nonblank cells in the range.
4	MAX	Returns the largest (maximum) value in the range.
5	MIN	Returns the smallest (minimum) value in the range.
6	PRODUCT	Returns the result of multiplying all numbers in the range.
7	STDEV.S	Calculates the standard deviation of values in the range by examining a sample of the values.
8	STDEV.P	Calculates the standard deviation of the values in the range by using all the values.
9	SUM	Returns the result of adding all numbers in the range together.
10	VAR.S	Calculates the variance of values in the range by examining a sample of the values.
11	VAR.P	Calculates the variance of the values in the range by using all of the values.
12	MEDIAN	Returns the value in the middle of a group of values.
13	MODE.SNGL	Returns the most frequently occurring number from a group of numbers.
14	LARGE	Returns the k-th largest value in a data set; k is specified using the last function argument. If k is left blank, Excel returns the largest value.

(continued)

Number	Function	Description
15	*SMALL*	Returns the *k*-th smallest value in a data set; *k* is specified using the last function argument. If *k* is left blank, Excel returns the smallest value.
16	*PERCENTILE.INC*	Returns the *k*-th percentile of values in a range, where *k* is a value from 0 to 1, inclusive.
17	*QUARTILE.INC*	Returns the quartile value of a data set, based on a percentage from 0 to 1, inclusive.
18	*PERCENTILE.EXC*	Returns the *k*-th percentile of values in a range, where *k* is a value from 0 to 1, exclusive.
19	*QUARTILE.EXC*	Returns the quartile value of a data set, based on a percentage from 0 to 1, exclusive.

The second argument, *options*, enables you to select which items the *AGGREGATE* function should ignore. These items can include hidden rows, errors, and *SUBTOTAL* and *AGGREGATE* functions. The following table summarizes the values available for the options argument and the effect they have on the function's results.

Number	Description
0	Ignore nested *SUBTOTAL* and *AGGREGATE* functions
1	Ignore hidden rows and nested *SUBTOTAL* and *AGGREGATE* functions
2	Ignore error values and nested *SUBTOTAL* and *AGGREGATE* functions
3	Ignore hidden rows, error values, and nested *SUBTOTAL* and *AGGREGATE* functions
4	Ignore nothing
5	Ignore hidden rows
6	Ignore error values
7	Ignore hidden rows and error values

Finding Unique Values Within a Data Set

Summarizing numerical values can provide valuable information that helps you run your business. It can also be helpful to know how many different values appear within a column. For example, you might want to display all of the countries in which Consolidated Messenger has customers. If you want to display a list of the unique values in a column, click any cell in the data set, display the Data tab and then, in the Sort & Filter group, click Advanced to display the Advanced Filter dialog box.

You can filter the original list or create a filtered copy of the list.

In the List Range field, type the reference of the cell range you want to examine for unique values, select the Unique Records Only check box, and then click OK to have Excel display the row that contains the first occurrence of each value in the column.

Important Excel treats the first cell in the data range as a header cell, so it doesn't consider the cell as it builds the list of unique values. Be sure to include the header cell in your data range!

In this exercise, you'll select random rows from a list of exceptions to identify package delivery misadventures to investigate, create an *AGGREGATE* formula to summarize the visible cells in a filtered worksheet, and find the unique values in one column of data.

SET UP You need the ForFollowUp_start workbook located in your Chapter12 practice file folder to complete this exercise. Open the ForFollowUp_start workbook, and save it as *ForFollowUp*. Then follow the steps.

1. Select cells **G3:G27**.

   The average of the values in the selected cells, the number of cells selected, and the total of the values in the selected cells appear in the AutoCalculate area of the status bar.

2. In cell **J3**, enter the formula =**AGGREGATE(1,1,G3:G27)**.

   The value *$15.76* appears in cell J3.

3. On the **Data** tab, in the **Sort & Filter** group, click **Advanced**.

   The Advanced Filter dialog box opens.

4. In the **List range** field, type **E2:E27**.

5. Select the **Unique records only** check box, and then click **OK**.

   Excel displays the rows that contain the first occurrence of each different value in the selected range.

Tip Remember that you must include cell E2, the header cell, in the List Range field so that the filter doesn't display two occurrences of Northeast in the unique values list. To see what happens when you don't include the header cell, try changing the range in the List Range field to E3:E27, selecting the Unique Records Only check box, and then clicking OK.

	A	B	C	D	E	F	G	H	I	J	K	L	M
2		ExceptionID	PackageID	Date	Center	Route	Cost	Investigate		Summary			
3		EX1000001	PI34920119	3/30/2007	Northeast	RT310	$ 12.08			$ 15.76			
4		EX1000002	PI34920120	3/30/2007	Midwest	RT892	$ 14.88						
5		EX1000003	PI34920121	3/30/2007	Northwest	RT424	$ 13.61						
8		EX1000006	PI34920124	3/30/2007	Central	RT341	$ 18.86						
11		EX1000009	PI34920127	3/31/2007	South	RT983	$ 19.87						
12		EX1000010	PI34920128	3/31/2007	Southwest	RT827	$ 18.01						

The Unique Records Only filter hides duplicate records.

6. On the **Data** tab, in the **Sort & Filter** group, click **Clear**.

   Excel removes the filter.

7. In cell **H3**, type the formula **=IF(RAND()<0.15,"Yes","No")**, and press Enter.

   A value of *Yes* or *No* appears in cell H3, depending on the *RAND* function result.

8. Select cell **H3**, and then drag the fill handle down until it covers cell **H27**.

   Excel copies the formula into every cell in the range H3:H27.

9. With the range **H3:H27** still selected, on the **Home** tab, in the **Clipboard** group, click the **Copy** button.

   Excel copies the cell range's contents to the Microsoft Office Clipboard.

10. Click the **Paste** arrow, and then in the **Paste** gallery that appears, click the first icon in the **Paste Values** group.

    Excel replaces the cells' formulas with the formulas' current results.

You can paste the results of formulas rather than the formulas themselves.

✖ CLEAN UP Save the ForFollowUp workbook, and then close it.

Defining Valid Sets of Values for Ranges of Cells

Part of creating efficient and easy-to-use worksheets is to do what you can to ensure the data entered into your worksheets is as accurate as possible. Although it isn't possible to catch every typographical or transcription error, you can set up a validation rule to make sure that the data entered into a cell meets certain standards.

To create a validation rule, display the Data tab on the ribbon and then, in the Data Tools group, click the Data Validation button to open the Data Validation dialog box. You can use the controls in the Data Validation dialog box to define the type of data that Excel should allow in the cell and then, depending on the data type you choose, to set the conditions data must meet to be accepted in the cell. For example, you can set the conditions so that Excel knows to look for a whole number value between 1000 and 2000.

Data validation rules are intended to ensure that worksheet users enter the correct information in a cell.

Setting accurate validation rules can help you and your colleagues avoid entering a customer's name in the cell designated to hold the phone number or setting a credit limit above a certain level. To require a user to enter a numeric value in a cell, display the Settings page of the Data Validation dialog box, and, depending on your needs, choose either Whole Number or Decimal from the Allow list.

If you want to set the same validation rule for a group of cells, you can do so by selecting the cells to which you want to apply the rule (such as a column in which you enter the credit limit of customers of Consolidated Messenger) and setting the rule by using the Data Validation dialog box. One important fact you should keep in mind is that, with Excel, you can create validation rules for cells in which you have already entered data. Excel doesn't tell you whether any of those cells contain data that violates your rule at the moment you create the rule, but you can find out by having Excel circle any worksheet cells containing data that violates the cell's validation rule. To do so, display the Data tab and then, in the Data Tools group, click the Data Validation arrow. On the menu, click the Circle Invalid Data button to circle cells with invalid data.

When you're ready to hide the data validation circles, click Clear Validation Circles in the Data Validation list.

Of course, it's frustrating if you want to enter data into a cell and, when a message box appears that tells you the data you tried to enter isn't acceptable, you aren't given the rules you need to follow. With Excel, you can create a message that tells the user which values are expected before the data is entered and then, if the conditions aren't met, reiterate the conditions in a custom error message.

You can turn off data validation in a cell by displaying the Settings page of the Data Validation dialog box and clicking the Clear All button in the lower-left corner of the dialog box.

In this exercise, you'll create a data validation rule limiting the credit line of Consolidated Messenger customers to $25,000, add an input message mentioning the limitation, and then create an error message if someone enters a value greater than $25,000. After you create your rule and messages, you'll test them.

 SET UP You need the Credit_start workbook located in your Chapter12 practice file folder to complete this exercise. Open the Credit_start workbook, and save it as *Credit*. Then follow the steps.

1. Select the cell range **J4:J7**.

   Cell J7 is currently blank, but you will add a value to it later in this exercise.

2. On the **Data** tab, in the **Data Tools** group, click **Data Validation**.

   The Data Validation dialog box opens and displays the Settings page.

You can specify the type of data allowed in a cell.

3. In the **Allow** list, click **Whole Number**.

   Boxes labeled Minimum and Maximum appear below the Data box.

4. In the **Data** list, click **less than or equal to**.

   The Minimum box disappears.

5. In the **Maximum** box, type **25000**.

6. Clear the **Ignore blank** check box.

7. Click the **Input Message** tab.

   The Input Message page is displayed.

The input message is intended to provide guidance to the worksheet user.

8. In the **Title** box, type **Enter Limit**. In the **Input Message** box, type **Please enter the customer's credit limit, omitting the dollar sign and any commas.**

9. Click the **Error Alert** tab. On the **Error Alert** page, in the **Style** list, click **Stop**.

   The icon that appears on your message box changes to the Stop icon.

You can enter a custom error message or use the default message for this type of error.

10. In the **Title** box, type **Error**, and then click **OK**.

11. Click cell **J7**.

   A ScreenTip with the title *Enter Limit* and the text *Please enter the customer's credit limit, omitting the dollar sign and any commas* appears near cell J7.

12. Type **25001**, and press Enter.

A stop box with the title Error opens. Leaving the Error Message box blank in the Data Validation dialog box causes Excel to use its default message.

Clicking Retry enables you to edit the bad value; clicking Cancel deletes the entry.

13. In the **Error** box, click **Cancel**.

14. Click cell **J7**.

15. Type **25000**, and press Enter.

16. On the **Data** tab, in the **Data Tools** group, click the **Data Validation** arrow and then, in the list, click **Circle Invalid Data**.

A red circle appears around the value in cell J4.

CAPTION

17. In the **Data Validation** list, click **Clear Validation Circles**.

The red circle around the value in cell K4 disappears.

✕ CLEAN UP Save the Credit workbook, and then close it. If you are not continuing directly to the next chapter, exit Excel.

Key Points

- A number of filters are defined in Excel. (You might find the one you want is already available.)

- Filtering an Excel worksheet based on values in a single column is easy to do, but you can create a custom filter to limit your data based on the values in more than one column as well.

- With the new search filter capability in Excel 2010, you can limit the data in your worksheets based on characters the terms contain.

- Don't forget that you can get a running total (or an average, or any one of several other summary operations) for the values in a group of cells. Just select the cells and look on the status bar: the result will be there.

- Use data validation techniques to improve the accuracy of data entered into your worksheets and to identify data that doesn't meet the guidelines you set.

Part 4

Microsoft PowerPoint 2010

13 Work with Slides 371

14 Work with Slide Text. 389

15 Format Slides 423

16 Add Simple Visual Enhancements. 447

17 Review and Deliver Presentations. 485

Chapter at a Glance

Add and delete slides, **page 371**

Add slides with ready-made content, **page 374**

Divide presentations into sections, **page 380**

Rearrange slides and sections, **page 384**

13 Work with Slides

In this chapter, you will learn how to

✔ Add and delete slides.

✔ Add slides with ready-made content.

✔ Divide presentations into sections.

✔ Rearrange slides and sections.

For each slide to accomplish its purpose, it needs to present its content in the most effective way. The layout of individual slides and the order of slides in the presentation contribute significantly to the logical development of your message.

In this chapter, you'll add slides with different layouts, delete slides, and change the layout of a slide. You'll also divide a presentation into sections and collapse and expand sections. Finally, you'll rearrange slides and sections in a presentation.

> **Practice Files** Before you can complete the exercises in this chapter, you need to copy the book's practice files to your computer. The practice files you'll use to complete the exercises in this chapter are in the Chapter13 practice file folder. A complete list of practice files is provided in "Using the Practice Files" at the beginning of this book.

Adding and Deleting Slides

When you create a presentation, you add a slide by clicking the New Slide button in the Slides group on the Home tab. By default in a new presentation, a slide added after the title slide has the Title And Content layout. Thereafter, each added slide has the layout of the preceding slide. If you want to add a slide with a different layout, you can select the layout you want from the New Slide gallery.

If you change your mind about including a slide, you can easily delete it by selecting it either on the Slides tab of the Overview pane or in Slide Sorter view and then pressing the Delete key. You can also right-click the slide in either the pane or the view and then click Delete Slide. To select a series of slides, click the first slide in the series and hold down the Shift key while you click the last slide. To select noncontiguous slides, click the first one and hold down the Ctrl key as you click additional slides.

If you change your mind about the layout of a slide, you don't have to delete it and then add a new one with the layout you want. Instead, you can change the layout of an existing slide by selecting the new layout from the Layout gallery.

In this exercise, you'll add a slide with the default layout and add slides with other layouts. You'll delete first a single slide and then a series of slides. Then you'll change the layout of a slide.

SET UP You need the ServiceA_start presentation located in your Chapter13 practice file folder to complete this exercise. Open the ServiceA_start presentation, and save it as *ServiceA*. Then follow the steps.

1. With slide **1** displayed, on the **Home** tab, in the **Slides** group, click the **New Slide** button (not its arrow).

   Keyboard Shortcut Press Ctrl+M to add a slide to the presentation.

   PowerPoint adds slide 2 to the presentation with the default Title And Content layout.

This layout accommodates a title and either text or graphic content—a table, chart, diagram, picture, clip art image, or media clip.

Troubleshooting The appearance of buttons and groups on the ribbon changes depending on the width of the program window. For information about changing the appearance of the ribbon to match our screen images, see "Modifying the Display of the Ribbon" at the beginning of this book.

2. In the **Slides** group, click the **New Slide** arrow.

   The New Slide gallery appears.

The World In Hand design template has nine predefined slide layouts.

3. In the gallery, click **Two Content**.

   PowerPoint adds slide 3, which has a placeholder for a title and two placeholders for text or graphic content.

4. In the **Slides** group, click the **New Slide** button.

   PowerPoint adds another slide with the Two Content layout.

   Tip You can also add new slides by pressing keyboard shortcuts while you're entering text on the Outline tab. For more information, see "Entering Text in Placeholders" in Chapter 14, "Work with Slide Text."

5. Continue adding slides from the IO gallery, selecting a different layout each time so that you can see what each one looks like.

   When you finish, the presentation contains 10 slides.

6. In the **Overview** pane, scroll to the top of the **Slides** tab. Then right-click slide **3**, and click **Delete Slide**.

   PowerPoint removes the slide from the presentation and renumbers all the subsequent slides.

7. On the **Slides** tab, click slide **5**. Then scroll to the bottom of the tab, hold down the Shift key, and click slide **9**.

8. With slides **5** through **9** selected, right-click the selection, and click **Delete Slide**.

   The presentation now has four slides.

 9. With slide **4** selected, on the **Home** tab, in the **Slides** group, click the **Layout** button.

   The Layout gallery appears. This gallery is the same as the New Slide gallery, but it applies the layout you choose to an existing slide instead of adding a new one.

10. In the gallery, click the **Title and Content** thumbnail.

✖ **CLEAN UP** Save the ServiceA presentation, and then close it without exiting PowerPoint.

Adding Slides with Ready-Made Content

If your presentation will contain information that already exists in a document created in Microsoft Word or another word processing program, you can edit that information into outline format and then import the outline into a PowerPoint presentation. The outline can be a Word document (.doc or .docx) or a Rich Text Format (RTF) file (.rtf).

For the importing process to work as smoothly as possible, the document must be formatted with heading styles. PowerPoint translates Heading 1 styles into slide titles, Heading 2 styles into bullet points, and Heading 3 styles into second-level bullet points, called *subpoints*.

If you often include a slide that provides the same basic information in your presentations, you don't have to re-create the slide for each presentation. For example, if you
create a slide that shows your company's product development cycle for a new product
presentation, you might want to use variations of that same slide in all new product
presentations. You can easily tell PowerPoint to reuse a slide from one presentation in
a different presentation. The slide assumes the formatting of its new presentation.

See Also For information about using a slide library to store slides for reuse, see the sidebar
"Working with Slide Libraries" following this topic.

Within a presentation, you can duplicate an existing slide to reuse it as the basis for a
new slide. You can then customize the duplicated slide instead of having to create it
from scratch.

In this exercise, you'll add slides by importing a Word outline. Then you'll reuse a slide
from an existing presentation. Finally, you'll duplicate an existing slide.

SET UP You need the ServiceB_start and Projects presentations and the Service-
Orientation document located in your Chapter13 practice file folder to complete this
exercise. Open the ServiceB_start presentation, and save it as *ServiceB*. Then follow
the steps.

1. On the **Home** tab, in the **Slides** group, click the **New Slide** arrow, and then below
   the gallery, click **Slides from Outline**.

   The Insert Outline dialog box opens. This dialog box resembles the Open
   dialog box.

2. Navigate to your **Chapter13** practice file folder, and then double-click the
   ServiceOrientation file.

   PowerPoint converts the outline into 12 slides.

3. In the **Overview** pane, click the **Outline** tab.

   On the Outline tab, each Heading 1 style from the ServiceOrientation document is
   now a slide title, each Heading 2 style is a bullet point, and each Heading 3 style
   is a subpoint.

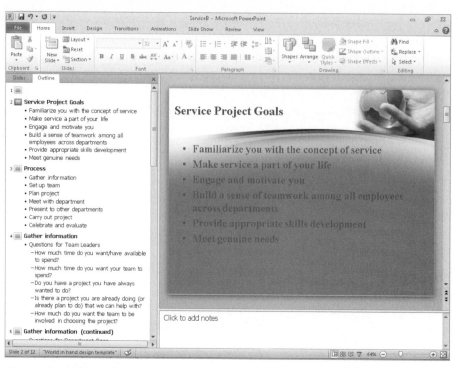

The text from the outline, shown on the Outline tab.

Tip You can start a new presentation from a Word outline. Click the File tab to display the Backstage view, and then click Open. In the Open dialog box, click All PowerPoint Presentations, and in the list of file types, click All Files. Then locate and double-click the outline document you want to use.

4. In the **Overview** pane, click the **Slides** tab, and then click the empty slide **1**.

5. On the **Home** tab, in the **Slides** group, click the **New Slide** arrow, and then below the gallery, click **Reuse Slides**.

   The Reuse Slides task pane opens on the right side of the window.

6. In the **Reuse Slides** task pane, click **Browse**, and then in the list, click **Browse File**.

   PowerPoint displays the Browse dialog box, which resembles the Open dialog box.

7. If the contents of your **Chapter13** practice file folder are not displayed, navigate to that folder now. Then double-click the **Projects** presentation.

   Thumbnails of all the slides in the presentation appear in the Reuse Slides task pane.

This presentation includes a series of diagrams related to a project workflow.

8. Scroll to the bottom of the task pane to see all the available slides, and then point to the last thumbnail.

   The thumbnail expands so that you can see the slide details, making it easier to select the slide you want.

9. Scroll back to the top of the task pane, and then click the first thumbnail.

   PowerPoint inserts the selected slide from the Projects presentation as slide 2 in the ServiceB presentation. The slide takes on the design of the presentation in which it is inserted.

The presentation now contains a diagram from the Projects *presentation.*

Tip If you want the slide to retain the formatting from the Projects presentation instead of taking on the formatting of the ServiceB presentation, select the Keep Source Formatting check box at the bottom of the Reuse Slides task pane.

10. Click the task pane's **Close** button.

11. With slide **2** selected on the **Slides** tab, in the **Slides** group of the **Home** tab, click the **New Slide** arrow. Then click **Duplicate Selected Slide**.

Tip You can also right-click the selected slide and then click Duplicate Slide.

PowerPoint inserts a new slide 3 identical to slide 2. You could now modify the existing slide content instead of creating it from scratch.

CLEAN UP Save the ServiceB presentation, and then close it.

Working with Slide Libraries

If your organization is running Microsoft SharePoint Server and has enabled slide libraries, and if PowerPoint Professional Plus is installed on your computer, you and your colleagues can store slides or even entire presentations in a slide library so that they are available for use in any presentation.

For example, suppose a graphically gifted person has developed a slide with a sophisticated chart showing the percentage of income derived from the sale of different categories of merchandise. He or she can store the slide in a slide library so that other people can use it in their presentations without having to take the time to develop a similar chart. Larger organizations might even have people on staff with responsibility for creating this type of slide, so that they can ensure that all presentations convey the same information in the same professional way.

To store slides in a slide library:

1. Display the Backstage view, click Save & Send, and then click Publish Slides.
2. In the right pane, click the Publish Slides button.

    The Publish Slides dialog box opens.
3. In the Publish Slides dialog box, select the check box for the slide you want to store in the library.
4. If the URL of your SharePoint slide library does not appear in the Publish To box, click the box, and type the URL.
5. Click Publish to store the slide in the slide library.

To insert a slide from a slide library:

1. Click the slide after which you want the new slide to appear.
2. On the Home tab, in the Slides group, click the New Slide arrow, and then click Reuse Slides.
3. In the Reuse Slides task pane, in the Insert Slide From box, type the URL of your SharePoint slide library, and then click the Go arrow.

    You can also click Browse, click Browse Slide Library, and then navigate to the URL of the library in the Select A Slide Library dialog box.
4. Double-click the thumbnail of the slide you want to insert in the active presentation.

Exporting Presentations as Outlines

When you want to use the text from a presentation in another program, you can save the presentation outline as an .rtf file. Many programs, including the Windows and Macintosh versions of Word and older versions of PowerPoint, can import outlines saved in .rtf with their formatting intact.

To save a presentation as an .rtf file:

1. Display the Backstage view, and then click Save As.

   The Save As dialog box opens.

2. In the File Name box, specify the name of the file.

3. Display the Save As Type list, and click Outline/RTF.

4. Navigate to the folder in which you want to store the outline, and click Save.

   PowerPoint saves the presentation's outline in .rtf format with the designated name in the designated folder.

Dividing Presentations into Sections

New in PowerPoint 2010 is the ability to divide slides into sections. Sections appear as bars across the Slides tab of the Overview pane in Normal view and across the workspace in Slide Sorter view. They do not appear in other views, and they do not create slides or otherwise interrupt the flow of the presentation.

Dividing a presentation into sections can be a great tool during content development. Because you can hide whole sections of slides, the sections make it easier to focus on one part of a presentation at a time. If you are working on a presentation with other people, you can name one section for each person to delineate who is responsible for which slides.

In this exercise, you'll divide a presentation into two sections, adding one in Normal view and the other in Slide Sorter view. After naming the sections, you'll hide their slides and then display first one section and then both sections.

SET UP You need the ServiceC_start presentation located in your Chapter13 practice file folder to complete this exercise. Open the ServiceC_start presentation, and save it as *ServiceC*. Then follow the steps.

1. With slide **1** displayed, on the **Home** tab, in the **Slides** group, click the **Section** button, and then click **Add Section**.

   On the Slides tab of the Overview pane, PowerPoint adds a section bar before slide 1.

   PowerPoint selects all the slides that are included in the new section.

2. On the **View Shortcuts** toolbar, click the **Slide Sorter** button.

3. Click slide **4**, click the **Section** button, and then click **Add Section**.

   PowerPoint adds a section bar before slide 4.

Again, PowerPoint selects the slides in the new section.

4. Right-click the second **Untitled Section** bar, and click **Rename Section**.

    The Rename Section dialog box opens.

5. In the **Section name** box, type **Process**, and then click **Rename**.

6. On the **View Shortcuts** toolbar, click the **Normal** button.

7. On the **Slides** tab of the **Overview** pane, click the **Untitled Section** bar above slide **1**.

    The section bar and all the slides in the section are selected.

You can select just one section of the presentation.

8. In the **Slides** group, click the **Section** button, and click **Rename Section**. Then in the **Rename Section** dialog box, type **Introduction** as the section name, and click **Rename**.

9. In the **Slides** group, click the **Section** button, and then click **Collapse All**.

   The slides are hidden under their section bars.

You can use sections to provide an "outline" of long presentations.

10. On the **Slides** tab, click the arrow to the left of **Introduction** to display only the slides in that section.

11. In the **Slides** group, click the **Section** button, and then click **Expand All**.

All the slides are now displayed.

 CLEAN UP Save the ServiceC presentation, and then close it.

Rearranging Slides and Sections

After you have created several slides, whether by adding them and entering text or by importing them from another presentation, you might want to rearrange the order of the slides so that they effectively communicate your message. You can rearrange a presentation in three ways.

- On the Slides tab, you can drag slides up and down to change their order.

- On the Slides tab, you can move entire sections up or down in a presentation.

- To see more of the presentation at the same time, you can switch to Slide Sorter view. You can then drag slide thumbnails or sections into the correct order.

In this exercise, you'll work on the Slides tab and in Slide Sorter view to logically arrange the slides in a presentation. You'll also delete a section you no longer need.

➡ **SET UP** You need the ServiceD_start presentation located in your Chapter13 practice file folder to complete this exercise. Open the ServiceD_start presentation, and save it as *ServiceD*. Then follow the steps.

1. In the **Overview** pane, on the **Slides** tab, click the slide **2** thumbnail, and then drag it downward to the space above the thumbnail for slide **4**, but don't release the mouse button yet.

The thumbnail itself remains in place, but a bar indicates where the slide will move to when you release the mouse button.

2. Release the mouse button.

PowerPoint moves the slide to its new location in the Process section and switches the numbers of slides 2 and 3.

Tip You can move slides from one open presentation to another in Slide Sorter view. Display both presentations in Slide Sorter view, and then on the View tab, in the Window group, click the Arrange All button. Then drag slides from one presentation window to the other.

3. To the left of **Introduction** in the first section bar, click the black **Collapse Section** button. Then repeat this step for the **Process** section.

   Even with these two sections collapsed, you can't see all the slides.

4. On the **View Shortcuts** toolbar, click the **Slide Sorter** button.

5. Use the **Zoom Slider** at the right end of the status bar to adjust the zoom percentage so that you can see all the slides.

   We set the zoom percentage to 80%.

The sections you collapsed in Normal view are still collapsed in Slide Sorter view.

6. In the **Selling** section, click slide **7**, and then drag it to the left until its bar sits to the left of slide **5**.

   PowerPoint renumbers the slides in the section.

7. Point to the **Planning** section bar, right-click it, and then click **Move Section Up**.

   The Planning section bar and all its slides move above the Selling section. PowerPoint renumbers the slides in both sections.

8. Switch to Normal view.

9. Click the white **Expand Section** button to expand the **Introduction** and **Process** sections.

   These two sections could easily be combined into one section.

10. Click the **Process** section bar. Then in the **Slides** group, click the **Section** button, and click **Remove Section**.

   PowerPoint removes the Process section bar.

The Introduction section now contains four slides.

✖ CLEAN UP Save the ServiceD presentation, and then close it.

Key Points

- You can add as many slides as you want. Most templates provide a variety of ready-made slide layouts to choose from.

- If you change your mind about a slide or its layout, you can delete it or switch to a different layout.

- You can create slides with content already in place by importing an outline or reusing existing slides. Both methods save time and effort.

- Grouping slides into sections makes it easy to focus on specific parts of the presentation.

- If you need to change the order of slides or sections, you can rearrange them on the Slides tab in Normal view or in Slide Sorter view.

Chapter at a Glance

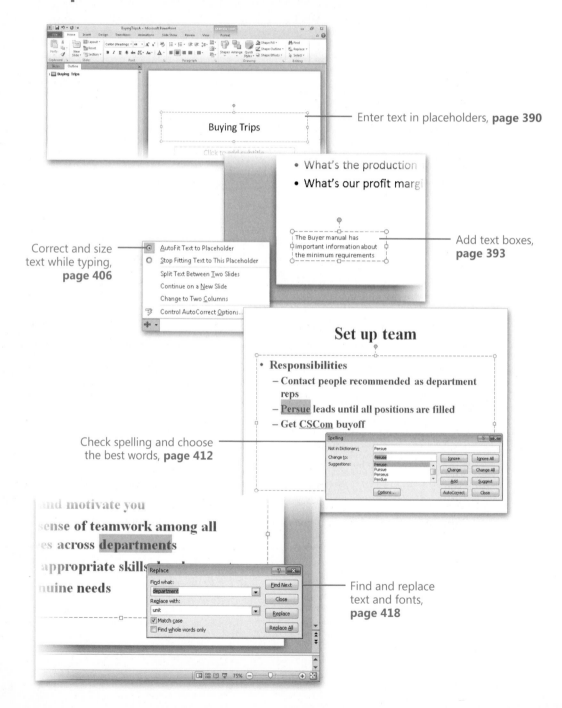

Enter text in placeholders, **page 390**

Correct and size text while typing, **page 406**

Add text boxes, **page 393**

Check spelling and choose the best words, **page 412**

Find and replace text and fonts, **page 418**

14 Work with Slide Text

In this chapter, you will learn how to

- ✔ Enter text in placeholders.
- ✔ Add text boxes.
- ✔ Edit text.
- ✔ Correct and size text while typing.
- ✔ Check spelling and choose the best words.
- ✔ Find and replace text and fonts.

In later chapters of this book, we show you ways to add fancy effects to electronic presentations so that you can really grab the attention of your audience. But no amount of animation, jazzy colors, and supporting pictures will convey your message if the words on the slides are inadequate to the task.

For most of your presentations, text is the foundation on which you build everything else. Even if you follow the current trend of building presentations that consist primarily of pictures, you still need to make sure that titles and any other words on your slides do their job, and do it well. So this chapter shows you various ways to work with text to ensure that the words are accurate, consistent, and appropriately formatted.

In this chapter, you'll learn how to enter and edit text on slides, on the Outline tab, and in text boxes. You'll see how the AutoCorrect feature helps you avoid typographical errors and the AutoFit feature makes the words you type fit in the available space. Then you'll see how the spell-checking feature can help you correct misspellings. Finally, you'll learn how to replace one word with another throughout a presentation by using the Find And Replace feature, which you also use to ensure the consistent use of fonts.

> **Practice Files** Before you can complete the exercises in this chapter, you need to copy the book's practice files to your computer. The practice files you'll use to complete the exercises in this chapter are in the *Chapter14* practice file folder. A complete list of practice files is provided in "Using the Practice Files" at the beginning of this book.

Entering Text in Placeholders

When you add a new slide to a presentation, the layout you select indicates with placeholders the type and position of the objects on the slide. For example, a Title And Content slide has placeholders for a title and either a bulleted list with one or more levels of bullet points and subpoints or an illustration such as a table, chart, graphic, or movie clip. You can enter text directly into a placeholder on a slide in the Slide pane, or you can enter text on the Outline tab of the Overview pane, where the entire presentation is displayed in outline form.

When you point to a placeholder on a slide, the pointer changes to an I-beam. When you click the placeholder, a blinking cursor appears where you clicked to indicate where characters will appear when you type. As you type, the text appears both on the slide and on the Outline tab.

In this exercise, you'll enter slide titles, bullet points, and subpoints, both directly in placeholders on a slide and on the Outline tab.

SET UP You don't need any practice files to complete this exercise. Open a new, blank presentation, and save it as *BuyingTripsA*. Then follow the steps.

1. In the **Slide** pane, click the slide's **Click to add title** placeholder.

   A selection box surrounds the title placeholder, and the cursor appears in the center of the box, indicating that the text you type will be centered in the placeholder.

2. Type **Buying Trips**. (Do not type the period.)

   By tradition, slide titles have no periods.

   Tip If you make a typing error while working through this exercise, press Backspace to delete the mistake, and then type the correct text. For information about more sophisticated ways of checking and correcting spelling, see "Correcting and Sizing Text While Typing" and "Checking Spelling and Choosing the Best Words," both later in this chapter.

3. In the **Overview** pane, click the **Outline** tab.

   Notice that the text you typed also appears there.

On the Outline tab, a slide icon appears adjacent to the slide title.

Troubleshooting The appearance of buttons and groups on the ribbon changes depending on the width of the program window. For information about changing the appearance of the ribbon to match our screen images, see "Modifying the Display of the Ribbon" at the beginning of this book.

4. In the **Slide** pane, click the **Click to add subtitle** placeholder.

5. Type **Ensuring Successful Outcomes**, and then press Enter to move the cursor to a new line in the same placeholder.

6. Type **Judy Lew, Purchasing Manager**.

   As you enter titles and bullet points throughout the exercises, don't type any ending punctuation marks.

7. On the Quick Access Toolbar, click the **Save** button.

   We won't tell you to save your work again in this exercise. Suffice it to say that you should save often.

8. Add a new slide with the **Title and Content** layout.

   See Also For information about adding slides, see "Adding and Deleting Slides" in Chapter 13, "Work with Slides."

   PowerPoint creates a slide with placeholders for a title and either a bulleted list or an illustration. The Outline tab now displays an icon for a second slide, and the status bar displays *Slide 2 of 2*.

9. Without clicking anywhere, type **Overview**.

   If you start typing on an empty slide without first selecting a placeholder, PowerPoint enters the text into the title placeholder.

10. On the **Outline** tab, click to the right of **Overview**, and then press Enter.

    PowerPoint adds a slide to the presentation, and an icon for slide 3 appears in the Outline pane.

11. Press the Tab key.

    The new slide changes to a bullet point on slide 2. The bullet is gray until you enter text for the bullet point.

12. Type **Preparing for a buying trip**, and then press Enter.

    PowerPoint adds a new bullet at the same level.

13. Type **Traveling internationally**, and then press Enter.

14. Type **Meeting the client**, and then press Enter.

15. Press Shift+Tab.

    On the Outline tab, the bullet changes into an icon for slide 3.

When you create a slide on the Outline tab, the new slide is displayed in the Slide pane.

16. Type **Preparing for a Buying Trip**, press Enter, and then press Tab.

17. Type **Know your needs**, and then press Enter.

18. On the **Home** tab, in the **Paragraph** group, click the **Increase List Level** button.

    PowerPoint creates a subpoint.

    Tip You can use the Increase List Level button to change slide titles to bullet points and bullet points to subpoints, both in the Slide pane and on the Outline tab. You can also use the Decrease List Level button to change subpoints to bullet points and bullet points to slide titles in both places. However, when you're entering text on the Outline tab, it's quicker to use keys—Tab and Shift+Tab—to perform these functions than it is to take your hands off the keyboard to use your mouse.

19. Type **Know your customers**, press Enter, and then type **Know the current trends**.

20. Press Ctrl+Enter.

Instead of creating another bullet, PowerPoint creates a new slide.

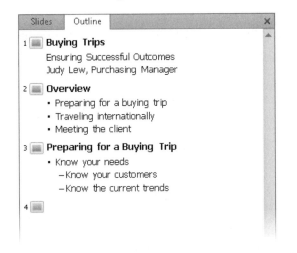

If you know what text you want to appear on your slides, it is often quicker to work on the Outline tab.

✖ **CLEAN UP** Save the BuyingTripsA presentation, and then close it.

Adding Text Boxes

The size and position of the placeholders on a slide are dictated by the slide's design. Every slide you create with a particular layout of a particular design has the same placeholders in the same locations, and the text you type in them has the same format.

If you want to add text that does not belong in a placeholder—for example, if you want to add an annotation to a graphic—you can create an independent text box and enter the text there. You can create a text box in two ways:

- You can click the Text Box button, click the slide where you want the text to appear, and then type. The text box grows to fit what you type on one line, even expanding beyond the border of the slide if necessary.

- You can click the Text Box button, drag a box where you want the text to appear on the slide, and then type. When the text reaches the right boundary of the box, the height of the box expands by one line so that the text can wrap. As you continue typing, the width of the box stays the same, but the height grows as necessary to accommodate all the text.

When you click inside a text box, the box is surrounded by a dashed border. You can then enter new text or edit existing text.

When the border is dashed, you can enter or edit text.

Clicking the dashed border changes it to a solid border. You can then manipulate the text box as a unit.

When the border is solid, you can manipulate the box.

You can move a text box by dragging its border, and you can copy it just as easily by holding down the Ctrl key while you drag. You can drag the blue squares and circles around the border of the box, which are called *sizing handles*, to change the size and shape of the text box. If you want the text in the text box to be oriented differently than the rest of the text on the slide, you can drag the green circle, which is called the *rotating handle*, to accomplish this purpose.

If you want to create a text box of a specific size or shape, you can right-click the box's border, click Format Shape, click Size in the Format Shape dialog box, and then change the settings. On the Text Box page of this dialog box, you can change the direction of text by displaying the Text Direction list and clicking one of the Rotate options. You can click Stacked in this list to keep the individual characters horizontal but make them run from top to bottom in the box instead of from left to right.

Tip If you want to change the size, shape, or behavior of a placeholder on an individual slide, you can use the same techniques as those you use with text boxes. If you want to make changes to the same placeholder on every slide, you should make the adjustments on the presentation's master slide. For more information about working with master slides, refer to *Microsoft PowerPoint 2010 Step by Step*, by Joyce Cox and Joan Lambert (Microsoft Press, 2010).

The Text Box page of the Format Shape dialog box.

On the Text Box page, you can also specify whether PowerPoint should shrink the text to fit the box if it won't all fit at the default size (18 points), and whether the text should wrap within the box.

To deselect the text box, you click a blank area of the slide. The border then disappears. If you want a text box to have a border when it's not selected, you can display the Format Shape dialog box, and on the Line Color page, select either Solid Line or Gradient Line. You can then fine-tune the border's color or gradient to achieve the effect you want.

In this exercise, you'll select and deselect a placeholder to see the effect on its border. You'll create one text box whose height stays constant while its width increases and another whose width stays constant while its height increases. You'll manipulate these text boxes by rotating and moving one of them and sizing the other.

SET UP You need the BuyingTripsB_start presentation located in your Chapter14 practice file folder to complete this exercise. Open the BuyingTripsB_start presentation, and save it as *BuyingTripsB*. Then follow the steps.

1. Move to slide **2**, and then on the slide, click the slide title.

   The cursor and dashed border indicate that the placeholder is selected for editing.

2. Point to the border of the placeholder, and when the pointer changes to a four-headed arrow, click the mouse button once.

   The placeholder is selected as a unit, as indicated by the solid border. Although you won't usually want to change the size or location of a text placeholder, while the placeholder has a solid border, you can size and move it just like any other text box. Your changes will affect only the placeholder on the current slide, not corresponding placeholders on other slides.

3. To deselect the placeholder, click outside it in a blank area of the slide.

4. Move to slide **5**, and then click anywhere in the bulleted list to display its placeholder.

5. On the **Insert** tab, in the **Text** group, click the **Text Box** button, and then point below and to the left of the placeholder for the bulleted list.

   The pointer shape changes to an upside-down *t*.

6. Click the slide to create a text box.

   A small, empty text box appears with a cursor blinking inside it.

Clicking the slide creates a single-line text box.

7. Type **Critical to get things off to a good start**.

   The width of the text box increases to accommodate the text as you type it.

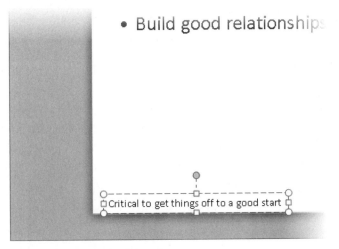

   The text box grows horizontally.

8. To rotate the text so that it reads vertically instead of horizontally, point to the green rotating handle that is attached to the upper-middle handle of the text box, and drag it 90 degrees clockwise.

   Tip You can also rotate a text box by selecting the box for manipulation, and then on the Format contextual tab, in the Arrange group, clicking the Rotate button. In the list that appears, you can select an option to rotate the text box by 90 degrees to the left or right or to flip it horizontally or vertically.

9. Point to the border of the box (not to a handle), and then drag the box up and to the right, until it sits at the right edge of the slide.

10. Right-click the border of the box, and then click **Format Shape**.

11. In the **Format Shape** dialog box, click **Line Color**. Then click **Solid Line**.

    The page changes to allow you to pick the line color you want.

The Line Color page of the Format Shape dialog box.

12. Click the **Color** button, and in the top row of the **Theme Colors** palette, click the orange box (**Orange, Accent 6**). Then click **Close**.

13. Click a blank area of the slide to deselect the text box so that you can see the orange border.

14. Move to slide **6**, and then in the **Text** group, click the **Text Box** button. On the left side of the area below the bulleted list, drag approximately **2** inches to the right and **0.5** inch down.

No matter what height you make the box, it snaps to a standard height when you release the mouse button.

15. Type **The Buyer manual has important information about the minimum requirements**.

The width of the box does not change, but the height of the box increases to accommodate the complete entry.

The text box grows vertically.

16. Click the border of the text box to select it as a unit. Then drag the solid border and the white sizing handles until the box is two lines high and the same width as the bullet points.

17. Click a blank area of the slide to deselect the text box.

    The border of the text box is no longer visible.

You can manually adjust the size and shape of a text box.

✖ **CLEAN UP** Save the BuyingTripsB presentation, and then close it.

Changing the Default Font for Text Boxes

When you create a text box, PowerPoint applies default settings such as the font, size, and style—regular, bold, and italic—as well as other effects, such as underline, small capitals, and embossing. To save yourself some formatting steps, you can change the default settings for the presentation you are working on.

To save the current settings as the new default:

1. In a new, blank presentation, create a text box and enter some text in it.
2. Select the text, and then on the Home tab, click the Font dialog box launcher.
3. Select the font, font style, size, color, underline style, and effects you want to apply to all the text boxes you create from now on in this presentation, and then click OK.

   You can also add other effects, such as a fill color, outline formatting, or a special effect.

   See Also For information about these other effects, refer to *Microsoft PowerPoint 2010 Step by Step*, by Joyce Cox and Joan Lambert (Microsoft Press, 2010).

4. Select the text box itself, right-click its border, and then click Set As Default Text Box.
5. Create another text box on the same slide, and then enter text in it.

   The text appears with the new default settings.

Editing Text

After you enter text in either a placeholder or a text box, you can change it at any time. You can insert new text by clicking where you want to make the insertion and simply typing. However, before you can change existing text, you have to select it by using the following techniques:

- **Word** Double-click the word to select the word and the space following it. Punctuation following the word is not selected.

- **Adjacent words, lines, or paragraphs** Drag through them. Alternatively, position the cursor at the beginning of the text you want to select, hold down the Shift key, and either press an arrow key to select characters one at a time or click at the end of the text you want to select.

- **Slide title** Click its slide icon on the Outline tab.

- **Bullet point or subpoint** Click its bullet on either the Outline tab or the slide.

- **All the text in a placeholder** Click inside the placeholder, click the Select button in the Editing group on the Home tab, and then click Select All.

   Keyboard Shortcut Press Ctrl+A after clicking inside the placeholder to select all the text.

- **All the objects on a slide** Select a placeholder (so that it has a solid border), click the Select button, and then click Select All. All the other objects on that slide are added to the selection. You can then work with all the objects as a unit.

   Tip Clicking Select and then Selection Pane displays the Selection And Visibility task pane, where you can specify whether particular objects should be displayed or hidden. You might want to hide an object if you're using the slide in similar presentations for two different audiences, one of which needs more detail than the other.

Selected text appears highlighted in the location where you made the selection—that is, on either the slide or the Outline tab.

To replace a selection, you type the new text. To delete the selection, you press either the Delete key or the Backspace key.

If you want to move or copy the selected text, you have three options:

- **Drag-and-drop editing** Use this feature, which is frequently referred to simply as *dragging*, when you need to move or copy text within the same slide or to a slide that is visible on the Outline tab without scrolling. Start by using any of the methods described previously to select the text. Then point to the selection, hold down the mouse button, drag the text to its new location, and release the mouse button. To copy the selection, hold down the Ctrl key while you drag.

- **Cut, Copy, and Paste buttons** Use this method when you need to move or copy text between two locations that you cannot see at the same time—for example, between slides that are not visible simultaneously on the Outline tab. Select the text, and click the Cut or Copy button in the Clipboard group on the Home tab. (The cut or copied item is stored in an area of your computer's memory called the *Microsoft Office Clipboard*, hence the name of the group.) Then reposition the cursor, and click the Paste button to insert the selection in its new location. If you click the Paste arrow instead of the button, PowerPoint displays a list of different ways to paste the selection.

Under Paste Options, buttons represent the ways in which you can paste the item.

Pointing to a button under Paste Options displays a preview of how the cut or copied item will look when pasted into the text in that format, so you can experiment with different ways of pasting until you find the one you want.

See Also For more information about the Clipboard, see the sidebar "About the Clipboard" later in this chapter.

- **Keyboard shortcuts** It can be more efficient to press key combinations to cut, copy, and paste selections than to click buttons on the ribbon. The main keyboard shortcuts for editing tasks are listed in the following table.

Task	Keyboard shortcuts
Cut	Ctrl+X
Copy	Ctrl+C
Paste	Ctrl+V
Undo	Ctrl+Z
Repeat/Redo	Ctrl+Y

Tip While moving and copying text on the Outline tab, you can collapse bullet points under slide titles so that you can see more of the presentation at one time. Double-click the icon of the slide whose bullet points you want to hide. Double-click again to redisplay the bullet points. To expand or collapse the entire outline at once, right-click the title of a slide, point to Expand or Collapse, and then click Expand All or Collapse All.

If you change your mind about a change you have made, you can reverse it by clicking the Undo button on the Quick Access Toolbar. If you undo an action in error, you can click the Redo button on the Quick Access Toolbar to reverse the change.

To undo multiple actions at the same time, you can click the Undo arrow and then click the earliest action you want to undo in the list. You can undo actions only in the order in which you performed them—that is, you cannot reverse your fourth previous action without first reversing the three actions that followed it.

Tip The number of actions you can undo is set to 20, but you can change that number by clicking the File tab to display the Backstage view, clicking Options to display the PowerPoint Options dialog box, clicking Advanced, and then in the Editing Options area of the Advanced page, changing the Maximum Number Of Undos setting.

In this exercise, you'll delete and replace words, as well as move bullet points and sub-points on the Outline tab and on slides.

SET UP You need the BuyingTripsC_start presentation located in your Chapter14 practice file folder to complete this exercise. Open the BuyingTripsC_start presentation, and save it as *BuyingTripsC*. Then follow the steps.

1. On the **Outline** tab, in the first bullet on slide **2**, double-click the word **buying**.

   When you select text on either the Outline tab or the slide, a small toolbar (called the *Mini Toolbar*) containing options for formatting the text appears. If you ignore the Mini Toolbar, it fades from view.

   See Also For information about using the Mini Toolbar, see "Changing the Alignment, Spacing, Size, and Look of Text" in Chapter 15, "Format Slides."

2. Press the Delete key.

3. In the slide **3** title, double-click **Buying**, and then press the Backspace key.

4. In the third bullet point on slide **5**, double-click **good**, and then type **lasting**, followed by a space.

   What you type replaces the selection. Notice that the text also changes in the Slide pane.

5. On slide **4**, click the bullet to the left of **Know the culture**.

   The entire bullet point is selected, including the invisible paragraph mark at the end.

   Tip When you want to work with a bullet point or subpoint as a whole, you need to ensure that the invisible paragraph mark at its end is included in the selection. If you drag across the text on the slide, you might miss the paragraph mark. As a precaution, hold down the Shift key and press End to be sure that the paragraph mark is part of the selection.

6. On the **Home** tab, in the **Clipboard** group, click the **Cut** button.

   Keyboard Shortcut Press Ctrl+X to cut the selection.

7. Click to the left of the word **Make** in the first bullet point on slide **5**, and then click the **Paste** button.

   Keyboard Shortcut Press Ctrl+V to paste the contents of the Clipboard.

   You have moved the bullet point from slide 4 to slide 5.

8. Display slide **3** in the **Slide** pane, and click the bullet point to the left of **Know your needs** to select the bullet point and its subpoints.

9. Drag the selection down and to the left of **Read the Buyer manual**.

   The bullet point and its subpoints move as a unit.

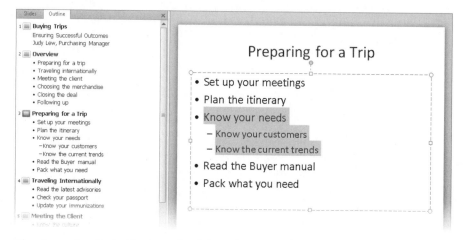

The change is reflected both on the slide and on the Outline tab.

10. On the Quick Access Toolbar, click the **Undo** button to reverse your last editing action.

    Keyboard Shortcut Press Ctrl+Z to undo the last editing action.

    The Redo button appears on the Quick Access Toolbar, to the right of Undo. When you point to the Undo or Redo button, the name in the ScreenTip reflects your last editing action—for example, Redo Drag And Drop.

11. On the Quick Access Toolbar, click the **Redo** button to restore the editing action.

    Keyboard Shortcut Press Ctrl+Y to restore the last editing action.

 CLEAN UP Save the BuyingTripsC presentation, and then close it.

About the Clipboard

You can view the items that have been cut or copied to the Clipboard in the Clipboard task pane, which you display by clicking the Clipboard dialog box launcher on the Home tab.

The Clipboard stores items that have been cut or copied from any presentation.

To paste an individual item at the cursor, you simply click the item in the Clipboard task pane. To paste all the items, click the Paste All button. You can point to an item, click the arrow that appears, and then click Delete to remove it from the Clipboard and the task pane, or you can remove all the items by clicking the Clear All button.

You can control the behavior of the Clipboard task pane by clicking Options at the bottom of the pane, and choosing the circumstances under which you want the task pane to appear.

To close the Clipboard task pane, click the Close button at the right end of its title bar.

Correcting and Sizing Text While Typing

We all make mistakes while typing text in a presentation. To help you ensure that these mistakes don't go uncorrected, PowerPoint uses the AutoCorrect feature to catch and automatically correct many common capitalization and spelling errors. For example, if you type *teh* instead of *the* or *WHen* instead of *When*, AutoCorrect immediately corrects the entry.

Tip If you don't want an entry you type to be corrected—for example, if you want to start a new paragraph with a lowercase letter—click the Undo button on the Quick Access Toolbar when AutoCorrect makes the change.

You can customize AutoCorrect to recognize misspellings you routinely type or to ignore text you do not want AutoCorrect to change. You can also create your own AutoCorrect entries to automate the typing of frequently used text. For example, you might customize AutoCorrect to enter the name of your organization when you type only an abbreviation.

In addition to providing the AutoCorrect feature to correct misspellings as you type, PowerPoint provides an AutoFit feature to size text to fit its placeholder. By default, if you type more text than will fit in a placeholder, PowerPoint reduces the size of the text so that all the text fits, and displays the AutoFit Options button to the left of the placeholder. Clicking this button displays a menu that gives you control over automatic sizing. For example, you can stop sizing text for the current placeholder while retaining the AutoFit settings for other placeholders.

Tip You can also change the AutoFit settings for a placeholder on the Text Box page of the Format Shape dialog box. In the Autofit area, you can change the default Shrink Text On Overflow setting to Do Not Autofit. You can also specify that instead of the text being sized to fit the placeholder, the placeholder should be sized to fit the text.

You can change the default AutoFit settings by clicking Control AutoCorrect Options on the AutoFit Options button's menu to display the AutoFormat As You Type page of the AutoCorrect dialog box.

Clear the AutoFit Title Text To Placeholder and AutoFit Body Text To Placeholder check boxes to stop making text fit in the placeholder.

In this exercise, you'll use AutoCorrect to fix a misspelled word and you'll add an AutoCorrect entry. Then you'll use AutoFit to size text so that it fits within its placeholder and to make a long bulleted list fit on one slide by converting its placeholder to a two-column layout.

 SET UP You need the CommunityServiceA_start presentation located in your Chapter14 practice file folder to complete this exercise. Open the Community-ServiceA_start presentation, and save it as *CommunityServiceA*. Then follow the steps.

1. Display slide **2**, and click the content placeholder.

2. Being careful for the purposes of this exercise to include the misspellings, type **Set up teh teem**, press the Enter key, and then type **Gather adn analyze data**.

   Almost immediately, AutoCorrect changes *teh* to *the* and *adn* to *and*. Notice that AutoCorrect does not change *teem* to *team*, or even flag it as a misspelling because *teem* is a legitimate word. PowerPoint cannot detect that you have used this homonym for *team* incorrectly. (A homonym is a word that sounds the same as another word but has a different meaning.)

3. Click the **File** tab to display the Backstage view, click **Options**, and then in the left pane of the **PowerPoint Options** dialog box, click **Proofing**.

4. In the **AutoCorrect options** area, click **AutoCorrect Options**.

   The AutoCorrect dialog box opens.

The AutoCorrect page of the AutoCorrect dialog box.

Troubleshooting If the AutoCorrect page is not active, click its tab to display its options.

The top part of the dialog box lists general rules for correcting errors such as capitalization mistakes. You can change any of these rules by clearing the associated check box.

5. In the lower part of the dialog box, scroll through the huge table of misspellings.

   When you type one of the entries in the first column, PowerPoint automatically substitutes the correct spelling from the second column. For this exercise, suppose you often misspell the word *category* as *catigory*.

6. In the **Replace** box above the table, type **catigory**, and then press the Tab key.

   The table below scrolls to show you similar words that are already in the AutoCorrect list.

7. In the **With** box, type **category**, and then click **Add**.

   Now if you type *catigory* in any presentation, PowerPoint will replace it with *category*.

8. Click **OK** to close the **AutoCorrect** dialog box, and then click **OK** again to close the **PowerPoint Options** dialog box.

9. On slide **2**, with the cursor to the right of the word **data**, press Enter, type **Assign to a catigory**, and then press Enter.

   PowerPoint changes the word *catigory* to *category*.

10. Display slide **1**, click the subtitle placeholder, and type **Community Service Committee**.

11. Without moving the cursor, hold down the Shift key, and click to the left of **Community** to select the three words you just typed. Then press Ctrl+C to copy the words to the Clipboard.

12. Open the **PowerPoint Options** dialog box, and then open the **AutoCorrect** dialog box.

13. With the cursor in the **Replace** box, type **csc**. Then click the **With** box, press Ctrl+V to paste in the words you copied to the Clipboard, and click **Add**.

14. Close the **AutoCorrect** dialog box, and then close the **PowerPoint Options** dialog box.

15. Display slide **3**, and click to the left of **Responsibilities**. Then type **csc**, and press the Spacebar.

    PowerPoint changes the initials *csc* to *Community Service Committee*.

Set up team

- **Community Service Committee Responsibilities**
  - Contact people recommended as department reps

AutoCorrect makes the replacement if you follow csc *with a space or a punctuation mark.*

16. Display slide **1**, and click at the right end of the title.

    Notice that the setting in the Font Size box in the Font group on the Home tab is 44.

17. Type **:** (a colon), press Enter, and then type **Planning, Selling, and Executing a Project**.

When you type the word *Project*, AutoFit reduces the size of the title to 40 so that it fits in the title placeholder.

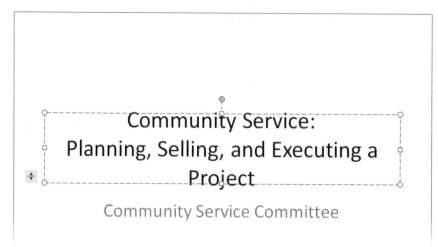

After AutoFit reduces the size of text, the AutoFit Options button appears to the left of the adjusted placeholder.

18. Click the **AutoFit Options** button.

    A menu of options appears.

You can click Stop Fitting Text To This Placeholder to reverse the size adjustment and prevent future adjustments.

19. Press the Esc key to close the menu without making a selection.

20. Display slide **8**, click at the right end of the last subpoint, and notice that the font size is 28. Then press Enter, and type **How do we know if we are successful?**

    The text size changes from 28 to 26.

21. Click the **AutoFit Options** button.

    The menu of options appears.

The menu for a bulleted list includes more options than the one for a title placeholder.

22. Click **Change to Two Columns**.

    The placeholder is instantly formatted to accommodate a two-column bulleted list.

23. Click a blank area of the slide.

    When the placeholder is not selected, it is easier to see the results.

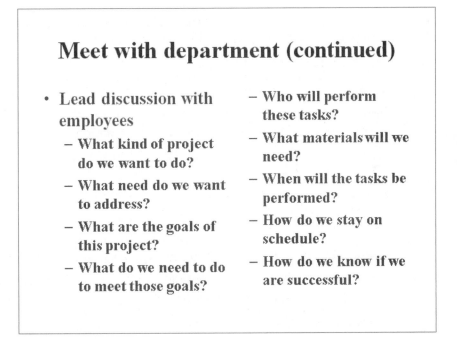

A two-column bulleted list.

CLEAN UP If you want, display the AutoCorrect dialog box, and remove the *catigory* and *csc* entries from the replacement table. Save the CommunityServiceA presentation, and then close it.

Checking Spelling and Choosing the Best Words

The AutoCorrect feature is very useful if you frequently type the same misspelling. However, most misspellings are the result of erratic finger-positioning errors or memory lapses. You can use two different methods to ensure that the words in your presentations are spelled correctly in spite of these random occurrences.

● By default, PowerPoint's spelling checker checks the spelling of the entire presentation—all slides, outlines, notes pages, and handout pages—against its built-in dictionary. To draw attention to words that are not in its dictionary and that might be misspelled, PowerPoint underlines them with a red wavy underline. You can right-click a word with a red wavy underline to display a menu with a list of possible spellings. You can choose the correct spelling from the menu or tell PowerPoint to ignore the word.

Tip To turn off this behind-the-scenes spell-checking, display the Backstage view, and click Options to open the PowerPoint Options dialog box. In the left pane, click Proofing, and then clear the Check Spelling As You Type check box.

● Instead of dealing with potential misspellings while you're creating a presentation, you can check the entire presentation in one session by clicking the Spelling button in the Proofing group on the Review tab. PowerPoint then works its way through the presentation, and if it encounters a word that is not in its dictionary, it displays the Spelling dialog box. After you indicate how PowerPoint should deal with the word, it moves on and displays the next word that is not in its dictionary, and so on.

The English-language version of Microsoft Office 2010 includes English, French, and Spanish dictionaries. If you use a word or phrase from a different language, you can mark it so that PowerPoint doesn't flag it as a misspelling.

You cannot make changes to the main dictionary in PowerPoint, but you can add correctly spelled words that are flagged as misspellings to the PowerPoint supplemental dictionary (called *CUSTOM.DIC*). You can also create and use custom dictionaries and use dictionaries from other Microsoft programs.

PowerPoint can check your spelling, but it can't alert you if you're not using the best word. Language is often contextual—the language you use in a presentation to members of a club is different from the language you use in a business presentation. To make sure you're using words that best convey your meaning in any given context, you can use the Thesaurus feature to look up alternative words, called *synonyms*, for a selected word.

Tip For many words, the quickest way to find a suitable synonym is to right-click the word, and point to Synonyms. You can then either click one of the suggested words or click Thesaurus to display the Research task pane.

In this exercise, you'll correct a misspelled word, mark a French phrase so that PowerPoint won't flag it as a misspelling, and check the spelling of an entire presentation. You'll then use the Thesaurus to replace a word on a slide with a more appropriate one.

SET UP You need the CommunityServiceB_start presentation located in your Chapter14 practice file folder to complete this exercise. Open the Community-ServiceB_start presentation, and save it as CommunityServiceB. Then follow the steps.

1. Display slide **2**, and right-click **infermation**, which PowerPoint has flagged as a possible error with a red wavy underline.

   PowerPoint doesn't know whether you want to format the word or correct its spelling, so it displays both a Mini Toolbar and a menu.

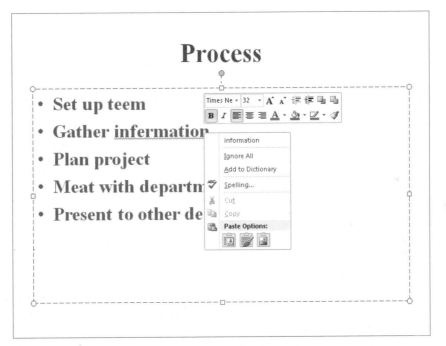

Right-clicking a flagged word displays options to format it or to correct it.

2. On the menu, click **information** to replace the misspelled word.

3. Move to slide **7**.

   The French words *Médecins* and *Frontières* have been flagged as possible errors.

4. Select **Médecins Sans Frontières**, and then on the **Review** tab, in the **Language** group, click the **Language** button, and then click **Set Proofing Language**.

   The Language dialog box opens.

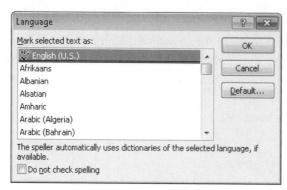

You can choose from a wide selection of languages in this dialog box.

5. Scroll down the list of languages, click **French (France)**, and then click **OK**.

   Behind the scenes, PowerPoint marks *Médecins Sans Frontières* as a French phrase, and the words no longer have red wavy underlines.

6. Click a corner of the slide so that no placeholders are selected, and then press Ctrl+Home.

7. On the **Review** tab, in the **Proofing** group, click the **Spelling** button.

   Keyboard Shortcut Press F7 to begin checking the spelling of a presentation.

   PowerPoint begins checking the spelling in the presentation. The spelling checker stops on the word *Persue* and displays the Spelling dialog box.

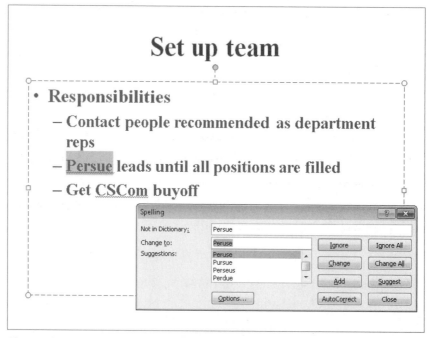

The words in the Suggestions list have the same capitalization as the possible misspelling.

8. In the **Suggestions** list, click **Pursue**, and then click **Change**.

   The spelling checker replaces *Persue* with the suggested *Pursue* and then stops on the word *CSCom*, suggesting *Como* as the correct spelling. For purposes of this exercise, assume that this is a common abbreviation for *Community Service Committee.*

9. Click **Add**.

   The term *CSCom* is added to the CUSTOM.DIC dictionary.

   Tip If you do not want to change a word or add it to the supplemental dictionary, you can click Ignore or Ignore All. The spelling checker then ignores either just that word or all instances of the word in the presentation during subsequent spell checking sessions.

   Next the spelling checker stops on *the* because it is the second of two occurrences of the word.

10. Click **Delete**.

    The duplicated word is deleted. Now the spelling checker identifies *employes* as a misspelling.

11. In the suggestions list, click **employees**, and then click **AutoCorrect**.

    PowerPoint adds the misspelling and the selected spelling to the AutoCorrect substitution table.

12. Click **Change** to change *succesful* to *successful.*

13. When a message box tells you that the spelling check is complete, click **OK**.

    This presentation still has spelling problems—words that are spelled correctly but that aren't correct in context. We'll leave it to you to proof the slides and correct these errors manually. In the meantime, we'll finish the exercise by using the Thesaurus to find a synonym.

14. On slide **1**, select the word **Executing** (but not the space following the word).

15. On the **Review** tab, in the **Proofing** group, click the **Thesaurus** button.

    Keyboard Shortcut Press Shift+F7 to activate the Thesaurus.

    The Research task pane opens on the right side of the screen, displaying a list of synonyms for the selected word.

The synonyms have the same capitalization as the selected word.

16. Below **Performing**, point to **Completing**, click the arrow that appears, and then click **Insert**.

    Tip If you don't see an obvious substitute for the selected word, click a word that is close in the Thesaurus list to display synonyms for that word.

17. At the right end of the **Research** task pane, click the **Close** button.

✖ CLEAN UP If you want, display the AutoCorrect dialog box, and remove the *employes* entry from the replacement table. To remove *CSCom* from the supplemental dictionary, display the Proofing page of the PowerPoint Options dialog box, and click Custom Dictionaries. Then in the Custom Dictionaries dialog box, click Edit Word List. Click CSCom, click Delete, and click OK three times. Then save and close the CommunityServiceB presentation.

Researching Information and Translating Text

In addition to the Thesaurus, the Research task pane provides access to a variety of informational resources. Display the Research task pane by clicking the Research button in the Proofing group and then enter a topic in the Search For box, specifying in the box below which resource PowerPoint should use to look for information about that topic. Clicking Research Options at the bottom of the Research task pane displays the Research Options dialog box, where you can specify which of a predefined set of reference materials and other Internet resources will be available from the list.

PowerPoint also comes with three translation tools with which you can quickly translate words and phrases, or even entire presentations.

- When the Mini Translator is turned on, you can point to a word or selected phrase to display a translation in the specified language. (You turn the Mini Translator on or off by clicking the Translate button in the Language group of the Review tab and then clicking Mini Translator.) When the box containing the translation is displayed, you can click the Expand button to display the Research task pane, where you can change the translation language. You can also copy the translated word or phrase, or hear it spoken for you.

  To change the default language used by the Mini Translator, click Choose Translation Language on the Translate menu. Then in the Translation Language Options dialog box, you can select from a list of languages, including Arabic, Chinese, Greek, Hebrew, Italian, Japanese, Korean, Polish, Portuguese, Russian, Spanish, and Swedish.

- To obtain the translation of a selected word, you can also click Translate Selected Text in the Translate menu to display the Research task pane. In the task pane, you can also type a word in the Search For box, specify the language you want, and then click Start Searching. PowerPoint consults the online bilingual dictionary for the language you chose and displays the result.

Finding and Replacing Text and Fonts

Sometimes a word you use might be correctly spelled but just not be the correct word. You can find and change specific text in a presentation by clicking the buttons in the Editing group on the Home tab to do the following:

- Click the Find button to locate each occurrence of a word, part of a word, or a phrase. In the Find dialog box, you enter the text, and then click Find Next. You can specify whether PowerPoint should locate only matches with the exact capitalization (also known as the *case*); in other words, if you specify *person*, you don't want PowerPoint to locate *Person*. You can also tell PowerPoint whether it should locate only matches for the entire text; in other words, if you specify *person*, you don't want PowerPoint to locate *personal*.

- Click the Replace button to locate each occurrence of a word, part of a word, or a phrase and replace it with something else. In the Replace dialog box, you enter the text you want to find and what you want to replace it with, click Find Next, and then click Replace to replace the found occurrence. You can also click Replace All to replace all occurrences. Again, you can specify whether to match capitalization and whole words.

You can also click the Replace arrow, and in the Replace list, click Replace Fonts to find and replace a font throughout a presentation. In the Replace Font dialog box, you can specify the font you want to change and the font you want PowerPoint to replace it with.

In this exercise, you'll first find and replace a word and then find and replace a font.

SET UP You need the CommunityServiceC_start presentation located in your Chapter14 practice file folder to complete this exercise. Open the Community-ServiceC_start presentation, and save it as *CommunityServiceC*. Then follow the steps.

1. On the **Home** tab, in the **Editing** group, click the **Replace** button.

   Keyboard Shortcut Press Ctrl+H to open the Replace dialog box.

   The Replace dialog box opens.

If you have already used the Find or Replace command, your previous Find What and Replace With entries carry over to this replace operation.

Tip To move a dialog box so that it doesn't hide the text, drag its title bar.

2. In the **Find what** box, type **department**, and then press Tab.

3. In the **Replace with** box, type **unit**.

4. Select the **Match case** check box to locate text that exactly matches the capitalization you specified and replace it with the capitalization you specified.

5. Click **Find Next**.

   PowerPoint finds and selects part of the word *departments* on slide 2.

If you select the Find Whole Words Only check box, PowerPoint does not match this instance of department.

6. Click **Replace**.

   PowerPoint replaces *departments* with *units*, and then locates the next match.

7. Click **Replace All**.

   A message box tells you that PowerPoint has finished searching the presentation and that the replace operation changed nine occurrences of the text.

8. Click **OK**, and then in the **Replace** dialog box, click **Close**.

   Because you selected Match Case for this replace operation, one occurrence of *Department* has not been changed. We'll leave it to you to change it manually.

9. Click a blank area of the current slide so that no placeholder is selected, press Ctrl+Home to move to slide **1**, and then click the title.

   Notice that *Calibri (Headings)* is displayed in the Font box in the Font group.

10. Display slide **2**, and click first the title and then any bullet point.

    Notice that the font used for these elements is Times New Roman. Let's change this font to make it consistent with the title slide.

11. Click a corner of the slide so that no placeholder is selected.

12. In the **Editing** group, click the **Replace** arrow, and then click **Replace Fonts**.

    The Replace Font dialog box opens.

The default setting is to replace all instances of the Arial font with the Agency FB font.

13. Display the **Replace** list, and click **Times New Roman**.

    The Replace list includes only Arial and the fonts in the presentation.

14. Display the **With** list, and click **Calibri**.

    The With list includes all the fonts available on your computer.

15. Click **Replace**.

    All the Times New Roman text in the presentation changes to Calibri.

16. Click **Close** to close the **Replace Font** dialog box.

✖ **CLEAN UP** Save the CommunityServiceC presentation, and then close it.

Key Points

- You can enter and edit text both on the Outline tab or directly on a slide, depending on which is most efficient.

- You can place text wherever you want it on a slide by using text boxes.

- PowerPoint provides assistance by correcting common spelling errors and adjusting the size of text so that it fits optimally on a slide.

- The spelling checker flags possible misspellings so that you can take care of them as you type. Or you can check the spelling of an entire presentation.

- You can take advantage of the Find and Replace features to ensure consistent use of terms and fonts throughout a presentation.

Chapter at a Glance

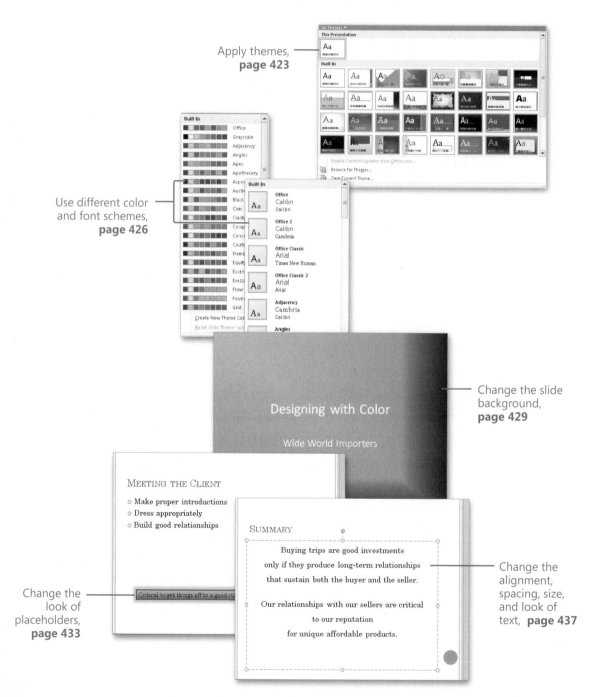

Apply themes,
page 423

Use different color
and font schemes,
page 426

Change the slide
background,
page 429

Change the
look of
placeholders,
page 433

Change the
alignment,
spacing, size,
and look of
text, **page 437**

15 Format Slides

In this chapter, you will learn how to

✔ Apply themes.

✔ Use different color and font schemes.

✔ Change the slide background.

✔ Change the look of placeholders.

✔ Change the alignment, spacing, size, and look of text.

An overall consistent look, punctuated by variations that add weight exactly where it is needed, can enhance the likelihood that your message will be well received and absorbed by your intended audience. To make your Microsoft PowerPoint 2010 presentations visually appealing, you can add enhancements to the presentation as a whole or to individual slides.

In this chapter, you'll apply a theme to a presentation and then change the theme's color and font schemes. You'll add color and shading to the background of slides and to the background of placeholders. Finally, you'll change the look of specific text elements.

> **Practice Files** Before you can complete the exercises in this chapter, you need to copy the book's practice files to your computer. The practice files you'll use to complete the exercises in this chapter are in the Chapter15 practice file folder. A complete list of practice files is provided in "Using the Practice Files" at the beginning of this book.

Applying Themes

When you create a presentation based on a template or a ready-made design, the presentation includes a theme—a combination of colors, fonts, formatting, graphics, and other elements that gives the presentation a coherent look. Even a presentation developed from scratch has a theme; the Office theme is applied by default. This theme consists of a white background, a very basic set of colors, and the Calibri font.

If you want to change the theme applied to a presentation, you can choose one from the Themes gallery. By using the Live Preview feature, you can easily try different effects until you find the one you want.

See Also For information about creating your own themes, refer to *Microsoft PowerPoint 2010 Step by Step*, by Joyce Cox and Joan Lambert (Microsoft Press, 2010).

In this exercise, you'll change the theme applied to one presentation that was created from scratch and to another that was created from a template.

SET UP You need the Landscaping_start and CompanyMeetingA_start presentations located in your Chapter15 practice file folder to complete this exercise. Open the presentations, and save them as *Landscaping* and *CompanyMeetingA*, respectively. Then follow the steps.

1. With the **Landscaping** presentation active, on the **Design** tab, in the **Themes** group, click the **More** button.

   The Themes gallery appears, displaying all the available themes.

The theme attached to this presentation is identified in the This Presentation area.

2. Point to each theme thumbnail in turn to see a live preview of what the presentation will look like with that theme applied.

   Notice that the themes are organized alphabetically and that their names appear in ScreenTips when you point to them.

3. Click the **Austin** thumbnail to apply that theme to the entire presentation.

4. Click the **Home** tab, and then on slide **1**, click the presentation's title.

   Instead of a white background with black text in the Calibri font, the presentation now has a green background design with title text in the Century Gothic font.

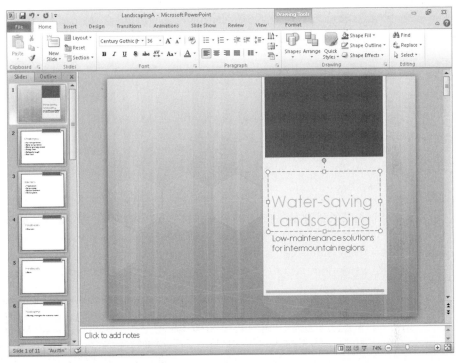

Most built-in themes have a distinctive title slide design that is modified for all the other slide layouts.

Troubleshooting The appearance of buttons and groups on the ribbon changes depending on the width of the program window. For information about changing the appearance of the ribbon to match our screen images, see "Modifying the Display of the Ribbon" at the beginning of this book.

5. On the **View** tab, in the **Window** group, click the **Switch Windows** button, and click **CompanyMeetingA** to switch to that presentation.

   This presentation already has a theme applied to it.

6. Display the **Themes** gallery, and then click the **Urban** thumbnail.

   The background of the presentation now has dark blue and teal accents, and the text is in blue Trebuchet and black Georgia.

✖ CLEAN UP Save and close the CompanyMeetingA and LandscapingA presentations.

Using Different Color and Font Schemes

Every presentation you create with PowerPoint 2010, even a blank one, has a set of colors, called a *color scheme*, associated with its theme. A color scheme consists of 12 complementary colors designed to be used for the following elements of a slide:

- **Text/Background** Use these four colors for dark text on a light background or light text on a dark background.

- **Accent 1 through Accent 6** Use these six colors for objects other than text.

- **Hyperlink** Use this color to draw attention to hyperlinks.

- **Followed Hyperlink** Use this color to indicate visited hyperlinks.

When you click color buttons such as the Font Color button in the Font group on the Home tab, the color palette displays 10 of the 12 colors with light to dark gradients. (The two background colors are not represented in these palettes.)

Understanding color schemes can help you create professional-looking presentations that use an appealing balance of color. You're not limited to using the colors in a presentation's color scheme, but because they have been selected by professional designers and are based on good design principles, using them ensures that your slides will be pleasing to the eye.

See Also For information about how scheme colors are allocated, refer to *Microsoft PowerPoint 2010 Step by Step*, by Joyce Cox and Joan Lambert (Microsoft Press, 2010). For information about using non-scheme colors, see the sidebar "Non–Color Scheme Colors" later in this chapter.

To view the color schemes you can apply to a presentation, you display the Colors gallery, which has Live Preview capabilities. When you find a color scheme you like, you simply click it to change the color scheme of all the slides in the presentation.

Tip To apply a color scheme only to a selected slide, right-click the scheme and then click Apply To Selected Slides

In addition to changing the color scheme, you can change the font scheme, which pro-vides two complementary fonts for each theme. The Fonts gallery lists the combinations in alphabetical order by theme. In each combination, the top font (called the *heading font*) is used for slides titles, and the bottom font (called the *body font*) is used for other slide text.

If none of the color schemes is exactly what you're looking for, you can create your own by clicking Create New Theme Colors at the bottom of the Colors gallery and assembling colors in the Create New Theme Colors dialog box. You can also create a custom font scheme by clicking Create New Theme Fonts at the bottom of the Fonts gallery and then specifying the font combination you want in the Create New Theme Fonts dialog box.

After you save either type of custom scheme, you can apply it to one or all of the slides in a presentation.

When you apply a different color scheme or font scheme to a presentation, your changes are stored with the presentation and do not affect the underlying theme.

Tip Also associated with each theme is an effects scheme. This scheme ensures that the shapes in the presentation have a consistent look. Clicking the Effects button in the Themes group of the Design tab displays a gallery of effect combinations to choose from.

In this exercise, you'll apply a different color scheme to a presentation, create your own scheme, change the color scheme of one slide, and then apply a different font scheme.

SET UP You need the CompanyMeetingB_start presentation located in your Chapter15 practice file folder to complete this exercise. Open the CompanyMeetingB_start presentation, and save it as *CompanyMeetingB*. Then follow the steps.

1. On the **Design** tab, in the **Themes** group, click the **Colors** button.

   The Colors gallery appears.

Built-In	
	Office
	Grayscale
	Adjacency
	Angles
	Apex
	Apothecary
	Aspect
	Austin
	Black Tie
	Civic
	Clarity
	Composite
	Concourse
	Couture
	Elemental
	Equity
	Essential
	Executive
	Flow
	Foundry
	Grid

   Create New Theme Colors...
   Reset Slide Theme Colors

   The color schemes show 8 of the 12 available colors.

2. In the gallery, point to a few color schemes, and watch the Live Preview effect on the active slide.

3. Click **Essential** to apply that color scheme to the presentation instead of the default color scheme of the Urban theme.

   Notice that the theme retains all of its other characteristics, such as the fonts and background graphic; only the colors change.

4. With slide **1** displayed, in the **Themes** group, click the **Colors** button.

5. Right-click the **Solstice** color scheme, and then click **Apply to Selected Slides**.

   PowerPoint applies the Solstice color scheme to only the title slide, changing its main background color from red to dark brown, but retaining the gold accent color.

6. On the **Design** tab, in the **Themes** group, click the **Fonts** button.

   The Fonts gallery appears.

Two fonts are assigned to each theme.

7. In the **Fonts** gallery, point to a few font schemes to display live previews of their effects on the active slide.

8. Click **Newsprint**.

   PowerPoint applies that font scheme to the presentation instead of the default font scheme of the Urban theme.

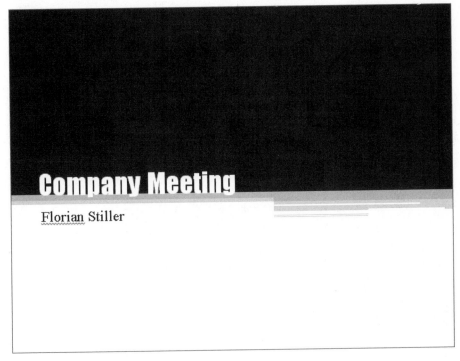

The title slide with the new font scheme.

✖ CLEAN UP Save the CompanyMeetingB presentation, and then close it.

Changing the Slide Background

In PowerPoint, you can customize the background of a slide by adding a solid color, a color gradient, a texture, or even a picture.

A color gradient is a visual effect in which a solid color gradually changes from light to dark or dark to light. PowerPoint offers several gradient patterns, each with variations. You can also choose a preset arrangement of colors from professionally designed backgrounds in which different colors gradually merge.

If you want something fancier than a solid color or a gradient, you can give the slide background a texture. PowerPoint comes with several built-in textures that you can easily apply to the background of slides. If none of these meets your needs, you might want to use a picture of a textured surface. For a dramatic effect, you can also incorporate an image or design of your own, although these are best reserved for small areas of the slide rather than the entire background.

In this exercise, you'll shade the background of one slide. Then you'll apply a textured background to all the slides in the presentation.

 SET UP You need the ColorDesign_start presentation located in your Chapter15 practice file folder to complete this exercise. Open the ColorDesign_start presentation, and save it as *ColorDesign*. Then follow the steps.

1. On the **Design** tab, in the **Background** group, click the **Background Styles** button.

   The Background Styles gallery appears.

   The gallery shows four solid colors and two gradients in each of four colors taken from the theme's color scheme.

2. In the gallery, point to each thumbnail in turn to see a live preview of its effects.

3. Click the third thumbnail in the second row (**Style 7**).

    Instantly, the background of all the slides in the presentation change to a blue gradient.

4. Click the **Background Styles** button again, and then at the bottom of the gallery, click **Format Background**.

    The Format Background dialog box opens.

The Fill page shows the settings that control the gradient.

5. Click the **Type** arrow to display the list of options, and then click **Rectangular**.

    Behind the dialog box, the active slide changes to reflect this setting.

6. Display the **Direction** list, and click the rightmost thumbnail (**From Top Left Corner**).

7. In the **Gradient stops** area, drag the middle handle on the slider (**Stop 2 of 3**) to the right until the **Position** setting is **80%**.

Behind the dialog box, you can see that 80 percent of the slide is now a lighter shade, with the gradient to dark occupying only about 20 percent.

8. Display the **Color** list, and then under **Theme Colors**, click the third box in the purple column (**Purple, Accent 4, Lighter 40%**).

9. Click **Close**.

PowerPoint applies the shaded background to the current slide only.

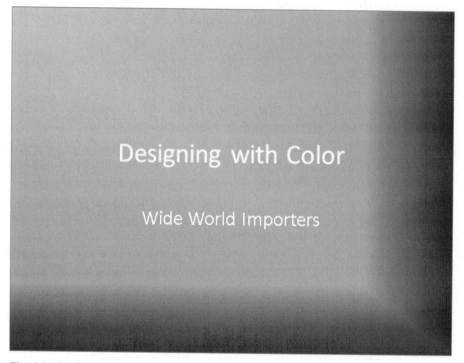

The title slide has a two-tone gradient that gives a raised effect.

10. Click the **Background Styles** button again, and then click **Format Background**.

11. In the **Format Background** dialog box, click **Picture or texture fill**.

The active slide shows a live preview of the default texture.

12. Display the **Texture** gallery, and then click **Purple mesh**.

13. Click the **Apply to All** button, and then click **Close**.

    PowerPoint applies the textured background to all the slides in the presentation.

14. In the **Themes** group, click the **More** button.

    The Themes gallery appears.

At the top of the gallery is a thumbnail reflecting the formatting you have applied to this presentation.

✖ **CLEAN UP** Save the ColorDesign presentation, and then close it.

Changing the Look of Placeholders

For a consistent look, you won't usually want to change the formatting of a presentation's placeholders. However, when you want to draw attention to an entire slide or an element of a slide, you can do so effectively by making specific placeholders stand out. You might also want to format text boxes that you have drawn manually on a slide.

See Also For information about drawing text boxes, see "Adding Text Boxes" in Chapter 14, "Work with Slide Text."

When you format a placeholder or a text box, you are essentially formatting a shape. You have the following options:

- Fill the background with a color, gradient, texture, pattern, or picture.
- Change the color and style of the shape's outline.
- Apply a style such as a shadow, reflection, or glow.
- Apply a three-dimensional effect.

In this exercise, you'll first apply a color to a text box. Then you'll change its border and give it a glow effect.

 SET UP You need the BusinessTravelA_start presentation located in your Chapter15 practice file folder to complete this exercise. Open the BusinessTravelA_start presentation, and save it as *BusinessTravelA*. Then follow the steps.

1. Display slide **5**, click anywhere in the free-standing text at the bottom of the slide, and then click the border of the text box to select the box for manipulation.

2. On the **Format** contextual tab, in the **Shape Styles** group, click the **Shape Fill** arrow.

   The Shape Fill palette appears.

Like other palettes, the Shape Fill palette reflects the theme's colors.

3. In the palette, point to a few colors in turn to see a live preview of its effects on the background of the text box.

4. Click the third shade in the orange column (**Orange, Accent 1, Lighter 40%**).

   The background of the text box is now a medium orange color.

5. Click the **Shape Fill** arrow again, and then below the palette, point to **Gradient**.

   The Gradient gallery appears.

This gallery offers light and dark versions of gradients in different directions.

6. Under **Dark Variations**, click the second thumbnail in the third row (**Linear Up**).

7. In the **Shape Styles** group, click the **Shape Outline** arrow, and under **Standard Colors**, click the **Dark Red** box.

8. Click the **Shape Outline** arrow again. Then below the palette, point to **Weight**, and in the list, click **3 pt**.

> **Tip** The abbreviation *pt* stands for *point*. A point is a unit of measurement used in the design and publishing industries. There are 72 points to the inch.

9. In the **Shape Styles** group, click the **Shape Effects** button.

A list of all the types of effects you can apply to the text box appears.

☐	P̲reset ▸
☐	S̲hadow ▸
☐	R̲eflection ▸
☐	G̲low ▸
☐	Soft E̲dges ▸
☐	B̲evel ▸
☐	3-D̲ Rotation ▸

Many possible effects are available with a couple of mouse clicks.

10. In turn, display the options for each type, and point to a few to see their live previews.

11. When you have finished exploring, point to **Glow**, and then click the first thumbnail in the last row (**Orange, 18 pt glow, Accent color 1**).

12. Click away from the text box to release the selection.

The text box is less likely to be overlooked now.

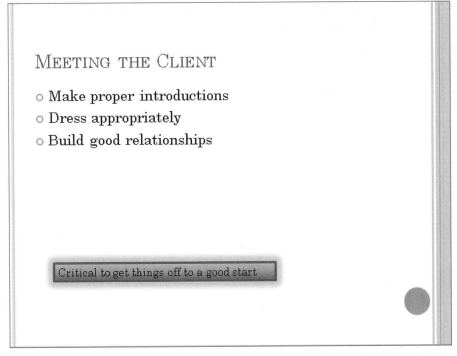

You can easily set off text boxes and placeholders with combinations of color, borders, and effects.

 CLEAN UP Save the BusinessTravelA presentation, and then close it.

Changing the Alignment, Spacing, Size, and Look of Text

In most PowerPoint templates, text appears as either a slide title or a bulleted list. The alignment and spacing of the text are controlled by the design built into the template. You can override these settings, which are collectively called *paragraph formatting*. Click anywhere in the paragraph, and then do the following:

● **Lists** Click the Bullets arrow to display a gallery of alternative built-in bullet symbols. You can click None to remove bullet formatting and create an ordinary paragraph. To switch to a numbered list, click the Numbering arrow, and then click the numbering style you want.

- **Alignment** Click one of the following alignment buttons in the Paragraph group on the Home tab:

  ○ Click the Align Text Left button to align text against the placeholder's left edge. Left-alignment is the usual choice for paragraphs.

  Keyboard Shortcut Press Ctrl+L to left-align text.

  ○ Click the Center button to align text in the middle of the placeholder. Center-alignment is often used for titles and headings.

  Keyboard Shortcut Press Ctrl+E to center text.

  ○ Click the Align Text Right button to align text against the placeholder's right edge. Right-alignment isn't used much for titles and paragraphs, but you might want to use it in text boxes.

  Keyboard Shortcut Press Ctrl+R to right-align text.

  ○ Click the Justify button to align text against both the left and right edges, adding space between words to fill the line. You might justify a single, non-bulleted paragraph on a slide for a neat look.

- **Line spacing** Click the Line Spacing button in the Paragraph group, and make a selection.

- **Paragraph spacing** Open the Paragraph dialog box, either by clicking the Line Spacing button and then clicking Line Spacing Options at the bottom of the menu or by clicking the dialog box launcher in the lower-right corner of the Paragraph group. You can then adjust the Before and After settings for the entire paragraph.

In addition to changing the look of paragraphs, you can manipulate the look of individual words by manually applying settings that are collectively called *character formatting*. After selecting the characters you want to format, you can make changes by using the commands in the Font group on the Home tab, as follows:

- **Font** Override the font specified by the font scheme by making a selection in the Font box.

- **Size** Manually control the size of text either by clicking the Increase Font Size or Decrease Font Size button or by setting a precise size in the Font Size box.

  Keyboard Shortcut Press Ctrl+Shift+> or Ctrl+Shift+< to increase or decrease font size.

Tip If you turn off AutoFit so that you can manually size text, you have two ways to adjust the size of placeholders to fit their text: by manually dragging the handles around a selected placeholder, or by clicking Resize Shape To Fit Text on the Text Box page of the Format Shape dialog box. For information about AutoFit, see "Correcting and Sizing Text While Typing" in Chapter 14, "Work with Slide Text."

- **Style** Apply attributes such as bold, italic, underlining, and shadow and strike-through effects to selected characters.

B *I* <u>U</u> **S** a̶b̶c̶

The character style buttons.

Keyboard Shortcut Press Ctrl+B to make text bold, Ctrl+I to make it italic, or Ctrl+U to underline it.

- **Color** Change the color of the selected characters by clicking the Font Color arrow and then clicking the color you want in the palette.

- **Case** Change the capitalization of the words—for example, you can change small letters to capital letters—by clicking the Change Case button and then clicking the case you want.

- **Character spacing** Increase or decrease the space between the letters in a selection by clicking the Character Spacing button and then clicking the option you want. You can also click More Spacing to display the Character Spacing page of the Font dialog box, where you can specify spacing more precisely.

Tip You can clear all manually applied character formatting from a selection by clicking the Clear All Formatting button.

To make it quick and easy to apply the most common paragraph and character formatting, PowerPoint displays the Mini Toolbar when you make a text selection. This toolbar contains the same buttons you'll find in the Font and Paragraph groups on the Home tab, but they're all in one place, adjacent to the selection. If you don't want to apply any of the Mini Toolbar formats, you can simply ignore it, and it will disappear.

Calibri (E ▾ 32 ▾ **A**ˆ ᴀˇ ⋮≡ ⋮≡ ⬚ ⬚
B *I* ≣ ≡ ≡ **A** ▾ ⬧ ▾ ⬚ ▾ ⬧

The Mini Toolbar.

After you have formatted the text on a slide, you might find that you want to adjust the way lines break to achieve a more balanced look. This is often the case with slide titles, but bullet points and regular text can sometimes also benefit from a few manually inserted line breaks. You can simply press Shift+Enter to insert a line break at the cursor.

This fine-tuning should wait until you have taken care of all other formatting of the slide element, because changing the font, size, and attributes of text can affect how it breaks.

In this exercise, you'll experiment with changing various types of character formatting and paragraph formatting to achieve the look you want. You'll also insert a few line breaks to balance the text on a slide.

SET UP You need the BusinessTravelB_start presentation located in your Chapter15 practice file folder to complete this exercise. Open the BusinessTravelB_start presentation, and save it as *BusinessTravelB*. Then follow the steps.

1. Display slide **3**, and in the fourth bullet point, double-click **Buyer**.

   The Mini Toolbar appears.

   Know your customers

   Know the current trends

   up your

   n the itin

   ad the Buyer manual

   ck what you need

   The Mini Toolbar is a shadow until you point to it.

2. Move the pointer over the Mini Toolbar to make it active, and then click the **Italic** button.

3. Display slide **4**, and in the **Slide** pane, drag diagonally across the four bullet points to select them.

4. On the **Home** tab, in the **Font** group, click the **Font Color** arrow. Then under **Standard Colors** in the palette, click the **Red** box.

Select

5. Display slide **5**, and click anywhere in the bulleted list. Then in the **Editing** group, click the **Select** button, and click **Select All**.

   All the text in the placeholder is selected. The text at the bottom is not selected because it is in a separate text box, not in the placeholder.

A⁺

6. In the **Font** group, click the **Increase Font Size** button until the setting in the **Font Size** box is **44**.

   Keyboard Shortcut Press Ctrl+Shift+> to increase the font size.

   Using the Increase Font Size and Decrease Font Size buttons takes the guesswork out of sizing text.

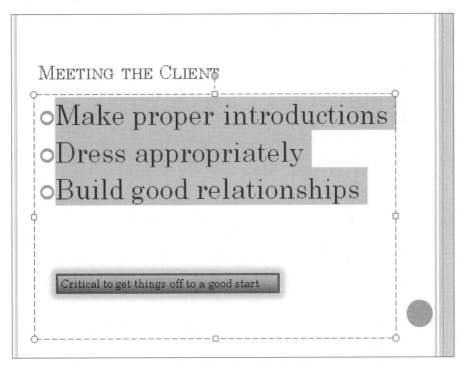

The first bullet point now spans the width of the placeholder.

7. In the **Font** group, click the **Clear All Formatting** button to return the font size to **24**.

8. Display slide **9**, and select both bullet points.

9. In the **Paragraph** group, click the **Bullets** arrow.

The Bullets gallery appears.

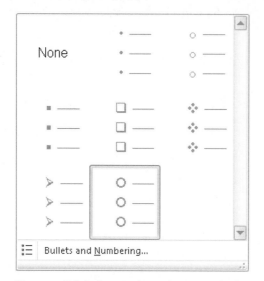

You can click Bullets And Numbering at the bottom of the gallery to create custom bullets.

10. In the gallery, click **None**.

The bullet points are converted to regular text paragraphs.

11. With both paragraphs still selected, in the **Paragraph** group, click the **Line Spacing** button, and then click **Line Spacing Options**.

The Paragraph dialog box opens.

You can set alignment, indentation, line spacing, and paragraph spacing all in one place.

12. In the **General** area, change the **Alignment** setting to **Centered**.

13. In the **Spacing** area, change the **Before** setting to **0 pt** and the **After** settings to **24 pt**. Then change the **Line Spacing** setting to **1.5 lines**.

14. Click **OK**.

15. In the first paragraph, click to the left of the word **only**, and press Shift+Enter to insert a line break.

16. Repeat step 15 to insert another line break before the word **that**.

17. In the second paragraph, insert a line break before the word **to** and another before the word **for**.

> The phrases of both paragraphs are now nicely balanced.

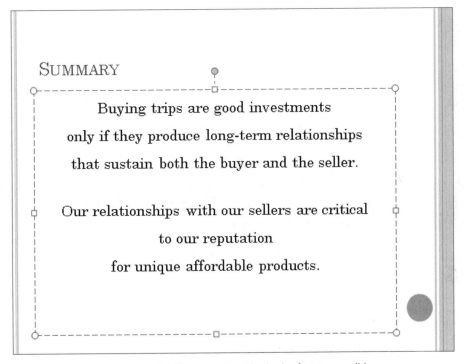

Line breaks can increase readability as well as the look of text on a slide.

✖ CLEAN UP Save the BusinessTravelB presentation, and then close it.

Non–Color Scheme Colors

Although working with the 12 colors of a harmonious color scheme enables you to create presentations with a pleasing design impact, you might want to use a broader range of colors. You can add colors that are not part of the color scheme by selecting the element whose color you want to change and then choosing a standard color from the Font Color palette or a custom color from the wide spectrum available in the Colors dialog box.

To apply a custom color:

1. Select text on a slide, and then on the Home tab, in the Font group, click the Font Color arrow.

2. At the bottom of the color palette, click More Colors.

   The Colors dialog box opens.

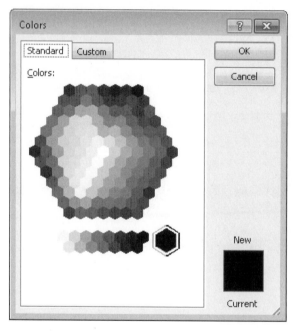

The Standard page of the Colors dialog box.

3. Click a color in the Colors spectrum, and then click OK.

   You can also click the Custom tab to display a color gradient where you can select a color based on precise Red/Green/Blue or Hue/Saturation/Luminescence settings.

After you use a color, it becomes available on all the palettes that appear when you click a button that applies color—for example, the Font Color button in the Font group on the Home tab. The color remains on the palettes even if you change the theme applied to the presentation.

Key Points

- Switching from one predefined theme to another is an easy way of changing the look of an entire presentation.

- You can apply a ready-made color scheme or font scheme to one or all the slides in a presentation, and you can create your own schemes.

- To dress up the background of one slide or of all the slides in a presentation, you can apply a solid color, a color gradient, a texture, or a picture.

- You can change the background, outline, and effect of specific placeholders or of text boxes.

- The formatting of paragraphs and text in a presentation can easily be changed by using the commands in the Focnt and Paragraph groups on the Home tab.

Chapter at a Glance

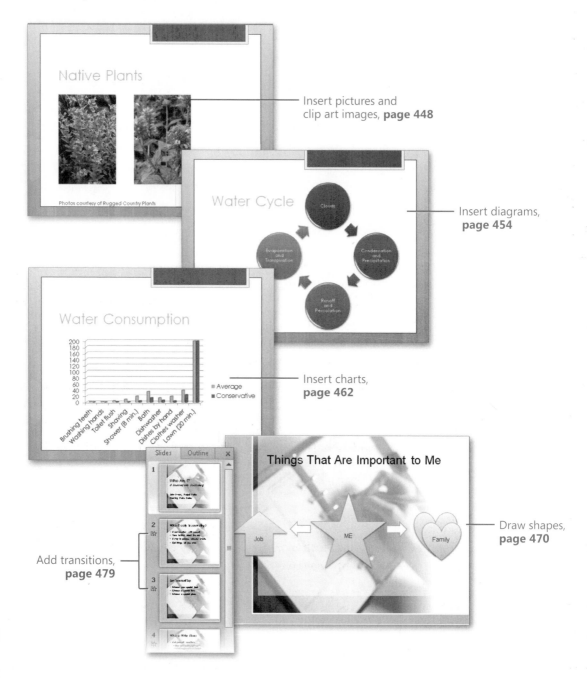

Insert pictures and clip art images, **page 448**

Insert diagrams, **page 454**

Insert charts, **page 462**

Draw shapes, **page 470**

Add transitions, **page 479**

16 Add Simple Visual Enhancements

In this chapter, you will learn how to

- ✔ Insert pictures and clip art images.
- ✔ Insert diagrams.
- ✔ Insert charts.
- ✔ Draw shapes.
- ✔ Add transitions.

With the ready availability of professionally designed templates, presentations have become more visually sophisticated and appealing. The words you use on your slides are no longer enough to guarantee the success of a presentation. These days, presentations are likely to have fewer words and more graphic elements. In fact, many successful presenters dispense with words altogether and use their slides only to graphically reinforce what they say when they deliver their presentations.

The general term *graphics* applies to several kinds of visual enhancements, including pictures, clip art images, diagrams, charts, and shapes. All of these types of graphics are inserted as objects on a slide and can then be sized, moved, and copied. For purposes of this chapter, we also consider transitions from one slide to another as a type of visual enhancement.

See Also For information about formatting and otherwise modifying graphics, refer to *Microsoft PowerPoint 2010 Step by Step*, by Joyce Cox and Joan Lambert (Microsoft Press, 2010).

In this chapter, you'll insert pictures and clip art images. You'll create a diagram and a chart, and you'll draw a simple illustration by using built-in shapes. Finally, you'll change the way slides move on and off the screen during a slide show.

> **Practice Files** Before you can complete the exercises in this chapter, you need to copy the book's practice files to your computer. The practice files you'll use to complete the exercises in this chapter are in the Chapter16 practice file folder. A complete list of practice files is provided in "Using the Practice Files" at the beginning of this book.

Inserting Pictures and Clip Art Images

You can add images created and saved in other programs as well as digital photographs to your Microsoft PowerPoint 2010 presentations. Collectively, these types of graphics are known as *pictures*. You might want to use pictures to make your slides more attractive and visually interesting, but you are more likely to use pictures to convey information in a way that words cannot. For example, you might display photographs of your company's new products in a presentation to salespeople.

If a slide has a content placeholder, you can insert a picture by clicking the Insert Picture From File button in the content placeholder. If the slide has no content placeholder, you can click the Picture button in the Images group on the Insert tab. Either way, the Insert Picture dialog box opens so that you can locate and insert the picture you want.

Tip Pictures you acquire from locations such as Web sites are often copyrighted, meaning that you cannot use them without the permission of the person who created them. Sometimes owners will grant permission if you give them credit. Professional photographers usually charge a fee to use their work. Always assume that pictures are copyrighted unless the source clearly indicates that they are license-free.

In addition to pictures you have acquired from various sources, you can insert clip art images into your slides. PowerPoint provides access to hundreds of professionally designed license-free clip art items that. These license-free graphics often take the form of cartoons, sketches, or symbolic images, but can also include photographs, animated drawings, and movies. In a PowerPoint presentation, you can use clip art to illustrate a point you are making, as interesting bullet characters, or to mark pauses in a presentation. For example, you might display a question mark image on a slide to signal a time in which you answer questions from the audience.

To add clip art to a slide, you can click the Clip Art button in a content placeholder, or you can click the Clip Art button in the Images group on the Insert tab. Either way, the Clip Art task pane opens. From this task pane, you can locate and insert the clip art image you want. You can search for clip art by keyword, search a specific Microsoft Clip Organizer collection, or search for specific files or media types, such as movies.

If your computer has an Internet connection, by default your search is expanded to include the thousands of free clip art images available on the Office.com Web site.

After you have inserted a picture, you can make it larger or smaller and position it anywhere you want on the slide.

Tip You can save PowerPoint slides as pictures that you can insert in other types of documents. Display the Save & Send page of the Backstage view, and click Change File Type in the center pane. Then click one of the formats listed under Image File Types in the right pane, and click Save As. In the Save As dialog box, specify a name and location, and then click Save. In the message box that appears, click Every Slide to save all the slides as images, or click Current Slide Only to save an image of the current slide.

In this exercise, you'll add pictures and clip art images to slides. After inserting them, you'll move and size them to fit their slides.

SET UP You need the WaterSavingA_start presentation and the Penstemon and Agastache pictures located in your Chapter16 practice file folder to complete this exercise. Open the WaterSavingA_start presentation, and save it as *WaterSavingA*. Be sure you have an Internet connection so that you can connect to Office.com. Then follow the steps.

1. Press Ctrl+End to move to slide **11**, and delete **<show pictures>**.

    Because you have deleted the text from the content placeholder, PowerPoint redisplays the content buttons.

2. In the content placeholder, click the **Insert Picture from File** button.

    The Insert Picture dialog box opens.

3. Navigate to your **Chapter16** practice file folder, click the **Penstemon** file, and then click **Insert**.

    Tip If a picture might change, you can ensure that the slide is always up to date by clicking the Insert arrow and then clicking Link To File to insert a link to the picture, or by clicking Insert And Link to both insert the picture and link it to its graphic file.

    PowerPoint inserts the picture in the middle of the content pane.

The picture is surrounded by a frame to indicate that it is selected. You use the handles around the frame to size and rotate the picture.

4. On the **View** tab, in the **Show** group, select the **Ruler** check box.

   Horizontal and vertical rulers are displayed across the top and down the left side of the Slide pane. The 0 mark on each ruler indicates the center of the slide. For clarity, we will refer to marks to the left of or above 0 as negative marks.

5. Point to the picture, and when you see a four-headed arrow attached to the pointer, drag to the left and down until its upper-left corner is almost level with the **−4** inch mark on the horizontal ruler and the **0.5** inch mark on the vertical ruler.

6. Point to the handle in the upper-right corner of the photo, and drag up and to the right until that corner sits about level with the **−1.5** inch mark on the horizontal ruler and the **1** inch mark on the vertical ruler.

   The photo increases in size. To make the picture smaller, you would drag in the opposite direction.

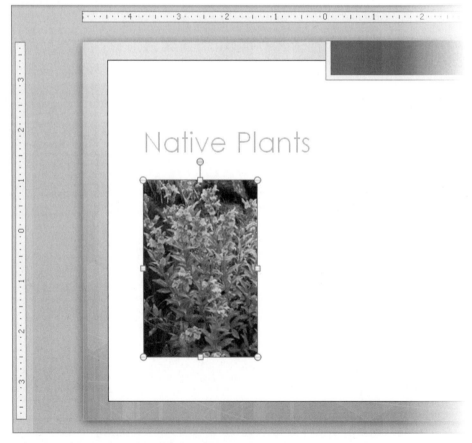

When you drag a corner handle, the photograph shrinks or grows proportionally.

Picture

7. On the **Insert** tab, in the **Images** group, click the **Picture** button, and then in the **Insert Picture** dialog box, double-click the **Agastache** file.

   You can add pictures or other images to a slide without an available content place-holder, and regardless of the slide layout.

8. Point to the handle in the lower-right corner of the photo, and drag down and to the right until the Agastache photo is about the same size as the Penstemon photo. Then click away from the photo to release the selection.

9. On the **Insert** tab, in the **Text** group, click the **Text Box** button, and then click below the lower-left corner of the Penstemon photo.

Text Box

10. In the text box, type **Photos courtesy of Rugged Country Plants**. Then select the text, make it 14 points and purple, and click a blank area of the slide.

    These photographs came from ruggedcountryplants.com and are used with permission of the owners.

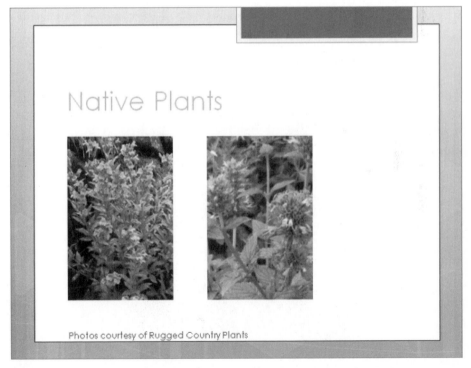

When you use photos you haven't taken yourself, you should always credit the source.

11. Move to slide **4**, and on the **Insert** tab, in the **Images** group, click the **Clip Art** button.

The Clip Art task pane opens.

12. In the **Search for** box at the top of the task pane, type **protect**. Then with the **Include Office.com content** check box selected, click **Go**.

Thumbnails of any clip art, movies, and sounds stored on your computer or on the Office.com Web site that have the associated keyword *protect* or *protection* appear in the task pane.

You can find free images of almost any concept by searching in the Clip Art task pane.

> **Tip** If you don't see a suitable image, you can click Find More At Office.com at the bottom of the task pane, and search for additional images there.

13. Scroll down to see all the images that are available, and when you are ready, point to the green and blue drawing of hands protecting a plant.

    A ScreenTip describes the image and gives its dimensions, file size, and format.

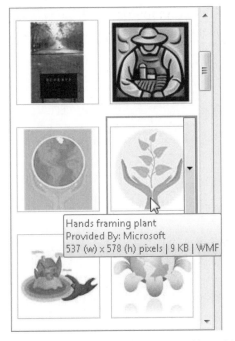

Hands framing plant
Provided By: Microsoft
537 (w) x 578 (h) pixels | 9 KB | WMF

This clip art file is in Windows Metafile (WMF) format.

14. Click the thumbnail once.

    PowerPoint inserts the image in the center of the slide.

15. At the right end of the title bar of the **Clip Art** task pane, click the **Close** button.

16. Drag the image to the lower-right corner of the slide, and then drag the upper-left corner handle until the image occupies about half of the slide. Click a blank area to release the selection.

    The image balances the text on the slide.

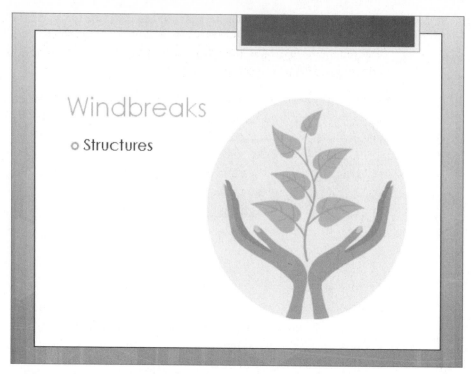

This image symbolizes people's efforts to protect plants.

CLEAN UP Save the WaterSavingA presentation, and then close it.

Inserting Diagrams

Sometimes the concepts you want to convey to an audience are best presented in diagrams, which depict processes, hierarchies, cycles, or relationships. You can easily create a dynamic, visually appealing diagram for a slide by using SmartArt Graphics, a powerful tool that comes with the Microsoft Office 2010 programs. SmartArt provides predefined sets of formatting for effortlessly putting together any of the following types of diagrams:

- **Process** These visually describe the ordered set of steps required to complete a task—for example, the approval process for the launch of a new book series.

- **Hierarchy** These illustrate the structure of an organization or entity—for example, a company's top-level management structure.

- **Cycle** These represent a circular sequence of steps, tasks, or events; or the relationship of a set of steps, tasks, or events to a central, core element—for example, the looping process for continually improving a product based on customer feedback.

- **Relationship** These show convergent, divergent, overlapping, merging, or containing elements—for example, how organizing your e-mail, calendar, and contacts can converge to improve your productivity.

On a slide that includes a content placeholder, you can click the placeholder's Insert SmartArt Graphic button to start the process of creating a diagram. You can also click the SmartArt button in the Illustrations Group on the Insert tab to add a diagram to any slide. In either case, you then select the type of diagram you want to create and click a specific layout to see a picture and description. When you find the diagram that best conveys your information, you click OK to insert the diagram with placeholder text that you can replace in an adjacent Text pane.

Graphic Formats

You can use picture and clip art files in a variety of formats, including the following:

- **BMP (bitmap)** This format stores graphics as a series of dots, or pixels. There are different qualities of BMP, reflecting the number of bits available per pixel to store information about the graphic—the greater the number of bits, the greater the number of possible colors.

- **GIF (Graphics Interchange Format)** This format is common for images that appear on Web pages because they can be compressed with no loss of information and groups of them can be animated. GIFs store at most 8 bits per pixel, so they are limited to 256 colors.

- **JPEG (Joint Photographic Experts Group)** This compressed format works well for complex graphics such as scanned photographs. Some information is lost in the compression process, but often the loss is imperceptible to the human eye. Color JPEG images store 24 bits per pixel, so they are capable of displaying more than 16 million colors. Grayscale JPEG images store 8 bits per pixel.

- **TIFF (Tag Image File Format)** This format can store compressed images with a flexible number of bits per pixel. Using tags, a single multipage TIFF file can store several images, along with related information such as type of compression and orientation.

- **PNG (Portable Network Graphic)** This format has the advantages of the GIF format but can store colors with 8, 24, or 48 bits per pixel and grayscales with 1, 2, 4, 8, or 16 bits per pixel. A PNG file can also specify whether each pixel blends with its background color and can contain color correction information so that images look accurate on a broad range of display devices. Graphics saved in this format are smaller, so they display faster.

After you create a diagram, you can move and size it to fit the slide, and with a few clicks, you can change the colors and look of its shapes to achieve professional looking results.

In this exercise, you'll add a cycle diagram, enter text, and then move and size it. You'll also format its shapes in simple ways.

SET UP You need the WaterSavingB_start presentation located in your Chapter16 practice file folder to complete this exercise. Open the WaterSavingB_start presentation, and save it as *WaterSavingB*. Display the rulers, and then follow the steps.

1. Display slide **6**, and then click the **Insert SmartArt Graphic** button in the content placeholder.

   The Choose A SmartArt Graphic dialog box opens.

By default, all the available layouts are listed in the center pane, but you can filter them by category. A picture and description of the selected layout appear in the right pane.

2. In the left pane, click each layout type in turn to see all the available layouts of that type in the center pane, and then click **Cycle**.

3. In the center pane, click each layout in turn to view a picture and description in the right pane.

4. When you finish exploring, click the second layout (**Text Cycle**), and then click **OK**.

   PowerPoint inserts a blank cycle diagram into the slide. The Design and Format contextual tabs appear on the ribbon.

5. On the **Design** tab, in the **Create Graphic** group, click the **Text Pane** button.

The Text pane opens.

You can use the same techniques to create bullet points and subpoints in the Text pane as you would on the Outline tab of the Overview pane.

Troubleshooting The appearance of buttons and groups on the ribbon changes depending on the width of the program window. For information about changing the appearance of the ribbon to match our screen images, see "Modifying the Display of the Ribbon" at the beginning of this book.

6. With the first bullet in the **Text** pane selected, type **Clouds**, and then press the Down Arrow key to move to the next bullet.

Troubleshooting Be sure to press the Down Arrow key and not the Enter key. Pressing Enter will add a new bullet point (and a new shape).

7. Pressing Shift+Enter after each word, type **Condensation**, **and**, and **Precipitation**. Then press the Down Arrow key.

8. Repeat step 7 to add **Runoff**, **and**, and **Percolation**. Then repeat it again to add **Evaporation**, **and**, and **Transpiration**.

9. You don't need the last bullet point, so on the **Design** tab, in the **Create Graphic** group, click the **Text Pane** button to close the Text pane.

   Tip You can also click the Close button in the upper-right corner of the Text pane.

10. In the diagram, click the **Text** placeholder, and click the border of the empty shape to select it for manipulation. Then press the Delete key.

   The diagram now has four sets of text and arrows.

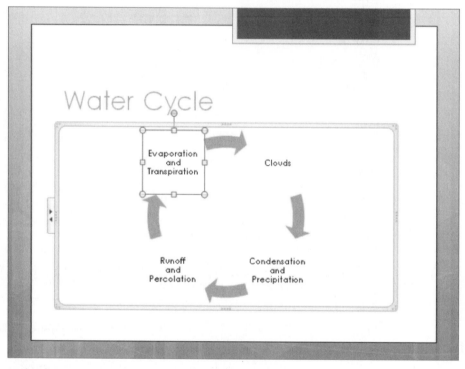

In this diagram, the arrows are more prominent than the text.

   Tip You can click the tab with left and right arrows on the left side of the diagram's frame to open the Text pane.

11. In the **Layouts** group, click the **More** button to view the available Cycle diagram layouts, and then click the first thumbnail in the first row (**Basic Cycle**).

The diagram changes to the new layout.

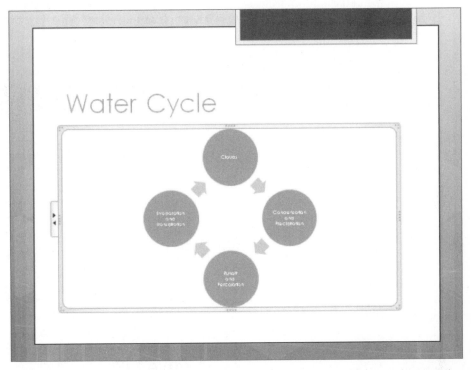

In this diagram, the text is contained in solid-color circles, and the arrows are less prominent.

12. Point to the handle (the four dots) in the middle of the right side of the diagram's frame, and when the pointer changes to a two-headed arrow, drag to the left until the frame is only as wide as the diagram. (Repeat the process as necessary.)

13. Point to a part of the frame where there is no handle, and when a four-headed arrow is attached to the pointer, drag the diagram until it sits in the lower-right corner of the white area of the slide.

14. Point to the handle in the upper-left corner of the frame and drag up and to the left until the frame sits at about the **–2.5** inch mark on both the horizontal and vertical rulers.

   Troubleshooting Remember that the 0 mark on both rulers is centered on the slide. You want the 2.5-inch marks to the left of and above the 0 marks.

   The diagram expands with its frame.

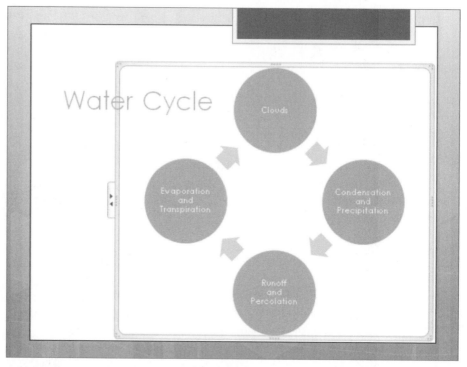

Because the diagram is an independent object, it can sit on top of the empty part of the title placeholder.

15. In the **SmartArt Styles** group, click the **Change Colors** button, and then in the gallery, under **Colorful**, click the second thumbnail (**Colorful Range - Accent Colors 2 and 3**).

   The shapes in the diagram assume the colors of the selected scheme.

16. In the **SmartArt Styles** group, click the **More** button.

   The SmartArt Styles gallery appears.

You can apply two-dimensional and three-dimensional styles from this gallery.

17. Under **3-D** in the gallery, click the first thumbnail in the first row (**Polished**).

18. Click outside the frame.

    You can now see the final result.

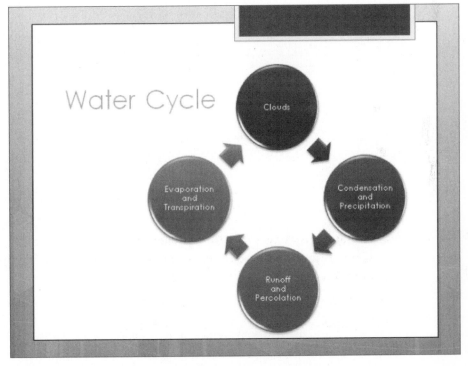

The colors and three-dimensional effect give the diagram pizzazz.

✖ **CLEAN UP** Save the WaterSavingB presentation, and then close it.

Converting Existing Bullet Points into Diagrams

You might decide after creating a bulleted list on a slide that a diagram would more clearly convey your point to your audience. You can easily convert a bulleted list to a SmartArt diagram with only a few clicks of the mouse button.

To create a diagram from an existing bulleted list:

1. Click anywhere in the placeholder containing the bulleted list you want to convert.

2. Right-click anywhere in the selected placeholder, and point to Convert To SmartArt.

3. Do one of the following:

   a. If the diagram layout you want appears in the gallery, click its thumbnail.

   b. If you don't see the layout you want, click More SmartArt Graphics. Then in the Choose A SmartArt Graphic dialog box, click the layout you want, and click OK.

4. Adjust the size, position, and look of the diagram in the usual way.

Inserting Charts

For those occasions when you want to display numeric data visually, you can add a chart to a slide. Charts make it easy to see trends that might not be obvious from looking at the numbers themselves.

On a slide that includes a content placeholder, you can click the placeholder's Insert Chart button to start the process of creating a chart. You can also click the Chart button in the Illustrations Group on the Insert tab to add a chart to any slide. In either case, you then select the type of chart you want. If your PowerPoint window is maximized, when you click OK, a sample chart of the type you selected is inserted in the current slide, and the PowerPoint window shrinks so that it occupies half the screen. An associated Microsoft Excel worksheet containing the data plotted in the sample chart is displayed in the other half. You use this worksheet to enter the information you want to plot, following the pattern illustrated by the sample data.

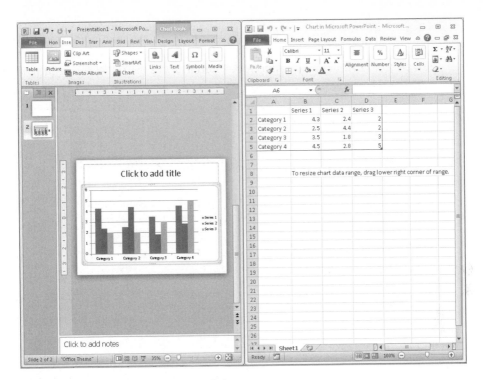

A sample chart and its associated worksheet.

The Excel worksheet is composed of rows and columns of cells that contain values, which in charting terminology are called *data points*. Collectively a set of data points is called a *data series*. Each worksheet cell is identified by an address consisting of its column letter and row number—for example, A2. A range of cells is identified by the address of the cell in the upper-left corner and the address of the cell in the lower-right corner, separated by a colon—for example, A2:D5.

When you replace the sample data in the worksheet, you immediately see the results in the chart in the adjacent PowerPoint window. Each data point in a data series is represented graphically in the chart by a data marker. The data is plotted against an x-axis—also called the *category axis*—and a y-axis—also called the *value axis*. (Three-dimensional charts also have a z-axis—also called the *series axis*.) Tick-mark labels along each axis identify the categories, values, or series in the chart. A legend provides a key for identifying the data series.

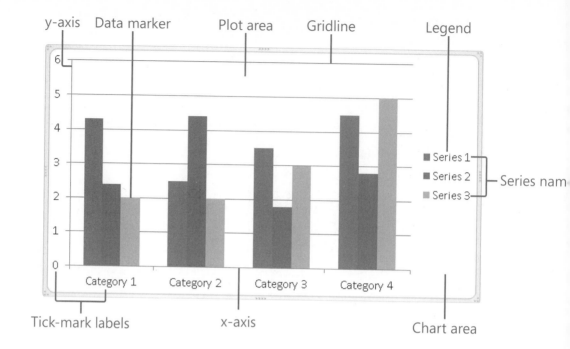

The major elements of a chart.

To enter data in a cell of the Excel worksheet, you first click the cell to select it. You can select an entire column by clicking the column header—the shaded box containing a letter at the top of each column—and an entire row by clicking the row header—the shaded box containing a number to the left of each row. You can select the entire worksheet by clicking the Select All button—the box at the junction of the column and row headers.

Having selected a cell, you can enter your data by typing it directly. However, if your data already exists in an Excel worksheet or a Microsoft Access or Microsoft Word table, you don't have to retype it. You can copy the data from its source program and paste it into the Excel worksheet that is linked to the slide.

After you've plotted your data in the chart, you can move and size the chart to suit the space available on the slide. You can edit the data—both the values and the column and row headings—at any time, and PowerPoint will replot the chart to reflect your changes.

In this exercise, you'll create a chart by pasting existing data into the associated Excel worksheet. You'll then size the chart, and edit its data.

SET UP You need the WaterConsumption workbook and the WaterSavingC_start presentation located in your Chapter16 practice file folder to complete this exercise. From Windows Explorer, open the WaterConsumption workbook in Excel by double-clicking the workbook's file name. Then open the WaterSavingC_start presentation, and save it as *WaterSavingC*. Ensure that the PowerPoint program window is maximized, and then follow the steps.

1. Display slide **7**, and then in the content placeholder, click the **Insert Chart** button.

   The Insert Chart dialog box opens.

You can choose from many types of charts in this dialog box.

2. With **Column** selected in the left pane, click the first thumbnail in the second row (**Clustered Cylinder**), and then click **OK**.

   PowerPoint inserts the chart into the slide and resizes its program window to occupy the left half of your screen. Excel starts and displays the data used to plot the chart in the right half of the screen.

3. From the Windows Taskbar, display the **WaterConsumption** worksheet. Then in the worksheet, point to cell **A3**, and drag down and to the right to cell **C13**.

   Excel selects all the cells in the range A3:C13.

4. On the Excel **Home** tab, in the **Clipboard** group, click the **Copy** button.

5. From the Windows Taskbar, display the **Chart in Microsoft PowerPoint** worksheet. Then in the worksheet, click cell **A1**.

6. On the Excel **Home** tab, in the **Clipboard** group, click the **Paste** button. Then click **OK** to acknowledge the message that Excel has inserted rows in the worksheet to accommodate the copied data.

Excel pastes in the data, and PowerPoint immediately replots the chart.

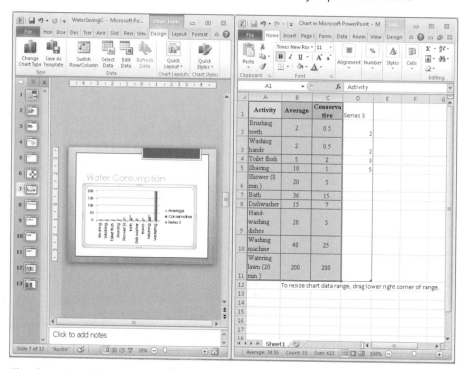

The chart plots all the data within the blue border in the worksheet.

7. To exclude the data in column D from the chart, in the worksheet, drag the handle in the lower-right corner of the blue border to the left, releasing it when cells **D1:D11** are shaded.

In the PowerPoint window, the chart now reflects the fact that only the Activity, Average, and Conservative columns are plotted.

8. In the upper-right corner of the Excel window, click the **Close** button to close the associated worksheet. Then close the **WaterConsumption** workbook.

   The PowerPoint window expands, giving you a better view of the chart.

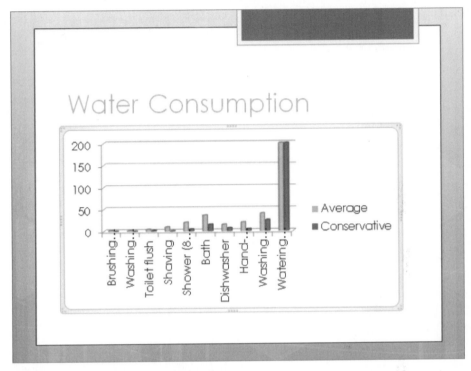

The copied data, plotted as a cylinder chart.

9. Point to the handle (the four dots) in the middle of the bottom of the frame, and drag downward until the frame sits at the bottom of the white area of the slide.

   When you release the mouse button, the chart area expands, but not enough for the category labels to be displayed in their entirety.

10. On the **Design** contextual tab, in the **Data** group, click the **Edit Data** button.

    The associated worksheet opens in Excel so that you can make changes to the plotted data.

11. Click cell **A9**, type **Dishes by hand**, and press Enter. Then in cell **A10**, type **Clothes washer**, and press Enter. Finally in cell **A11**, replace **Watering lawn (20 min.)** with **Lawn (20 min.)**, and press Enter. Then close the Excel worksheet.

Tip If the chart isn't selected (surrounded by a frame) in the PowerPoint window when you make changes to the data in the Excel window, the chart won't automatically update. If this happens, click the chart before proceeding.

PowerPoint replots the chart with the new category labels.

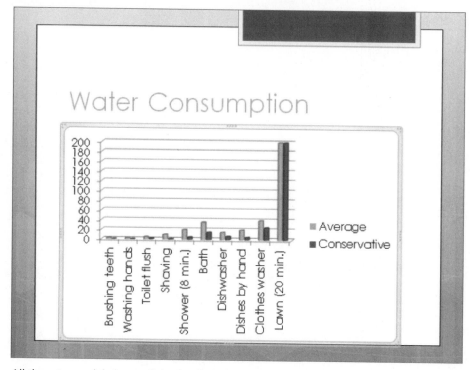

All the category labels now fit in the chart area.

12. Point to the handle in the middle of the right side of the frame, and drag to the right until the frame sits at the edge of the white area on that slide. Then click outside the chart frame.

PowerPoint has rotated the labels so that the chart area can expand even more.

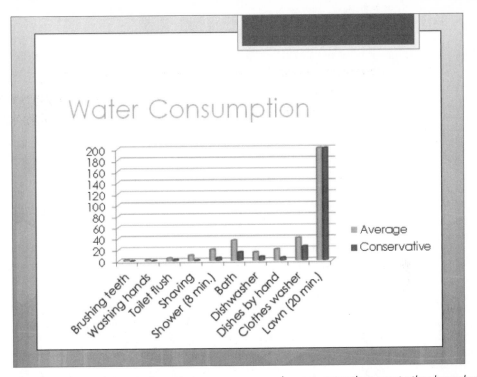

The chart shows that watering a lawn consumes much more water than most other household water usages.

Tip By default, the chart is plotted based on the series in the columns of the worksheet, which are identified in the legend. If you want to base the chart on the series in the rows instead, click the Switch Row/Column button in the Data group on the Design contextual tab. The worksheet must be open for the button to be active. (To open the worksheet, right-click the chart, and then click Edit Data.)

 CLEAN UP Save the WaterSavingC presentation, and then close it.

Drawing Shapes

To emphasize the key points in your presentation, you might want to include shapes in addition to text. PowerPoint provides tools for creating several types of shapes, including stars, banners, boxes, lines, circles, and squares. With a little imagination, you'll soon discover ways to create drawings by combining shapes.

To create a shape in PowerPoint, you click the Shapes button in the Illustrations group on the Insert tab, click the shape you want to insert, and then drag the crosshair pointer across the slide.

Tip To draw a circle or a square, click the Oval or a Rectangle shape, and hold down the Shift key while you drag.

After you draw the shape, it is surrounded by a set of handles, indicating that it is selected. (You can select a shape at any time by simply clicking it.) The handles serve the following purposes:

- You can drag the pale blue sizing handles to change the size of a shape.

- If a shape has a yellow diamond-shaped adjustment handle next to one of the sizing handles or elsewhere on the shape, the shape is adjustable. You can use this handle to alter the appearance of the shape without changing its size.

- You can drag the green rotating handle to adjust the angle of rotation of a shape.

The three types of shape handles.

You can copy or cut a selected shape or multiple shapes and then paste the shapes elsewhere in the same presentation, in another presentation, or in any Office program.

To move a shape from one location to another on the same slide, you simply drag it. You can create a copy of a selected shape by dragging it while holding down the Ctrl key or by clicking the Copy arrow in the Clipboard group on the Home tab and then clicking Duplicate.

After drawing a shape, you can modify it by using the buttons on the Format contextual tab that appears when a shape is selected. For example, you can:

- Add text to a shape. PowerPoint centers the text as you type, and the text becomes part of the shape.

- Change the size and color of the shape and its outline.

- Apply special effects, such as making the shape look three-dimensional.

Having made changes to one shape, you can easily apply the same attributes to another shape by clicking the shape that has the desired attributes, clicking the Format Painter button in the Clipboard group on the Home tab, and then clicking the shape to which you want to copy the attributes. If you want to apply the attributes of a shape to all shapes in the active presentation, right-click the shape and then click Set As Default Shape. From then on, all the shapes you draw in the active presentation will have the new default attributes.

When you have multiple shapes on a slide, you can group them so that you can copy, move, and format them as a unit. You can change the attributes of an individual shape— for example, its color, size, or location—without ungrouping the shapes. If you do un-group the graphics, you can regroup the same shapes by selecting one of them and then clicking Regroup in the Group list.

In this exercise, you'll draw several shapes, add text to them, and change their colors. Then you'll duplicate and copy a shape and switch one shape for another.

SET UP You need the JournalingA_start presentation located in your Chapter16 practice file folder to complete this exercise. Open the JournalingA_start presentation, and save it as *JournalingA*. Display the rulers, and then follow the steps.

1. Display slide **5**, and on the **Insert** tab, in the **Illustrations** group, click the **Shapes** button.

   The Shapes gallery appears.

Many different types of shapes are grouped by category in the Shapes gallery.

2. Under **Stars and Banners** in the gallery, click the **5-Point Star** shape, and then drag the crosshair pointer in the middle of the slide to draw a star shape that spans the shadow of the hand in the background graphic.

   Tip If you click a shape button and then change your mind about drawing the shape, you can release the shape by pressing the Esc key.

   Pale blue handles surround the shape to indicate that it is selected.

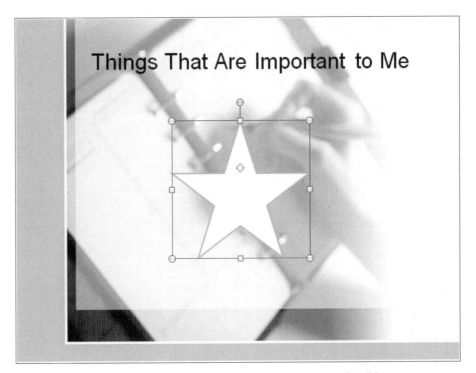

When a shape is selected, the Format contextual tab appears on the ribbon.

3. On the **Format** tab, in the **Insert Shapes** group, click the **More** button to display the **Shapes** gallery. Then under **Block Arrows**, click the **Right Arrow** shape, and draw a small arrow to the right of the star.

4. With the arrow still selected, hold down the Ctrl key, and drag a copy of the arrow to the left of the star.

    Troubleshooting Be sure to release the mouse button before you release the Ctrl key. Otherwise you'll move the shape instead of copying it.

5. With the shape still selected, in the **Arrange** group, click the **Rotate** button, and then click **Flip Horizontal**.

    You could have drawn a Left Arrow shape, but this technique ensures that the two arrows have the same proportions.

    Tip You can rotate or flip any type of image. Rotating turns a shape 90 degrees to the right or left; flipping turns a shape 180 degrees horizontally or vertically. You can also rotate a shape to any degree by dragging the green rotating handle.

6. Adjacent to the left arrow, add a scroll shape, and adjacent to the right arrow, add a heart shape.

All the shapes have the same outline and interior colors.

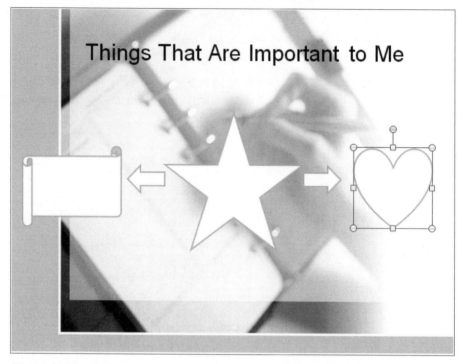

You can build a picture with the shapes available in the Shapes gallery.

7. With the heart selected, on the **Home** tab, in the **Clipboard** group, click the **Copy** arrow, and then in the list, click **Duplicate**.

PowerPoint pastes a copy of the shape on top of the original.

8. Point to the handle in the upper-left corner of the new shape, and drag down and to the right to make the second heart smaller than the first.

9. On the **Format** tab, in the **Insert Shapes** group, click the **Text Box** button, click the center of the star, and then type **ME**.

See Also For information about working with text boxes, see "Adding Text Boxes" in Chapter 14, "Work with Slide Text."

Don't worry that you can barely see the text; you'll fix that in a later step.

10. Repeat step 9 to add the word **Education** to the scroll shape and **Family** to the heart shape.

11. Click the scroll shape (don't click the text), hold down the Shift key, click the star shape, and then click the two hearts.

12. With all four shapes selected, in the **Shape Styles** group, click the **More** button to display the **Shape Styles** gallery.

13. Point to several thumbnails to see live previews of their effects, and then click the last thumbnail in the fourth row (**Subtle Effect – Light Blue, Accent 6**).

    The color of the interior and outline of the shapes changes, as does the color of the text.

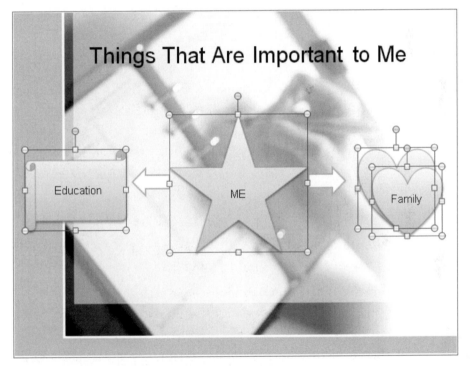

The text stands out after you change the shape style.

14. Click a blank area of the slide to release the selection, and then click the scroll shape (don't click its text).

15. In the **Insert Shapes** group, click the **Edit Shape** button, point to **Change Shape**, and under **Block Arrows**, click the third shape (**Up Arrow**).

    The scroll changes to the selected shape, with all formatting and text intact.

16. Double-click the word **Education**, and type **Job**. Then click outside the shape to release the selection.

    You can now see the results.

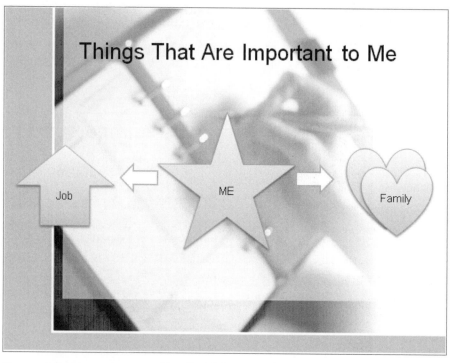

You can tell a story using a combination of shapes and text.

17. Select all the shapes on the slide. Then on the **Format** tab, in the **Arrange** group, click the **Group** button, and in the list, click **Group**.

    The shapes are grouped together as one object.

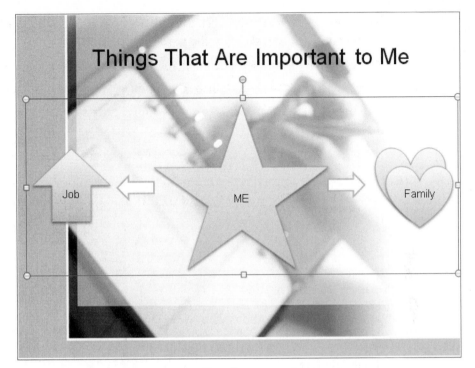

When shapes are grouped, one set of handles surrounds the entire group.

18. In the **Shape Styles** group, click the **Shape Outline** arrow, and then under **Standard Colors** in the palette, click the last color (**Purple**).

    [Shape Outline ▾]

    The outlines around the shapes change to purple.

19. Point to any shape in the group, and when the pointer has a four-headed arrow attached to it, drag downward about a half inch.

    The entire group moves.

20. Click the left arrow. In the **Shape Styles** group, click the **Shape Fill** arrow and change the shape's color to purple.

    [Shape Fill ▾]

    Even though the shapes are grouped, you can still change the attributes of one of the shapes.

21. With the left arrow still selected, on the **Home** tab, in the **Clipboard** group, click the **Format Painter** button, and then click the right arrow.

    Both arrows are now purple.

22. Click away from the selected shape, and then click any shape to select the group.

23. On the **Format** tab, in the **Arrange** group, click the **Group** button, and then click **Ungroup**.

    The group is disbanded, and the individual shapes are now selected.

✖ **CLEAN UP** Save the JournalingA presentation, and then close it.

Connecting Shapes

If you want to show a relationship between two shapes, you can connect them with a line by joining special handles called *connection points*.

To connect shapes:

1. Click one of the shapes you want to connect. Then on the Format tab, in the Insert Shapes group, display the Shapes gallery, and under Lines, click one of the Connector shapes.

2. Point to the selected shape.

   Red connection points appear, and the pointer changes to a crosshair.

3. Point to a connection point, and then drag over to the other shape (don't release the mouse button).

4. When connection points appear on the other shape, point to a connection point, and release the mouse button.

   Red handles appear at each end of the line, indicating that the shapes are connected.

   Troubleshooting If a blue handle appears instead of a red one, the shapes are not connected. Click the Undo button on the Quick Access Toolbar to remove the connection line, and then redraw it.

Adding Transitions

When you deliver a presentation, you can move from slide to slide by clicking the mouse button or you can have PowerPoint replace one slide with the next at predetermined intervals. You can avoid abrupt breaks between slides by employing transitions that control the way slides move on and off the screen.

PowerPoint comes with the following categories of built-in transition effects:

- **Subtle** This category includes fades, wipes, and a shutter-like effect.

- **Exciting** This category includes more dramatic effects such as checkerboards, ripples, turning, and zooming.

The connector between two connection points.

After you have drawn the connector, you can format it by changing its color and weight. You can then set the formatted line as the default for all future connectors in this drawing. If you move a connected shape, the line moves with it, maintaining the relationship between the shapes.

- **Dynamic Content** This category holds the background of the slides still and applies a dynamic effect to the title and other content, such as rotating or flying onto the slide.

Each slide can have only one transition. You set transitions from the Transitions tab in Normal view or Slide Sorter view, for one slide at a time, for a group of slides, or for an entire presentation. This tab is new in PowerPoint 2010, reflecting the importance of transitions in ensuring a smooth flow for your presentations. (Previously, transitions were included on the Animations tab because they were considered just another form of animation.)

In addition to selecting the type of transition, you can specify the following:

- The sound
- The speed
- When the transition occurs

In this exercise, you'll apply a transition to a single slide, and apply the same transition to all the slides in the presentation. You'll also add sound to the transition and set the transition speed.

SET UP You need the JournalingB_start presentation located in your Chapter16 practice file folder to complete this exercise. Open the JournalingB_start presentation, and save it as *JournalingB*. Then follow the steps.

1. Display slide **2** in Normal view. Then on the **Transitions** tab, in the **Transition to This Slide** group, click each thumbnail in the gallery to see its effects.

2. To the right of the gallery, click the **Down** button, and continue previewing the effects of each transition.

3. When you have finished exploring, click the **More** button to display the entire gallery, and then click the **Cover** thumbnail in the **Subtle** category.

PowerPoint demonstrates the Cover transition effect on slide 2 and indicates that the transition has been applied by placing an animation symbol below the slide number on the Slides tab of the Overview pane. (There is no indication on the slide itself.)

You have applied an animation to one slide.

4. In the **Transition to This Slide** group, click the **Effect Options** button, and then click **From Top-Left**.

5. In the **Timing** group, click the **Apply To All** button.

   An animation symbol appears below each slide number on the Slides tab.

6. On the **Slides** tab in the **Overview** pane, click the animation symbol below slide **3**.

   The Slide pane turns black, and then PowerPoint demonstrates the Cover transition from slide 2 to slide 3.

7. Display slide **1**. In the **Transition to This Slide** group, click the **More** button, and then in the **Transitions** gallery, click the **None** thumbnail.

   PowerPoint removes the animation symbol from below the slide 1 thumbnail.

*Because you will usually start a presentation with the title slide displayed,
there is no need for a transition on this slide.*

8. On the **View Shortcuts** toolbar at the right end of the status bar, click the **Reading View** button.

   PowerPoint switches to Reading view and displays slide 1.

9. At the bottom of the screen, click the **Next** button repeatedly to see the transitions of the first few slides, and then press Esc to return to Normal view.

10. On the **View Shortcuts** toolbar, click the **Slide Sorter** button.

11. In **Slide Sorter** view, click slide **2**, hold down the Shift key, and then click slide **7** to select all the slides that have transitions.

12. In the **Timing** group, click the **Sound** arrow, and then click **Wind**.

   Tip If you want to associate a sound file of your own with a slide transition, click Other Sound at the bottom of the Sound list. Then in the Add Audio dialog box, find and select the sound file you want to use, and click Open.

13. In the **Timing** group, click the **Duration** up arrow until the duration shows as **02.00**.

14. In the **Preview** group, click the **Preview** button to preview the transition effect again. Then if you want, preview it again in Reading view.

PowerPoint demonstrates the transition of each selected slide with the sound specified in step 13.

✖ CLEAN UP Save the JournalingB presentation, and then close it.

Key Points

- When you add pictures or photographs to a slide, keep in mind that using pictures you don't own without permission, especially for business purposes, can breach the copyright of the owner. Limited use for non-commercial purposes is usually allowed as long as you acknowledge the source.

- Thousands of free clip art images are available to help you add visual interest to your slides.

- With SmartArt, you can create a variety of professional-looking diagrams with a few mouse clicks.

- Charts present numeric data in an easy-to-grasp visual format. You can choose from 11 types with many variations.

- Shapes can add interest to a slide and draw attention to key concepts. However, they can become tiresome and produce an amateurish effect if they are overused.

- Avoid abrupt transitions by having one slide smoothly replace another. You can control the transition type, its speed, and when it takes place.

Chapter at a Glance

Set up presentations for delivery, **page 486**

Preview and print presentations, **page 491**

Prepare speaker notes and handouts, **page 495**

Finalize presentations, **page 502**

Deliver presentations, **page 509**

17 Review and Deliver Presentations

In this chapter, you will learn how to

✔ Set up presentations for delivery.

✔ Preview and print presentations.

✔ Prepare speaker notes and handouts.

✔ Finalize presentations.

✔ Deliver presentations.

When it is time to deliver the Microsoft PowerPoint 2010 presentation you have worked so hard to create, taking the time for a few final tasks helps to ensure a successful outcome.

Before exposing a new presentation to the eyes of the world, you should check a few settings and proof the text of the slides, preferably on paper, where typographic errors seem to stand out much better than they do on the screen. When you are satisfied that the presentation is complete, you can prepare for your moment in the spotlight by creating speaker notes. You might also want to create handouts to give to your audience, to remind them later of your presentation's message.

When all these tasks are complete, you should remove extraneous information before declaring the presentation final.

If you will deliver the presentation from your computer as an electronic slide show, it pays to become familiar with the tools available in Slide Show view, where instead of appearing in a window, the slide occupies the entire screen. You navigate through slides by clicking the mouse button or by pressing the Arrow keys, moving forward and backward one slide at a time or jumping to specific slides as the needs of your audience dictate. During the slide show, you can mark slides with an on-screen pen or highlighter to emphasize a point.

In this chapter, you'll set up a slide show for delivery, preview a presentation, and print selected slides. You'll remove the properties attached to a presentation and prevent other people from making further changes to it. Finally, you'll see how to deliver a presentation, including marking up slides while showing them.

> **Practice Files** Before you can complete the exercises in this chapter, you need to copy the book's practice files to your computer. The practice files you'll use to complete the exercises in this chapter are in the *Chapter17* practice file folder. A complete list of practice files is provided in "Using the Practice Files" at the beginning of this book.

Setting Up Presentations for Delivery

In the old days, presentations were delivered by speakers with few supporting materials. Little by little, "visual aids" such as white board drawings or flip charts on easels were added, and eventually, savvy speakers began accompanying their presentations with 35mm slides or transparencies projected onto screens. To accommodate these speakers, early versions of PowerPoint included output formats optimized for slides of various sizes, including 35mm slides and the acetate sheets used with overhead projectors.

Although technology has evolved to the point where most presentations are now delivered electronically, PowerPoint 2010 still accommodates those output formats, as well as formats designed for printing on paper. Usually, you'll find the default on-screen format adequate for your needs. If you have a wide-screen monitor, or if you know you'll be using a delivery method other than your computer for your presentation, you should set the format of the presentation before you begin developing your content so that you place elements appropriately for the final size of your slides.

By default, slides are sized for an on-screen slide show with a width-to-height ratio of 4:3 (10 × 7.5 inches). The slides are oriented horizontally, with slide numbers starting at 1. You can change these settings in the Page Setup dialog box, where you can select from the following slide sizes:

- **On-screen Show** For an electronic slide show on screens of various aspects (4:3, 16:9, or 16:10)

- **Letter Paper** For a presentation printed on 8.5 × 11 inch U.S. letter-size paper

- **Ledger Paper** For a presentation printed on 11 × 17 inch legal-size paper

- **A3 Paper, A4 Paper, B4 (ISO) Paper, B5 (ISO) Paper** For a presentation printed on paper of various international sizes

- **35mm Slides** For 35mm slides to be used in a carousel with a projector

- **Overhead** For transparencies for an overhead projector

- **Banner** For a banner for a Web page

- **Custom** For slides that are a nonstandard size

If you want the same identifying information to appear at the bottom of every slide, you can insert it in a footer. You can specify the date and time, the slide number, and custom text in the Header And Footer dialog box, which shows a preview of where the specified items will appear on the slide.

If you are going to deliver a presentation before an audience and will control the progression of slides manually, the default settings will work well. However, provided the slides have been assigned advancement times on the Transitions tab, you can set up the presentation to run automatically, either once or continuously. For example, you might want to set up a product demonstration slide show in a store or at a tradeshow so that it runs automatically, looping until someone stops it. All it takes is a few settings in the Set Up Show dialog box.

In this exercise, you'll explore the Page Setup dialog box and experiment with slide orientation. You'll add footer information to every slide in a presentation, and then turn the presentation into a self-running slide show.

SET UP You need the ServiceOrientationA_start presentation located in your Chapter17 practice file folder to complete this exercise. Open the ServiceOrientationA_start presentation, and save it as *ServiceOrientationA*. Then follow the steps.

1. On the **Design** tab, in the **Page Setup** group, click the **Page Setup** button.

   The Page Setup dialog box opens.

   By default, the slides in a presentation are sized for an on-screen slide show with a width-to-height ratio of 4:3.

2. Display the **Slides sized for** list, and toward the bottom, click **35mm Slides**.

   The Width setting changes to 11.25 inches and the Height setting changes to 7.5 inches.

3. Display the **Slides sized for** list again, and click **Banner**.

The Width setting changes to 8 inches, and the Height setting changes to 1 inch. This format is useful if you want to design a presentation that will display in a frame across the top or bottom of a Web page.

Tip Obviously the current presentation with its long title and many bulleted lists is not suitable for the Banner format. If you want to create a banner, be sure to set the format before you begin developing the content of your presentation so that you choose words and graphics that fit within the space available.

4. Set the size of the slides to **On-screen Show (4:3)**. Then in the **Slides** area, click **Portrait**, and click **OK**.

The slide width changes to 7.5 and its height changes to 10 inches. This orientation is useful if you want to compare two presentations side by side in Reading view.

Slide
Orientation ▾

5. In the **Page Setup** group, click the **Slide Orientation** button, and then click **Landscape**.

Header
& Footer

6. On the **Insert** tab, in the **Text** group, click the **Header & Footer** button.

The Header And Footer dialog box opens with the Slide page displayed.

By default, the slides in this presentation do not display footer information.

7. In the **Include on slide** area, select the **Date and time** check box. Then with **Fixed** selected, type today's date in the text box.

    PowerPoint indicates on the thumbnail in the Preview area that the date will appear in the lower-left corner of the slide. The date will appear in the format in which you typed it.

8. Select the **Slide number** check box.

    The thumbnail in the Preview area shows that the slide number will appear in the lower-right corner.

9. Select the **Footer** check box, and then type your name in the text box.

    Your name will appear in the center of the slide.

10. Select the **Don't show on title slide** check box, and click **Apply to All**. Then display slide **2**.

    The specified footer information appears at the bottom of the slide.

Service project goals

- Familiarize you with the concept of service
- Make service a part of your life
- Engage and motivate you
- Build a sense of teamwork among all employees across units
- Provide appropriate skills development
- Meet genuine needs

April 17, 2010   Sidney Higa   2

You have entered footer information for all slides except the title slide.

Set Up Slide Show

11. On the **Slide Show** tab, in the **Set Up** group, click the **Set Up Slide Show** button.

    The Set Up Show dialog box opens.

By default, the presentation is set for presenter delivery and to include all slides.

12. In the **Show type** area, click **Browsed at a kiosk (full screen)**.

    When you click this option, the Loop Continuously Until 'Esc' check box in the Show Options area becomes unavailable so that you cannot clear it. Any narration or animation attached to the presentation will play with the presentation unless you select the Show Without Narration or Show Without Animation check box.

    See Also For information about narration, and animation, refer to *Microsoft PowerPoint 2010 Step by Step*, by Joyce Cox and Joan Lambert (Microsoft Press, 2010).

13. Click **OK**.

14. To test the show, display slide **1**, and on the **View Shortcuts** toolbar, click the **Reading View** button.

    The presentation runs continuously, using the transition effect and advancement time applied to all its slides.

    See Also For information about transitions, see "Adding Transitions" in Chapter 16, "Add Simple Visual Enhancements."

    Tip If the presentation has no advancement time applied to its slides, you should click Manually in the Advance Slides area of the Set Up Show dialog box.

15. When the presentation starts again at slide 1, press Esc to stop the slide show and return to Normal view.

Now when you are ready to run the presentation, you can navigate to the folder where it is stored, and double-click it. When the presentation opens, switch to Slide Show view to start the presentation. You can press Esc to stop the slide show at any time.

✖ **CLEAN UP** Save the *ServiceOrientationA* presentation, and then close it.

Previewing and Printing Presentations

Even if you plan to deliver your presentation electronically, you might want to print the presentation to proof it for typographical errors and stylistic inconsistencies. Before you print, you can preview your presentation to see how the slides will look on paper. You preview a presentation on the Print page in the Backstage view, where the presentation appears in the right pane.

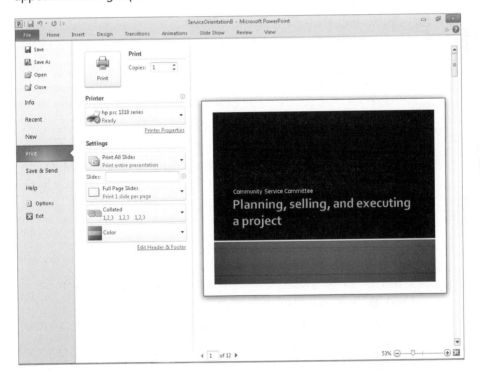

The Print page of the Backstage view.

You can click the Next Page or Previous Page button in the lower-left corner of the pane to move among the slides. To zoom in on part of a slide, click the Zoom In and Zoom Out buttons on the Zoom Slider in the lower-right corner. Click the Zoom To Page button to fit the slide to the pane.

If you will print a color presentation on a monochrome printer, you can preview in grayscale or black and white to verify that the text is legible against the background.

Tip In Normal view, you can see how your slides will look when printed on a monochrome printer by clicking either the Grayscale or the Black And White button in the Color/Grayscale group on the View tab.

When you're ready to print, you don't have to leave the Backstage view. You can simply click the Print button to print one copy of each slide on the default printer. If the default settings aren't what you want, you can make the following changes on the Print page:

- **Number of copies** Click the arrows to adjust the Copies setting.

- **Which printer** If you have more than one printer available, specify the printer you want to use and set its properties (such as paper source and image compression).

- **Which slides to print** You can print all the slides, the selected slides, or the current slide. To print only specific slides, click the Slides box, and enter the slide numbers and ranges separated by commas (no spaces). For example, enter 1,5,10-12 to print slides 1, 5, 10, 11, and 12 .

- **What to print** From the Print Layout gallery, specify whether to print slides (one per page), notes pages (one half-size slide per page with space for notes), or an outline. You can also print handouts, specifying the number of slides that print on each page (1, 2, 3, 4, 6, or 9) and their order.

You select what to print from this gallery.

● **Whether to frame slides** Click this option below the Print Layout and Handouts galleries to put a frame around the slides on the printed page.

● **Whether to scale slides** If you haven't set the size of the slides to match the size of the paper in the printer, click this option to have PowerPoint automatically reduce or increase the size of the slides to fit the paper when you print them.

See Also For information about setting the size of slides, see "Setting Up Presentations for Delivery" earlier in this chapter.

● **Print quality** Click this option if you want the highest quality printed output.

● **Print comments and ink markup** Click this option if electronic or handwritten notes are attached to the presentation and you want to review them along with the slides.

● **Collate multiple copies** If you're printing multiple copies of a presentation, specify whether complete copies should be printed one at a time.

● **Color range** Specify whether the presentation should be printed in color (color on a color printer and grayscale on a monochrome printer), grayscale (on either a color or a monochrome printer), or pure black and white (no gray on either a color or a monochrome printer).

● **Edit the header or footer** Click this option to display the Header And Footer dialog box.

See Also For information about adding footers to slides, see "Setting Up Presentations for Delivery" earlier in this chapter.

In this exercise, you'll preview a presentation in grayscale, select a printer, and print a selection of slides.

SET UP You need the ServiceOrientationB_start presentation located in your Chapter17 practice file folder to complete this exercise. Open the ServiceOrientationB_start presentation, and save it as *ServiceOrientationB*. Then follow the steps.

1. Click the **File** tab to display the Backstage view, and then click **Print**.

   The right side of the Print page displays the first slide as it will print with the current settings.

2. Under **Settings**, click **Color**, and then click **Grayscale**.

   The preview shows the slide in black, white, and shades of gray.

3. Click the **Next Page** button to move through the slides, until slide **12** is displayed.

4. On the **Zoom Slider**, click the **Zoom In** button several times, and then use the horizontal scroll bar that appears to scroll all the way to the left.

It's easier to examine the date in the footer of the magnified slide.

- Informal discussion of results
  - What might be done better next tim
  - Projects for next year

April 17, 2010   Sidney Higa

You can use the Zoom Slider to zoom in on parts of a slide.

5. Click the **Zoom to Page** button to return to the original zoom percentage.

6. In the middle pane, click the setting for your printer.

A list displays the names of all the printers installed on your computer.

7. In the list, click the printer you want to use.

Tip After choosing a printer, you can customize its settings for this particular print operation by clicking Printer Properties to display the Properties dialog box. For example, if the printer you have selected has duplex capabilities, you might want to specify that it should print slides on both sides of the page.

8. Under **Settings**, in the **Slides** box, type **1-3,5**, and then press Tab.

In the right pane, PowerPoint displays a preview of slide 1. Below the preview, the slide indicator changes to *1 of 4*, and you can now preview only the selected slides.

9. Click **Full Page Slides**, and below the gallery that appears, click **Frame Slides**.

10. At the top of the middle pane, click the **Print** button.

PowerPoint prints slides 1, 2, 3, and 5 with frames in shades of gray on the selected printer.

 CLEAN UP Save the ServiceOrientationB presentation, and then close it.

Preparing Speaker Notes and Handouts

If you will be delivering your presentation before a live audience, you might want some speaker notes to guide you. Each slide in a PowerPoint presentation has a corresponding notes page. As you create each slide, you can enter notes that relate to the slide's content by simply clicking the Notes pane and typing. If you want to include something other than text in your speaker notes, you must switch to Notes Page view by clicking the Notes Page button in the Presentation Views group on the View tab. When your notes are complete, you can print them so that they are readily available to guide the presentation.

Tip In Presenter view, you can see your notes on one monitor while you display the slides to your audience on another monitor. For information about Presenter view, see the sidebar "Setting Up Presenter View" later in this chapter.

As a courtesy for your audience, you might want to supply handouts showing the presentation's slides so that people can take notes. Printing handouts requires a few decisions, such as which of the nine available formats you want to use and whether you want to add headers and footers, but otherwise, you don't need to do anything special to create simple handouts.

Tip The layout of PowerPoint notes pages and handouts is controlled by a special kind of template called a *master*. Usually, you'll find that the default masters are more than adequate, but if you want to make changes, you can. For information about customizing masters, refer to *Microsoft PowerPoint 2010 Step by Step*, by Joyce Cox and Joan Lambert (Microsoft Press, 2010).

In this exercise, you'll enter speaker notes for some slides in the Notes pane. Then you'll switch to Notes Page view, and insert a graphic into one note and a diagram into another. Finally, you'll print both speaker notes and handouts.

SET UP You need the Harmony_start presentation and the YinYang graphic located in your Chapter17 practice file folder to complete this exercise. Open the Harmony_start presentation, and save it as *Harmony*. Then follow the steps.

1. With slide **1** displayed, drag the splitter bar between the **Slide** pane and the **Notes** pane upward to enlarge the Notes pane.

2. Click anywhere in the **Notes** pane, type **Welcome and introductions**, and then press Enter.

3. Type **Logistics**, press Enter, and then type **Establish knowledge level**.

4. Display slide **2**, and in the **Notes** pane, type **Talk about the main concepts**.

5. Display slide **3**, and in the **Notes** pane, type **Complementary energies**, and then press Enter twice.

6. On the **View** tab, in the **Presentation Views** group, click the **Notes Page** button.

   Slide 3 is displayed in Notes Page view. The zoom percentage is set so that the entire notes page fits in the window.

7. On the **Insert** tab, in the **Images** group, click the **Picture** button.

8. In the **Insert Picture** dialog box, navigate to your **Chapter17** practice file folder, and then double-click the **YinYang** graphic.

9. Drag the image down below the note you typed in step 5.

   The picture is visible in Notes Page view.

You might want to add images to your speaker notes to remind yourself of concepts you want to cover while the slide is displayed.

10. Below the scroll bar, click the **Next Slide** button to move to slide **4**. Then click the border around the text placeholder to select it, and press Delete.

11. On the **Insert** tab, in the **Illustrations** group, click the **SmartArt** button. In the left pane of the **Choose a SmartArt Graphic** dialog box, click **Hierarchy**, and then in the middle pane, double-click the second thumbnail in the last row (**Hierarchy List**).

    A diagram with six shapes and placeholder text is inserted into the page. Don't worry about its placement for now; you will fix that later.

    See Also For information about how to work with SmartArt diagrams, see "Inserting Diagrams" in Chapter 16, "Add Simple Visual Enhancements." For information about using SmartArt to customize diagrams, refer to Microsoft PowerPoint 2010 Step by Step, by Joyce Cox and Joan Lambert (Microsoft Press, 2010).

12. Open the **Text** pane, click the first placeholder in the hierarchy, and type the following, pressing the Down Arrow key or the Enter key as indicated:

    Focus (Down Arrow)

       Health (Down Arrow)

       Creativity (Enter)

       Relationships (Enter)

       Community (Down Arrow)

    Follow (Down Arrow)

       Knowledge (Down Arrow)

       Career (Enter)

       Fame (Enter)

       Fortune

    Tip If you have trouble seeing the notes at this zoom percentage, click the Zoom In button on the Zoom Slider in the lower-right corner of the window.

    The speaker notes now include a diagram expressing visually the concepts to be emphasized during the presentation.

13. Use the formatting options available in the **SmartArt Styles** group on the **Design** tab to format the diagram any way you want, and then move and size the diagram to fit in the space below the slide.

We used the Moderate Effect style and the Gradient Loop – Accent 1 colors.

Diagrams can give you an at-a-glance reminder of important concepts.

14. On the **View** tab, in the **Presentation Views** group, click the **Normal** button.

The diagram is not visible in Normal view.

15. Display slide **3**.

The YinYang graphic is not visible in this view either.

Header & Footer

16. Switch to Notes Page view, and then on the **Insert** tab, in the **Text** group, click the **Header & Footer** button.

The Header And Footer dialog box opens with the Notes And Handouts page displayed.

On the Notes And Handouts page, you can insert a header and a footer.

17. Select the **Date and Time** check box, and then click **Fixed**.

18. Select the **Header** check box, and then in the text box, type Harmony in Your Home.

19. Select the **Footer** check box, and then in the text box, type Wide World Importers.

20. Click **Apply to All**.

The notes page reflects your specifications.

21. Switch to Normal view, and then display the **Print** page of the Backstage view.

22. On the **Print** page, under **Settings**, click **Full Page Slides**, and then click **Notes Pages**.

23. Click the **Slides** box, type **1-4**, and then click the **Print** button.

    You now have a copy of the speaker notes to refer to during the presentation.

24. Display the **Print** page of the Backstage view again, and under **Settings**, click **Notes Pages**, and under **Handouts** in the gallery, click **3 slides**.

    The first page of the handouts is previewed in the right pane.

When you print three slides per page, PowerPoint adds lines for notes to the right of each slide image.

25. Change the **Slides** setting to **1-3**, and then click the **Print** button.

✖ CLEAN UP Save the Harmony presentation, and then close it.

Enhanced Handouts

If you want to provide audience handouts that include notes as well as pictures of the slides, you can send the presentation to a Microsoft Word document and then develop the handout content in Word.

To create handouts in Word:

1. Display the Save & Send page of the Backstage view, and under File Types in the middle pane, click Create Handouts.

2. In the right pane, click the Create Handouts button.

   The Send To Microsoft Word dialog box opens.

In two of the five available formats, you can enter notes along with the pictures of the slides.

3. Click the notes format you want.

4. If the slide content might change, under Add Slides To Microsoft Word Document, click Paste Link.

5. Click OK.

   Word starts and opens a document set up to contain the handout format you selected. If you selected Outline Only, the text of the presentation appears in the document as a bulleted list.

Finalizing Presentations

These days, many presentations are delivered electronically, either by e-mail or from a Web site. As you develop a presentation, it can accumulate information that you might not want in the final version, such as the names of people who worked on the presentation, comments that reviewers have added to the file, or hidden text about status and assumptions. If your presentation will never leave your computer, you don't have to worry that it might contain something that you would rather other people did not see. However, if the presentation file is going to be shared with other people, you will want to remove this identifying and tracking information before you distribute the presentation.

To examine some of the information attached to a presentation, you can display the properties on the Info page of the Backstage view. You can change or remove some of the properties in the Properties pane, or you can display the Document Panel or the Properties dialog box by clicking Properties at the top of the pane and clicking the option you want. However, to automate the process of finding and removing all extraneous and potentially confidential information, PowerPoint provides a tool called the *Document Inspector.*

The Document Inspector removes many different types of information.

Tip When rearranging the objects on a slide, you might drag an object to one side while you decide whether to include it. The Off-Slide Content option in the Document Inspector dialog box detects any stray content that you might have overlooked. The Document Inspector also looks for invisible content on the slide. This is content you might have hidden by displaying the Selection And Visibility task pane and then clearing the object's check box. (To display the Selection And Visibility pane, click the Select button in the Editing group on the Home tab, and then click Selection Pane.)

After you run the Document Inspector, you see a summary of its search results, and you have the option of removing all the items found in each category.

PowerPoint also includes two other finalizing tools:

- **Check Accessibility** This tool checks for presentation elements and formatting that might be difficult for people with certain kinds of disabilities to read. It reports its findings in the Accessibility Checker task pane, and offers suggestions for fixing any potential issues.

- **Check Compatibility** This tool checks for the use of features not supported in earlier versions of PowerPoint. It presents a list of features that might be lost or degraded if you save the presentation in an earlier PowerPoint file format.

After you have handled extraneous information and accessibility and compatibility issues, you can mark a presentation as final and make it a read-only file, so that other people know that they should not make changes to this released presentation. This process does not lock the presentation, however; if you want to make additional changes to the presentation, you can easily turn off the final status.

In this exercise, you'll examine the properties attached to a presentation, remove personal information from the file, and then mark the presentation as final.

 SET UP You need the Meeting_start presentation located in your Chapter17 practice file folder to complete this exercise. Open the Meeting_start presentation, and save it as *Meeting*. Then follow the steps.

1. Display the **Info** page of the Backstage view.

   The Properties pane on the right side of the window displays the standard properties associated with this presentation.

Properties ▾

Size	82.3KB
Slides	11
Hidden slides	0
Title	Company Meeting
Categories	Meetings

Related Dates

Last Modified	Today, 10:44 AM
Created	4/24/2006 4:46 PM
Last Printed	Never

Related People

Author	☐ Joyce Cox
	☐ Joan Lambert
	Add an author
Last Modified By	☐ Sidney Higa

Related Documents

📁 Open File Location

Show All Properties

PowerPoint controls some of the properties, such as the size and dates; you can add and change others, such as the assigned categories and authors.

2. At the bottom on the **Properties** pane, click **Show All Properties**.

The pane expands to show all the properties.

3. Click the property adjacent to **Status**, and type Done.

4. At the top of the pane, click **Properties**, and click **Advanced Properties**. Then in the **Meeting Properties** dialog box, click the **Summary** tab.

   This page includes some of the properties you might want to change in a convenient format.

Meeting Properties	?	X

General | **Summary** | Statistics | Contents | Custom

Title: Company Meeting

Subject:

Author: Joyce Cox;Joan Lambert

Manager: Florian Stiller

Company: Online Training Solutions, Inc.

Category: Meetings

Keywords:

Comments: Copyright © 2010 Online Training Solutions, Inc.

Hyperlink base:

Template: Flow

☑ Save preview picture

OK   Cancel

The Summary page of the Properties dialog box.

5. Click in the **Subject** box, type Morale event, and then click **OK**.

   The Subject property in the Properties pane reflects your change.

6. Save your changes to the presentation.

7. Display the **Info** page of the Backstage view again. Then in the center pane, click **Check for Issues**, and click **Inspect Document**.

   In the Document Inspector dialog box, you can inspect for six types of content.

8. Clear the **Custom XML Data** check box. Then with the **Comments and Annotations**, **Document Properties and Personal Information**, **Invisible On-Slide Content**, and **Presentation Notes** check boxes selected, click **Inspect**.

The Document Inspector reports its findings.

This presentation includes properties that you might not want others to be able to view.

9. To the right of **Document Properties and Personal Information**, click **Remove All**.

PowerPoint removes the presentation's properties.

10. Close the **Document Inspector** dialog box.

In the Properties pane, all the properties have been cleared.

11. In the center pane of the **Info** page, click **Protect Presentation**, and then click **Mark as Final**.

    A message tells you that the presentation will be marked as final and then saved.

12. Click **OK** in the message box, and then click **OK** in the confirmation box that appears after the document is marked as final.

    The presentation's final status is now indicated on the Info page.

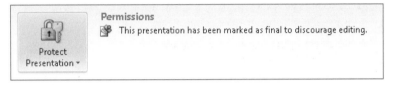

Marking as final discourages but does not prevent editing.

13. Click any tab on the ribbon to return to the presentation.

    The title bar indicates that this is a read-only file, and the ribbon tabs are hidden.

The information bar explains that this presentation has been marked as final.

14. Click the **Home** tab to display its commands, most of which are inactive.

15. On the title slide, double-click the word **Company**, and press the Delete key.

    Nothing happens. You cannot change any of the objects on the slides unless you click the Edit Anyway button in the information bar to remove the final status.

✖ **CLEAN UP** Close the Meeting presentation.

Setting Up Presenter View

If your computer can support two monitors, or if you will be presenting a slide show from your computer through a projector, you might want to check out Presenter view. In this view, you can control the presentation on one monitor while the audience sees the slides in Slide Show view on the delivery monitor or the projector screen.

To deliver a presentation on one monitor and use Presenter view on another:

1. Open the PowerPoint presentation you want to set up.

2. On the Slide Show tab, in the Set Up group, click Set Up Slide Show.

   The Set Up Show dialog box opens. When your computer is set up to use multiple monitors, the settings in the Multiple Monitors area are active.

3. In the Multiple Monitors area, click the Display Slide Show On arrow, and then in the list, click the name of the monitor you want to use to show the slides to your audience.

   The slides will display full-screen on the specified monitor.

4. Select the Show Presenter View check box, and then click OK.

5. With the title slide of the presentation active, switch to Slide Show view.

   The title slide is displayed full screen on the delivery monitor, and Presenter view is displayed on the control monitor. As the presenter, you can see details about what slide or bullet point is coming next, see your speaker notes, jump directly to any slide, black out the screen during a pause in the presentation, and keep track of the time.

6. On the control monitor, use the Presenter view tools to control the presentation.

Delivering Presentations

To deliver a presentation to an audience, you first click the Slide Show button to display the slides full screen. Then depending on how you have set up the presentation, you can either click the mouse button without moving the mouse to display the slides in sequence, or you can allow PowerPoint to display the slides according to the advancement timings you have set on the Transitions tab.

See Also For information about advancement timings, see "Adding Transitions" in Chapter 16, "Add Simple Visual Enhancements."

If you need to move to a slide other than the next one or the previous one, you can move the mouse pointer to display an inconspicuous navigation toolbar in the lower-left corner of the slide. You can use this toolbar in the following ways:

- To move to the next slide, click the Next button.
- To move to the previous slide, click the Previous button.
- To jump to a slide out of sequence, click the Navigation button, click Go To Slide, and then click the slide.

  Tip You can also display the Navigation button's menu by right-clicking the slide.

- To end the presentation, click the Navigation button, and then click End Show.

  Keyboard Shortcuts To display a list of keyboard shortcuts for carrying out presentation tasks, click the Navigation button, and then click Help. For example, you can press the Spacebar, the Down Arrow key, or the Right Arrow key to move to the next slide; press the Page Up key or the Left Arrow key to move to the previous slide; and press the Esc key to end the presentation.

During a presentation, you can reinforce your message by drawing on the slides with an electronic "pen" or changing the background behind text with a highlighter. You simply click the Pen button on the toolbar that appears when you move the mouse, click the tool you want, and then begin drawing or highlighting. The pen color is determined by the setting in the Set Up Show dialog box, but you can change the pen color during the presentation by clicking the Pen button, clicking Ink Color, and then selecting the color you want.

In this exercise, you'll move around in a presentation in various ways while delivering it. You'll also use a pen tool to mark up one slide, change the color of the markup, and then mark up another.

SET UP You need the SavingWater_start presentation located in your Chapter17 practice file folder to complete this exercise. Open the SavingWater_start presentation, and save it as *SavingWater*. Then follow the steps.

1. With slide **1** selected in Normal view, on the **View Shortcuts** toolbar, click the **Slide Show** button.

   PowerPoint displays the title slide after implementing its applied transition effect.

2. Click the mouse button to advance to slide **2**.

   The slide contents ripple onto the screen.

3. Press the Left Arrow key to move back to the previous slide, and then press the Right Arrow key to display the next slide.

4. Move the mouse.

   The pointer appears on the screen, and barely visible in the lower-left corner, the shadow toolbar appears.

   Troubleshooting If the pop-up navigation toolbar doesn't seem to appear, move the pointer to the lower-left corner of the screen and move it slowly to the right. The four toolbar buttons should become visible in turn. If they don't, press the Esc key to end the slide show. Then display the Backstage view, and click Options. In the PowerPoint Options dialog box, click Advanced, and in the Slide Show area, select the Show Popup Toolbar check box, and click OK.

5. Move the pointer to the bottom of the screen and to the left until the **Next** button appears. Then click the **Next** button to display slide **3**.

6. Right-click anywhere on the screen, and then click **Previous** to redisplay slide **2**.

7. Right-click anywhere on the screen, point to **Go to Slide**, and then in the list of slide names, click **11 Soil Amendment**.

8. Display the toolbar, click the **Navigation** button, and then click **Next** to display slide **12**.

9. Use various navigation methods to display various slides in the presentation until you are comfortable moving around.

10. Right-click anywhere on the screen, and then click **End Show**.

    The active slide appears in Normal view.

    Tip If you click all the way through to the end of the presentation, PowerPoint displays a black screen to indicate that the next click will return you to the previous view. If you do not want the black screen to appear at the end of a presentation, display the PowerPoint Options dialog box, and click Advanced. Then in the Slide Show area, clear the End With Black Slide check box, and click OK. Then clicking while the last slide is displayed will return you to the previous view.

11. Display slide **11**, and switch to Slide Show view.

12. Right-click anywhere on the screen, point to **Pointer Options**, and then click **Highlighter**.

   Tip When the pen or highlighter tool is active in Slide Show view, clicking the mouse button does not advance the slide show to the next slide. You need to switch back to the regular pointer to use the mouse to advance the slide.

13. On the slide, highlight the words **10 tons**.

14. Right-click anywhere on the screen, point to **Pointer Options**, and then click **Pen**.

15. On the slide, draw a line below the words **per acre per year**.

   PowerPoint draws the line in the color specified in the Set Up Show dialog box as the default for this presentation.

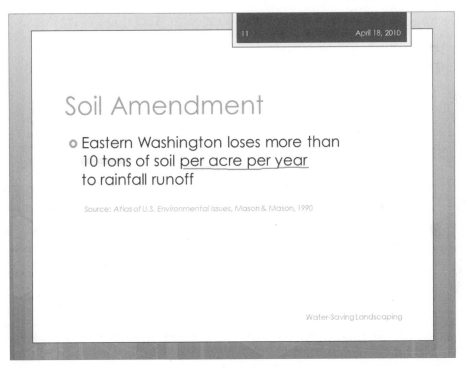

You can emphasize a point with the highlighter or pen.

16. Right-click the screen, point to **Pointer Options**, and then click **Erase All Ink on Slide**.

   The highlight and line are erased.

17. Press the Spacebar to move to the next slide.

18. Display the toolbar, click the **Pen** button, point to **Ink Color**, and then under **Standard Colors** in the palette, click the **Dark Red** box.

19. Draw a line below the words **Prevent erosion**.

20. Right-click anywhere on the screen, point to **Pointer Options**, and then click **Arrow**.

    The pen tool changes back to the regular pointer, and you can now click the mouse button to advance to the next slide.

21. Press Esc to stop the presentation.

    A message asks whether you want to keep your ink annotations.

22. Click **Discard**.

    The active slide is displayed in Normal view.

✖ CLEAN UP Save the SavingWater presentation, and then close it.

Key Points

- It's most efficient to set up your presentation in its intended output format before you begin adding content.

- To proof a presentation on paper, you can print it in color, grayscale, or black and white, depending on the capabilities of your printer.

- You can easily create speaker notes to facilitate a presentation delivery, or print handouts so that your audience can easily follow your presentation.

- Finalizing a presentation ensures that it doesn't contain personal or confidential information and that people are alerted before making further changes.

- Knowing how to use all the navigation toolbar buttons, commands, and keyboard shortcuts to navigate in Slide Show view is important for smooth presentation delivery.

- To emphasize a point, you can mark up slides during a presentation by using a pen in various colors or a highlighter.

Part 5

Microsoft
OneNote 2010

18 Explore OneNote 2010 515

19 Create and Configure Notebooks. 539

20 Create and Organize Notes 563

Chapter at a Glance

Navigate in the OneNote program window, **page 516**

Drama Club

Performance Sunday
☐ Need to get a hat!

Pasted from: http://www.contoso.c

Notebooks: ‹   General   Unfiled Notes
📘 Personal   ⌃
    📄 General   OneNote kee
    📄 Unfiled Notes
📘 My Notebook   ⌃
    📄 Miscellaneous
    📄 Recipes   How are OneNote
    📄 Shopping
    📄 To Do
    📄 Travel

N.. ▾ ‹
OneNote
OneNote
OneNote Basics
What's 515

Explore OneNote in the default notebook, **page 526**

N | ← → ⟲ ▭▭ ▭▭ | ⤓   OneNote keeps track of stuff at Work, Home, or Sch - Microsoft OneNote

File   Home   Insert   Share   Draw   Review   View

Normal Full Page Dock to   Hide   Page   Rule Hide   Paper   Zoom Zoom ⟲ 100%   New   New Docked New Side kee
View   View   Desktop Authors Color Lines Page Title Size   Out   In   □ 100% Window   Window   Note
                                                                          □ 75%
      Views   Authors   Page Setup   Zoom   Window

Gather, organize, search, an
ideas, thoughts, clippings
meeting notes, lect
event p

How are OneNote pages different?

Work in the OneNote program window, **page 519**

N | ← → ⟲ ▭▭ ▭▭ | ⤓   Appetizers - Microsoft OneNote   ▬   ▭   ☒

File   Home   Insert   Share   Draw   Review   View

Info
Open   Share Notebook
New
            1. Select Notebook:
Share
Save As   📘 My Notebook   ▾
Send
Print   2. Share On:

                🌐 Web
                   Access from any computer or browser.
                   Share with others (optional).

                   Network

OneNote Options   ? ☒

General
Display   🔍 Change how OneNote looks.
Proofing
Save & Backup   Display
Send to OneNote
Audio & Video   ☑ Place OneNote icon in the notification area of the taskbar ⓘ
Language   ☐ Create all new pages with rule lines
Advanced   ☐ Dock new Side Note windows to the side of the desktop ⓘ
                 ☐ Page tabs appear on the left
Customize Ribbon ☑ Show the floating New Page button near page tabs
Quick Access Toolbar ☑ Navigation bar appears on the left
                 ☐ Vertical scroll bar appears on the left
Add-Ins   ☑ Show note containers on pages
Trust Center   ☐ Disable screen clipping notifications

Customize OneNote, **page 535**

                                              OK   Cancel

18 Explore OneNote 2010

In this chapter, you will learn how to

✔ Navigate in the OneNote program window.

✔ Work in the OneNote program window.

✔ Explore OneNote in the default notebook.

✔ Customize OneNote.

Microsoft OneNote 2010 is a handy program that makes it possible to electronically collect and store pieces of information. You can use OneNote to:

● Collect, save, and safeguard information in one place.

● Take notes in a class or meeting.

● Organize information in a way that is logical to you.

● Search for information when you need it.

After you spend a short time using OneNote, you will undoubtedly find many uses for it. OneNote 2010 is available in all editions of Microsoft Office 2010, and is equally useful for business and personal purposes.

As with all organizational systems, OneNote is most effective if you use it on a regular basis. By developing consistent data collection and storage practices, you will be able to most efficiently locate stored information whenever you need it. Eventually, you might even wonder how you ever survived without it.

In this chapter, you'll explore the OneNote working environment and storage structure, learn how to move around and work in OneNote, and look at the options for customizing OneNote to better fit the way you work.

> **Practice Files** You don't need any practice files to complete the exercises in this chapter. For more information about practice file requirements, see "Using the Practice Files" at the beginning of this book.

Navigating in the OneNote Program Window

In the same way that the Windows operating system information storage structure reflects that of a physical office, (with a desktop, folders, and files), the OneNote storage structure reflects that of a tabbed notebook. You might have a notebook for each project you work on, or one notebook in which you track business information and another in which you track personal information. Each notebook is divided into sections, and each section is divided into pages. If you want to extend the analogy, you can even format the background of a notebook page to resemble various types of ruled paper.

See Also For information about changing the background of a notebook page, see "Creating Sections and Pages," in Chapter 19, "Create and Configure Notebooks."

In Windows Explorer, each notebook is represented by a folder in your Documents\OneNote Notebooks folder. Each section of a notebook is stored as an .one file within the notebook folder. (Although you would usually move sections within OneNote itself, it is possible to move or copy a section to a different notebook in Windows Explorer by moving or copying the section file to a different notebook's folder.

A typical OneNote notebook storage structure.

When you start OneNote 2010 for the first time, the program opens a sample notebook named Personal. Thereafter when you start OneNote, the notebook you worked with in the previous OneNote session opens.

Information about the content of open OneNote notebooks is shown in four areas of the OneNote program window.

Navigation Bar   Notebook header   Content pane   Page Tabs Bar

The default appearance of the OneNote program window.

● The Navigation Bar on the left side of the program window displays information about the notebooks that are stored in the default notebook location. When collapsed, as it is by default, the Navigation Bar displays a button for each notebook. When expanded, the Navigation Bar displays the hierarchical structure of each notebook. You expand and collapse the Navigation Bar by clicking the button in its upper-right corner.

The expanded Navigation Bar.

● The content pane in the center of the program window displays the active notebook page. On pages that you create, the page title appears at the top of the page, along with the date and time the page was most recently modified.

- The notebook header above the content pane displays section tabs that you can click to move between sections of the active notebook.

- The Page Tabs Bar to the right of the content pane displays page tabs you can click to move between pages of the active section. By default, the Page Tabs Bar displays a tab for each page in the current section. You can filter the display of tabs to make it easier to locate specific content.

You can collapse and expand the Page Tabs Bar by clicking the button in its upper-right corner.

Keyboard Shortcuts Press Alt+Page Up to display the first page in the currently visible set of page tabs; press Alt+Page Down to display the last page in the currently visible set. Press Ctrl+Shift+[to increase the width of the Page Tabs Bar; press Ctrl+Shift+] to decrease the width of the Page Tabs Bar.

Working with Multiple Notebooks

You can have multiple notebooks open at one time, either in the same OneNote window or in separate OneNote windows.

Keyboard Shortcut Press Ctrl+M to open a second instance of the current OneNote window.

To open a notebook in the current OneNote window:

1. On the Open page of the Backstage view, click the Open Notebook button.
2. Browse to your Documents\OneNote Notebooks folder.
3. Click the folder representing the notebook you want to open, and click Open. In the notebook folder, click the Open Notebook file, and then click Open.

   Tip The Open Notebook file is a Table Of Contents file that contains pointers to the content within the notebook.

When you work with multiple notebooks in the same OneNote window, you can easily switch between them by clicking a notebook's button on the Navigation Bar.

Keyboard Shortcut Press Ctrl+G, the Down Arrow or Up Arrow key, and then Enter to switch to a different notebook on the Navigation Bar.

If you don't need to access an open notebook any more, you can close it. Closed notebooks do not appear on the Navigation Bar.

To close a notebook:

- On the Navigation Bar, right-click the notebook button, and then click Close This Notebook.

Working in the OneNote Program Window

As you do in other Office programs, you work with OneNote notebook content by using the commands on the ribbon and Quick Access Toolbar, and with the OneNote program, and OneNote notebook files in the Backstage view.

Working from the Ribbon and Quick Access Toolbar

Unlike in other Office 2010 programs, the ribbon in OneNote is collapsed by default to provide more space for the notebook page.

The OneNote ribbon includes the File tab and six other tabs:

- **Home** This tab includes buttons that represent commands for formatting note-book content, inserting and locating content tags, and coordinating notebook content with Microsoft Outlook 2010.

  See Also For information about content tags, see the sidebar "Tagging Content" in Chapter 20, "Create and Organize Notes."

The Home tab of the OneNote ribbon.

  Troubleshooting The appearance of buttons and groups on the ribbon changes depending on the width of the program window. For information about changing the appearance of the ribbon to match our screen images, see "Modifying the Display of the Ribbon" at the beginning of this book.

  See Also For information about interactions between OneNote and Outlook, see "Creating Sections and Pages" in Chapter 19, "Create and Configure Notebooks."

- **Insert** This tab includes commands for inserting, linking to, and attaching images, files, audio and video recordings, time stamps, and special symbols.

The Insert tab of the OneNote ribbon.

  See Also For information about inserting various types of content, see Chapter 20, "Create and Organize Notes."

- **Share** This tab includes commands for sharing a notebook with other OneNote users and for managing a multiuser notebook.

The Share tab of the OneNote ribbon.

See Also For information about multiuser notebooks, see "Creating a Notebook for Use by Multiple People" in Chapter 19, "Create and Configure Notebooks."

- **Draw** This tab includes commands for inserting and manipulating handwritten content.

The Draw tab of the OneNote ribbon.

See Also For information about writing in a notebook, see "Entering Content Directly onto a Page" in Chapter 20, "Create and Organize Notes."

- **Review** This tab includes commands for working with the of text stored on notebook pages, including checking spelling and grammar; researching word choices; and translating content either by using the Office translation tools or through an online service.

The Review tab of the OneNote ribbon.

See Also For information about reviewing content, see "Correcting Spelling and Grammatical Errors" in Chapter 3, "Edit and Proofread Text."

● **View** This tab includes commands for changing the appearance of the OneNote window and of notebook pages, for magnifying your view of notebook content, and for working with multiple program windows.

The View tab of the OneNote ribbon.

In OneNote, the default Quick Access Toolbar displays the Back, Undo, Dock To Desktop, and Full Page View buttons. As with other Office 2010 programs, you can change the location of the Quick Access Toolbar and customize it to include any commands to which you want to have one-click access.

Customize Quick Access Toolbar menu

The default OneNote Quick Access Toolbar.

From the Customize Quick Access Toolbar menu, you can add the Forward, Redo, Print, Print Preview, Favorite Pens, and Favorite Highlighter buttons. You can add other buttons from the Quick Access Toolbar page of the OneNote Options window or by right-clicking a command on the ribbon and then clicking Add To Quick Access Toolbar.

See Also For information about creating handwritten content with pens and highlighters, see "Entering Content Directly onto a Page" in Chapter 20, "Create and Organize Notes."

Tip If you prefer to work with the ribbon collapsed to maximize the available notebook page space, add all the commands you use frequently to the Quick Access Toolbar and display it below the ribbon, directly above the workspace. For information, see "Customizing the Quick Access Toolbar" in Chapter 1, "Explore Office 2010."

Working in the Backstage View

As with other Office 2010 programs, clicking the File tab at the left end of the OneNote ribbon displays the Backstage view. Commands related to managing OneNote and OneNote files (rather than notebook content) are organized on the following pages of the Backstage view:

● **Info** From this page, you can share, close, or view the properties of a notebook, view the synchronization status of your local copy of a shared notebook (the copy that is on your computer) with the original notebook (the copy that is in the central storage location), and open backup copies of notebooks.

The Info page of the Backstage view.

● **Open** From this page, you can open an existing notebook either by browsing to and selecting the notebook's Table Of Contents file or by selecting a recently closed notebook from a list on the page.

● **New** From this page, you can create a new notebook on your local computer, on a computer that you access on your local network, on a SharePoint site, or on a Web site.

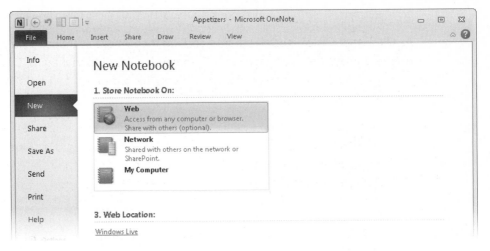

The New page of the Backstage view.

See Also For information about new notebooks, see "Creating a Notebook for Use by One Person" and "Creating a Notebook for Use by Multiple People" in Chapter 19, "Create and Configure Notebooks."

● **Share** From this page, you can share a notebook with other OneNote users by storing it on a computer that you access on your local network, on a SharePoint site, or on a Web site.

The Share page of the OneNote Backstage view.

See Also For information about sharing notebooks, see "Creating a Notebook for Use by Multiple People" in Chapter 19, "Create and Configure Notebooks."

● **Save As** From this page, you can save the current page or section in one of several file formats, or save the current notebook as a OneNote Package (a distributable OneNote file), a PDF file, or an XPS file.

The Save As page of the Backstage view.

● **Send** From this page, you can send the current page content to Outlook or to Microsoft Word. If you want to send information from the current page to some-one, you can embed the page content in the body of an e-mail message or attach the page to a message as a OneNote (.one) file, a Web (.mht) file, or a Portable Document Format (.pdf) file. You can copy the page content into a Word document, or if you use Word as your blog editor, you can copy the page content to a blog post form.

The Send page of the Backstage view.

● **Print** From this page, you can preview and print a notebook page, a group of pages, or an entire section of a notebook.

You can click Print and choose settings in the Print dialog box, or click Print Preview and choose settings in the Print Preview And Settings dialog box.

The Print Preview And Settings dialog box.

● **Help** From this page, you can access information about your Office installation, manage product activation and product keys, and access support resources, program options, and program updates.

Exploring OneNote in the Default Notebook

The default installation of OneNote 2010 includes one notebook, named *Personal*, which has one section, named *General*. This section has four pages of information about OneNote and examples of the types of information you can collect in OneNote and ways that you can work with it.

In this exercise, you'll take a quick tour of the Personal notebook while moving among sections and pages, and displaying different views of a page.

 SET UP You don't need any practice files to complete this exercise; just follow the steps.

1. On the **Start** menu, point to **All Programs**, click **Microsoft Office**, and then click **Microsoft OneNote 2010**.

   OneNote starts. If this is the first time you've used OneNote, the first page of the General section of the Personal notebook is displayed.

2. If the **Personal** notebook isn't open, do one of the following to open it:

   ○ If the **Personal** notebook is shown on the **Navigation Bar**, click its button.

   ○ If the **Personal** notebook is not shown on the **Navigation Bar**, display the **Open** page of the Backstage view, and click the **Open Notebook** button. In the **Open Notebook** dialog box, browse to your **Documents\OneNote Notebooks** folder, double-click the **Personal** folder, and then double-click **Open Notebook**.

   Troubleshooting If your school or organization has a specialized OneNote environment, the Personal notebook might not be available. You can follow along with this exercise by substituting any available notebook.

   With the default settings, the ribbon is collapsed at the top of the program window, the Navigation Bar is collapsed on the left side of the program window, and the Page Tabs Bar is open on the right side of the program window.

   Troubleshooting If the program window doesn't appear as described, don't worry; we'll show you how to adjust the settings in this exercise.

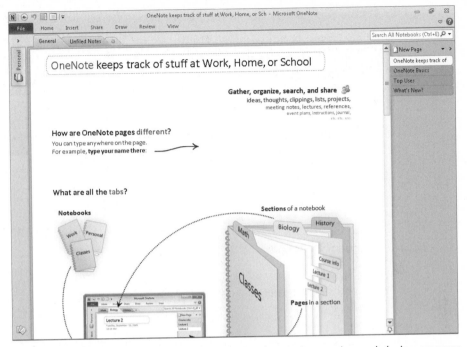

You can change the area available to the notebook page by opening and closing program window elements.

The current notebook is indicated by the active (boxed) notebook button on the Navigation Bar. The current section is indicated by the active (top) tab in the notebook header. The current page is indicated in the window title bar, in the dotted box at the top of the page, and on the active page tab.

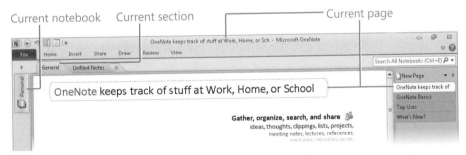

You can easily identify your location within the notebook organizational structure.

3. At the top of the **Navigation Bar**, click the **Expand Navigation Bar** button.

   The expanded Navigation Bar displays the notebook and the two sections within it, which correspond to the tabs in the notebook header.

4. On the **Navigation Bar**, in the **Personal** notebook, click **Unfiled Notes**.

OneNote displays the Unfiled Notes section. This is a holding area for content that you send to OneNote from other programs. You can also create content directly in this section if you haven't decided on an organizational structure for the content.

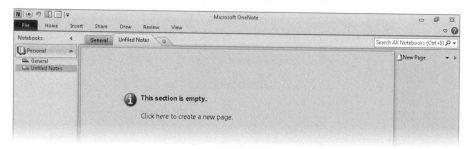

Until you add content to the Unfiled Notes section, it is empty.

See Also For information about sending content to OneNote from other Office 2010 programs, see "Creating Sections and Pages" in Chapter 19, "Create and Configure Notebooks," and "Sending Content to OneNote" in Chapter 20, "Create and Organize Notes."

The Unfiled Notes section is part of the OneNote program rather than part of a specific notebook; you have only one Unfiled Notes section, and it is shared by all your notebooks.

Tip You can open the Unfiled Notes section when working in any notebook by clicking the Unfiled Notes button located at the bottom of the Navigation Bar.

5. On the **Navigation Bar**, on the right side of the **Personal** notebook button, click the **Collapse** button.

The sections of the Personal notebook disappear from the Navigation Bar.

6. In the notebook header, point to the **General** tab.

A ScreenTip displays the complete path to the storage location of the section file (the .one file). Notice that the file name matches the section name.

Point to a section tab to display its storage location.

7. Click the **General** tab to redisplay the **General** section of the **Personal** notebook. Then scroll down the page to view its content.

Tip An image of a video thumbnail is embedded near the bottom of the page. Clicking the Click Here link to the right of the thumbnail displays a Web page from which you can play the video "How to organize stuff in OneNote 2010." This is a short video, without narrative, that provides a very basic overview of notebooks, sections, and pages.

8. At the top of the **Page Tabs Bar**, click the **Collapse Page Tabs** button.

   The Page Tabs Bar shrinks to about half its former width. When truncated, the same name is displayed for the first and second pages.

9. In the **Page Tabs Bar**, point to the second page tab.

   A ScreenTip displays the entire page title, *OneNote Basics*.

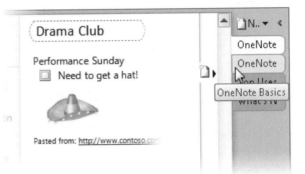

When the Page Tabs Bar is collapsed, pointing to any page tab displays the full page name.

See Also For information about the New Page icon that appears to the left of the page tabs when you point to them, see "Creating Sections and Pages" in Chapter 19, "Create and Configure Notebooks."

10. Click the **OneNote Basics** page tab. Then scroll down the page to view its content.

    At the top of the page are images of several types of content you can create in a notebook by using the tools that are built into OneNote.

You can create tables, charts, lists, equations, and more by using the tools in OneNote.

See Also For information about inserting and creating content on notebook pages, see Chapter 20, "Create and Organize Notes."

11. View the content of the **Top Uses** and **What's New** pages. Then display the **Info** page of the Backstage view, and click the **Settings** button for the **Personal** notebook.

A menu of actions you can take with the notebook expands.

From the Info page, you can work with the currently active notebook.

12. On the **Settings** menu, click **Close**.

The Personal notebook closes. Only the Unfiled Notes section remains open in the OneNote program window.

13. Display the **Open** page of the Backstage view.

The Open page includes a list of notebooks you've recently closed.

Tip Clicking the pushpin button to the right of a notebook in the Recently Closed Notebooks list "pins" that notebook to the list so that it stays on the list regardless of how many other notebooks you close.

From the Open page, you can open a notebook you've recently closed or click Open and browse to a notebook.

14. In the **Recently Closed Notebooks** list, click **Personal**.

    The Personal notebook reopens.

15. At the top of the program window, click the collapsed **View** tab of the ribbon.

    The ribbon temporarily expands.

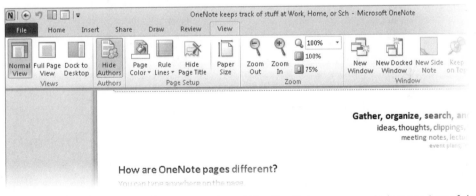

Options in the Views group change your view of the OneNote program window, not just of the selected notebook.

Dock to Desktop

16. In the **Views** group, click the **Dock to Desktop** button.

Keyboard Shortcut Press Ctrl+Alt+D to dock the OneNote window.

The ribbon collapses. The OneNote program window becomes a vertical pane on the right side of the screen.

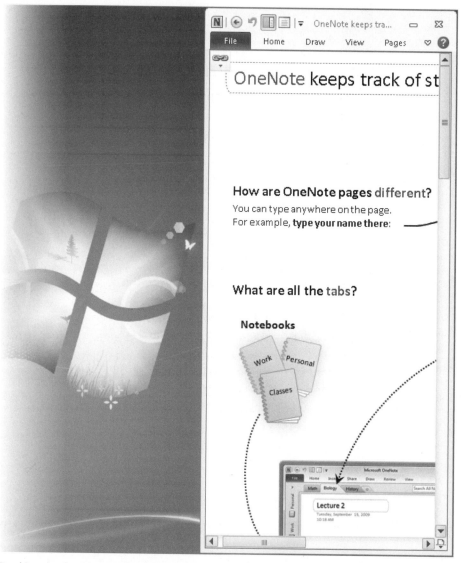

Docking the OneNote program window allows you to see more of your desktop.

17. Experiment with the docked OneNote window.

    You can't move the docked window by dragging its title bar. You can change the width of the window by dragging its left edge. When the window width is at its narrowest, the Quick Access Toolbar and ribbon tabs are not visible.

    Tip Other open windows on the screen might resize when you change the width of the docked OneNote window. Maximizing another window while OneNote is docked resizes that window to fill the entire screen other than the vertical space taken by the docked OneNote window. The docked window space is not available to other windows.

18. In the docked OneNote window, click the collapsed **View** tab.

    Only a subset of the commands previously available from this tab is available in the docked window.

19. In the **Views** group, click the **Normal View** button.

    The program window returns to its normal size.

    Tip You can also undock the window by clicking the active Dock To Desktop button on the Quick Access Toolbar.

20. On the Quick Access Toolbar, click the **Full Page View** button.

    Keyboard Shortcut Press F11 to enable or disable Full Page view.

    The Navigation Bar and Page Tabs Bar close entirely, and the content pane fills the width of the program window. The Pages tab appears on the ribbon.

21. Double-click the **Pages** tab to permanently expand it.

    The tab contains commands for moving among pages, locating content, and creating, deleting, or moving notebook pages.

Next Page

22. In the **Navigate** group, click the **Next Page** button two times.

   Keyboard Shortcut Press Ctrl+Page Down to display the next page in the current section. Press Ctrl+Page Up to display the previous page in the section. Press Alt+Home to display the first page in the section. Press Alt+End to display the last page in the section.

   OneNote displays the Top Uses page in Full Page view.

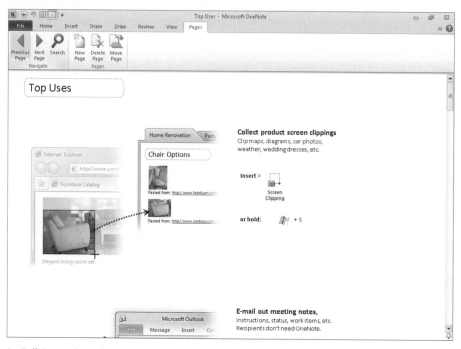

In Full Page view, the Navigation Bar and Page Tabs Bar are hidden.

23. On the Quick Access Toolbar, click the active **Full Page View** button.

   OneNote returns to Normal view, and the Pages tab disappears from the ribbon.

 CLEAN UP Close the Personal notebook, but leave OneNote open.

Customizing OneNote

In this book, we discuss the default behavior of OneNote—the way the program works if you don't change any of its settings. As with all Office programs, there are a number of adjustments—major and minor—that you can make to modify the program to suit your needs. The majority of these are available from the OneNote Options dialog box, which you open by clicking Options in the Backstage view.

The Display page of the OneNote Options dialog box.

Like the Options dialog box in other Office 2010 programs, the OneNote Options dialog box presents a wide variety of settings divided into category-specific pages. Many of the settings you can control in OneNote are the same as those available in other Office programs. The OneNote Options dialog box includes the following pages:

● **General** On this page, you can set options that are common to the Office 2010 programs, including user interface options, the default font, and the user name and initials that identify changes you make to notebook content.

● **Display** On this page, you can change the location and appearance of OneNote features and tools.

● **Proofing** On this page, you can set the AutoCorrect options and spelling options for use in OneNote, as well as the spelling options that are common to the Office 2010 programs.

● **Save & Backup** On this page, you can specify the default locations in which OneNote saves files, configure automatic backup options or start a backup procedure, and configure file optimization options.

● **Send to OneNote** On this page, you can specify where OneNote stores content that you send from Outlook, send from a Web page, and print from a program to OneNote.

● **Audio & Video** On this page, you can specify audio and video recording settings and enable OneNote to search for spoken words within audio and video recordings.

● **Language** On this page, you can specify the languages used by the dictionary and spelling checker, the language priority order for buttons, tabs, and Help content, and the ScreenTip display language.

● **Advanced** On this page, you can set a variety of options including those for linking notes that you take from a docked OneNote window to other programs, optimizing OneNote operations when the computer is running on battery power, and working with tags and passwords.

Investigate this dialog box at your own convenience.

Key Points

- OneNote simplifies the process of collecting and storing electronic information.

- OneNote 2010 supports multiple notebooks, computers, and users, and has many useful new features.

- OneNote 2010 stores information in the Documents\OneNote Notebooks folder. Each "notebook" consists of a folder containing a .one file corresponding to each section within the notebook.

- The default OneNote 2010 installation includes a notebook containing examples and ideas for using OneNote in your home, school, or business environment.

- You can customize many aspects of the appearance and behavior of OneNote to fit your needs.

Chapter at a Glance

Create a notebook for use by one person, **page 540**

Create a notebook for use by multiple people, **page 543**

Create sections and pages, **page 550**

19 Create and Configure Notebooks

In this chapter, you will learn how to

✔ Create a notebook for use by one person.

✔ Create a notebook for use by multiple people.

✔ Create sections and pages.

In Chapter 18, "Explore OneNote 2010," we discussed the basic Microsoft OneNote 2010 data storage structure (notebooks, sections, and pages) and took a tour of the sample notebook that comes with OneNote. As you'll see in this chapter, there are many ways of structuring a notebook. The important thing is to create a structure that is easy for you to move around in so that you can easily find the information you want when you want it.

With OneNote 2010, you can create notebooks for your personal use on one computer, for use on multiple computers, and for use by multiple people. The ability to contribute and edit content in a shared notebook simultaneously with other people opens up many possibilities for collaboration.

In this chapter, you'll create a OneNote notebook on your computer and learn how to create a notebook that you can access from more than one computer or in which you can collaborate on content with other people. You'll create sections and section groups in your notebook, and add pages and subpages to the notebook so that you are ready to start storing information.

> **Practice Files** You don't need any practice files to complete the exercises in this chapter. For more information about practice file requirements, see "Using the Practice Files" at the beginning of this book.

Creating a Notebook for Use by One Person

OneNote 2007 included several notebook templates that created notebooks containing sections and pages customized for their intended use. OneNote 2010 doesn't include any notebook templates; you simply create a basic notebook and then create the sections and pages you want within it.

You can create a basic notebook, add content to it, and then organize the content into pages and sections, or you can create an organizational structure and then add content to the pages and sections. The best method will vary depending on the way you plan to use the notebook—whether you are collecting a wide variety of information or working on a highly structured.

If you work on only one computer, simply create the notebook in the default location (your Documents\OneNote Notebooks folder). If you work on more than one computer (such as a desktop computer and a portable computer) and have read/write access from both computers to a shared location, you can create a notebook that you can access from more than one computer. An appropriate shared location might be any of the following:

- A shared folder on your primary computer
- A folder on a shared network location
- A removable storage drive (such as a USB flash drive) that you move between computers
- A Microsoft SharePoint site document library
- A Web site

The first two locations are accessible only when you're working on the same network as the storage location; the last two are accessible only when you have an Internet connection; and the removable storage drive is accessible from any location.

See Also For information about sharing notebooks with other people over a network, on a SharePoint site, or on a Windows Live SkyDrive site, see "Creating a Notebook for Use by Multiple People" later in this chapter.

If you store the notebook in a shared folder on your primary computer, you can open it from any other computer for which you have the same logon credentials. Choose a storage location that will be available when you need it; for example, if you turn off your desktop computer while traveling with your portable computer, a notebook stored on the desktop computer might not be accessible.

In this exercise, you'll create a simple notebook in the default storage location on your computer.

SET UP You don't need any practice files to complete this exercise. Start OneNote, and then follow the steps.

1. Display the Backstage view, and then in the left pane, click **New**.

    The New page displays options for creating local and shared notebooks.

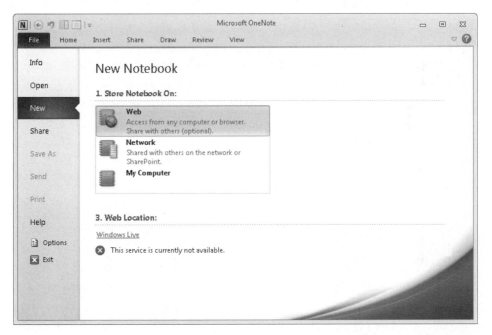

The New page is divided into numbered areas that lead you through the process of creating a notebook. Only steps 1 and 3 are visible until you select the storage location.

2. On the **New** page, under **1. Store Notebook On**, click **My Computer**.

    The page content changes to include options specific to creating a local notebook.

3. In the **2. Name** box, enter **My SBS Notes**.

    Important The name of this notebook includes SBS, for *Step by Step*, so that you can easily differentiate it from your own notebooks.

4. In the **3. Location** box, confirm that the path specifies your **Documents\OneNote Notebooks** folder as the location of the new notebook.

This is all the information you need to provide to create the notebook.

After you select the type of storage location, corresponding options appear on the page.

5. In the lower-right corner of the **New** page, click the **Create Notebook** button.

OneNote displays the new notebook.

A new notebook includes one section and one untitled page.

✖ CLEAN UP Retain the My SBS Notes notebook for use in later exercises.

Creating a Notebook for Use by Multiple People

With Microsoft Office 2010, Microsoft has placed a strong emphasis on collaboration, specifically on the ability for multiple people (referred to as *authors*) to work together to create a document. OneNote is no exception—multiple people can access and contribute to an individual notebook that is stored in a central location.

OneNote creates an offline copy of the notebook on each computer from which the notebook is accessed. OneNote synchronizes each offline copy with the original notebook when the computer reconnects to the shared location and OneNote is running.

If you know in advance that you plan to share a notebook, you can do so at the time you create it; otherwise, you can share an existing notebook at any time.

Sharing a New or Existing Notebook

When creating a shared notebook, you select a storage location that is accessible either over your network or over the Internet, depending on the access requirements of the people with whom you want to share the notebook.

If you create a notebook for use on only one computer and later decide you want to share it with other authors, you can easily do so.

- If your primary computer can be accessed through a network or workgroup, you can share the notebook from its original location.

- If your primary computer cannot be accessed through a network or workgroup, or if you do not log on to your primary and secondary computers with the same credentials, you can move the notebook to a shared location.

To share the active notebook, follow these steps:

1. On the Share tab, in the Shared Notebook group, click Share This Notebook.

   The Share page of the Backstage view opens.

2. Select the location from which you want to share the notebook, as follows:

   ○ To share the notebook with any Internet user, click Web in the Share On section. Then in the Web Location section, click or browse to the site.

Sharing a notebook over the Web allows authors to access it from any location.

Troubleshooting When sharing a notebook over the Web, you should be able to do so by storing the notebook on a Windows Live SkyDrive site. At the time of writing this book, that option is unavailable, but hopefully it will be working by the time you read this.

○ To share the notebook with co-workers from a computer that is on your organization's internal network, click Network in the Share On section. In the Network Location section, enter the UNC address of the network location (in the format \\server\share\folder), click the location in the Recent Locations list, or click Browse and then, in the Select Folder dialog box, navigate to the network location and click Select.

To share a notebook over a network, choose a network location to which all authors have access.

Tip If the Network Location box contains a SharePoint site address, clicking the Browse button opens that site; if you need to enter credentials to access the site, OneNote prompts you to do so.

○ To share the notebook with co-workers from a SharePoint document library, click Network in the Share On section. In the Network Location section, enter the URL of the document library or click the document library in the Recent Locations list.

3. On the Share page of the Backstage view, click the Share button.

   OneNote saves the notebook in the selected location and displays a confirmation dialog box.

You can let other authors know the location of the shared notebook by sending an e-mail message initiated by OneNote.

4. If you want to inform other people about the location of the shared notebook at this time, click E-mail A Link. Otherwise, click No, Thanks.

   If you click E-mail A Link, your default e-mail program starts, if it isn't already running, and creates an e-mail message with the subject *Invitation to OneNote notebook*. The message body includes a link to the shared notebook.

The standard e-mail message includes the location of the shared notebook.

After you share a notebook on a Web or network location, the Share page of the Backstage view changes to reflect that.

Other OneNote users can open a shared notebook either by clicking the link in the notification e-mail message or by browsing to the storage location of the shared notebook from the Open page of the Backstage view.

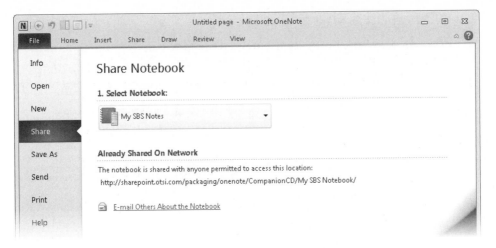

You can notify other people of the location of a shared notebook at any time by clicking the link on the Share page of the Backstage view.

To create a new notebook in a shared location, follow these steps:

1. Display the New page of the Backstage view.

2. Select the location in which you want to create the notebook, as follows:

   ○ To share the notebook with any Internet user from a Windows Live Sky Drive site, click Web in the Store Notebook On section. Then in the Web Location section, click or browse to the site.

   ○ To share the notebook with co-workers from a computer that is on your organization's internal network, click Network in the Store Notebook On section. In the Network Location section, enter the UNC address of the network location, click the location in the Recent Locations list, or click Browse and then, in the Select Folder dialog box, navigate to the network location and click Select.

   ○ To share the notebook with co-workers from a SharePoint document library, click Network in the Store Notebook On section. In the Network Location section, enter the URL of the document library or click the document library in the Recent Locations list.

3. On the New page of the Backstage view, click the Create Notebook button.

Managing a Shared Notebook

In OneNote, people who contribute to a notebook are referred to as *authors*. OneNote 2010 tracks the contributions of each notebook author. By default, other author's initials (as identified in the OneNote Options dialog box) are shown next to his or her edits; if you prefer, you can hide the authors' initials.

Author's initials

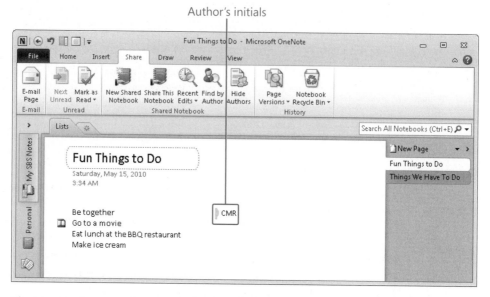

The commands you use to manage the shared notebook content are available from the Share tab on the ribbon.

Troubleshooting The appearance of buttons and groups on the ribbon changes depending on the width of the program window. For information about changing the appearance of the ribbon to match our screen images, see "Modifying the Display of the Ribbon" at the beginning of this book.

You can locate changes made to the notebook content within a specific time frame or by author. You can also view prior versions of a page, and roll back to a prior version if you want to discard the changes made since that version.

OneNote saves all prior versions of a page and indicates when and by whom they were changed.

By default, shared notebooks are synchronized when any author makes changes. You can check the synchronization status of your local copy of a shared notebook from the Shared Notebook Synchronization dialog box, which you open by clicking the View Sync Status button on the Info page of the Backstage view or by right-clicking the notebook on the Navigation Bar and then clicking Notebook Sync Status.

Your local copy of a shared notebook automatically reflects changes made by other authors unless you change the default setting in the Shared Notebook Synchronization dialog box.

The Sync Automatically Whenever There Are Changes option is selected by default. If you prefer, you can choose to work offline and sync only when you click the Sync Now button in this dialog box.

When the Navigation Bar is expanded, the ActiveSync icon to the right of the notebook name indicates the synchronization status of the shared notebook.

Synchronization status

A green check mark on the ActiveSync icon indicates that your local copy is synchronized with the shared notebook.

When OneNote is not actively synchronizing the primary notebook with the copies on other computers, one of the following indicators appears on the icon:

- A green check mark indicates a successful synchronization.
- A yellow caution triangle indicates a synchronization error.
- A red slashed circle indicates that the local copy of the notebook is offline.

Creating Sections and Pages

As we discussed briefly in the previous topic, you can create content and then move it into an organizational structure, or you can create an organizational structure and then create content within it. In this topic, we discuss creating storage structures within OneNote.

A new notebook contains one untitled section and one untitled page. You can easily create new pages on which to collect information and subdivide pages into subpages. You can also create new sections in which to organize the pages. You can further organize information by grouping sections together in section groups.

So how do you know whether to create a page, subpage, section, or section group? The answer is determined by the following:

- The nature of the information you are collecting. In a Customer Records notebook, you might want to include a section for each client, and in a Project Records notebook, you might want one section per project.

- The volume of information. There is no point in collecting information unless you can quickly and easily retrieve it when you need it. On an ideal page, all the information is visible at a glance, without too much scrolling. If you have to scroll, maybe some of the information should be organized on subpages. Similarly, in an ideal section, all the pages and subpages are visible at a glance on the Page Tabs Bar. If there are too many page tabs, maybe some of the pages should be organized in new sections. And if not all the sections are visible in the notebook header at a glance, maybe it's time to organize the sections in section groups.

The important thing to remember is that the organizational structure of a notebook should be dynamic—in other words, it should change as the information in the notebook changes.

Creating Pages and Subpages

When first created, each section contains one blank, untitled page. You can add plain blank pages, blank pages of a special size or with a special background, or specialized pages containing content templates for you to replace with your own content.

Blank page options include the following:

- Specific sizes, including Statement, Letter, Tabloid, Legal, A3–A6, B4–B6, Postcard, Index Card, and Billfold

- Simple backgrounds, including College Ruled, Small Grid, or 16 solid colors

- Nearly 70 decorative backgrounds displaying illustrated or photographic elements in the title bar, corner, margin, or background of an otherwise blank page

Specialized page options are based on content templates, which are divided into the following categories:

- Academic templates, including Simple and Detailed Lecture Notes, Lecture Notes And Study Questions, Math/Science Class Notes, and History Class Notes

- Business templates, including Project Overview and six types of Meeting Notes

- Planners templates, including three types of To Do Lists

You can quickly create a new page or subpage in the current section by selecting an option from the New Page menu at the top of the Page Tabs Bar.

Common or recently selected page templates are available from the New Page menu.

Clicking Page Templates on the New Page menu displays the Templates task pane. You can preview any page template by clicking it in the list. The first time you click a template in the task pane, OneNote creates a page based on that template; subsequent clicks apply the selected template to the created page.

OneNote □ ▭ ✕

♡ ❓

Notebooks (Ctrl+E) 🔍 ▾ | Templates ▾ ✕

New Page ▾ ›

Add a page

Things to Do

Create a new page at the end of the
current section, based on the
template you choose.

ings We Have To Do

▲ **Academic**
Simple Lecture Notes
Detailed Lecture Notes
Lecture Notes and Study Questions
Math/Science Class Notes
History Class Notes
▷ **Blank**
▷ **Business**
▷ **Decorative**
▲ **Planners**
Simple To Do List
Prioritized To Do List
Project To Do List

🌐 Templates on Office.com

Choose default template

Set the default template for new
pages in the current section.

No Default Template ▾

Create new template

Save current page as a template

Additional page templates are available from Microsoft Office Online.

Tip You can't apply a template from the Templates task pane to an existing page, but you can apply a background color or create your own page template. For more information, see the "Formatting Notes, Pages, and Sections" section of "Entering Content Directly onto a Page" in Chapter 20, "Create and Organize Notes."

Naming Sections and Pages

A new section is named simply *New Section*, followed by a number to differentiate it from other new sections you create (New Section 1, New Section 2, and so on). To change the name of a section, right-click the section tab in the notebook header, click Rename, enter the section name you want, and then press Enter or click away from the section tab. A section name can have up to 50 characters.

A new page isn't named at all. OneNote identifies it as *Untitled page*. To assign a name to a page, you enter text in the title box located in the upper-left corner of the page.

Page title box   Page Tabs Bar (minimized)

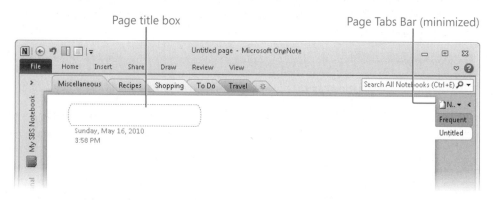

The date and time the page was created appear below the page title box.

You can enter as much text as you want in the title box; after the first eight characters, the box expands to fit the text. When the text exceeds the maximum for the page width, it wraps to the next line. You could enter thousands of characters in the title box, but we recommend that you keep page titles short. Because OneNote processes the title text each time it displays the page, long titles slow down the program response time, and you can't use the program while it is processing the text.

When the Page Tabs Bar is expanded at its default width, the first 21 characters of the page title appear on the page tab; when it's collapsed, only the first eight characters are visible. You can increase the width of the expanded Page Tabs Bar by pointing to the border between the active page and the tab area and then, when the cursor changes to a double-headed arrow, dragging the border to the left.

Keyboard Shortcuts Press Ctrl+Shift+[to increase the width of the Pages Tabs Bar. Press Ctrl+Shift+] to decrease the width of the Pages Tabs Bar.

The Page Tabs Bar is part of the program window, so when you switch between pages, sections, or notebooks, its width doesn't change. The configuration of common elements such as the Navigation Bar and Page Tabs Bar remains constant, and changing them for one page changes them for all pages.

Creating Sections and Section Groups

You have fewer options to consider when creating sections than when creating pages, because there is only one type of section. Unlike pages, sections don't have special templates. You can change a section color to differentiate it from other sections, perhaps as a visual reminder to yourself, and you can safeguard a section by assigning an access password to it.

See Also For information about changing a section color, see the "Page and Section Backgrounds" section of "Entering Content Directly onto a Page" in Chapter 20, "Create and Organize Notes."

When a notebook contains a lot of information, you might want to create a section group. This useful organizational tool is an entirely separate set of sections and pages within a notebook. You can move sections to and among section groups.

In this exercise, you will rename existing sections and pages, add pages and subpages to a section, and then add a section and a section group to a notebook.

SET UP You need the My SBS Notes notebook you created earlier in this chapter to complete this exercise. Open the My SBS Notes notebook, expand the Navigation Bar and the Page Tabs Bar, and then follow the steps.

1. In the notebook header, right-click the **New Section 1** tab, and then click **Rename**.

   The tab name is selected for editing.

2. Type **Work**, and then press Enter.

   The section name changes on the section tab and on the Navigation Bar.

3. On the **Untitled** page, click in the page title box, and then type **Notes**.

   As you type, the page name changes on the Page Tabs Bar.

4. On the **Page Tabs Bar**, click the **New Page** arrow and then, in the list, click **Simple To Do List**.

   OneNote creates a new page, titled *To Do List*. On the Page Tabs Bar, the To Do List page tab follows the Notes page tab.

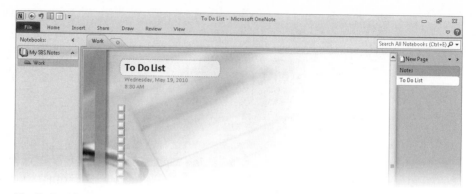

The To Do List page includes a background image and a checklist. You insert tasks in the space to the right of the check boxes.

Tip Scroll to the bottom of the To Do List page for information about reordering checklist items.

5. On the **Page Tabs Bar**, click the **New Page** arrow, and then click **Page Templates**.

   The Templates task pane opens on the right side of the program window.

6. In the **Templates** task pane, click the **Business** category and then, in the list, click **Simple Meeting Notes 1**.

   OneNote creates a page named *Meeting Title*. The page has a background image and a structure for basic meeting notes.

7. In the **Templates** task pane, in the **Business** category, click **Informal Meeting Notes 1**.

   The format of the existing Meeting Title page changes.

The Informal Meeting Notes 1 page includes a background image, a numbered agenda, an action item checklist, and areas for meeting details, announcements, discussion, summary, and notes about the next meeting.

8. In the upper-right corner of the **Templates** task pane, click the **Close** button.

   The task pane closes.

9. On the **Page Tabs Bar**, point to the **Notes** page tab.

   A New Page button appears on the right side of the content pane, to the left of the Page Tabs Bar. A black triangle points from the New Page button to the top of the page tab list.

10. Move the pointer down the page tab list to the **Meeting Title** page.

    The New Page icon moves down the list with the pointer.

11. Point to the **New Page** button.

    A thick black bar appears between the page tabs.

The bar indicates where a new page will be inserted when you click the button.

12. If necessary, move the pointer to position the insertion bar at the end of the page tab list. Then click the **New Page** button.

   Keyboard Shortcut Press Ctrl+N to create a new page at the end of the current section. Press Ctrl+Alt+N to create a new page following the current page.

   OneNote creates an untitled page at the location of the insertion bar.

13. On the **Page Tabs Bar**, right-click the **Untitled** page tab, and then click **Make Subpage**.

   Keyboard Shortcut Press Ctrl+Alt+] to make the current page a subpage. Press Ctrl+Alt+[to bring a subpage up one level.

   On the Page Tabs Bar, the name of the Untitled page tab is indented to indicate that it is now a subpage of the Meeting Title page.

The page tabs of subpages are indented to differentiate them from page tabs.

14. Click the **Meeting Title** page tab. At the top of the **Page Tabs Bar**, click the **New Page** arrow, and then, in the list, click **New Subpage**.

    Keyboard Shortcut Press Ctrl+Shift+Alt+N to create a new subpage for the current page.

    OneNote creates a second Untitled subpage.

15. Point to the **Meeting Title** page tab, and then click the **Collapse** button that appears at its right side.

    The subpages collapse under the Meeting Title page tab.

Collapsed subpages

You can collapse subpages to save space.

16. In the notebook header, to the right of the **Work** section tab, click the **Create New Section** button.

    Keyboard Shortcut Press Ctrl+T to create a new section.

    OneNote creates a section containing one blank untitled page. The section name, *New Section 1*, is selected for editing.

17. Type **Ideas**, and then press Enter.

18. In the **Navigation Bar**, right-click the **My SBS Notes** notebook, and then click **New Section Group**.

    OneNote creates a section group and selects the section group's name for editing.

19. Type **Analysis**, and then press Enter.

    The section group appears on the Navigation Bar and in the notebook header, represented by a stack of section tabs.

Section group

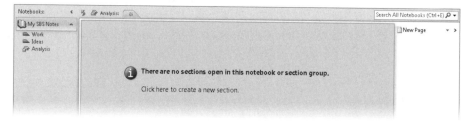

Section groups appear on the Navigation Bar at the same level as sections within the notebook.

20. On the **Navigation Bar** or the notebook header, click the **Analysis** section group.

    The section group contains no sections or pages; it is only a container for sections.

A new section group doesn't contain anything.

21. On the **Navigation Bar**, drag the **Ideas** section to the **Analysis** section group.

    The selected section and its pages move to the section group.

You can move sections to a section group or create new sections and pages directly in the section group.

✖ **CLEAN UP** Close the My SBS Notes notebook.

Key Points

- You can create a notebook for your own personal use on one computer or on multiple computers.

- When planning your information-storage system, you start with a blank notebook and add sections and pages.

- The organizational structure of a notebook is dynamic and can change to reflect the information you collect.

- You collect information on pages. When you have a lot of information on one page, individual items of information might be easier to find if you organize them on subpages.

- You can create pages based on decorative or functional page templates. Functional page templates include content templates that guide you in placing your own content.

- Pages are contained within sections. You can create additional sections to organize different types of information, and you can organize sections in section groups.

Chapter at a Glance

Work with note containers, **page 564**

Enter content directly onto a page, **page 565**

Send content to OneNote, **page 579**

Capture audio and video notes, **page 585**

20 Create and Organize Notes

In this chapter, you will learn how to

✔ Work with note containers.

✔ Enter content directly onto a page.

✔ Send content to OneNote.

✔ Capture audio and video notes.

✔ Take notes on the side.

In Chapter 19, "Create and Configure Notebooks," we discussed creating Microsoft OneNote notebooks, sections, and pages within which to store electronic information. In this chapter, we move on to the task of collecting and storing the information.

OneNote 2010 provides two primary ways to collect information: the OneNote program window and the OneNote Side Note utility. In addition, options in other programs—such as the Send To OneNote command on the Windows Internet Explorer Tools menu, and the Send To OneNote 2010 printer available when printing from any Windows program—make it easy to collect information without starting or switching to OneNote.

You can store almost any type of electronic information in a OneNote notebook, including text, graphics, photos, Web clippings and pages, hyperlinks, audio clips, and video clips. You can store as much or as little information as you want on each individual page.

In this chapter, you'll insert text, graphics, handwritten notes, screen clippings, Web notes, and media clips into note containers on pages of a OneNote notebook by using various methods.

> **Practice Files** Before you can complete the exercises in this chapter, you need to copy the book's practice files to your computer. The practice files you'll use to complete the exercises in this chapter are in the Chapter20 practice file folder. A complete list of practice files is provided in "Using the Practice Files" at the beginning of this book.

Working with Note Containers

Each piece of information you store on a notebook page exists within a note container. Similar to a text box that you might use to position text in a Microsoft Word document or on a Microsoft PowerPoint slide, a note container consists of a frame that has a move handle and a sizing handle. Each object (such as a text block, image, or URL) within the note container has an object selector.

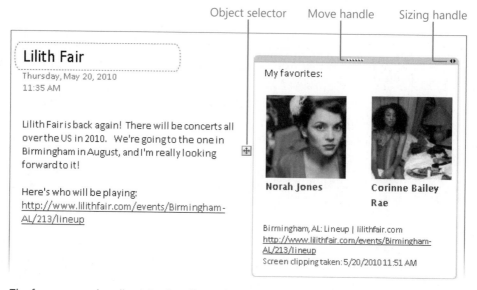

The frame, move handle, sizing handle, and object selector are visible only when you point to the content within the note container.

Unlike a text box in other programs, you don't have to insert a note container on the page before entering content into it—simply click anywhere on the page and type or paste content, or insert content from another source, to create the container. A note container can contain any sort of content, such as text, images, handwritten notes, screen clippings, or Web notes (Web page content you send to OneNote directly from Internet Explorer).

You can manipulate a note container on the page in the same way that you would manipulate a text box or other type of content frame in a word-processing or graphics program. You can change its size, relocate it on the page, and cut, copy, or delete it.

The contents of an entire page may be stored in one note container or in many note containers. While you work in OneNote, the frame of the active note container is visible, but the frames of the other note containers are not. Pointing to the content displays the note container's frame, and pointing to an object within the active container displays the object selector. You can manipulate individual objects within the container by dragging, clicking, or right-clicking the associated object selector.

Entering Content Directly onto a Page

The simplest type of information you will store in a OneNote notebook, and probably the most common, is text. You can enter text by typing directly on the notebook page or by pasting it from another source. But you aren't limited to simple text entry. You can insert attachments, formatted file contents, images, multimedia objects, and handwritten notes, all with a minimum amount of effort.

Tip When deciding how much information to include on a notebook page, consider whether you want to scroll down the page. If you want to see all the information at a glance, limit the content to about 30 lines of standard text.

Referencing External Files

When conducting research, you might identify an entire file of information—such as a document, image, or video clip—that you want to include in your notebook. You can store this information in the following three ways:

- Link to the external file on a local drive, network drive, or Web site by clicking the Link button in the Links group on the Insert tab, browsing to the file, and then clicking OK.

- Insert the file as an attachment by clicking the Attach File button in the Files group on the Insert tab, browsing to the file, and then clicking Insert.

  Keyboard Shortcut Press Alt+N+F to attach a document or file to the current page.

- Insert the file's contents on the page by clicking the File Printout button in the Files group on the Insert tab, browsing to the file, and then clicking OK.

  Keyboard Shortcut Press Alt+N+O to insert the contents of a document or file on the current page.

Linked file   Attached file   Inserted file

Opening a linked file requires access to the file location; attached and inserted files are part of the notebook.

Tip The name of the File Printout button is somewhat misleading. Clicking this button sends the contents of the external file that you select into the note container, in the same way that you send a file's contents to a printer. It does not print the OneNote page or notebook.

Tip OneNote automatically inserts the date and time when you send content from another source to OneNote. (For more information, see the sidebar "Inserting the Date & Time" later in this chapter.)

Creating Handwritten Notes

On any computer that has a mouse, you can enter "handwritten" notes by using a pen tool that you control with the mouse. On a Tablet PC, you can enter handwritten notes by using the tablet pen, just as you would in other handwriting-enabled programs.

You can draw notes on a notebook page or on top of other content.

Tip OneNote automatically saves all your changes as you make them, so you don't need to. For this reason, you won't ever be prompted to choose whether to save a notebook when you close it.

Inserting Images

You can insert and attach image files just as you can document files. You can insert an image at a size that is scaled to fit the available space by using the Insert Picture command, or you can insert an image at its full size by using the File Printout command.

Inserting an image by using the File Printout command inserts an image icon, the image path, and the image.

To insert scaled versions of one or more photos or other image files onto a OneNote notebook page:

1. On the Insert tab, in the Images group, click the Picture button to insert the image at a size that is scaled to fit the available space.

2. In the Insert Picture dialog box, select the image file or image files that you want to insert on the page, and then click Insert.

You can easily change the size of an image on the page.

To change a scaled image to its full size:

- Right-click the image, and then click Restore To Original Size.

To manually resize an inserted image:

1. Click the image (not the note container).

   Sizing handles appear in the corners and at the center of each side of the image.

2. Drag a sizing handle to resize the image.

   ○ Drag a round corner sizing handle to maintain the image's aspect ratio.

   ○ Drag a square edge handle to resize the image in one direction only.

Using the new Screen Clipping tool, you can insert clip art (free graphics, photos, sounds, and movies) into your notes, but there is no built-in command for doing so. You must do one of the following:

● Insert the clip art into another Office document, such as a Word document, cut or copy the clip art from the document, and then paste it onto the notebook page.

● From the Start menu, open the Microsoft Office Clip Organizer, locate and copy the clip art you want, and then paste it onto the notebook page.

See Also For information about inserting screen clippings, see "Sending Content to OneNote" later in this chapter.

Formatting Notes, Pages, and Sections

You can change the appearance of text in notes in much the same way that you do in other Office 2010 programs. OneNote supports character-level formatting such as font, size, and color, and simple styles such as headings and titles.

Paragraph Formatting

OneNote 2010 provides several standard paragraph formatting options, including:

● Alignment (left, center, or right)

● Spacing (before, after, and within a paragraph)

● Lists (bulleted and numbered)

● Indent level

The paragraph formatting options settings aren't as complete as those in Word and the other Office 2010 programs, but they are a great improvement over what was available in OneNote 2007.

Outline Levels

You can assign outline levels (1 through 5) to paragraphs by indenting the paragraph. An icon appears to the left of each paragraph when you point to the paragraph. You can select all the content within the level headed by the paragraph by clicking the icon, and you can collapse or expand the content within the level by double-clicking the icon. You can also hide levels, which gives you the equivalent of an outline view.

To change the paragraph indentation for the purpose of assigning an outline level:

1. Click to place the cursor at the beginning of the paragraph, or drag to select multiple paragraphs.

2. Press the Tab key to increase the level, or press the Backspace key or Shift+Tab to decrease the level.

To select all text of a specific outline level within a note:

● Right-click the note container header, click Select, and then click the outline level you want to select.

You can create an outline view by indenting paragraphs.

Keyboard Shortcuts Press Alt+Shift+*level number* (for example, Alt+Shift+1) to show all content through the specified outline level. Press Alt+Shift+0 to expand all outline levels. Press Alt+Shift+Plus Sign to expand a collapsed outline. Press Alt+Shift+Minus Sign to collapse an expanded outline.

Page and Section Backgrounds

By default, a OneNote notebook page has a blank white background. You can modify the appearance of the page in several ways. For example, you can:

- Change the page size, orientation, and margins.

- Change the page background to any of 16 background colors. The available colors are muted so they don't obscure the page content.

- Display any of four horizontal rule line patterns (Narrow, College, Standard, and Wide) or four grid line patterns (Small, Medium, Large, and Very Large).

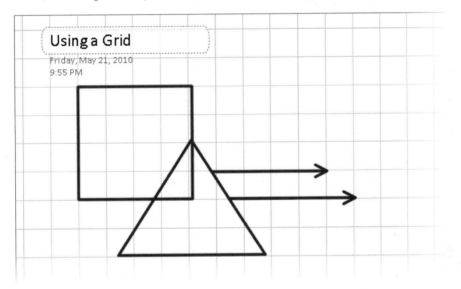

A notebook page displaying large grid rule lines that you can use to align content.

- Hide rule lines and grid lines (while leaving them in place for alignment purposes) or change the line color to any of 17 colors.

    Keyboard Shortcut Press Ctrl+Shift+R to show or hide rule lines.

These and other options are available on the View tab, in the Page Setup group.

Tip Changing the size, orientation, background, or other attribute of a page does not affect other pages of the notebook.

You can change the color of a section tab and its Page Tabs area by right-clicking the page tab, clicking Section Color, and clicking the color you want.

In this exercise, you'll enter text; insert, attach, and manipulate images; and create a handwritten note by using the OneNote writing tools.

→ **SET UP** You need the SBS Content Entry notebook, the Landscaping presentation, and the Cabo, California_Poppy, Desert, and ADatumLogo images located in the Chapter20 practice file folder. Open the SBS Content Entry notebook, and then follow the steps.

1. On the **Text Notes** page, click to place the cursor on the page, and then type **Collecting information in OneNote is easy!**

   OneNote creates a visible note container when you type the first character and then expands the note container to fit the remaining text.

When working with simple text entries, you can increase the available page space by collapsing the ribbon.

2. In the **Page Tabs** area, click the **External Files** page tab.

3. On the **Insert** tab, in the **Files** group, click the **File Printout** button.

   The Choose Document To Insert dialog box opens.

   See Also For information about the File Printout button, see the "Referencing External Files" section of this topic.

4. Browse to the **Chapter20** practice file folder. Click the **Landscaping** presentation, and then click **Insert**.

   OneNote inserts the presentation file as an attachment, the *Inserted From* reference, and then each slide of the presentation, at its full size. Each slide is an individually sizable object.

   Tip When inserting an image on a blank page, you don't need to create a note container; OneNote does it for you.

5. In the **Page Tabs** area, click the **Images** page tab.

6. On the **Insert** tab, in the **Images** group, click the **Picture** button.

   The Insert Picture dialog box opens.

7. If necessary, browse to the **Chapter 20** practice file folder. Click the **ADatumLogo** image, and then click **Insert**.

   The inserted image appears on the page.

OneNote creates a note container for the image.

Troubleshooting The appearance of buttons and groups on the ribbon changes depending on the width of the program window. For information about changing the appearance of the ribbon to match our screen images, see "Modifying the Display of the Ribbon" at the beginning of this book.

8. Click the inserted image.

   Within the note container, a dotted outline appears around the image to indicate that it can be manually resized on the notebook page. Sizing handles appear on each side and in each corner of the inserted image.

9. Drag the bottom handles to change the height of the image, making it smaller and approximately square.

10. Right-click the image, and then click **Make Text in Image Searchable**.

Notice that by default, OneNote searches the text of the embedded image.

OneNote searches text in images, such as the words A Datum Corporation *shown in this image.*

11. Click to place the cursor to the right of the logo. Then on the **Insert** tab, in the **Files** group, click the **Attach File** button.

The Choose A File Or A Set Of Files To Insert dialog box opens.

12. If necessary, browse to the **Chapter20** practice file folder. Click the **Cabo** image, hold down the Shift key, and then click the **Desert** image.

The three images (the two you clicked and the one in-between) are selected in the dialog box.

Files in dialog boxes may be represented by thumbnails as shown here, by program icons, or by words, depending on your Windows settings.

13. In the **Choose a file or a set of files to insert** dialog box, click **Insert**.

The icons and file names representing the attached images appear on the page.

14. Point to the **California_Poppy** image.

A ScreenTip containing file information is displayed.

Pointing to an attached file icon displays a ScreenTip; double-clicking the icon opens the file.

Troubleshooting The displayed icons represent the program that is set up on your computer as the default program for this file type (the program in which the file opens when you double-click it). If your default programs are different from ours, the icons shown on your notebook page won't match the icons shown here.

15. Double-click the **California_Poppy** image. If a warning message appears, select the **Don't show this again** check box, and then click **OK**.

The image opens in the default program for viewing .jpg files.

Tip Unless you've changed the settings on your computer, the default program to view .jpg files is Windows Photo Viewer.

16. Close the image window to return to OneNote.

17. In the **Page Tabs** area, click the **Handwritten Notes** page tab.

18. On the **Draw** tab, in the **Tools** group, click the **Blue Pen (.05 mm)** button.

19. Point to the notebook page.

    The pointer shape changes from an arrow to a blue dot.

20. By dragging the pen on the notebook page, draw a picture depicting a possible business logo.

21. On the **Draw** tab, in the **Tools** group, click the **Select & Type** button.

22. Click to place the cursor on the page to the right of the note containing the logo (not in the same note container), and type **Logo idea**. Then drag the note container for the typed words to the left, to overlap the note container for the drawing.

    The content of both note containers is visible where they overlap.

You can move note containers on the page to arrange notes the way you want.

23. Experiment on your own with additional pens, colors, and commands from the Writing Tools toolbar.

 CLEAN UP Close the SBS Content Entry notebook.

Tagging Content

You can identify content that fits into specific categories by attaching a visual identifier, a *tag*, to the content. Tags are not only icons, however—they function as a property attached to the content. You can locate specific content based on the tags attached to it. OneNote 2010 includes nearly 30 built-in tags. You can modify any built-in tag, and also create your own tags.

```
Customize Tags                          [?] [X]

All Tags:

  □  To Do (Ctrl+1)                        [▲]
  ☆  Important (Ctrl+2)
  ?  Question (Ctrl+3)                      [▼]
  ᴬA  Remember for later (Ctrl+4)
  ᴬA  Definition (Ctrl+5)                   [X]
  /  Highlight (Ctrl+6)
  ▣  Contact (Ctrl+7)
  ⌂  Address (Ctrl+8)
  ☎  Phone number (Ctrl+9)
  ☎  Web site to visit
  ♀  Idea
  🔒  Password
  !  Critical
  ■  Project A
  ▪  Project B
  ▦  Movie to see
  ▨  Book to read
  ♪  Music to listen to
  ▣  Source for article
  ◉  Remember for blog
  ▤  Discuss with <Person A>
  ▤  Discuss with <Person B>
  ▤  Discuss with manager
  ▨  Send in e-mail
  ▨  Schedule meeting
  ▨  Call back
  ▨  To Do priority 1
  ▨  To Do priority 2
  ▨  Client request

  [ New Tag... ]  [ Modify Tag... ]

             [    OK    ]   [  Cancel  ]
```

The built-in content tags.

You apply a tag to a paragraph by right-clicking the paragraph, clicking Tag, and then clicking the tag you want to apply. You apply a tag to the active paragraph by clicking the tag in the Tags gallery on the Home tab.

Alternatively, you can use the keyboard shortcuts in the following table to work with tags.

To do this	Press this
Apply, mark, or clear the To Do tag	Ctrl+1
Apply or clear the Important tag	Ctrl+2
Apply or clear the Question tag	Ctrl+3
Apply or clear the Remember for later tag	Ctrl+4
Apply or clear the Definition tag	Ctrl+5
Apply or clear a custom tag	Ctrl+6
Apply or clear a custom tag	Ctrl+7
Apply or clear a custom tag	Ctrl+8
Apply or clear a custom tag	Ctrl+9
Remove all note tags from the selected notes	Ctrl+0
Move the selected page tab up	Alt+Shift+Up Arrow
Move the selected page tab down	Alt+Shift+Down Arrow
Move the insertion point to the page title	Ctrl+Shift+T

Sending Content to OneNote

The tools available in OneNote make collecting on-screen information in a OneNote notebook incredibly simple. You can send content from any screen to OneNote as a screen clipping, or send an entire Web page as a Web note. When viewing a Web page, you can send the entire page to your notebook without leaving Internet Explorer.

You can specify what you want OneNote to do with screen clippings, Web notes, and content that you print to OneNote from another program (by using the Print command and selecting the Send To OneNote 2010 printer) by setting the default action on the Send To OneNote page of the OneNote Options dialog box.

You can change how OneNote deals with content sent from other programs and from the Internet.

For Web notes and content printed to OneNote, the options are:

- **Always ask where to send** After capturing a Web note or printing to the OneNote Printer, you can select the section in which you want to save the content.

- **To current page** OneNote inserts the Web note into a new note container on the active notebook page.

- **To new page in current section** OneNote creates a new page in the active section and inserts the Web note into a note container at the top of the new page.

- **Set default location** You choose a specific location to which all Web notes and printed content are sent. This location is usually the Unfiled Notes section, from which you can move content into any notebook.

For screen clippings, the options are:

- **Always ask where to send** After capturing a screen clipping, you can select the section in which you want to save the clipping.

- **To Clipboard only** OneNote copies the screen clipping to the Microsoft Office Clipboard. You can paste it into OneNote or another program by using the Paste command in that program.

- **Set default location** You choose a specific location to which all Web notes are sent. This location is usually the Unfiled Notes section, from which you can move content into any notebook.

Collecting Screen Clippings

You can use the Screen Clipping tool to capture an image of anything that is visible on your computer screen. When the Screen Clipping tool is active, a transparent white overlay appears on the screen. Drag with your mouse (or pen, if you're using a Tablet PC) to define the area you want to "clip." As you drag, the white overlay becomes clear in the area you define. When you release the mouse button or lift the pen, the selected area is clipped.

Using the default settings, you can use one method to add a screen clipping to the active notebook page, and another method to send a screen clipping to a new page in any section of an active OneNote notebook.

To add a screen clipping to the active notebook page, follow these steps:

1. Display the content you want to clip.
2. Open the OneNote notebook and display the page to which you want to add the screen clipping.
3. On the Insert tab, in the Images group, click the Screen Clipping button.

   The OneNote window minimizes to the taskbar, and the Screen Clipping tool starts.
4. Capture the screen clipping you want.

   When you release the Screen Clipping tool, OneNote reappears, and the screen clipping is inserted into a note container on the page.

To send a screen clipping to a new page, follow these steps:

1. Display the content you want to clip.
2. In the notification area of the taskbar, right-click the OneNote icon, and then click Create Screen Clipping.

   Keyboard Shortcut Press the Windows logo key+S to start the Screen Clipping tool.

   The Screen Clipping tool starts.

3. Capture the screen clipping you want.

When you release the Screen Clipping tool, the Select Location In OneNote dialog box opens.

You can send a screen clipping to any section of an open notebook, or to the Unfiled Notes section.

Tip If you've selected a screen clipping option on the Send To OneNote page of the OneNote Options dialog box other than Always Ask Where To Send, the dialog box will not appear; instead, the option you selected will be invoked.

4. In the Select Location In OneNote dialog box, click the section to which you want to send the screen clipping, and then click Send To Selected Location. If the notebook to which you want to send the screen clipping is not open, click the Unfiled Notes section.

See Also For more information about the Unfiled Notes section, see "Exploring OneNote in the Default Notebook" in Chapter 18, "Explore OneNote 2010."

5. Display OneNote.

The selected section is active. The screen clipping appears on a new page in the section.

A screen clipping.

If you clipped content from a Web page, the notebook page tab name matches the Web page title. If you clipped content from the desktop or from another program, the notebook page tab name is *Screen clipping taken:*, followed by the date. In either case, the page title box at the top of the page is empty.

Collecting Web Notes

From Internet Explorer, you can send an entire Web page to OneNote.

To capture a Web note, follow these steps:

1. In Internet Explorer, display the Web page you want to send to OneNote.

2. On the Tools menu, click Send To OneNote.

3. In the Select Location In OneNote dialog box, click the section to which you want to send the screen clipping, and then click Send To Selected Location. If the notebook to which you want to send the screen clipping is not open, click the Unfiled Notes section.

   OneNote creates a new page in the selected section and inserts the Web page content in a note container on the page.

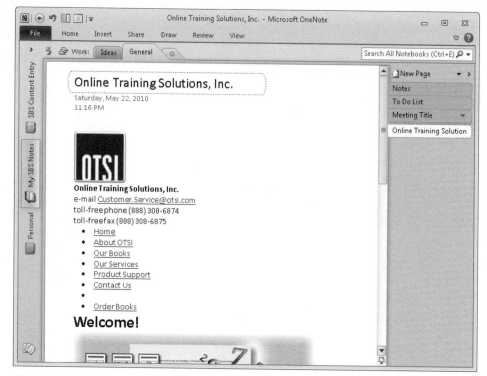

The Web page title is reflected in the notebook page title box and on the page tab.

Depending on the complexity of the content, the page layout in OneNote might not precisely reflect the on-screen layout.

Inserting the Date and Time

OneNote automatically inserts the date and time in certain locations, including the following:

- At the top of a notebook page, below the page title box, when you create a page
- In a note container, when you insert a screen clipping

You can insert date and time information in other locations.

To insert the date or time on a notebook page

1. Click to place the cursor where you want the date and time to appear on the page.

2. On the Insert tab, in the Time Stamp group, click the Date button, the Time button, or the Date & Time button.

   Keyboard Shortcuts Press Alt+N+D to insert the current date. Press Alt+Shift+T to insert the current time. Press Alt+Shift+F to insert the current date and time.

Capturing Audio and Video Notes

If your computer system includes a microphone, such as a built-in microphone or a free-standing or headset microphone, you can record audio directly into a file stored on a OneNote notebook page. (You'll get the best results by using a headset microphone.) Similarly, if your system includes a built-in or external webcam, you can record video directly into a file stored on a OneNote notebook page.

You can record audio that is playing on your computer, or audio that you speak, sing, or otherwise communicate through a microphone.

Tip If you haven't already configured your audio input device, you can do so by using the Microphone Setup Wizard available from the Speech Recognition window of Control Panel.

You can record video that you capture by using a webcam. The quality of the video you capture depends greatly on the webcam, lighting, and other factors not specific to OneNote. Many portable computers have built-in webcams that will automatically work with OneNote. If you don't have a built-in webcam, you can purchase one that connects to your desktop or portable computer through a USB cable.

Video is recorded and displayed in a window separate from the OneNote program window. You can move it around the screen by dragging its title bar, change its size by dragging the window frame, and minimize, maximize, or restore it by clicking the buttons on the window's title bar. If you're working on a Windows 7 computer, you can use the new window-management techniques such as Snap To Screen and Shake to manage the video window as you would any other.

The first time you record an audio or video clip, OneNote prompts you to indicate whether you want to configure the recordings so that OneNote can search the audio recording or the audio track of the video recording for spoken words. By enabling the Audio Search feature, spoken words matching the search criteria you enter in the Search box will be included in search results. For this feature to work effectively, the audio recording must be of a high quality, words must be spoken clearly, and the spoken language must match that of the OneNote user interface. Audio Search is currently supported for nine languages: English, Spanish, German, French, Italian, Traditional Chinese, Simplified Chinese, Japanese, and Korean.

In this exercise, you'll record and play back an audio clip and a video clip in OneNote.

SET UP You don't need any practice files, but you do need to have a microphone and webcam installed to complete the exercise in its entirety. Display a blank notebook page, and then follow the steps.

1. In the page title box, type **My Recordings**. Then press Enter.

   OneNote creates a note container below the timestamp.

2. On the **Insert** tab, in the **Recording** group, click the **Record Audio** button.

   If you haven't previously made an Audio Search selection, the Audio Search dialog box opens.

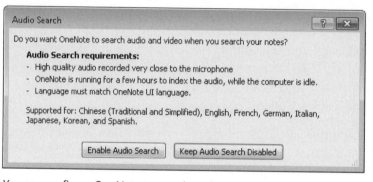

You can configure OneNote to search spoken words in audio and video recordings.

3. If the **Audio Search** dialog box opens, and you want to make a selection at this time, click **Enable Audio Search** or **Keep Audio Search Disabled**. Otherwise, click the **Close** button on the window title bar, and OneNote will prompt you again later.

   Tip If you have a lot of audio and video content stored in a notebook, enabling the Audio Search feature can slow down the search process. You can change your Audio Search setting at any time by selecting or clearing the Enable Searching Audio And Video Recordings For Words check box on the Audio & Video page of the OneNote Options dialog box.

   OneNote inserts a Windows Media Audio (.wma) file icon, a file name that matches the page name, and the recording start time, and displays the Audio & Video Recording contextual tab of the ribbon. *(Recording...)* appears at the beginning of the page name in the program window title bar to indicate that you're currently recording an audio or video clip.

Recording indicators   Recording timer

You can pause a recording session.

4. Speak, sing, or otherwise deliver approximately 30 seconds of audio content. (Go ahead—take a chance on your favorite song!)

   As the recording progresses, the timer in the Playback group on the Recording tab indicates the length of the recording.

5. When you finish, click the **Stop** button in the **Playback** group on the **Recording** tab.

   Keyboard Shortcut Press Ctrl+Alt+S to stop the recording or playback of an audio or video clip.

   The Recording tab changes to the Playback tab.

6. Point to the **My Recordings** audio file icon.

   The note container becomes visible, and a Play button appears to the left of the note container. You can play a recording by clicking the Play button on the Playback tab or the Play button to the left of the note container.

7. Click the **Play** button.

Keyboard Shortcut Press Ctrl+Alt+P to play the most recently active audio or video recording on the page.

OneNote plays your audio recording. (If you can't hear it, check that your computer's speaker volume is turned up.) Additional commands for controlling the playback become active on the Playback tab.

You can skip backward and forward through a recording by clicking the Rewind and Fast Forward buttons.

8. On the **Playback** tab, in the **Playback** group, watch the progress of the timer. After the first 15 seconds of the recording, click the **Rewind 10 Seconds** button.

Keyboard Shortcuts Press Ctrl+Alt+Y to rewind the playback 10 seconds. Press Ctrl+Alt+U to fast forward the playback 10 seconds.

9. When the audio playback is finished, click the **Record Video** button in the **Recording** group on the **Playback** tab.

OneNote inserts a Windows Media Video (.wmv) file icon, a file name that matches the page name, and the recording start time. A video window opens on the page, displaying video captured by your webcam.

The recording controls for video recordings are the same as for audio recordings.

The Playback tab changes to the Recording tab, and *(Recording...)* appears at the beginning of the page name in the program window title bar.

10. Record a short video segment, and then click the **Pause** button.

   The picture in the video window freezes.

11. Click the **Pause** button again to restart the recording. Record another short video segment, and then click the **Stop** button.

12. On the **Playback** tab, in the **Playback** group, click the **Play** button to play your video recording.

   Note that there is no pause or transition between the two video segments you recorded.

CLEAN UP Retain the My Recordings page for future reference, if you want to, or delete it by right-clicking the page tab and then clicking Delete.

Missing the OneNote Icon?

If the OneNote icon does not appear in the notification area when the program is running, follow these steps to verify that the feature is turned on:

1. In the Backstage view, click Options.
2. In the left pane of the OneNote Options dialog box, click Display.
3. On the Display page, select the Place OneNote Icon In The Notification Area Of The Taskbar check box.
4. Click OK to close the dialog box and save your changes.

If the check box is selected and the icon still doesn't appear, follow these steps to verify that the icon is not hidden:

1. At the left end of the notification area of the status bar, click the Show Hidden Icons button, and then click Customize.
2. In the Notification Area Icons window of Control Panel, scroll down the Icons list to locate Microsoft OneNote Quick Launcher.
3. In the associated Behaviors list, click Show Icon And Notifications.

   The icon will now appear in the notification area at all times.

You can specify which icons appear in the notification area.

4. Click OK to close the dialog box and save your changes.

Taking Notes on the Side

It's not necessary to start OneNote each time you want to take notes or otherwise store information. You can also enter information into a Side Note—a simplified version of the OneNote program window. You can quickly open a Side Note by clicking the OneNote icon located in the notification area of the Windows Taskbar.

Keyboard Shortcut Press Ctrl+Shift+M to open a Side Note.

You can also open a Side Note from within the OneNote program window by clicking the New Side Note button, in the Window group, on the View tab.

A standard Side Note is a minimized version of a OneNote page, with the Navigation Bar and Page Tabs area hidden, that displays a subset of the ribbon.

You can dock a Side Note to the desktop or display it in the full OneNote window by clicking the view buttons on the Quick Access Toolbar.

You work with content in a Side Note in the same way you work with it in the OneNote program window—because, in fact, that is precisely what you are doing. If you click the Full Page View button in the Side Note window (and then enlarge the window to provide perspective), you'll find yourself working on a page in the Unfiled Notes section.

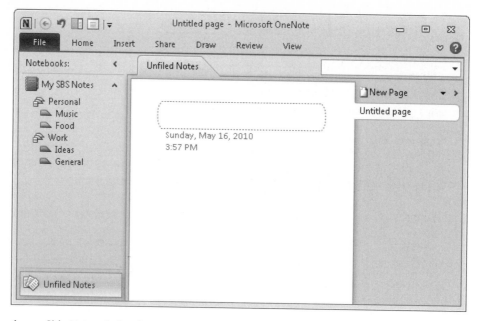

A new Side Note window is a page in the Unfiled Notes section; you can navigate to any notebook, section, or page from the Full Page view of the Side Note window.

The purpose of the Side Note window is to provide a small and easily accessible interface to OneNote. Because of the small size of the Side Note window, only a subset of the ribbon tabs may be visible at a time.

See Also For more information about the ribbon in OneNote, see "Working in the OneNote Program Window" and "Exploring OneNote in the Default Notebook" in Chapter 18, "Explore OneNote 2010."

When the Keep On Top button in the Window group on the View tab is active, you can position the Side Note in a convenient location on your screen, changing its size as necessary, and enter information as you want to. When the Side Note window is on top, it may get in the way of other windows, information, or commands that you might want to access, so you'll want to choose a location that doesn't interfere with your work. You can change the height or width of the window by dragging any side or corner of it.

Right-clicking the OneNote icon on the taskbar displays a list of options for collecting information.

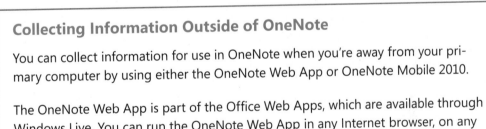

From the taskbar, you can start a variety of OneNote actions.

You can change the action that occurs when you click the OneNote icon to suit your needs. For example, if you frequently record audio, you might make that the default action. The available actions are Open New Side Note (the default), Open OneNote, Start Recording Audio, and Create Screen Clipping.

To change what happens when you click the OneNote icon:

● On the taskbar, right-click the OneNote icon, click OneNote Icon Defaults, and then click the action you want.

Collecting Information Outside of OneNote

You can collect information for use in OneNote when you're away from your primary computer by using either the OneNote Web App or OneNote Mobile 2010.

The OneNote Web App is part of the Office Web Apps, which are available through Windows Live. You can run the OneNote Web App in any Internet browser, on any computer; all you need is a Windows Live ID.

If you have a mobile device running Windows Mobile, such as a Windows phone, you can collect information by using OneNote Mobile 2010, which is available as part of Office Mobile 2010, and then synchronize data with a local or network notebook by using the built-in Microsoft ActiveSync software.

See Also For more information about the OneNote Web App, visit the Office Web Apps page at workspace.officelive.com/office-web-applications/. For more information about OneNote Mobile 2010, visit www.microsoft.com/office/2010/mobile/.

Key Points

- Notes are stored on a page in note containers. Each object within a note container can be manipulated separately.

- You can resize images inserted on a page and open file attachments directly from a page.

- You can use the OneNote writing tools to create handwritten notes and drawings.

- You can collect and store selected images of anything displayed on your screen by using the Screen Clipping tool.

- You can collect and store an entire Web page by using the Send To OneNote command on the Internet Explorer Tools menu.

- You can jot down quick notes without interfering with other program windows, by using Side Notes.

- You can display the OneNote icon in the notification area of the taskbar and choose the action that occurs when you click the icon.

Glossary

absolute reference A cell reference, such as =$B$3, that doesn't change when you copy a formula containing the reference to another cell.

action button In PowerPoint, a predefined button that you can insert into a presentation and use to define hyperlinks.

add-in A supplemental program that can be used to extend program functions.

adjustment handle A diamond-shaped handle used to adjust the appearance but not the size of most AutoShapes. For example, you can adjust a rounded rectangle to be more or less rounded.

arguments In Excel, the specific data a function requires to calculate a value.

aspect ratio The ratio of the width of an image to its height.

attribute Individual items of character formatting, such as size or color, which determine how text looks.

auditing The process of examining a worksheet for errors.

AutoComplete The Excel functionality that completes data entry for a cell based on similar values in other cells in the same column.

AutoCorrect A feature that automatically detects and corrects misspelled words, grammatical errors, and incorrect capitalization. You can add custom AutoCorrect entries.

AutoFill The Excel functionality that extends a series of values based on the contents of a single cell. See also *Fill Series*.

AutoRepublish An Excel technology that maintains a link between a Web document and the worksheet on which the Web document is based, and updates the Web document whenever the original worksheet is saved.

Backstage view A new view in Office 2010 programs, accessed by clicking the File tab, that gathers program management and file management tasks into a single location.

balloon In the Print Layout view or Web Layout view of Word, a box that shows comments and tracked changes in the margins of a document, making it easy to see and respond to them.

blog A frequently updated online journal or column. Blogs are often used to publish personal or company information in an informal way. Short for *weblog*.

browser A program with which users view Web documents.

building block Frequently used text saved in a gallery, from which it can be inserted quickly into a document.

cell A box formed by the intersection of a row and column in a worksheet or a table, in which you enter information.

cell address See *cell reference*.

cell range A group of cells.

cell reference In an Excel worksheet, the letter and number combination, such as C16, that identifies the location of a cell by the column letter and row number.

character spacing The distance between characters in a line of text. Character spacing can be adjusted by pushing characters apart (expanding) or squeezing them together (condensing).

character style A combination of any of the character formatting options identified by a style name.

Click and Type A feature that allows you to double-click a blank area of a Word document to position the cursor in that location, with the appropriate paragraph alignment already in place.

clip art A piece of ready-made art, often appearing as a bitmap or a combination of drawn shapes.

Clipboard A storage area shared by all Office programs, on which cut or copied items are stored.

color scheme A set of 12 balanced colors that you can apply to slides, notes pages, or audience handouts. A color scheme consists of light and dark background colors, light and dark text colors, six accent colors, and two colors for hyperlinks.

column header In an Excel worksheet, a shaded rectangular area at the top of each column that displays a letter. You can click a column header to select an entire column. See also *row header*.

comment An annotation that is associated with text or an object to provide context-specific information or reviewer feedback.

conditional format A format that is applied only when cell contents meet certain criteria.

conditional formula A formula that calculates a value by using one of two different expressions, depending on whether a third expression is true or false.

connection points A point on a shape where another drawing object can be connected.

connector A link between two connection points.

content pane The pane of a program window in which the active file appears.

content placeholder See *placeholder*.

contextual tab A tab containing commands that are relevant only when you have selected a particular object type. See also *tab*.

credentials See *logon credentials*.

cursor An on-screen representation of the point at which text or graphics will be inserted.

custom slide show A subset of slides extracted from a presentation.

data bar A horizontal line within a cell that indicates the relative magnitude of the cell's value.

data consolidation Summarizing data from a set of similar cell ranges.

data marker A customizable symbol or shape that identifies a data point on a chart. A data marker can be formatted with various sizes and colors.

data point An individual value plotted in a chart and represented together with other data points by bars, columns, lines, pie or doughnut slices, dots, and various other shapes referred to as *data markers*. Data markers of the same color constitute a data series.

data series Related data points that are plotted in a chart. One or more data series in a chart can be plotted. A pie chart has just one data series.

data source A file containing variable information, such as names and addresses, that is merged with a main document containing static information.

demoting In an outline, changing a heading to body text or to a lower heading level; for example, changing from Heading 5 to Heading 6. See also *promoting*.

dependent A cell with a formula that uses the value from a particular cell. See also *precedent*.

design template A file that contains masters that control the styles used in a presentation, including placeholder sizes and positions; background design, graphics, and color schemes; fonts; and the type and size of bullets.

destination file The file that a linked or embedded object located in a source file is inserted into. When you change information in a destination file, the information is not updated in the source file.

dialog box launcher On the ribbon, a button in the lower-right corner of a group that opens a dialog box or task pane containing settings related to the group.

digital signature Data that binds a sender's identity to the information being sent. A digital signature may be bundled with any message, file, or other digitally encoded information, or transmitted separately. Digital signatures are used in public key environments and provide authentication and integrity services.

drag-and-drop editing See *dragging*.

dragging A way of moving an object by pointing to it, holding down the mouse button, moving the mouse pointer to the desired location, and then releasing the mouse button.

drawing object Any graphic you draw or insert, which can be changed and enhanced. Drawing objects include AutoShapes, curves, lines, and WordArt.

drop cap An enlarged, decorative capital letter that appears at the beginning of a paragraph.

embedding To insert the contents of a file into another file. See also *linking*.

embedded object An object created with one program and embedded into a document created by another program. Embedding the object, rather than simply inserting or pasting it, ensures that the object retains its original format. If you double-click the embedded object, you can edit it with the toolbars and menus from the program used to create it.

encrypting To programmatically disguise content to hide its substance.

endnote A note that appears at the end of a section or document and that is referenced by text in the main body of the document. An endnote consists of two linked parts, a reference mark within the main body of text and the corresponding text of the note. See also *footnote*.

Excel table An Excel object with which you can store and refer to data based on the name of the table and the names of its columns and rows.

Extensible Markup Language (XML) A format for delivering structured data. XML tags describe the content of a document, whereas HTML tags describe how the document looks. XML is extensible because it allows designers to create custom tags.

field A placeholder that tells Word to supply the specified information in the specified way. Also, the set of information of a specific type in a data source, such as all the last names in a contacts list. In Excel, a column of data used to create a PivotTable.

field name A first-row cell in a data source that identifies data in the column below.

file format The structure or organization of data in a file. The file format is usually indicated by the file name extension.

file name extension A set of characters added to the end of a file name that identifies the file type or format.

fill handle The square at the lower-right corner of a cell that can be dragged to indicate other cells that should hold values in the series defined by the active cell.

FillSeries The ability to extend a series of values based on the contents of two cells, where the first cell has the starting value for the series and the second cell shows the increment. See also *AutoFill*.

filter A rule that Excel uses to determine which worksheet rows to display.

filtering Displaying files or records in a data source that meet certain criteria; for example, filtering a data source so that you see only the records for people who live in a particular state. Filtering does not delete files, it simply changes the view so that you see only the files that meet your criteria.

First Line Indent marker The triangle-shaped control, on the top of the horizontal ruler, that indicates the position of the first line of the paragraph.

font A graphic design applied to a collection of numbers, symbols, and characters. A font describes a certain typeface, along with other qualities such as size, spacing, and pitch.

font effect An attribute, such as superscript, small capital letters, or shadow, that can be applied to a font.

font size The height (in points) of a collection of characters, where one point is equal to approximately 1/72 of an inch.

font style The emphasis placed on a font by using formatting such as bold, italic, underline, or color.

footer One or more lines of text in the bottom margin area of a page in a document or slide in a presentation, typically containing elements such as the page number and the name of the file. See also *header*.

footnote A note that appears at the end of a page, section, chapter, or publication that explains, comments on, or provides references for text in the main body of a document. A footnote consists of two linked parts, a reference mark within the main body of the document and the corresponding text of the note. See also *endnote*.

format In Excel, a predefined set of characteristics that can be applied to cell contents.

formula A sequence of values, cell references, names, functions, or operators in a cell of a table or worksheet that together produce a new value. A formula always begins with an equal sign (=).

Formula AutoComplete The Excel functionality with which you can enter a formula quickly by selecting functions, named ranges, and table references that appear when you begin to type the formula into a cell.

formula bar The area just above the worksheet grid that displays the active cell's formula and within which you can edit the formula.

function A predefined formula.

gallery List boxes that organize items by category, display them in flexible column- and row-based layouts, and represent them with images and text. Depending on the type of gallery, live preview is also supported.

Goal Seek An analysis tool in Excel that finds the value for a selected cell that would produce a given result from a calculation.

gridlines In a table, thin lines that indicate the cell boundaries in a table. Table gridlines do not print when you print a document. In a chart, lines that visually carry the values on the y-axis across the plot area.

group On a ribbon tab, an area containing buttons related to a specific document element or function.

grouping Assembling several objects, such as shapes, into a single unit so that they act as one object. Grouped objects can easily be moved, sized, and formatted.

handle A small circle, square, or set of dots that appears at the corner or on the side of a selected object and facilitates moving, sizing, reshaping, or other functions pertaining to the object.

handout master A template that defines the layout for the printed handout pages distributed to a presentation's audience.

Hanging Indent marker The triangle-shaped control, on the bottom of the horizontal ruler, that indicates the left edge of the second and subsequent lines of the paragraph.

header In Word, a line, or lines, of content in the top margin area of a page in a document, typically containing elements such as the title, page number, or name of the author. In Excel, an area of the worksheet that appears above the contents of the worksheet grid when you print the worksheet or view it in Layout View.

Help button The button located at the right end of the ribbon and labeled with a question mark (?), that provides access to the program-specific Help system.

HTML See *Hypertext Markup Language*.

hyperlink The text or graphic that you click to go to a file, a location in a file, or a Web site. Hyperlinks usually appear underlined and in color, but sometimes the only indication is that when you point to them, the pointer changes to a hand.

Hypertext Markup Language (HTML) An application of the Standard Generalized Markup Language (SGML) that uses tags to mark elements in a document to indicate how Web browsers should display these elements to the user and should respond to user actions.

hyphenating Splitting a word that would otherwise extend beyond the right margin of the page.

icon set A conditional format that uses distinct visual indicators to designate how a value compares to a set of criteria.

indent marker One of four controls located on the horizontal ruler that indicate how far text is indented from the left or right margin.

index A list of the words and phrases that are discussed in a printed document, along with the page numbers they appear on.

index entry A field code that marks specific text for inclusion in an index. When you mark text as an index entry, Word inserts an XE (Index Entry) field formatted as hidden text.

index entry field The XE field, including the braces ({ }), that defines an index entry.

justifying Making all lines of text in a paragraph or column fit the width of the document or column, with even margins on each side.

keyboard shortcut Any combination of keystrokes that can be used to perform a task.

kiosk mode A display mode in which a single window takes over the whole screen and the desktop is inaccessible.

landscape The orientation of a picture, page, or worksheet where the width is greater than the height.

Left Indent marker The square-shaped control, on the bottom of the horizontal ruler, that indicates how far text is indented from the left margin.

legend A key in a chart that identifies the colors and names of the data series or categories that are used in the chart.

line break A manual break that forces the text that follows it to the next line. Also called a *text wrapping break*.

link In Excel, a formula that has a cell show the value from another cell.

linked object An object that is created in a source file to which a link is inserted into a destination file, maintaining a connection between the two files. The linked object in the destination file can be updated when the source file is updated.

linking To insert a pointer to a file into another file. See also *embedding*.

Live Preview A feature that temporarily displays the effect of applying a specific format to the selected element.

locked cell A cell that cannot be modified if its worksheet is protected.

logon credentials The user name and password that identify and authenticate you when accessing a computer, network, or site.

macro An action or a set of actions you can use to automate tasks. Macros are recorded in the Visual Basic for Applications programming language.

mail merge The process of merging information into a main document from a data source, such as an address book or database, to create customized documents, such as form letters or mailing labels.

mailto hyperlink A special type of hyperlink with which a user creates an e-mail message to a particular e-mail address.

main document In a mail merge operation in Word, the document that contains the text and graphics that are the same for each version of the merged document.

manual page break A break inserted to force subsequent information to appear on the next page.

margin The blank space outside the printing area of a page.

master A slide or page on which you define formatting for all slides or pages in a presentation. Each presentation has a set of masters for slides, as well as masters for speaker notes and audience handouts.

Merge And Center An operation that combines a contiguous group of cells into a single cell. Selecting a merged cell and clicking the Merge And Center button splits the merged cells into the original group of separate cells.

merge field A placeholder inserted in the main document that is replaced with variable information from a data source during the merge process.

merging To combine table cells to create one cell that spans two or more columns or rows.

Microsoft Office Clipboard See *Clipboard*.

Microsoft PowerPoint Viewer A viewer with which you can display presentations on a computer that does not have PowerPoint installed.

Mini Toolbar A toolbar that is typically displayed after you select text on a slide so that you can quickly format the text.

move handle The handle with which you can drag a docked toolbar. The move handle is represented by a row of four dots at the left end of the toolbar.

named range A group of related cells defined by a single name.

Navigation task pane In Word, a task pane that displays an outline of a document's headings, or thumbnails of a document's pages, and allows you to jump to a heading or page in the document by clicking it. Also provides content search capabilities.

nested table A table inserted into a cell of a table that is being used to arrange information on a page.

Normal view In PowerPoint, a view that displays three panes: Overview, Slide, and Notes.

note container In OneNote, the smallest data storage unit. Notes on a page are stored within note containers; each note container can be individually manipulated.

note separator A set of characters that separates document text from footnotes or endnotes. The default separator is a horizontal line.

notebook header In OneNote, the area above the content pane that displays the notebook name, section tabs, and section groups.

notes master In PowerPoint, a template that defines the formatting and content used by speaker notes pages.

Notes pane In PowerPoint, the pane in Normal view in which you type notes that you want to accompany a slide. You print these notes as speaker notes pages.

object An item, such as a graphic, video clip, sound file, or worksheet, that can be inserted into a PowerPoint slide and then selected and modified.

object selector In OneNote, the handle that appears to the left of a text paragraph, graphic, table, or other individually selectable item within a note container or on a page. You click the object selector to select the object.

.one file The OneNote data file format. Each .one file contains the content of one section. The .one file name is the same as the section name in the program window; changing one changes the other. See also *section*.

orphan The first line of a paragraph printed by itself at the bottom of a page.

Outline tab In PowerPoint, the tab of the Overview pane that shows all the text of the slides displayed as an outline.

Overview pane In PowerPoint, the pane that appears in Normal view on the left side of the program window and that contains the Slides and Outline tabs.

Package for CD In PowerPoint, a feature to help you gather all the components of a presentation and store them to a CD or another type of removable media so that they can be transported to a different computer.

page In OneNote, a titled data storage unit within a section.

Page Tabs area In OneNote, the area to the right of the content pane from which you can select and manipulate pages within the active section.

paragraph style A combination of character formatting and paragraph formatting that is named and stored as a set. Applying the style to a paragraph applies all the formatting characteristics at one time.

Paste Options A button that appears after you paste an item from the Microsoft Office Clipboard into your document, and which provides options for how the item appears in the document.

path A sequence of folders (directories) that leads to a specific file or folder. A backslash is used to separate each folder in the path. For example, the path to a file called *invoice.txt* might be C:\Documents\July\invoice.txt.

PDF file The Portable Document Format is an Adobe Systems specification for electronic documents that can't be edited without specific software. PDF-format files have a .pdf file name extension.

photo album In PowerPoint, a specific kind of presentation into which you can insert and arrange collections of digital images.

Pick From List The Excel functionality that allows you to enter a value into a cell by choosing the value from the set of values already entered into cells in the same column.

PivotChart A chart that is linked to a PivotTable and that can be reorganized dynamically to emphasize different aspects of the underlying data.

PivotTable A dynamic worksheet that can be reorganized by a user.

pixel The smallest element used to form the composition of an image on a computer monitor. Computer monitors display images by drawing hundreds or thousands of pixels arranged in columns and rows. The number of pixels a monitor displays is expressed by its screen resolution.

placeholder A area on a slide designed to contain a specific type of content that you supply.

plot area In a two-dimensional chart, the area bounded by the axes, including all data series. In a three-dimensional chart, the area bounded by the axes, including the data series, category names, tick-mark labels, and axis titles.

point The unit of measure for expressing the size of characters in a font, where 72 points equals 1 inch.

pointing to Pausing a pointing device over an area of the display.

portrait The orientation of a picture or page where the page is taller than it is wide.

post A message published on a blog, message board, or help board.

precedent A cell that is used in a formula.

primary key In Excel, a field or group of fields with values that distinguish a row of data from all other rows.

promoting In an outline, to change body text to a heading, or to change a heading to a higher-level heading.

property Settings of a file that you can change, such as the file's name and read-only status, as well as attributes that you can't directly change, such as the file's size and creation date.

pull quote Text taken from the body of a document and showcased in a text box to create visual interest.

query Selection criteria for extracting information from a data source for use in the mail merge process.

Quick Access Toolbar A small, customizable toolbar, independent of the ribbon that displays frequently used commands.

Quick Style In Word, a collection of character and paragraph formatting that makes formatting documents and objects easier. Quick Styles appear in the Quick Styles gallery and are organized into ready-made Quick Style sets that are designed to work together to create an attractive and professional-looking document.

Quick Table In Word, a table with sample data that you can customize.

range A group of related cells.

read-only A setting that allows a file to be read or copied, but not changed or saved. If you change a read-only file, you can save your changes only if you give the file a new name.

record In Excel, a collection of data about a person, a place, an event, or some other item. Records are the logical equivalents of rows in a table.

reference mark The number or symbol displayed in the body of a document when you insert a footnote or endnote.

refresh To update the contents of one document when the contents of another document are changed.

relative reference A cell reference in a formula, such as =B3, that refers to a cell that is a specific distance away from the cell that contains the formula. For example, if the formula =B3 were in cell C3, copying the formula to cell C4 would cause the formula to change to =B4. See also *absolute reference*.

ribbon A user interface design that organizes commands into logical groups, which appear on separate tabs.

Rich Text Format (RTF) A format for text and graphics interchange that can be used with different output devices, operating environments, and operating systems.

rotating handle A small green handle that you can use to adjust the angle of rotation of a shape.

row header In an Excel worksheet, a shaded rectangular area to the left of each row containing a number. You can click a row header to select an entire row. See also *column header*.

scenario In Excel, an alternative data set with which you view the impact of specific changes on your worksheet.

screen clipping A captured image of content shown on the screen. OneNote provides a tool for defining, capturing, and importing screen clippings directly into the program window.

screen resolution The amount of information displayed on a monitor, expressed as the number of pixels wide by the number of pixels high.

ScreenTip A note that appears on the screen to provide information about a button, tracked change, or comment, or to display a footnote or endnote. ScreenTips also display the text that will appear if you choose to insert a date or AutoText entry.

search filter A filter in which you type a string of characters and have Excel display every value within an Excel table, data set, or PivotTable that contains that character string.

section In OneNote, an organizational unit containing a group of pages that you can view separately from other notebook content. See also *.one file*.

section break In Word, a mark you insert to show the end of a section. A section break stores the section formatting elements, such as the margins, page orientation, headers and footers, and sequence of page numbers.

section group In OneNote, a subdivision of a notebook containing a group of sections that you can view separately from other notebook sections.

selection area An area in a document's left margin in which you can click and drag to select blocks of text.

sharing Making a file available for more than one user to open and modify simultaneously.

sheet tab In Excel, the indicator for selecting a worksheet, located at the bottom of the workbook window.

shortcut menu A menu that shows a list of commands relevant to a particular item. To display the shortcut menu for an item, right-click the item.

sizing handle A small circle, square, or set of dots that appears at the corner or on the side of a selected object. You drag these handles to change the size of the object horizontally, vertically, or proportionally.

Slicer An Excel tool with which you can filter an Excel table, data list, or PivotTable while indicating which items are displayed and which are hidden.

slide library A SharePoint document library designed for storing and reusing PowerPoint slides.

slide master In PowerPoint, the set of slides that stores information about a presentation's design template, including font styles, placeholder sizes and positions, background design, and color schemes.

Slide pane In PowerPoint, the area in Normal view that shows the currently selected slide as it will appear in the presentation.

slide timing The time each slide in a slide show is displayed.

Slides tab In PowerPoint, the tab in the Overview pane that displays thumbnails of all the slides in the presentation.

SmartArt graphic A predefined set of shapes and text used as a basis for creating a diagram.

soft page break A page break that Word inserts when text reaches the bottom margin of a page.

Solver An Excel add-in that finds the optimal value for one cell by varying the results of other cells.

sort To reorder selected paragraph or cell content based on a criterion such as alphabetical order.

source file A file containing an object that is inserted in or linked to a destination file.

source program The program used to create a linked object or embedded object. To edit the object, you must have the source program installed on your computer.

sparkline In Excel, a compact chart that summarizes data visually within a single worksheet cell.

splitting To separate a cell into two or more cells.

status bar The horizontal bar at the bottom of a program window displaying program controls and information related to the current file.

subentry An index entry that falls under a more general heading; for example, "Mars" and "Venus" might be subentries of the index entry "planets."

subpage In OneNote, a page that is subordinate to another page. Subpages are linked to the corresponding page and move with the page as a unit.

subpoint A subordinate item below a bullet point in a list.

switch In fields, a setting that refines the results of the field; for example, by formatting it in a particular way.

tab An organizational element of the ribbon that displays related groups of buttons.

tab leader A repeating character (usually a dot or dash) that separates text before the tab from text or a number after it.

tab stop A location on the horizontal ruler that indicates how far to indent text or where to begin a column of text.

tabbed list A list that arranges text in simple columns separated by left, right, centered, or decimal tab stops.

table One or more rows of cells commonly used to display numbers and other items for quick reference and analysis. Items in a table are organized into rows and columns.

table of authorities A list of the references in a legal document, such as references to cases, statutes, and rules, along with the numbers of the pages the references appear on.

table of contents A list of the headings in a document, along with the numbers of the pages the headings appear on.

table of figures A list of the captions for pictures, charts, graphs, slides, or other illustrations in a document, along with the numbers of the pages the captions appear on.

table style A set of formatting options, such as font, border style, and row banding, that are applied to a table. The regions of a table, such as the header row, header column, and data area, can be variously formatted.

tablet pen The pen that comes with a Tablet PC and is used to interact with items on the screen.

tag A text string used in HTML and XML to identify a page element's type, format, or appearance. Many elements have start and end tags that define where the element starts and stops.

target A path that identifies a linked object, such as a location in a document or a Web page.

template A file that can contain predefined formatting, layout, text, or graphics, and that serves as the basis for new presentations, workbooks, or documents with a similar design or purpose.

text box A movable, resizable container used to give text a different orientation from other text on the slide or in the document.

text wrapping The way text wraps around an object on the page.

text wrapping break A manual break that forces the text that follows it to the next line. Also known as a *line break*.

theme A set of unified design elements that combine color, fonts, and graphics to provide a professional look for a presentation, workbook, or document.

3-D reference In Excel, a pattern for referring to the workbook, worksheet, and cell from which a value should be read.

thumbnail A small representation of an item, such as an image, a page of content, or a set of formatting, obtained by scaling a snapshot of it. Thumbnails are typically used to provide visual identifiers for related items.

tick-mark A small line of measurement, similar to a division line on a ruler, that intersects an axis in a chart.

title bar The horizontal bar at the top of a window that contains the name of the window. Most title bars also contain boxes or buttons for closing and resizing the window.

tracer arrow In Excel, an arrow that indicates the formulas to which a cell contributes its value (a dependent arrow) or the cells from which a formula derives its value (a precedent arrow).

trendline On a chart or graph, a projection of future data (such as sales) based on past performance.

UNC address The Universal Naming Convention (UNC) address is the full address identifying the location of a folder or resource on a network, generally expressed as \\server name\share name\folder name.

Unfiled Notes section In OneNote, the information storage unit that exists in the program but outside of any specific notebook.

validation rule In Excel, a test that data must pass to be entered into a cell without generating a warning message.

View Shortcuts toolbar A toolbar located at the right end of the status bar that contains tools for switching between views of document content and changes the display magnification.

watch The display of a cell's contents in a separate window even when the cell is not visible in the Excel workbook.

what-if analysis Analysis of the contents of a worksheet to determine the impact that specific changes have on your calculations.

widow The last line of a paragraph printed by itself at the top of a page.

wildcard character A text character that can be used to represent one or many characters when conducting a search. Common wildcards include the question mark (?), which represents a single character, and the asterisk (*), which represents one or more characters.

Windows logo key A keyboard key, labeled with the Windows logo, that is used for many Windows shortcuts. For example, pressing the Windows logo key displays or hides the Start menu.

word wrap The process of breaking lines of text automatically to stay within the page margins of a document or window boundaries.

WordArt object A text object you create with ready-made effects to which you can apply additional formatting options.

workbook The basic Excel file, consisting of one or more worksheets.

worksheet A data page in an Excel workbook.

workspace An Excel file type (.xlw) that allows you to open several files at once.

XML See *Extensible Markup Language*.

XPS A Microsoft specification that describes the architecture of the XPS Document file format, which is a fixed-layout format that is based on XML, preserves document formatting, and enables file sharing.

Index

Symbols & Numbers

$ (dollar sign) in absolute references, 294
= (equal sign) in formulas, 286
error code, 301
#DIV/0! error code, 301
#NAME? error code, 301
#REF! error code, 301
#VALUE! error code, 301
[ ] (square brackets) in formulas, 289, 299
3-D borders, 128
3-D references, 604
35mm slides, 486

A

A3 Paper slide size, 486
A4 Paper slide size, 486
absolute references in formulas, 307, 595
   changing to relative references, 294
   dollar sign ($) in, 294
accent colors, 426
accessibility, checking, 219, 503
action button, 595
active cells, 260
   in cell group, 261
   in filtering, 349
active document, closing, 48
ActiveSync icon (OneNote), 550
adding values together, 286
add-ins (Word)
   defined, 595
   settings for, 24
adjusting shapes, 470
adjustment handles, 595
Advanced Filter dialog box, 358-359
advanced options (Word), 22
AGGREGATE function, 357-359
Align Center button (Word), 155
Align Center Right button (Word), 156, 163
Align Text Left button (PowerPoint), 438
Align Text Right button (PowerPoint), 438

aligning text, 121-122, 125-126, 438
   around pictures, 169
   with tab stops, 121
   in tables, 155-156, 163
alignment, cell, 318
alt text in tables, 159
alternative words. *See* Thesaurus
And option in filters, 353
angle of text in text boxes, 394
animation, turning off, 490
annotating graphics, 393
Apply To All button (PowerPoint), 481
arguments, 296
   defined, 288, 595
   error codes for, 301
Arrange All button, 59
Arrange Windows dialog box (Excel), 243, 251
arranging slides, 386
arranging workbook windows, 243
arrows
   button, 8, 311
   filter, 348, 350-351
   tracer, 301-302, 304-305
Artistic Effects button (Word), 173
aspect ratio, 595
Attach File button (OneNote), 565, 575
attachments (OneNote)
   inserting, 565, 572, 575
   keyboard shortcut for, 565
attributes (PowerPoint)
   applying, 439
   defined, 595
audio input devices, 585
audio notes (OneNote)
   appearance of, 586
   playing, 588
   recording, 586, 587
   rewinding, 588
   searchability, activating, 585
Audio Search dialog box (OneNote), 586
Audio Search (OneNote), 585-586
Audio & Video Recording contextual tab
      (OneNote), 586
auditing, 595
auditing errors, 300, 595

author name, viewing, 220
authors (OneNote), hiding names, 548
AutoCalculate, 355, 359
AutoComplete, 257, 595
AutoCorrect
  adding to, 91
  customizing, 406
  defined, 595
  fixing spelling errors with, 88-89
  limitations of, 407
  modifying, 409
  options, setting, 20, 89
  synonyms, 416
AutoCorrect dialog box (Word), 89, 136
AutoCorrect Options button (Excel), 275
AutoExpansion (Excel), 275
AutoFill (Excel)
  defined, 257, 595
  entering data series, 256
AutoFill Options button (Excel), 258, 260
AutoFilter, 348
AutoFit
  changing default settings , 406
  reducing text size with, 411
AutoFit Options button (PowerPoint), 406, 410
AutoFormatting options, 136
automatic slide shows, 491
automating tasks with macros, 601
AutoRecover options (Word), 20, 41
AutoRepublish, 595
AutoText, 190
AVERAGE function, 287, 355
AVERAGEIF function, 297-298, 300
AVERAGEIFS function, 297, 299
averages
  calculating, 297
  viewing with AutoCalculate, 355, 359

B

B4 (ISO) Paper slide size, 486
B5 (ISO) Paper slide size, 486
Background Styles button (Excel), 430
Background Styles gallery (Excel), 430
backgrounds, document
  appropriate use of, 176
  color, applying, 176
  gradients, applying, 177
  overview of, 168
  pictures as, applying, 179
  textures, applying, 178
backgrounds, OneNote notebook, 571

backgrounds, slide
  applying, 433
  changing , 429, 433
  colors, 426
  formatting placeholder, 436
backgrounds, worksheet
  deleting images from, 341-342, 344
  patterns, creating, 341, 343
  repeating images in, 341, 343
  watermarks, 341
Backspace key, 64, 390
Backstage view
  defined, 595
  displaying, 6
Backstage view (OneNote), 522
Backstage view (PowerPoint), 493, 502
Backstage view (Word), 18, 38, 43, 208, 217
  displaying, 48
  Help page, 16
  Info page, 15
  New page, 16
  opening documents from, 46
  Print page, 16
  Recent page, 16
  Share page, 16
banded rows in tables, 161
Banner slide size, 486
banners, 488
bilingual dictionary, 83, 87
Bing decision engine, 270
bitmaps, 455
Black And White button (PowerPoint), 492
black and white, printing in, 492-493
black numbered steps in book, xx
black screen, removing from end of PowerPoint
    presentation, 510
blank documents, creating, 38, 41
blank OneNote pages, 551, 558
Blank Page button (Word), 183
blank pages, inserting, 183
blocking content in Word, 25
blog posts, creating, 39
blogs, 595
blue numbered steps in book, xx
Blue Pen (.05 mm) button (OneNote), 577
BMP file format, 455
Bold button (Word), 18-19, 113, 148
bolding text, 18-19, 113, 148, 311, 313, 439
book exercise format, xviii
book help, xxv
book practice files, xxi
booklets, printing, 208
Borders button (Word), 123, 128, 162

Borders And Shading dialog box (Word), 124, 128, 162, 181
borders, document
  3-D, 128
  adding, 123-124, 128
  around cells, 162
  page, 181
borders, PowerPoint text box, 395, 398
borders, worksheet
  adding to cells, 312, 314
  adding to images, 340
bound documents, previewing, 209
Breaks button (Word), 120, 125, 146, 216
breaks, column, 140, 146, 595
breaks, line
  defined, 599
  inserting, 120, 125, 439
  keyboard shortcut for, 121
breaks, page
  deleting, 214
  inserting, 212
  keyboard shortcut for, 215
  manual, 599
  soft, 212, 603
breaks, section
  for columns, 140, 142
  defining, 605
  deleting, 214
  formatting mark for, 214, 216
  inserting, 214, 216
  overview of, 214
brightness, adjusting, 171
Browse By Page button, 50
Browse dialog box (PowerPoint), 376
browsers. *See* Web browsers
browsing objects, 50
building blocks. *See also* header/footers;
    Quick Parts
  cover pages, 183, 186
  creating, 94, 194
  defined, 93, 595
  deleting, 185
  entering in existing text, 96
  gallery of, 184, 190
  inserting, 94
  keyboard shortcuts for, 94
  overview of, 93, 168
  page numbers, 183, 189, 190
  properties, viewing, 185
  saving, 95
  text boxes, 183, 191, 196
Building Blocks Organizer, 184, 190
bullet points in slides. *See also* subpoints
  changing into diagrams, 462
  collapsing on Outline tab, 402
  converting to regular text, 442

bulleted lists in documents, 69, 71, 131-133.
    See also lists
Bullets button (PowerPoint), 437, 442
Bullets button (Word), 131-132
Bullets gallery (PowerPoint), 437, 442
buttons. *See also specific button names*
  adding to Quick Access Toolbar, 32, 244, 251
  arrows on, 8, 311
  default action, changing, 8
  inactive, 11
  moving, 32
  pictures of, xx
  ScreenTips for. *See* ScreenTips
  separator between, 32-33

C

Calculate Now button (Excel), 287
calculations. *See* formulas
capitalization, 118-119. *See also* uppercase
  changing, 439
  searching for, 266
cascading workbook windows, 243, 251
case, 118-119
  changing, 439
  searching for, 266
categories. *See* galleries
category axes in charts, 463
category axis, 608
cell addresses, 463
cell groups, 261
Cell Margins button, 159
Cell Styles gallery, 316-317
cells, Word table
  borders, 162
  deleting, 153
  inserting, 153
  merging, 153, 155
  setting width of, 159
  shading, 162
  splitting, 154
cells, worksheet. *See also* ranges
  absolute references, 294, 307, 595
  active, 260-261, 349
  aligning, 318
  borders, 312, 314
  contiguous, in formulas, 290
  copying, 258, 261
  defined, 595
  deleting, 238, 240
  deleting contents/formatting of, 311
  entering data in, 256, 258
  filtering. *See* filters, Excel
  finding sum of, 286
  formatting, copying, 258, 260

cells, worksheet *(continued)*
  individual, selecting, 260
  inserting, 238, 240
  monitoring values in, 303, 304
  moving, 238, 240
  moving to, 260
  noncontiguous, adding to formulas, 290
  noncontiguous, formatting, 314
  number formatting in, 319
  pasting formulas in, 291
  references, 294-295, 301, 595
  shading, 312-314, 324
  splitting, 606
  visible, summarizing, 355, 357
Center button (PowerPoint), 438
Center button (Word), 125, 129, 143, 189, 198
Center Tab button (Word), 148
centering text, 121-122, 125, 143
  with Click And Type, 121
  in header/footers, 189
  keyboard shortcut for, 121, 143
  in tables, 155
  in WordArt objects, 198
certification, xii
Change Case button (PowerPoint), 439
Change Colors button (PowerPoint), 460
Change Colors gallery (PowerPoint), 460
Change Styles button (Word), 101, 104
changes, redoing/undoing, 270, 402
chapter thumb tabs, xix
character formatting, 438. *See also* fonts
  appropriate use of, 119
  attributes, 595
  bolding, 18-19, 113, 148, 311, 313, 439
  case, 118
  clearing, 118, 439
  copying, 114, 173, 258, 260
  for individual characters, 439
  underlining, 113, 149
character spacing, 111
  changing, 117, 439
Character Spacing list, 439
character styles, 100, 130. *See also* Quick Styles
characters, non-printing, 53, 56. *See also*
    formatting marks
Chart button (PowerPoint), 462
charts
  adding to slides, 462
  associated Excel worksheets, 462
  category axes, 463
  copying Excel data, 466
  data markers, 463, 596
  data points, 463, 596
  data series, 256-258, 276, 463, 596

editing data, 467
entering data, 464
excluding data from, 466
hiding data, 466
legends, 463, 599
selecting for automatic updates, 468
series axes, 463
sizing, 467
switching rows/columns, 469
tick-mark labels, 463, 607
value axes, 463
Check Accessibility tool (PowerPoint), 503
Check Compatibility tool (PowerPoint), 503
checkerboard transition, 479
checking spelling, 42, 269, 272, 412, 415, 520
  adding new words to dictionary, 269, 272
  with AutoCorrect, 88-89
  with shortcut menu, 88, 90
  with Spelling and Grammar dialog box, 88
  turning off, 412
  typos, 63
Choose A File Or A Set Of Files To Insert dialog box
    (OneNote), 575
Choose A SmartArt Graphic dialog box
    (PowerPoint), 456
Choose Document To Insert dialog box
    (OneNote), 572
CLEAN UP paragraphs, xx
Clear All Formatting button (PowerPoint), 439, 441
Clear Formatting button (Word), 118
clearing
  filters, 350-353
  formatting, 118, 439
  table styles, 323
  validation rules, 363
Click And Type
  centering text with, 121
  defined, 595
clip art. *See also* pictures
  defined, 596
  free from Office.com, 448
  inserting, 168, 174
  inserting in notes, 569
  inserting in slides, 448
  saving, 174
  searching for, 174, 452
Clip Art button (PowerPoint), 448, 452
Clip Art button (Word), 168, 174
Clip Art task pane (PowerPoint), 448, 452
Clipboard, 66, 72, 401, 405, 596, 600
clippings (OneNote), 579
  adding to notebooks, 581
  capturing, 581
  displaying, 582

options for, 580
sending to new page, 581
Close button, xxviii, 5
Close button (Excel), 467
Close button (OneNote), 557
Close button (Word), 48, 51
Close Header and Footer button (Word), 190, 216
Close Task Pane button (PowerPoint), 378
closing
Clipboard task pane, 72
dialog boxes, 12
documents, 48, 51
Help window, xxviii
programs, 5
collaborating on OneNote notebooks, 543
Collapse button (OneNote), 528, 559
Collapse Page Tabs button (OneNote), 529
Collapse Section button (PowerPoint), 385
collapsing
bullet points, 402
OneNote notebooks, 528
OneNote Page Tabs Bar, 529
OneNote subpages, 559
collating printed documents, 217, 493
Color button (Word), 171
Color gallery (Word), 171
color gradients, 429
color of pen, 509
color of Word user interface, 18
color palettes, 426
color scales, 335, 336
color schemes
applying to slides, 426
creating, 426, 444
defined, 596
viewing, 426
coloring backgrounds, 176, 426
coloring pictures, 171
Colors button (PowerPoint), 427
Colors dialog box (Excel), 321
Colors dialog box (PowerPoint), 444
Colors gallery (PowerPoint), 426
column breaks, 140, 146
column headers, 261, 356, 596
Columns button (Word), 141
Columns dialog box (Word), 144
columns, document, 139. *See also* table columns
applying to entire document, 141
formatting, 140
hyphenating text in, 141, 145
indenting text in, 145
justifying, 141-142
margins, 143
overview of, 140
section/column breaks in, 140, 142

separated by tab stops, 147-148, 606
spacing, changing, 144
Columns gallery, 140, 141
columns, table
deleting, 153
inserting, 153
resizing, 153
setting width of, 159
columns, worksheet
changing multiple, 237
copying, 261
deleting, 238
error code, 301
filtering. *See* filters
formatting, 312
hiding, 238-239
inserting, 237, 239
labels, and filtering, 349
labels, as range names, 283
labels, hiding, 249
moving, 261
selecting, 261
unhiding, 238
width, changing, 237
width errors, 301
combining cells, 153-155, 601
commands. *See also* ribbon
adding to Quick Access Toolbar, 32, 244, 251
from previous versions, adding, 7
comments
balloons for, 595
defined, 596
in worksheet ranges, 282
printing, 493
comparing worksheet values, 335-337
compatibility
checking, before distributing document, 219
with earlier versions of PowerPoint, 503
with earlier versions of Word, 44
Compatibility Mode, 45
conditional formatting, 332-338, 596
Conditional Formatting Rules Manager, 333, 335, 337
conditional formulas, 296, 596
conditional functions, 297
conditions, setting. *See* validation rules
connecting shapes on slides, 478
connection points on slides, 478, 596
connectors, 596
content pane, 596
content placeholders on slides, 448, 451
content templates (OneNote), 552, 556
contextual tabs, 596
contiguous cells, adding to formulas, 290

continuous slide shows, 490
contrast, adjusting, 171
contributors to OneNote notebooks, 548
Convert button, 45
Convert Text To Table dialog box (Word), 156
Convert To Text button (Word), 152
converting bullet points to regular text, 442
converting bulleted lists to diagrams, 462
converting Excel tables to ranges, 277
converting tables to text, 152
converting text to tables, 152, 156
converting Word documents to Web pages, 23
Copy button (PowerPoint), 401, 466
Copy button (Word), 66, 70
copying
    cells, 258, 261
    character formatting, 114
    chart data from Excel, 466
    data, 263
    formatting, 114, 173, 258, 260
    formulas, 291, 294
    pictures, 173
    ranges, 261
    shape formatting, 471, 478
    shapes, 471
    slides from other presentations, 375
    text, 66-67, 401-402
    text boxes, 394
    worksheet columns/rows, 261
    worksheets, 233-235
copyrights, 448
correcting mistakes automatically, 406
Corrections button (Word), 171
COUNT function, 287, 297
COUNTA function, 297
COUNTBLANK function, 297
COUNTIF function, 297
COUNTIFS function, 297, 299
counting entries, 287
counts, viewing with AutoCalculate, 355, 359
Cover Page button (Word), 185
cover pages, 183, 186
Create button (Word), 39
Create Names From Selection dialog box
    (Excel), 283
Create New Building Block dialog box (Word),
    94, 194
Create New Section button (OneNote), 559
Create New Theme Colors dialog box
    (PowerPoint), 426
Create New Theme Fonts dialog box
    (PowerPoint), 426
Create Notebook button (OneNote), 542, 547
crediting pictures, 451
criteria, function, 299
Crop button (Word), 170

cropping pictures, 170
currency, in Excel worksheets, 329, 331
cursor
    defined, 596
    function of, 38
    keyboard shortcuts for, 47, 49
    moving, 49-50
    paging up or down with, 47
    placing, 47
    status bar display for, 47
Custom AutoFilter dialog box (Excel), 353
custom slide shows, 596
custom slide sizes, 486
Custom XML Data check box, 506
CUSTOM.DIC dictionary, 412, 415
Customize Quick Access Toolbar button, 33
Customize Ribbon page, 27
Customize Status Bar menu, 8
Cut button (PowerPoint), 401, 404
Cut button (Word), 66, 70, 193
cutting text, 66, 70, 193, 263
    vs. copying, 67
    keyboard shortcut for, 67, 193, 402
cycle diagrams, 454

D

data bars, 337
    defined, 596
    gradient fill in, 334
    and negative values, 335
data consolidation, 596
data entry
    ensuring accuracy of, 361
    in multiple cells, 257
    techniques, summarized, 257
data entry tools
    AutoComplete, 257
    AutoFill, 256
    AutoFill Options button, 258, 260
    Fill Series, 256
    overview of, 255
    Pick From Drop-Down List, 257, 259
data markers, 463, 596
data points, 463, 596
data series, 463
    defined, 596
    entering, 256-258
    in Excel tables, 276
    types of, 257
data source of charts, 596
data types, 348
Data Validation dialog box (Excel), 361, 364
date and time (OneNote), 584

dates
  filtering, 348, 351
  in footers, 487
  formatting, 329, 330
days, filling cells with series, 258
decimal alignment, 121, 127
Decimal Tab button (Word), 127
Decrease Font Size button (PowerPoint), 438
Decrease Indent button (Word), 120, 129
Decrease List Level button (PowerPoint), 392
defining filter rules, 350
Delete button (Word), 153
Delete dialog box (Excel), 238, 240
Delete key, 64
deleting
  background images, 341, 344
  building blocks, 185
  cells, 238, 240
  Clipboard items, 405
  columns, 238
  conditional formatting rules, 333
  custom styles, 317
  data, 311
  page/section breaks, 214
  ranges, 284
  rows, 238
  sections, 386
  slides, 371
  tab stops, 122
  table rows/columns/cells, 153
  text, 64, 66, 68, 71, 403
  watches, 303, 307
  worksheets, 234, 236
delivering presentations, 495, 512
demoting
  outline headings, 596
  text, 392
dependents, 302, 596
deselecting
  text, 66
  text boxes, 395
Design contextual tab, 277
design templates, 596. See also templates
    (OneNote); templates (PowerPoint);
    templates (Word)
destination files, 596, 600
diagrams
  adding text, 457
  changing colors, 460
  creating from bulleted list, 462
  cycle, 454
  hierarchy, 454, 600
  moving, 456, 459
  in notes pages, 498
  opening Text pane, 458

predefined sets of formatting, 455
process, 454, 603
relationship, 455, 604
sizing, 456, 459
in slides, 455-456
viewing layouts, 459
dialog box launcher, 7, 596
dialog boxes
  closing, 12
  displaying, 7
  displaying errors in, 302
  filtering criteria, 349
  Help buttons, xxv
  moving, 419
dictionaries
  adding words to, 269, 272
  bilingual, 83, 87
  in PowerPoint, 412
  supplemental, 412, 415
digital signatures, 596
directory paths, 603
disability accessibility, 503
display effects. See transitions
distributing documents
  electronically, 219
  in XPS format, 223
dividing cells, 154
dividing presentations into sections, 380
Dock to Desktop button (OneNote), 532
docking OneNote window, 532
docking Side Notes to desktop, 591
document format, setting default, 20
document headings, 51
document history, 16
Document Inspector (PowerPoint), 502, 505
Document Inspector (Word), 219, 221
document navigation, 78
document outlines, 52
Document Panel, 502
document properties, 15, 219-220
Document Properties panel, 229-231
document statistics, 93
document summaries, 221
Document Themes folder, 107
documents. See also saving documents
  blank, creating, 41
  blank, opening, 38
  closing, 48, 51
  compatibility with earlier versions, 44
  creating, 38-41
  default format, setting, 20
  formatting in columns, 141. See also columns,
    document
  full-screen display, 52, 56
  inserting in other documents, 97

documents *(continued)*
  location, specifying, 23
  maximizing, 59
  moving to top, 55
  navigating, 47, 56-57, 71
  opening, 46, 48
  printing with default settings, 34
  read-only, opening as, 46
  recently opened, 16, 46
  renaming when saving, 43
  repairing, 46
  scrolling through, 47, 50
  selecting, 65
  sharing, 16
  side-by-side display, 55
  splitting into two panes, 53
  switching between, 53, 59
  translating, 84
  viewing multiple, 59
  zooming in/out, 53
Documents library, 46
.docx format, 43-45
dollar sign ($) in absolute references, 294
Draft button, 58
Draft view, 52
drag-and-drop editing, 66, 71, 401
dragging in Excel
  to copy formulas, 292
  to fill cells, 256
  to resize images, 340
  to select cells, 260
dragging objects, 597
Draw tab (OneNote ribbon), 520
drawing objects
  defined, 597, 600
  overview of, 167
drawing pictures in OneNote, 577
drawing shapes in PowerPoint, 470
drawing tables in Word, 151. *See also* tables
drawing text boxes in Word, 196
Drop Cap dialog box (Word), 202
drop caps
  defined, 597
  inserting, 202
duplex printing, 217
duplicating shapes, 471, 474
duplicating slides, 375, 378

E

Edit Data button (PowerPoint), 467
Edit Formatting Rule dialog box (Excel), 334-337
Edit Name dialog box (Excel), 284
Edit Shape button (PowerPoint), 476

Effect Options button (PowerPoint), 481
effects. *See* text effects
Effects button (PowerPoint), 427
effects schemes, 427
efficiency, improving, 6, 227
e-mailing link to OneNote notebook, 546
embedded fonts in Word, 21
embedded objects, 597
Encarta dictionary, 270
encrypting, 597
endnotes, 597
enhanced handouts, 501
entering data series, 256
entering Excel data, 255-256
entering ranges in formulas, 295
entering text, 41, 64
  in OneNote, 565, 572
  on Outline tab, 390
  in Slide pane, 390
  in text boxes, 394
equal sign (=) in formulas, 286
erasing slide markup, 511
errata page, xxv
Error button (Excel), 301
Error Checking dialog box (Excel), 302, 305
error codes
  #####, 301
  common, summarized, 301
  #DIV/0!, 301
  #NAME?, 301
  #REF!, 301
  #VALUE!, 301
error messages
  adding icons to, 365
  Cancel button, 366
  displaying default, 366
  displaying with validation rules, 363, 364
  Retry button, 366
errors, Excel
  auditing, 300
  changing settings for, 302
  deleting, 390
  displaying custom messages, 298
  displaying in dialog box, 302, 305
  finding information about, 301, 305
  ignoring, 302
  ignoring in AGGREGATE function, 358
  messages, 298
  reference, 301
  settings, changing, 302
  tracing dependents to identify, 301
  tracing precedents to identify, 301
  ways to reduce, 412
errors, spelling, 42, 88-90

Evaluate Formula dialog box (Excel), 303, 306
examining formulas, 303, 306
Excel 2007
  data bars in, 334
  icon sets in, 335
Excel 2010
  data bars in, 334
  ease of use, improving, 227
  file formats, 44
  icon sets in, 335
  online version, xi
  program window, customizing, 241
  starting, 4, 227, 229
  user interface, customizing, 241
Excel, earlier versions of. *See also* Excel 2007
  Paste Options button , 261
  pasting in, 261
Excel formats, 229
Excel Options dialog box
  Customize The Quick Access Toolbar page,
    244, 251
  Customize The Ribbon page, 246, 252
Excel table styles. *See* table styles
Excel tables
  AutoExpansion, 275
  columns, adding/removing, 276
  converting to range, 277
  creating, 275, 277
  data, adding, 275, 277
  data series in, 276
  defined, 597
  Design contextual tab, 277
  fill color, 324
  filtering. *See* filters
  formatting, 322
  formulas in, 276, 277, 293
  in formulas, 289
  names, adding to formulas, 295
  overview of, 255
  renaming, 276, 278
  resize handle, 276
  rows, adding/removing, 276
  summarizing data in, 276, 277
  table style gallery, 275
  Total row, 276
Excel workbooks
  arranging multiple windows, 243, 251
  copying worksheets, 233, 235
  creating, 228, 230
  default, 228
  defined, 608
  display font, changing, 313, 315
  displaying side by side, 243
  Document Properties panel, 229

filtering ranges, 284
  properties, 229-232
  saving, 229, 232
  switching between, 227, 243, 251
  themes. *See* themes, Excel
Excel worksheets
  backgrounds, 341-344
  columns. *See* columns, worksheet
  copying, 233, 235
  creating, 233
  defined, 604
  deleting, 234, 236
  displaying, 233
  filtering. *See* filters
  hiding, 234, 235
  images, adding, 339, 342
  purpose of, 233
  renaming, 233, 235
  reordering, 234-235
  rows. *See* rows, worksheet
  searching, 264
  tab color, changing, 234-235
  unhiding, 234, 236
exiting. *See* closing
Expand button (Mini Translator), 87
Expand Navigation Bar button (OneNote), 527
Expand Section button (PowerPoint), 386
Expand The Ribbon button, 8, 33
expanding ribbon, 8, 33
exporting presentations as outlines, 380
Extensible Markup Language (XML), 597
external files, linking in OneNote, 565, 572

F

fancy effects. *See* WordArt objects
field names, 597
fields, 597
file embedding, 597
file formats
  converting, 45
  defined, 597
  overview of, 44
  saving Word documents as, 21
  setting default, 20
file information
  defined, 603
  for documents, 15
  for PowerPoint presentations, 502-506
  for workbooks, 229-232
file locations of Word documents, specifying, 23
file name extensions, 43-44, 597
File Printout button (OneNote), 565-566, 572
File tab, 6, 15

files
  inserting in documents, 97
  switching between, 53
fill color
  adding to cells, 312, 314
  adding to Excel table, 324
  data bars, 334
Fill Days option, 258
Fill Effects dialog box (Word), 176
fill handle, 256, 597
  controlling data series entry, 257
  copying formulas with, 292
  repeating values with, 257, 259
fill operations, 258
Fill Weekdays option, 258
FillSeries
  defined, 257, 597
  entering data series, 256
filter arrows, 348, 350-351
filter panel, 349
filtering
  defined, 597
  OneNote page tabs, 518
  ranges, 284
filters, 347-348
  active cells in, 349
  and AVERAGE function, 355
  AutoFilter, 348
  clearing, 350, 352-353
  creating, 348, 353
  and data types, 348
  date, 348, 351
  defined, 348, 597
  filter panel display, 349
  for highest or lowest value, 349
  labels in, 349
  options menu, 348
  removing, 350, 352-353
  rules, defining, 350
  Search box, 349, 352
  search filter, defined, 349
  and SUBTOTAL function, 357
  and SUM function, 355
  summarizing data, 355, 357
  Top 10 filter, 349
  turning off, 350
finalizing
  documents, 219, 223
  presentations, 503
Find And Replace dialog box, 48, 75, 264, 266
  clearing formatting from, 269
  Go To tab, displaying, 48
  options summarized, 265
  Replace tab, displaying, 76
Find button (PowerPoint), 418

Find button (Word), 73, 76
Find dialog box (PowerPoint), 418
Find Format dialog box (Excel), 265, 267
Find text, 420
finding fonts, 420
finding formatting, 130
finding information about errors, 301
finding maximum/minimum value in
    worksheets, 287
finding text, 73, 76, 418. *See also* Navigation
    task pane
  advanced options for, 74, 77
  in bilingual dictionary, 83
  keyboard shortcut for, 73
  matching case when, 75
  and replacing, 75, 78
  ScreenTips with page numbers for, 74
  search direction, specifying, 75
  sound-alikes, 75
  wildcards in searches, 75
finding worksheet data, 264-266
first line indent, 120, 597
First Line Indent marker, 597
fitting slides to page when printing, 493
flipping shapes, 473
flying onto slide effect, 480
folder paths, 603
folders, creating, when saving documents, 40, 43
followed hyperlink colors, 426
Font box, 438
Font button (Word), 114
Font Color button (PowerPoint), 426, 439-440, 444
Font Color button (Word), 117
Font dialog box (Word), 112, 116
font effects. *See* text effects
Font gallery, 114
font schemes in PowerPoint, 426, 428
font size
  changing, 111, 116, 313
  defined, 597
  incrementing, 116
  keyboard shortcuts for adjusting, 116
Font Size box, 438
font style, 111, 597
fonts. *See also* character formatting
  applying, 115
  attributes for, 111
  available, 111
  changing, 319, 438
  color, 111, 117
  default, 111
  defined, 99, 597
  embedding in Word documents, 21
  replacing, 418, 420
  in themes, changing, 109

Fonts button (PowerPoint), 428
Fonts gallery (PowerPoint), 426, 428
footers in slides, 487, 598. *See also* header/footers
   in documents
  adding to notes pages, 499
  adding to slides, 489
  editing before printing, 493
  excluding from title slide, 489
footnotes, 598
foreign languages, specifying in Word, 21
Format As Table dialog box (Excel), 275, 277
Format Background dialog box (PowerPoint), 431
Format Cells dialog box (Excel), 312, 316
Format Painter button, 114, 173, 317, 471, 478
Format Shape dialog box, 394
formats
  Excel, 229
  conditional, 332-338, 596
  default, setting, 20
  Rich Text Format (RTF), 374, 380, 604
formatting. *See also* character formatting; fonts;
   themes (Excel); themes (PowerPoint); themes
   (Word)
  alignment, 318
  automatically, 136
  in bold, 18-19, 113, 148, 311, 313, 439
  buttons, 311-312
  cell, 258, 260, 311
  clearing, 269, 311
  columns, 140, 312
  conditional, 332-338, 596
  copying, 173, 317
  currency, 329, 331
  dates, 329-330
  defined, 598
  finding/replacing, 130
  fonts, 313, 319
  with Format Painter, 317
  ignoring, in cell copying, 258
  inserting and, 237, 239
  italics, 314
  labels, 309-310
  Mini Toolbar, 312
  noncontiguous cells, 314
  numbers, 319, 327, 329, 331
  OneNote notes, 569
  pasting and, 263
  phone numbers, 328, 331
  placeholder backgrounds, 436
  previewing, 10
  retaining for reused slides , 378
  row, changing, 312
  searching for, 265, 267
  shapes, 471, 478
  Special formats, 328

tables, 160
time, in cells, 319
tools for, 311-312
formatting marks
  displaying, 56
  keyboard shortcut for, 68
  section break indicator, 214, 216
  showing/hiding, 68, 149
Formula AutoComplete, 288, 295-296, 598
formula bar
  changing data in, 266
  contents of, 260
  defined, 598
  Excel display font, changing, 313, 315
  hiding, 249
formula box
  editing formulas in, 286
  phone numbers in, 328
Formula button (Word), 158
Formula dialog box (Word), 158
formulas, Excel
  absolute references in, 307
  conditional, 296
  contiguous cells in, 290
  copying and pasting, 291, 294
  creating, 286, 288, 295
  defined, 286
  details, displaying, 303
  displaying messages with, 296
  editing, 286
  entering ranges in, 295
  equal sign (=) in, 286
  erroneously treated as text, 286
  errors. *See* errors, Excel
  examining, 303, 306
  Excel tables in, 289, 293, 295
  in Excel tables, 276, 277
  Formula AutoComplete, 288, 295-296
  functions in, 286
  ignoring values in, 357
  making ranges available for, 282
  multiple worksheets and, 243
  noncontiguous cells in, 290
  ranges in, 282, 288
  relative references in, 291, 307
  revising, 286
  searching in, 266
  square brackets in, 289
  troubleshooting, 286
  unrecognized text in, 301
formulas, Word, 158
  constructing, 158
  defined, 598
  referencing cells in, 158
Forward button, 57

French dictionary, 412
frequently misspelled words, correcting, 88
full name. *See* user name
Full Page View button (OneNote), 533-534
Full Screen Reading button, 56
Full Screen Reading view, 52, 56
Function Arguments dialog box (Excel), 296-297
functions
　adding to formulas, 286
　AGGREGATE, 357, 359
　arguments, 296
　arguments, defined, 288
　and AutoCalculate, 355
　automatic recalculation of, 354
　AVERAGE, 287
　AVERAGEIF, 297, 298, 300
　AVERAGEIFS, 297, 299
　conditional, 297
　constructing, 158
　COUNT, 287, 297
　COUNTA, 297
　COUNTBLANK, 297
　COUNTIF, 297
　COUNTIFS, 297, 299
　defined, 286, 598
　IF, 296, 360
　IFERROR, 297
　MAX, 287
　MIN, 287
　multiple criteria in, 299
　NOW(), 287
　PMT(), 287
　RAND, 354, 360
　RANDBETWEEN, 354
　SUBTOTAL, 355
　SUM, 287, 295
　SUMIF, 297
　SUMIFS, 297, 299, 300
　volatile, 354
funnel icon in filter arrow, 350

G

galleries
　building blocks, 595
　closing without making selection, 13
　defined, 598
　of thumbnails, 10
GIF file format, 455
Go To Footer button (Word), 189
Goal Seek, 598
Gradient gallery, 435
grammar checker, 91. *See also* spelling, checking

graphics. *See* building blocks; drawing objects;
　images (Excel); images (OneNote); images
　(PowerPoint); images (Word); SmartArt
　graphics
graphics file formats
　BMP, 455
　GIF, 455
　JPEG, 455
　PNG, 455
　TIFF, 455
grayed-out buttons, 11
grayscale
　previewing before printing in, 492
　printing in, 493
Grayscale button (PowerPoint), 492
gridlines (Excel), 598
gridlines (OneNote), 571
Group button (PowerPoint), 476
grouping
　OneNote sections. *See* section groups (OneNote)
　related data, 282
　shapes, 476, 598
groups, ribbon, 7, 598
　customizing, 27
　removing, 30
Grow Font button (Word), 116

H

handles, 450
　adjustment, 595
　around shapes, 470
　defined, 598
　rotating, 604
　sizing, 605
Handout masters, 495, 598
handouts
　creating in Word, 501
　enhanced, 501
　printing, 492
handwritten notes (OneNote), 520, 567, 577
hanging indent, 120, 598
　adjusting, 126
　in columns, adjusting, 145
Hanging Indent marker, 598
Header And Footer dialog box (PowerPoint), 487,
　488, 493, 499
Header button (Word), 188, 216
Header & Footer button (PowerPoint), 488, 499
header/footers in documents. *See also* footers in
　slides
　centering text in, 189
　closing, 190, 216
　defined, 598

different first page, 216
editing, 216
hiding, 54
inserting, 188
moving to, 189
navigating between, 188
overview of, 183
settings inheritance, 183, 216
headers, column and row
changing formatting with, 312
displaying unique values, 359, 360
filter arrow in, 351
and SUBTOTAL function, 356
headers, page, 598
headers, slide
adding to notes pages, 499
editing before printing, 493
headings, document, 51
height, row, 237
Help button, xxv, 8, 598
Help, on Office Online Web site, xxvii
Help page (OneNote Backstage view), 525
Help page (Word), 16
Help window
closing, xxviii
displaying, 8
navigating, xxviii
opening, xxvi
printing from, xxix
searching in, xxviii
showing all of topics, xxix
table of contents, displaying, xxvii
topics, displaying, xxvii
help with book, xxv
hidden characters, displaying, 53
hidden formatting marks, displaying, 68
hidden rows, ignoring in AGGREGATE function, 358
hidden text, clearing before distributing
document, 219
hidden worksheets, displaying, 234, 236
hiding
author names in OneNote, 548
columns, 238, 239
Document Properties panel, 230
formatting marks, 149
formula bar, 249
headers/footers in Word, 54
labels, 249
Mini Toolbar in Word, 18
non-printing characters, 56
ribbon, 59, 249
rows, 238
text, 53
tracer arrows, 302, 305-306
worksheets, 234-235

hierarchy diagrams, 454
highlighting during presentations, 509
highlighting objects. *See* selecting
highlighting text. *See also* selecting text
color selection for, 117
removing highlighting, 118
Home tab, 6
Home tab (OneNote), 519
Home tab (Word), 10
horizontal scroll bar, 47
HTML (Hypertext Markup Language), 598, 600
hyperlinks, 426, 598
Hypertext Markup Language (HTML), 598, 600
hyphenating text
defined, 598
in columns, 141, 145
Hyphenation button (Word), 145

I

icon sets
defined, 598
in Excel, 335
rules, changing, 335, 337
IF function, 296-297, 299, 360
IFERROR function, 297
ignoring errors, 302
images (Excel)
attributes, changing, 340
background, 341-344
borders, adding, 340
moving, 343
position, changing, 340
resizing, 340, 343
shape, changing, 340
worksheets, adding to, 339, 342
images (OneNote)
aspect ratio, 595
attaching to files, 575
displaying ScreenTips, 576
inserting, 568, 572-574
opening, 576
resizing, 569
scaling, 568
images (PowerPoint), 448
annotating, 393
crediting, 451
linking for automatic updating, 449
moving, 450
notes pages, adding to, 496
sizing, 450-451
slides, adding to, 448-449

images (Word)
  and line spacing, 169
  artistic effects, adding, 173
  as backgrounds, 179
  brightness, adjusting, 171
  contrast, adjusting, 171
  copying, 173
  correcting, 171
  cropping, 170
  incomplete display, 169
  inserting, 168-169, 173
  modifying, 168
  overview of, 167
  recoloring, 171
  resizing, 170
  styles, applying, 172
  text alignment around, 169
  troubleshooting, 169
Important paragraphs, xx
importing outlines, 374
inactive buttons, 11
Increase Font Size button (PowerPoint), 438, 441
Increase Indent button (Word), 120, 126, 133, 148
Increase List Level button (PowerPoint), 392
increasing/decreasing space between letters, 439
indent markers, 120
  defined, 599
  moving, 126
indenting columns, 145
indenting lists, 132-133
indenting text
  first line, 120, 597
  hanging indent, 120, 126, 145
  left, 120, 126, 600
  right, 120, 126
index entry fields, 599
indexes, 599
Info page (OneNote Backstage view), 502, 522
initials. *See* user name
Insert Above button (Word), 153
Insert Below button (Word), 153, 155
Insert Cells dialog box (Word), 153
Insert Chart button (PowerPoint), 462, 465
Insert Chart dialog box (PowerPoint), 465
Insert dialog box (Excel), 238, 240
Insert Function dialog box (Excel), 276, 286, 296
Insert Left button (Word), 153
Insert Options button (Excel), 237, 239
Insert Outline dialog box (PowerPoint), 375
Insert Picture dialog box (Excel), 339, 342
Insert Picture dialog box (OneNote), 568, 573
Insert Picture dialog box (PowerPoint), 448, 449, 451
Insert Picture dialog box (Word), 169

Insert Picture From File button (PowerPoint), 448, 449
Insert Right button (Word), 153
Insert SmartArt Graphic button (PowerPoint), 455, 456
Insert tab (OneNote), 519
Insert tab (Word), 11
Insert Table dialog box (Word), 150
Insert Table gallery (Word), 150
Insert Worksheet button (Excel), 233
inserting
  cells, 238, 240
  columns, 237, 239
  line breaks, 439
  rows, 237, 239
  slides, 448
  text, 64
inspecting documents, 219, 221, 502, 505
international languages, specifying in Word, 21
Internet Explorer. *See* Web browsers
Internet links, 426, 600
Italic button (PowerPoint), 440
italicizing text, 314, 439

J

JPEG file format, 455
Justify button (PowerPoint), 438
Justify button (Word), 125, 142
justifying text, 121, 125
  in columns, 141, 142
  defined, 599
  keyboard shortcut for, 121, 142
  in PowerPoint, 438

K

Keep On Top button (OneNote), 592
Keep Text Only button (Word), 87
Keyboard Shortcut paragraphs, xx
keyboard shortcuts, 599
  for attaching documents, 565
  for bolding text, 113
  for building blocks, 94
  for centering text, 121, 143
  for clearing formatting, 118
  for copying text, 67
  for creating blank OneNote pages, 558
  for creating OneNote sections, 559
  for creating OneNote subpages, 558, 559
  for cursor movement, 47
  for cursor placement, 49
  for cutting text, 67, 193

for docking OneNote window, 532
for document navigation, 55, 71, 78
for editing text, 402
for finding text, 73
for Font dialog box display, 116
for font size, 116
for formatting marks, 68
for Go To tab of Find And Replace dialog box, 48
for Help window display, 8
for hiding/displaying rule lines in OneNote, 571
for inserting date and time, 584
for inserting documents in OneNote, 565
for inserting page breaks, 215
for justifying text, 121, 142
for left-aligning text, 121
for line breaks, 121
for minimizing/expanding ribbon, 8
moving cursor with, 47
for navigating OneNote, 534
for OneNote tags, 579
for opening OneNote windows, 518
for opening Side Notes, 591
for outline levels in OneNote, 570
for Page Tabs Bar, 518
for pasting text, 67
for printing, 208
for repeating editing, 67, 146
for replacing text, 76, 130
for Research task pane, 79
for rewinding audio/video notes, 588
for right-aligning text, 121
for saving document, 41
for Screen Clipping tool in OneNote, 581
for selecting all, 65, 142
for underlining text, 113
for undoing editing, 67
keywords, 221, 229, 231
kiosk mode (PowerPoint), 599

L

labels, row and column
in filters, 349
formatting, 309-310
hiding, 249
as range names, 283
Landscape orientation, 208, 599
Language button (PowerPoint), 413
Language dialog box (PowerPoint), 413
languages, specifying additional in Word, 21
languages, translating, 271, 273, 417
launcher, dialog box, 7, 596
Layout button (PowerPoint), 374
Layout dialog box (Word), 200

Layout gallery (PowerPoint), 372
layouts, slide
applying, 374
changing existing slides, 372
diagram, 459
selecting from New Slide gallery, 371
Ledger Paper slide size, 486
left indent
adjusting, 120, 126
defined, 599
Left Indent marker, 599
Left Tab button (Word), 126
left-aligning text, 121
legacy commands, 7, 27
legacy compatibility, 44
legends
in charts, 463
defined, 599
Letter Paper slide size, 486
libraries, slide, 379, 605
Line And Paragraph Spacing button (Word), 122
line breaks
defined, 599
inserting, 120, 125, 439
keyboard shortcut for, 121
line spacing
changing, 438
pictures and, 169
Line Spacing button (PowerPoint), 438, 442
Line Spacing button (Word), 127
lines, selecting, 65, 103
Link button (OneNote), 565
linked objects, 599
linking
defined, 599
to external files in OneNote, 565, 572
text boxes, 196
links, 426, 600
list boxes. *See* galleries
lists. *See also* tabbed lists
converting text into, 131-132
ending, 131
indenting, 132-133
modifying, 131
multiple levels, creating, 131, 135
overview of, 130
sorting, 131, 135
undoing formatting of, 131
Live Preview, 10, 424
defined, 599
disabling, 18
Paste, 262
of styles, 316
loan payments, calculating with PMT()
function, 288

local OneNote notebooks, 541
locked cells, 599
logon credentials, 599
lowercase. *See* case

M

machine translator, 84
macros, 599
magnification level, 249
  adjusting, 53, 102
  displaying multiple pages, 55, 209
  to full page, 176
  overview of, 242
  by percentage, 56
  specific zoom level, 242
mail merge, 599
Mailings tab (Word), 14
mailto hyperlinks, 599
main documents, 599
managing ranges, 284
manual page breaks, 599
margins
  changing, 206, 208, 211, 216
  of columns, 143
  defined, 599
  gallery of, 209
  mirroring, 210
  specifying, 119
  in tables, 159
Margins button (Word), 12, 119, 216
marking documents as final, 223
marking presentations as final, 503
marking slides, 509
masters
  defined, 599
  handouts, 495
  notes pages, 495, 602
mathematical functions in tables. *See* formulas,
    Excel; functions
MAX function, 287
Maximize button, 59
maximizing documents, 59
maximum value in worksheets
  advantage of identifying, 281
  finding, 287
Meeting Properties dialog box (PowerPoint), 505
Merge And Center, 599
Merge Cells button (Word), 153, 155-156
merge fields, 599
Merge List button (Word), 70
merging
  bullet points, 71
  cells, 153, 155, 599

messages, entry, 363-364
messages, error
  adding icons to, 365
  displaying custom, 298, 363-364
  displaying default, 366
  displaying with validation rules, 363-364
microphones, configuring, 585
Microsoft Bing decision engine, 270
Microsoft certification, xii
Microsoft Encarta dictionary, 270
Microsoft Excel 2010
  data bars in, 334
  ease of use, improving, 227
  file formats, 44
  icon sets in, 335
  online version, xi
  program window, customizing, 241
  starting, 4, 227, 229
  user interface, customizing, 241
Microsoft Knowledge Base, xxix
Microsoft Office 2010
  common user interface, 3
  compatibility with earlier versions, 44
  online applications, xi
  software suite comparison, xi
  themes in, 322
Microsoft Office Clipboard, 66, 72, 401, 405,
    596, 600
Microsoft Office Compatibility Pack, 45
Microsoft Office Online Web site
  clip art images, 448
  Help from, xxvii
  templates on, 39
  themes from, 107
Microsoft Office Specialist (MOS), xii
Microsoft OneNote 2010. *See also* notebooks
    (OneNote)
  advanced options, 536
  audio/video options, 536
  Backstage view, 522
  customizing, 535
  display options, 536
  docking to desktop, 532-533
  docking window, 532
  drawing pictures in, 577
  entering text in, 572
  external files, inserting, 572
  file format, 602
  Full Page View, 533
  handwritten content, 520
  Help, accessing, 525
  inserting content in, 519
  language options, 536
  Navigation Bar, 517, 526-527
  navigation keyboard shortcuts, 534

online version, xi
opening images from, 576
Page Tabs Bar, collapsing, 529
Page Tabs Bar, default location of, 526
Pages tab, expanding, 533
page titles, displaying, 529
paragraph formatting, 569
printing from, 525
product activation, 525
program window, 516, 521, 526, 527
proofing options, 536
ribbon, 519, 531
saving options, 536
saving pages, 524
screen clippings from, 579-582
sending items to, 580
sending pages to Outlook/Word, 524
Side Notes, 591
starting, 4, 526
storage structure, 516
tags, 578-579
translating content, 520
undocking, 533
Unfiled Notes section, 528
Microsoft PowerPoint Viewer, 600
Microsoft Product Support Services, xxix
Microsoft SharePoint
file location, setting default, 20
sharing notebooks from, 545, 547
Microsoft Translator service, 84
Microsoft Update service, 10
Microsoft Word 2010. *See also* documents
compatibility with earlier versions, 44
file formats, 44
first time starting, 10
handouts, creating, 501
Help button, xxvi
Help window, opening, xxvi
OneNote pages, sending to, 524
online version, xi
starting, 4, 10
views in, 52
MIN function, 287
Mini Toolbar, 65, 312, 439, 440
character formatting with, 111
defined, 600
hiding, 18
Mini Translator, 82, 84, 417
Minimize button, 5
Minimize The Ribbon button, 8, 59
minimizing
documents, 5
ribbon, 8, 59

minimum value in worksheets
advantage of identifying, 281
finding, 287
mirroring margins, 210
misspellings. *See* spelling, checking
mistakes, correcting automatically. *See*
AutoCorrect
mobile devices, OneNote on, 593
monitoring values in cells, 303-304
monitors, multiple, 508
months, entering series with AutoFill, 256
More button (PowerPoint), 424
MOS (Microsoft Office Specialist), xii
move handles, 600
Move or Copy dialog box (Excel), 233, 235
Move Up button (Word), 28
moving
cells, 238, 240
to cells, 260
diagrams, 456, 459
dialog boxes, 419
images, 343
pictures, 450
shapes, 471
slides, 384
tables, 152-153
text, 401
text boxes, 394, 397
worksheet columns, 261
Multilevel List button (Word), 131
multi-line text boxes, 393
multiple criteria in functions, 299

N

Name box, creating ranges with, 283, 285
Name Manager dialog box (Excel), 284-285
named ranges. *See* ranges
naming
documents, 43
OneNote pages/sections, 554-555
narration in slides, turning off, 490
navigating
documents, 71
Help window, xxviii
OneNote, 534
OneNote page tabs, 518
tables, 152
Navigation Bar (OneNote), 517
collapsing, 517
default location of, 526
expanding, 517, 527
Navigation button (OneNote), 510

Navigation task pane, 77. *See also* finding text
defined, 600
displaying, 50
editing while open, 74
Search tab, displaying, 73
navigation toolbar, 509-510
nested tables, 600
New Folder button (Word), 40, 43
New Formatting Rule dialog box (Excel), 333, 335
New Name dialog box (Excel), 282, 286
New Page arrow (OneNote), 555, 559
New Page button (OneNote), 557
New page (OneNote Backstage view), 522, 541
New Side Note button (OneNote), 591
New Slide button (PowerPoint), 372-373, 375
New Slide gallery (PowerPoint), 371, 373
New Table Quick Style dialog box (Excel), 322, 323
Next Page button, 47, 50, 56
Next Page button (OneNote), 534
Next Page button (Print Page), 493
Next Slide button (PowerPoint), 497
noncontiguous cells, adding to formulas, 290
nonprinting characters
displaying, 53
keyboard shortcut for, 68
section break indicator, 214, 216
showing/hiding, 56, 68, 149
nonstandard color schemes, 444
Normal button (PowerPoint), 382, 498
Normal view
creating slide sections in, 384
defined, 600
in PowerPoint, 53
Normal View button (OneNote), 533
note containers (OneNote), 564
automatic creation of, 572
contents of, 564
defined, 600
inserting, 564
modifying, 564-565
object selectors for, 564
note separators, 600
notebook headers, 518, 600
notebooks (OneNote), 516. *See also* pages
(OneNote); sections (OneNote)
appearance of, 517
authors, 548
backgrounds, changing, 571
backup copies, opening, 522
closing, 518
collaboration on, 543
collapsing, 528
creating, 522, 540-542, 547
e-mailing link to, 546

entering text in, 565
green check mark icon, 550
hierarchy, displaying, 517
images, inserting, 568
local, creating, 541
moving sections, 516
multiple, working with, 518
multiuser, 520
offline copies, 543
opening, 518, 522, 530, 546
organizing, 551
Personal, 516, 526
pinning to Recently Closed list, 530
populating, 540
printing, 525
properties, viewing, 522
red slashed circle icon, 550
saving, 524, 567
screen clippings, 579-582
scrolling pages in, 565
sending Web pages to, 579
settings, 530
setup of, 516
sharing, 520, 523, 540, 544-547
spelling/grammar checks, 520
storing, 540
synchronizing, 543, 549-550
templates, 552
Web sharing, 544, 547
yellow caution triangle icon, 550
Notes masters, 495, 600
notes (OneNote)
audio, 585
clip art, inserting, 569
formatting, 569
handwritten, 577
images, inserting, 568
outline levels, 570
Tablet PC, entering with, 567
video, 585
from Web pages, 579-583
Notes Page button (PowerPoint), 495, 496
Notes Page view (PowerPoint), 53, 494
notes pages (PowerPoint)
adding to slides, 495, 497
adding diagrams, 498
adding headers/footers, 499
adding pictures, 496
handwritten, 567
printing, 492, 499
Notes pane, 600
notes, PowerPoint. *See* notes pages (PowerPoint)
NOW() function, 287

numbered lists. *See also* lists
    creating, 131, 133
    numbering value, setting, 134
    number style, changing, 132
    restarting numbering, 133
numbered steps, xx
Numbering button (PowerPoint), 437
Numbering button (Word), 131, 133
numbers. *See also* values
    adding text to values, 329, 332
    currency, formatting, 329, 331
    dates, formatting, 329, 330
    displaying visually, 462
    formatting, 319, 327, 329, 331
    negative, and data bars, 335
    negative, displaying, 329
    phone numbers, formatting, 328, 331
    specifying in validation rules, 364

O

object commands. *See* contextual tabs
object selectors (OneNote), 564, 600
objects
    embedded, 597
    linked, 600
Office 2010
    common user interface, 3
    compatibility with earlier versions, 44
    online applications, xi
    software suite comparison, xi
    themes in, 322
Office Online Web site
    clip art images, 448
    Help from, xxvii
    templates on, 39
    themes from, 107
Office Open XML formats, 44
Office Professional Plus, xi
Office Standard, xi
Office theme, 320
Office Themes
    copying worksheets, 234
Office Web Apps, xi
.one format, 600
OneNote 2010. *See also* notebooks (OneNote)
    advanced options, 536
    audio/video options, 536
    Backstage view, 522
    customizing, 535
    display options, 536
    docking to desktop, 532-533
    docking window, 532
    drawing pictures in, 577

    entering text in, 572
    external files, inserting, 572
    file format, 600
    Full Page View, 533
    handwritten content, 520
    Help, accessing, 525
    inserting content in, 519
    language options, 536
    Navigation Bar, 517, 526-527
    navigation keyboard shortcuts, 534
    online version, xi
    opening images from, 576
    Page Tabs Bar, collapsing, 529
    Page Tabs Bar, default location of, 526
    page titles, displaying, 529
    Pages tab, expanding, 533
    paragraph formatting, 569
    printing from, 525
    product activation, 525
    program window, 516, 521, 526, 527
    proofing options, 536
    ribbon, 519, 531
    saving options, 536
    saving pages, 524
    screen clippings from, 579-582
    sending items to, 580
    sending pages to Outlook/Word, 524
    Side Notes, 591
    starting, 4, 526
    storage structure, 516
    tags, 578-579
    translating content, 520
    undocking, 533
    Unfiled Notes section, 528
OneNote icon, 581
    action associated with, changing, 593
    activating, 590
    missing, 590
OneNote Mobile 2010, 593
OneNote Options dialog box, 535-536, 579, 590
OneNote Web App, 593
online applications, xi
online bilingual dictionary, 83, 87
On-screen Show slide size, 486
Open dialog box, 46, 48
Open Notebook button (OneNote), 518, 526
Open Notebook dialog box (OneNote), 526
Open page (OneNote Backstage view), 522
Open XML formats, 44
opening
    diagram Text pane, 458
    documents, 46, 48
    OneNote notebooks, 518, 522, 526, 530, 546
Options dialog box, 7, 17
order of conditional formatting rules, 333

order of worksheets, 234-235
organizing OneNote notebooks, 551
orientation, page
  changing, 206, 208
  defined, 602
orphans
  defined, 212, 600
  setting options for, 212, 215
Outline button, 57
outline levels, assigning in OneNote, 570
outline, shapes, 435
Outline tab, 392, 600
Outline view (Word), 52
outlines, PowerPoint
  exporting presentations as, 380
  importing into slides, 375
  opening as presentations, 376
  printing, 492
outlines, Word, importing to PowerPoint, 374
Outlining tab, 57
Overhead slide size, 486
Overview pane, 600
overwriting documents when saving, 41

P

Package for CD, 600
page borders, applying, 181
Page Borders button (Word), 181
Page Break button (Word), 215
Page Break Preview (Excel), 52
page breaks
  deleting, 214
  inserting, 212
  keyboard shortcut for, 215
  manual, 599
  soft, 212, 603
Page Color button (Word), 13, 176
page colors (Word), 13
Page Layout tab (Word), 11
Page Layout view (Excel), 52
page length, defining. *See* margins
Page Number button (Word), 189
page numbers
  formatting, 190
  inserting, 183, 189
page orientation, changing, 206, 208
Page Setup button (PowerPoint), 487
Page Setup dialog box (PowerPoint), 486-487
Page Setup dialog box (Word), 12, 206, 208
Page Tabs area (OneNote)
  color, changing, 571
  defined, 602

Page Tabs Bar (OneNote), 518, 554
  collapsing, 529
  collapsing/expanding, 518
  default location of, 526
  expanding, 554
  keyboard shortcut for, 518
page tabs (OneNote)
  filtering, 518
  navigating, 518
  ScreenTips on, 529
  selecting, 529
  truncating names on, 529
pages (OneNote)
  blank, 551, 558
  creating, 552, 555, 558
  defined, 600
  keyboard shortcuts for creating, 558
  naming, 554-555
  organizing, 551
  subpages, creating, 558-559
  templates, applying, 556
  titles, entering, 554
pagination, 212, 215
paper size, changing, 206, 208
Paragraph dialog box (PowerPoint), 438, 442
Paragraph dialog box (Word), 212, 214
  opening, 123
  tab alignment, 122
paragraph formatting (OneNote), 569-570
paragraph formatting (PowerPoint), 437
paragraph formatting (Word)
  aligning, 120-122, 125-126
  borders, 123-124, 128
  defined, 119
  shading, 128
paragraph indenting
  first line, 120, 597
  hanging indent, 120, 126, 145
  left, 120, 126, 600
  right, 120, 126
paragraph marks, 56. *See also* non-printing
    characters
paragraph spacing, 122, 127, 148, 438
paragraph styles, 100. *See also* Quick Styles
  defined, 600
  finding/replacing, 130
paragraphs
  aligning, 121
  first letter, formatting, 202
  keeping lines together, 215
  keeping with next, 212
  overview of, 119
  selecting, 65, 71
  width, defining. *See* margins
Paste All button (Word), 72

Paste button (PowerPoint), 401, 404, 466
Paste button (Word), 66, 70
Paste gallery, 261
Paste Live Preview, 261-262
Paste Options button (Excel), 261-262
Paste Options button (PowerPoint), 402
Paste Options button (Word), 67, 600
Paste Special dialog box (Excel), 262
pasting text, 66, 70, 263, 401
   from Clipboard, 404-405
   in earlier versions of Excel, 261
   formulas in cells, 291
   keyboard shortcut for, 67, 402
   options for, 70
   Paste Live Preview, 261
   previewing, 261
   specialized, 263
   undoing, 262
   without formatting, 191
paths, 601
pattern, background, 341, 343
Pause button (OneNote), 589
pausing video notes (OneNote), 589
PDF files, 601
Pen button (PowerPoint), 511
pen color, 509
pen tool (OneNote), 567, 577
personal information, clearing before distributing
   document, 219, 222
Personal notebook (OneNote), 516, 526
phone numbers
   formatting, 328, 331
   troubleshooting, 328
photo albums, 601
photos. *See* images (Excel); images (OneNote);
   images (PowerPoint); images (Word)
Pick From Drop-Down List
   data entry, 257, 259
   defined, 257, 601
Picture button (OneNote), 568, 573
Picture button (PowerPoint), 448, 451, 496
Picture button (Word), 168, 169,
Picture Styles gallery, 172
Picture Tools Format contextual tab, 340
pictures. *See* images (Excel); images (OneNote);
   images (PowerPoint); images (Word)
pinning OneNote notebooks to Recently Closed
   list, 530
PivotCharts, 601
PivotTable fields, 597
PivotTables, 601
pixels, 601
placeholders in slides, 393
   AutoFit settings, 406
   content, 448

   defined, 601
   effects, 436
   filling with color, 434
   formatting, 434
   formatting background, 436
   outline, 435
   selecting all text in, 441
   size/position of, 393
   sizing to fit text, 439
Play button (OneNote), 587-589
playing audio notes (OneNote), 588
plot area, 601
plus signs between keys, xx
PMT() function, 287
PNG file format, 455
pointing, 601
points (unit of measure), 436, 601
populating OneNote notebooks, 540
Portrait orientation, 208, 601
Position button (Word), 198
position of placeholders, 393
posts, blog, 601
PowerPoint 2010
   file formats, 45
   online version, xi
   starting, 4
PowerPoint Options dialog box, 407
PowerPoint Viewer, 600
practice files, xxi
precedents, Excel
   defined, 301, 601
   tracing, to identify errors, 301
preformatted tables. *See* Quick Tables
preparing presentations for delivery, 491
presentations. *See also* templates (PowerPoint)
   controlling audience view, 508
   delivering, 495, 512
   displaying properties, 503
   dividing into sections, 380
   exporting as outlines, 380
   highlighting during, 509
   looping continuously, 490
   marking as final, 503
   marking slides during, 509
   preparing for delivery, 491
   previewing, 495
   printing, 492, 495
   rearrange, 384
   removing ending black screen, 510
   removing information from, 502, 506
   saving as.rtf file, 380
   themes, 423-425
   transitions. *See* transitions
   for Web page banners, 488

Presenter view, 495, 508
previewing
  Paste Live Preview, 261
  color effects (Word), 13
  cut or copied items before pasting, 402
  documents, 52, 57, 207-210
  OneNote templates, 552
  presentations, 491, 495
  table styles, 161
  Word templates, 39
Previous Page button, 47
Previous Screen button, 57
primary key column, 601
Print button, xxix, 217, 218, 492, 495
Print dialog box (OneNote), 525
Print Layout view, 52, 54, 207
Print page (OneNote Backstage view), 493, 525
Print page (Word Backstage view), 208, 217
Print Preview And Settings dialog box
    (OneNote), 525
Print Preview button (OneNote), 525
print previewing, 52, 57, 207-210
print quality, 493
printers, 217-218
printing
  booklets, 208
  collating, 217
  with default settings, 217, 218
  duplex, 217
  frames around slides, 493
  Help topics, xxix
  keyboard shortcut for, 208
  number of copies, setting, 218
  OneNote items, 525, 580
  pages per sheet, setting, 208
  presentations, 491-492, 495
  from Quick Access Toolbar, 34
  settings for, 217
  speaker notes, 499
  Word documents, 34
process diagrams, 454
product activation (OneNote), 525
product support, xxix
professionally designed color schemes, 426
program icon, 5
program user. See user name
program window
  manipulating, 5
  minimizing, 5
  overview of, 5, 8, 10
  resizing, 5
  scrolling contents of, 47
program window (Excel)
  customizing, 241
  maximizing space, 249

programs
  closing, 5
  previous versions, adding commands from, 7
  starting, 4
promoting outline headings, 601
promoting text, 392
proofreading, importance of, 87, 92
properties
  defined, 601
  for documents, 15
  for PowerPoint presentations, 502-506
  for workbooks, 229-232
Properties dialog box, 221, 229, 231, 502
protecting documents by marking as final, 223
pull quotes. See quote boxes

Q

queries, 601
Quick Access Toolbar
  buttons, adding, 31-32, 244, 251
  buttons, positioning, 245
  customizing, 5, 32, 521
  defined, 601
  exporting customizations, 245
  improving efficiency with, 6
  legacy commands, adding, 7
  location, 244
  moving, 5
  overview of, 3
  printing from, 34
  removing buttons, 245
  resetting, 32-34, 245
  specifying for active document, 33
Quick Parts. See building blocks
Quick Parts button (Word), 95, 190, 194
Quick Parts gallery, 194
Quick Print button, 34
Quick Styles, 100. See also style sets
  applying, 103-104
  changing style set, 100
  defined, 601
  live preview of, 102
Quick Styles button (Word), 200
Quick Styles gallery, 100
  displaying, 103
  navigating in, 102
Quick Tables. See also tables, Word
  defined, 601
  inserting, 164
  overview of, 151, 163-164
Quick Tables gallery, 164

quote boxes
  defined, 601
  inserting, 191
  replacing text in, 191
quotes (quotation marks) in text strings, 330-332

R

RAND function, 354, 360
RANDBETWEEN function, 354
random rows, selecting, 354
random values, generating, 354
ranges
  cell, defined, 260, 282, 595, 600, 601
  changing definition of, 284
  comments, 282
  copying, 261
  creating, 282-284
  deleting, 284
  displaying, 283
  editing, 284-285
  filtering, 284
  in formulas, 282, 295
  managing, 284
  names, in formulas, 283, 288
  selecting, 260
  setting availability of, 282
Reading View button (PowerPoint), 482, 490
Reading view (PowerPoint), 53
read-only, 503
  defined, 601
  opening documents as, 46
rearranging
  presentations, 384
  slides, 386
recalculation time, displaying/updating, 287
Recent page, opening documents from, 46
recent Word documents, displaying, 16
recoloring pictures, 171
Record Audio button (OneNote), 586
Record Video button (OneNote), 588
recording notes. *See* audio notes (OneNote); video
    notes (OneNote)
records, defined, 601
red wavy lines under words, 42
Redo button, 5, 68, 402, 404
redoing editing, 67, 270, 402
reducing text size using AutoFit, 411
reference marks, 601
reference materials, specifying, 81
references
  absolute, 294, 307, 595
  cell, defined, 595
  errors, 301

relative, 291-294, 307, 604
  types of, 294-295
References tab (Word), 14
refreshing, defined, 602
related data, grouping, 282
relationship diagrams, 455
relative references, 307
  changing to absolute references, 294, 295
  defined, 291, 602
  usefulness of, 292
Rename dialog box (Word), 30
Rename Section dialog box (PowerPoint), 382
renaming
  Excel tables, 276, 278
  sections, 382
  tabs, 30
  worksheets, 233, 235
repairing documents, 46
Repeat button (Word), 68, 113
Repeat Insertion button (Word), 146
repeating background images, 341, 343
repeating editing, 68, 113, 146
repeating values with fill handle, 257, 259
Replace button (PowerPoint), 418, 420
Replace dialog box (PowerPoint), 418
Replace Font dialog box (PowerPoint), 418, 420
replacing data, 264, 268
replacing fonts, 418
replacing text
  keyboard shortcut for, 76, 130
  options for, 76
  in PowerPoint, 401, 418, 420
  in Word, 75, 78
Research button (PowerPoint), 417
Research button (Word), 80
Research Options dialog box (Word), 81
Research task pane, 79, 270, 412, 415, 417
  Bing decision engine, 270
  Encarta dictionary, 270
  keyboard shortcuts for, 79
  opening, 81, 86
  Thesaurus, 270, 273
  translation tools, 271, 273
researching information, 417
resetting
  Quick Access Toolbar customization, 34
  ribbon customization, 31
resize handle, 276
resizing
  images in Excel, 340, 343
  images in OneNote, 569, 574
  pictures, 170
  program window, 5
  table elements, 153
  tables, 152, 157

Restore Down/Maximize button, 5
restoring data, 270
retaining formatting for reused slides , 378
Reuse Slides task pane, 376
reusing slides, 375, 378
reversing changes, 402
Review tab (OneNote ribbon), 520
Review tab (Word), 14
revising formulas, 286
revisions, clearing before distributing
    document, 219
Rewind 10 Seconds button (OneNote), 588
rewinding audio notes (OneNote), 588
ribbon
    button appearance, xiv
    button separators, 32
    character formatting with, 112
    commands, adding to, 33
    commands no longer on, 27
    commands on, xiii
    customizing, 3, 26-29, 32
    decreasing width of, xiv
    defined, 602
    dynamic nature of, xiv
    expanding, 8, 33, 531
    exporting customizations, 248
    groups, 7
    groups, removing, 27-28, 30
    hiding and displaying, 249
    legacy commands, 27
    location of, 5
    Main Tabs, 246
    minimizing, 8, 59
    moving commands on, 28
    in OneNote, 519
    overview of, xiii, 3
    resetting, 31, 245
    restoring, 249
    tabs, 6, 246-247, 252
    tabs, removing, 27-28
    Tool Tabs, 246
ribbon tabs, 6
    adding groups to, 247
    changing groups on, 247
    changing order of, 246, 252
    customizing, 247, 252
    hiding, 246
    removing, 27-28
    removing groups from, 247
Rich Text Format (RTF)
    defined, 602
    outlines, importing, 374
    saving presentations as, 380
right indent, 120, 126
right-aligning text, 121-122

Right Tab button (Word), 149
ripple slide transition, 479
Rotate button (PowerPoint), 473
rotating effect in slide transitions, 480
rotating handles, 602
rotating shapes, 470, 473
rotating text, 394, 397
row headings, 261, 602
rows, Excel table
    adding and removing, 276
    creating, 275
rows, Word table
    deleting, 153
    inserting, 153
    resizing, 153
    setting properties of, 159
rows, worksheet
    changing height, 237
    changing multiple, 237
    copying, 261
    deleting, 238
    filtering. *See* filters
    formatting, 312
    hidden, and SUM and AVERAGE functions, 355
    hidden, in AGGREGATE function, 358
    hiding, 238
    inserting, 237, 239
    labels, as range names, 283
    labels, hiding, 249
    random, selecting, 354
    selecting, 261
    unhiding, 238
RTF (Rich Text Format) files
    defined, 604
    outlines, importing, 374
    saving presentations as, 380
rule lines (OneNote), 571
Ruler check box, 450
rulers and gridlines
    displaying, 53, 120
    hiding, 56
    markers on, 120
    setting tab stops with, 121
rules
    conditional formatting, 332-338, 596
    filter, defining, 350
rules, validation
    creating, 361
    defined, 607
    entry messages with, 363, 364
    error messages with, 363, 364
    and existing data, 362
    overview of, 361
    requiring numeric values, 362
    setting for multiple cells, 362

specifying minimum and maximum, 364
specifying whole numbers, 364
turning off, 363
validation circles, 362, 366
violations, displaying, 362, 366
running
  Excel 2010, 4, 227, 229
  OneNote 2010, 4, 526
  PowerPoint 2010, 4
  programs, 4
  Word 2010, 4, 10
running heads, xix

S

sample data, creating with RANDBETWEEN
    function, 354
sample templates, 39
Save As command, 41, 229, 231
Save As dialog box (Excel), 231
Save As dialog box (PowerPoint), 380
Save As dialog box (Word), 39, 42-43
Save As page (OneNote Backstage view), 524
Save As Type arrow (Word), 40
Save button (PowerPoint), 391
Save button (Word), 5, 39, 41-42
Save Current Theme dialog box (Excel), 322, 326
saving conditional formatting rules, 333
saving documents, 39, 42
  automatically, 41
  creating folders for, 43
  as earlier format, 45
  folders, creating for, 40
  in new location, 40, 43
  as new version, 41
  keyboard shortcut for, 41
  overwriting when, 41
saving OneNote items, 524, 567
saving presentations, 380
saving themes, 107, 109
saving workbooks, 229-232
scaling
  OneNote images, 568
  printed pages, 208
  slides when printing, 493
scenarios, 602
Screen Clipping button (OneNote), 581
screen clippings from OneNote, 579
  adding to notebooks, 581
  capturing, 581
  defined, 602
  displaying, 582
  options for, 580
  sending to new page, 581

Screen Clipping tool, 569, 581
ScreenTips
  customizing display of, 7
  defined, 602
  displaying, xxv, 7, 10, 18
  feature descriptions, hiding in, 19
  language, specifying, 21
  for OneNote images, 576
  for search results, 74
scroll bar, navigating with, 47
scrolling pages in OneNote, 565
Search box, filtering and, 349, 352
searching. *See also* finding text
  in audio notes, 585
  for clip art images, 452
  filters for, 349, 602
  in Help window, xxviii
  wildcards for, 75, 604
  for Word templates, 39
  in worksheets, 264-266
section breaks
  for columns, 140, 142
  defining, 602
  deleting, 214
  formatting mark for, 214, 216
  inserting, 214, 216
  overview of, 214
Section button (PowerPoint), 381, 383
section groups (OneNote), 555
  adding sections to, 560
  creating, 559
  defined, 602
  opening, 560
section tabs (OneNote), 571
sections (OneNote)
  color, changing, 555
  creating, 555, 559
  defined, 602
  grouping. *See* section groups (OneNote)
  keyboard shortcut for creating, 559
  naming, 554-555
sections (PowerPoint)
  creating in Slide Sorter view, 382
  deleting, 386
  dividing presentations into, 380, 384
  rearranging, 386
sections (Word), changing margins, 208
See Also paragraphs, xx
Select Browse Object button, 48, 50
Select button (PowerPoint), 441
Select button (Word), 142, 153
Select Location In OneNote dialog box, 582-583
Select & Type button (OneNote), 577

selecting
  cells, 260
  outline levels in OneNote, 570
  ranges, 260
  tables, 153
  worksheet columns/rows, 261
selecting all, 142
  keyboard shortcut for, 65
  in placeholders, 441
  with Select button, 214
selecting text, 65, 68, 71, 141, 401
  by line, 103
  deselecting, 66
  in tables, 155
selection area, 65, 602
selections, creating ranges from, 283
Send page (OneNote Backstage view), 524
sentences, selecting, 65
series axis, 463, 608
series, data, 463
  defined, 596
  entering, 256-258
  in Excel tables, 276
  types of, 257
Set Numbering Value dialog box (Word), 134
SET UP paragraphs, xx
Set Up Show dialog box (PowerPoint), 487,
    490, 508
Set Up Slide Show button (PowerPoint), 490
setting a watch, 303-304
setting up automatic slide shows, 491
setting up presentations, 491
setting workbook properties, 229, 231
SGML, 600
Shading button (tables), 163
shading cells in Excel worksheets, 312, 314,
    324, 334
shading cells in Word tables, 162
shading paragraphs, 128
shadow effect, 439
Shape Effects button (PowerPoint), 436
Shape Fill button (PowerPoint), 434
Shape Outline button (PowerPoint), 435
Shapes button (PowerPoint), 470-471
Shapes gallery (PowerPoint), 471
shapes, PowerPoint
  adjusting, 470
  connecting, 478, 596
  copying, 471, 473
  copying formatting, 471, 478
  drawing, 470
  duplicating, 471, 474
  effects, changing, 436
  filling with color, 434

  flipping, 473
  formatting, 434, 471
  grouping, 476
  moving, 471
  outline, changing, 435
  rotating, 470, 473
  setting default formatting, 471
  sizing, 470, 474
  text, adding, 471, 474
Share button (OneNote), 546
Share page (OneNote Backstage view), 523
Share tab (OneNote ribbon), 520
Share This Notebook button (OneNote), 544
Shared Notebook Synchronization dialog box
    (OneNote), 549
SharePoint
  file location, setting default, 20
  sharing notebooks from, 545, 547
sharing OneNote notebooks, 520, 523, 540,
    544, 547
  e-mailing link to, 546
  from SharePoint, 545, 547
  on internal network, 545, 547
  on Web, 544, 547
sharing Word documents, 16
sharing workbooks, 602
Sheet Background dialog box (Excel), 341, 343
sheet tabs, 602
shortcut menus, 602
shortcuts. *See* keyboard shortcuts
Show Hidden Icons button (OneNote), 590
Show/Hide ¶ button (Word), 53, 68, 149
Show Table of Contents button, xxvii
Shrink Font button (Word), 116
shrinking text to fit text box, 395
shutter effect for slide transitions, 479
sidebars, Word
  inserting, 192
  resizing, 193
Side Notes
  docking to desktop, 591
  keeping on top, 592
  keyboard shortcut for, 591
  modifying, 591
  opening, 591
  resizing, 592
side-by-side page display, 55
single-line text boxes, 393
size of placeholders, 393, 439
size of slides, 486
size of text, 438
sizing charts, 467
sizing diagrams, 456, 459
sizing handles, 602

sizing pictures, 170, 450-451
sizing shapes, 470, 474
sizing slides, 488
sizing text boxes, 394
Slicers, 602
slide backgrounds
    applying, 433
    changing , 429, 433
    colors, 426
    formatting placeholder, 436
slide layouts
    applying, 374
    changing existing slides, 372
    diagram, 459
    selecting from New Slide gallery, 371
slide libraries, 379, 602
slide markup
    erasing, 511
    printing, 493
slide masters, 602
slide numbers in footers, 487
Slide Orientation button (PowerPoint), 488
Slide pane
    adding text in, 390
    defined, 602
Slide Show button (PowerPoint), 509-510
Slide Show view (PowerPoint), 485, 491
slide shows
    looping continuously, 490
    starting automatic, 491
slide size, changing, 486
Slide Sorter button (PowerPoint), 381, 482
Slide Sorter view (PowerPoint), 53, 482
    creating sections in, 382
    rearranging slides in, 385
slide timing, 603
slide transitions
    adding to presentations, 479, 483
    animating, 481
    defined, 607
    dynamic content, 480
    exciting, 479
    removing animation, 481
    sounds, adding, 482
    subtle, 479
    timing, 483
    viewing, 482
slides
    adding, 371, 374
    applying color scheme to selected, 426
    changing order within presentations, 386
    charts in, 462
    clip art images in, 448
    copying from other presentations, 375

custom shows, 596
date/time in, 489
deleting, 371, 374
diagrams in, 455-456
displaying full screen, 509
displaying preview, 494
dividing into sections, 384
duplicating, 375, 378
footers, 489
highlighting during presentations, 512
importing outlines, 374, 375
in slide libraries, 379
libraries, 379, 605
masters, 605
moving, 384
notes in. *See* notes pages (PowerPoint)
number, adding, 489
pictures in. *See* images (PowerPoint)
previewing, 494
printing, 492
rearranging, 386
rearranging in Slide Sorter view, 385
renaming sections, 382
reusing, 378
saving as pictures, 448
size, changing, 486
sizing, 488
text, adding, 390
timing, 605
titles, 390, 607
Slides tab, 384, 603
SmartArt button (PowerPoint), 455, 497
SmartArt graphics, 454, 603. *See also* diagrams
SmartArt Styles gallery, 460
smart cut and paste, 69
soft page breaks, 212, 603
software support, xxix
Solver, 603
Sort button (Word), 131, 135, 154
Sort Text dialog box (Word), 137
sorting
    defined, 603
    lists, 131, 135
    tables, 154
    text, 137
sounds, associating with slide transitions, 482
source documents, 603
source file, 600
source programs, 603
spaces, automatic insertion of, 69
spacing
    character, 439
    between columns, 144
    paragraph, 122, 127, 148, 438

Spanish dictionary, 412
sparklines, 603
speaker notes
    adding diagrams, 498
    adding headers/footers, 499
    adding to slides, 495, 497
    preparing, 501
    printing, 492, 499
Special formats (number), 328
special text. *See* text effects
Spelling And Grammar dialog box (Word), 88, 91
Spelling button (PowerPoint), 412, 414
spelling, checking, 42, 269, 272, 412, 415, 520
    adding new words to dictionary, 269, 272
    with AutoCorrect, 88-89
    with shortcut menu, 88, 90
    with Spelling and Grammar dialog box, 88
    turning off, 412
    typos, 63
Spelling dialog box (Excel), 272
Spelling & Grammar button (Word), 88, 91
Split Cells button (Word), 154
splitting cells, 154, 603
splitting documents, 53
spreadsheets. *See* worksheets
square brackets [ ] in formulas, 289, 299
stacking
    text, 394
    windows, 59
Standard Generalized Markup Language
    (SGML), 600
Start button, 4
Start menu, 4
starting
    Excel 2010, 4, 227, 229
    OneNote 2010, 4, 526
    PowerPoint 2010, 4
    programs, 4
    Word 2010, 4, 10
statistics, document, 93
status bar
    AutoCalculate on, 355
    cursor location on, 47
    customizing, 8
    default items on, 9
    defined, 603
Stop button (OneNote), 587, 589
storing OneNote notebooks, 540
strikethrough effect, 439
strings, text, 330-332
Style dialog box (Excel), 316-317
style sets. *See also* Quick Styles
    changing, 100, 104
    displaying list of, 101
    live preview of, 101

styles, picture, 172
styles, table
    adding to Cell Styles gallery, 317
    applying, 316, 323
    clearing, 323
    creating, 316-317, 322-323
    default, changing, 323
    defined, 606
    deleting, 317
    overview of, 316
    previewing, 161, 316
subentries, index, 603
subpages (OneNote)
    collapsing, 559
    creating, 558
    defined, 603
    keyboard shortcut for, 558-559
subpoints, 603
SUBTOTAL function
    and column headers, 356
    and filters, 357
    AVERAGE operation, 356
    compared to AGGREGATE, 357
    COUNT operation, 356
    COUNTA operation, 356
    function_num argument, defined, 355
    ignoring in AGGREGATE function, 358
    introduced, 355
    limitations of, 357
    MAX operation, 356
    MIN operation, 356
    operations, summarized, 356
    PRODUCT operation, 356
    STDEV.P operation, 356
    STDEV.S operation, 356
    SUM operation, 356
    syntax, 355
    VAR.P operation, 356
    VAR.S operation, 356
SUM function, 287, 295, 355
SUMIF function, 297
SUMIFS function, 297, 299-300
summaries, viewing, 221
summarizing data. *See also* formulas, Excel;
    functions
    with AutoCalculate, 355, 359
    in Excel tables, 276, 277
summary formulas and conditional formatting, 336
supplemental dictionaries, 412, 415
switches, 603
Switch Row/Column button (PowerPoint), 469
Switch Windows button (PowerPoint), 425

switching
  documents, 59
  effect of, 321
  files, 53
  presentations, 425
  rows/columns in charts, 469
  themes
  workbooks, 227
Sync Now button (OneNote), 550
synchronizing OneNote notebooks, 543, 549-550
synonyms, 412, 415-416. *See also* Thesaurus
  defined, 79
  displaying more, 416
  searching for, 79, 85

T

tab bar, 233
tab leaders, 603
tab stops. *See also* tabbed lists
  center-aligned, setting, 148
  default, 121
  defined, 603
  deleting, 122
  moving, 122
  precisely placing, 122
  right-aligned, setting, 149
  setting, 121, 122
tabbed lists. *See also* tab stops
  defined, 603
  entering text for, 147
  formatting text in, 148
  overview of, 147
  setting up, 147
Table button (Word), 154, 164
table cells
  borders, 162
  deleting, 153
  inserting, 153
  merging, 153, 155
  setting width of, 159
  shading, 162
  splitting, 154
table columns
  deleting, 153
  inserting, 153
  resizing, 153
  setting width of, 159
Table Properties dialog box (Word), 159
table styles
  adding to Cell Styles gallery, 317
  applying, 316, 323
  clearing, 323
  creating, 316-317, 322-323

  default, changing, 323
  defined, 603
  deleting, 317
  overview of, 316
  previewing, 161, 316
Table Styles gallery, 160-161
tables, Excel
  AutoExpansion, 275
  columns, adding/removing, 276
  converting to range, 277
  creating, 275, 277
  data, adding, 275, 277
  data series in, 276
  defined, 597
  Design contextual tab, 277
  fill color, 324
  filtering. *See* filters
  formatting, 322
  formulas in, 276, 277, 293
  in formulas, 289
  names, adding to formulas, 295
  overview of, 255
  renaming, 276, 278
  resize handle, 276
  rows, adding/removing, 276
  summarizing data in, 276, 277
  table style gallery, 275
  Total row, 276
tables of authorities, 603
tables of contents
  defined, 603
  for Help window, xxvii
tables of figures, 603
tables, Word, 139. *See also* Quick Tables
  aligning text in, 156, 163
  alt text, entering, 159
  banded rows, 161
  borders around cells, 162
  calculations in, 158
  cell width, setting, 159
  centering text in, 155
  column width, setting, 157, 159
  components of, 152
  converting to/from regular text, 152, 156
  creating, 150, 154
  cutting and pasting, 153
  defined, 603
  deleting rows/columns/cells, 153
  drawing, 151
  entering text, 152, 155
  formatting, 160
  formatting text in, 155
  headings, rotating, 163
  inserting rows/columns/cells, 153, 155-156
  margin settings, 159

tables, Word *(continued)*
 merging cells, 153, 155
 move handle, 152, 153, 157
 moving, 153
 navigating in, 152
 overview of, 149
 previewing, 154
 resizing, 153, 157
 row properties, setting, 159
 saving as Quick Tables, 165
 selecting elements in, 153, 155
 shading cells, 162
 size handle, 152, 157
 sorting, 154
 splitting cells, 154
 total rows, 161
 width, setting, 159
Tablet PC, entering notes with, 567
tablet pens, 603
tabs, 6
 customizing, 26
 defined, 603
 keyboard, 56. *See also* nonprinting characters
 Outline, 392, 602
 Overview pane, 392
 removing, 27, 28
 renaming, 30
 Slides, 384, 605
Tag Image File Format (TIFF), 455
tagging documents, 221
tags (OneNote)
 applying, 579
 defined, 603
 keyboard shortcuts for, 579
 overview of, 578
technology certification, xii
templates (OneNote)
 creating pages from, 552, 556
 defined, 603
 previewing, 552
Templates task pane (OneNote), 552, 556
templates (Word)
 defined, 603
 displaying, 16
 previewing, 39
 recently used, 39
 sample, installed with Word, 39
 searching for, 39
text
 aligning, 438
 applying attributes to, 439
 capitalization, changing, 439
 character spacing, changing, 439
 color, changing, 439

 deleting, 403
 in diagrams, 457
 direction, changing, 394
 editing, 404
 entering, 390
 entering/editing in text boxes, 394
 finding, 418
 finding/replacing, 420
 formatting effects, 444
 formatting in columns, 140
 line spacing, changing, 438
 in numbers, 329, 332
 outside of placeholders, 393
 placeholders for, 393
 promoting/demoting, 392
 replacing, 418
 rotating, 394, 397
 selecting all in placeholder, 441
 in shapes, 471, 474
 shrinking to fit text box, 395
 size, changing, 438
 sizing to fit placeholder, 406
 stacking, 394
 in templates, 437
 wrapping in text boxes, 395
Text Box button, 393, 396, 451, 474
text boxes, 393
 adding borders, 395, 398
 adding to slides, 451
 changing effect, 436
 changing outline, 435
 copying, 394
 creating, 400
 default font,changing, 400
 defined, 603
 deselecting, 395
 drawing, 196
 entering/editing text, 394
 filling with color, 434
 inserting, 191
 linking, 196
 manipulating, 394
 moving, 394, 397
 multi-line, 393
 overview of, 183
 positioning, 196
 replacing text in, 191
 saving to Quick Parts Gallery, 194
 sidebars, inserting, 192
 sidebars, resizing, 193
 single-line, 393
 sizing, 394
 wrapping text within, 395
text boxes (OneNote). *See* note containers
  (OneNote)

text colors, 426
Text Direction button (Word), 163
text effects
    applying, 101, 105, 116
    live preview of, 105
Text Effects button (Word), 101, 105
text, entering, 41, 64
    in OneNote, 565, 572
    on Outline tab, 390
    in Slide pane, 390
    in text boxes, 394
text, hiding, 53
Text Highlight Color arrow (Word), 34
Text Highlight Color button (Word), 117
Text Pane button (PowerPoint), 457
text, selecting, 65, 68, 71, 141, 401
    by line, 103
    deselecting, 66
    in tables, 155
text size
    changing, 111, 116, 313
    incrementing, 116
    keyboard shortcuts for adjusting, 116
text strings, quotation marks in, 330, 332
text wrapping
    defined, 604
    in text boxes, 395
    around WordArt, 199
textured backgrounds, 178, 430
Theme Colors button (Word), 107
theme colors (Word)
    changing, 107, 117
    previewing effects of, 13
Theme Fonts button (Word), 108
Themes button (Word), 13, 106-107
themes (Excel)
    active, and available colors, 321
    applying, 320
    changing, 322, 326
    colors in palette, 321
    creating, 322
    default, 320
    defined, 320, 604
    in other Office programs, 322
    Office theme, 320
    switching, effect of, 321
Themes gallery, 424
themes (PowerPoint), 423
    applying different, 425
    live previews of, 424
    switching , 424
themes (Word)
    applying, 106, 107
    color set, changing, 108

font set, changing, 109
from Microsoft Office Online Web site, 107
gallery of, 13
live preview of, 107
mixing and matching, 107
overview of, 106
saving, 107, 109
Thesaurus, 270, 273, 412, 416
    finding synonyms in, 85
    overview of, 79
Thesaurus button (PowerPoint), 415
Thesaurus button (Word), 79, 85
three-dimensional borders, 128
three-dimensional references, 604
thumb tabs, xix
thumbnails, 384, 605
    defined, 604
    galleries of, 10
tick-mark labels in charts, 463, 604
TIFF file format, 455
time
    in footers, 487
    formatting cells for, 319
    in OneNote, inserting, 584
time of recalculation, using NOW() function to
        display, 287
timing, slide, 605
Tip paragraphs, xx
title bars, 5, 604
titles
    document, 220
    slide, 390
Toolbar, Mini, 65, 312, 439, 440
    character formatting with, 111
    defined, 600
    hiding, 18
toolbar, navigation, 509-510
Toolbar, Quick Access
    buttons, adding, 31-32, 244, 251
    buttons, positioning, 245
    customizing, 5, 32, 521
    defined, 604
    exporting customizations, 245
    improving efficiency with, 6
    legacy commands, adding, 7
    location, 244
    moving, 5
    overview of, 3
    printing from, 34
    removing buttons, 245
    resetting, 32-34, 245
    specifying for active document, 33

tools, data entry
    AutoComplete, 257
    AutoFill, 256
    AutoFill Options button, 258, 260
    FillSeries, 256
    overview, 255
    Pick From Drop-Down List, 257, 259
tools, formatting. *See* formatting
tools, research, 270. *See also* Research task pane
Top 10 AutoFilter dialog box (Excel), 349, 352
Top 10 filter, 349
total rows in tables, 161, 276
totals, viewing with AutoCalculate, 355, 359
tracer arrows, 301-302, 304, 306
    defined, 604
    hiding, 302, 305-306
tracing dependents to identify errors, 302
tracing precedents to identify errors, 301, 304
transitions
    adding to presentations, 479, 483
    animating, 481
    dynamic content, 480
    exciting, 479
    removing animation, 481
    sounds, adding, 482
    subtle, 479
    timing, 483
    viewing, 482
Translate button (PowerPoint), 417
Translate button (Word), 82, 86
translating text, 271, 273, 417
    entire documents, 84
    in Excel, 271
    in OneNote, 520
    options for, 86
    in Word, 82, 86
Translation Language Options dialog box
        (Word), 84
transparencies, 486
transposing data in paste operations, 263
trendlines, 604
troubleshooting formulas, 286
Troubleshooting paragraphs, xx
Trust Center dialog box (Word), 25
Trust Center (Word), 24-25
trusted locations, setting, 25
turning effect in slide transitions, 479
two monitors, 508
typos. *See* spelling, checking

U

UNC addresses, 604
Underline button (Word), 113
underlining text, 113, 439
undo actions, changing default number of, 403
Undo button, 5, 68, 70, 270, 353, 402, 404
undocking OneNote, 533
undoing editing
    keyboard shortcut for, 67, 402
    procedure for, 68, 70, 270, 402
Unfiled Notes section (OneNote), 528, 604
ungrouping shapes, 478
Unhide dialog box (Excel), 234, 236
unhiding rows/columns, 238
unique values
    displaying, 358, 359
    and headers, 359, 360
updating charts automatically, 468
updating pictures automatically, 449
uppercase. *See* case
user input in exercises, xx
user input, validating. *See* validation rules
user interface. *See also* ribbon
    color scheme, changing, 18
    common to Office programs, 3
    customizing, 241
    elements, navigating, 48
user interface objects in text, xx
user name
    AutoText for, changing, 190
    common to Office programs, 3
    entering, 10
    setting, 19

V

validation circles
    displaying, 362, 366
    hiding, 363, 366
validation rules
    creating, 361
    defined, 604
    entry messages with, 363-364
    error messages with, 363-364
    and existing data, 362
    minimum and maximum, specifying, 364
    overview of, 361

requiring numeric values, 362
setting for multiple cells, 362
turning off, 363
validation circles, 362-363, 366
violations, displaying, 362, 366
whole numbers, specifying, 364
value axes in charts, 463, 608
values. *See also* numbers
adding together, 286
average, viewing with AutoCalculate, 355, 359
comparing , 334-337
count, viewing with AutoCalculate, 355, 359
filtering for highest or lowest, 349, 353
ignoring in calculations, 357
maximum and minimum, 281, 287
monitoring, 303, 304
replacing, 264
searching for, 264
searching in, 266
sum of, 286
testing, 332-338
total, viewing with AutoCalculate, 355, 359
unique, displaying, 358-359
vertical scroll bar, 47
video notes (OneNote)
appearance of, 586
manipulating video in, 585
pausing, 589
playing, 588
recording, 585, 588
rewinding, 588
searchability, activating, 585
View Ruler button (Word), 120
View Shortcuts toolbar, 9, 52, 604
View Sync Status button (OneNote), 549
View tab (Excel), 242
View tab (OneNote), 521
View tab (Word), 14, 52
Viewer, Microsoft PowerPoint, 600
viewing color schemes, 426
viewing workbook properties, 229
views, Normal
creating slide sections in, 384
defined, 601
in PowerPoint, 53
views, Notes Page, 53, 494, 602
views, Reading, 53, 482, 490
views, Slide Sorter, 53, 482
creating sections in, 382
defined, 605
rearranging slides in, 385
views, Web Layout, 52, 607
visible cells, summarizing, 355, 357
volatile functions, 354

W

watch
defined, 604
deleting, 303, 307
setting, 303-304
Watch Window
defined, 303
deleting a watch, 303, 307
setting a watch, 303, 304
watermarks as background images, 341
Web App (OneNote), 593
Web Apps (Office), xi
Web browsers
defined, 595
previewing documents in, 52, 57
Web Layout button, 57
Web Layout view (Word), 52
Web notes (OneNote), 579
capturing, 583
creating, 583
default location for, 581
options for, 580
Web page banner presentations, 486, 488
Web pages
converting Word documents into, 23
sending to OneNote notebooks, 579
what-if analysis, 604
white space between Word pages, hiding, 54
wide margins, 210, 216
widows
defined, 212, 604
setting options for, 212, 215
width, column, 237
wildcards in searches, 75, 604
Windows Live Translator, 84
Windows logo key, 604
Windows Photo Viewer, 576
windows, stacking, 59
windows, workbook
arranging multiple, 243, 251
cascading, 243, 251
wipe transition effect, 479
Word 97-2003, saving documents as, 21
Word 2010. *See also* Word documents
compatibility with earlier versions, 44
file formats, 44
first time starting, 10
handouts, creating, 501
Help window, opening, xxvi
OneNote pages, sending to, 524
online version, xi
starting, 4, 10
views in, 52

word choice, researching, 270
word count, 93
Word Count button (Word), 93
Word Count dialog box (Word), 93
Word documents. *See also* saving documents
  blank, creating, 41
  blank, opening, 38
  closing, 48, 51
  compatibility with earlier versions, 44
  creating, 38-41
  default format, setting, 20
  formatting in columns, 141. *See also* columns,
    document
  full-screen display, 52, 56
  inserting in other documents, 97
  location, specifying, 23
  maximizing, 59
  moving to top, 55
  navigating, 47, 56-57, 71
  opening, 46, 48
  printing with default settings, 34
  read-only, opening as, 46
  recently opened, 16, 46
  renaming when saving, 43
  repairing, 46
  scrolling through, 47, 50
  selecting, 65
  sharing, 16
  side-by-side display, 55
  splitting into two panes, 53
  switching between, 53, 59
  translating, 84
  viewing multiple, 59
  zooming in/out, 53
Word Help button, 598
Word Options dialog box (Word), 17, 19
  AutoRecover settings, 41
  Recent page options, changing, 16
Word outlines, importing to PowerPoint, 374
Word tables, 139. *See also* Quick Tables
  aligning text in, 156, 163
  alt text, entering, 159
  banded rows, 161
  borders around cells, 162
  calculations in, 158
  cell width, setting, 159
  centering text in, 155
  column width, setting, 157, 159
  components of, 152
  converting to/from regular text, 152, 156
  creating, 150, 154
  cutting and pasting, 153
  defined, 606
  deleting rows/columns/cells, 153
  drawing, 151

  entering text, 152, 155
  formatting, 160
  formatting text in, 155
  headings, rotating, 163
  inserting rows/columns/cells, 153, 155-156
  margin settings, 159
  merging cells, 153, 155
  move handle, 152, 153, 157
  moving, 153
  navigating in, 152
  overview of, 149
  previewing, 154
  resizing, 153, 157
  row properties, setting, 159
  saving as Quick Tables, 165
  selecting elements in, 153, 155
  shading cells, 162
  size handle, 152, 157
  sorting, 154
  splitting cells, 154
  total rows, 161
  width, setting, 159
word wrap, 604
WordArt button, 198
WordArt objects
  centering, 198
  converting text into, 197
  defined, 604
  inserting, 197, 198
  overview of, 197
  positioning, 198
  starting new lines in, 198
  styles, applying, 200
  text wrapping, 199
words
  adding to dictionary, 269, 272
  selecting, 65, 68
workbooks
  arranging multiple windows, 243, 251
  copying worksheets, 233, 235
  creating, 228, 230
  default, 228
  defined, 604
  display font, changing, 313, 315
  displaying side by side, 243
  Document Properties panel, 229
  filtering ranges, 284
  properties, 229-232
  saving, 229, 232
  switching between, 227, 243, 251
  themes. *See* themes, Excel
worksheet cells. *See also* ranges
  absolute references, 294, 307, 595
  active, 260-261, 349
  aligning, 318

borders, 312, 314
contiguous, in formulas, 290
copying, 258, 261
defined, 596
deleting, 238, 240
deleting contents/formatting of, 311
entering data in, 256, 258
filtering. *See* filters, Excel
finding sum of, 286
formatting, copying, 258, 260
individual, selecting, 260
inserting, 238, 240
monitoring values in, 303, 304
moving, 238, 240
moving to, 260
noncontiguous, adding to formulas, 290
noncontiguous, formatting, 314
number formatting in, 319
pasting formulas in, 291
references, 294-295, 301, 596
shading, 312-314, 324
splitting, 606
visible, summarizing, 355, 357
worksheet columns
changing multiple, 237
copying, 261
deleting, 238
error code, 301
filtering. *See* filters
formatting, 312
hiding, 238-239
inserting, 237, 239
labels, and filtering, 349
labels, as range names, 283
labels, hiding, 249
moving, 261
selecting, 261
unhiding, 238
width, changing, 237
width errors, 301
worksheets, Excel
backgrounds, 341-344
columns. *See* columns, worksheet
copying, 233, 235
creating, 233
defined, 604
deleting, 234, 236
displaying, 233
filtering. *See* filters
hiding, 234, 235
images, adding, 339, 342
purpose of, 233

renaming, 233, 235
reordering, 234-235
rows. *See* rows, worksheet
searching, 264
tab color, changing, 234-235
unhiding, 234, 236
workspaces, 604
Wrap Text button (Word), 199
wrapping text
defined, 604
in text boxes, 395
around WordArt, 199

X

XML data, removing before distributing
document, 222
XML (Extensible Markup Language), 597, 604
XML file formats, 44
XPS format
defined, 608
printing documents to, 223

Y

y-axis, 463

Z

zeros in number formatting, 329
Zoom button (Word), 9, 53, 55, 56, 209
Zoom control, 242
Zoom dialog box (Excel), 242, 250
Zoom dialog box (Word), 55, 56, 209
Zoom In button (PowerPoint), 494
Zoom In button (Word), 56
Zoom Level button (Word), 176, 185
Zoom Out button (Word), 56, 102, 191
Zoom Slider, 9, 385
Zoom To Page button (PowerPoint), 494
Zoom To Selection button (Excel), 242, 249
zooming effect in slide transitions, 479
zooming in/out, 249
adjusting, 53, 102
displaying multiple pages, 55, 209
to full page, 176
overview of, 242
by percentage, 56
specific zoom level, 242

About the Authors

Joyce Cox

Joyce has 30 years' experience in the development of training materials about technical subjects for non-technical audiences, and is the author of dozens of books about Office and Windows technologies. She is the Vice President of Online Training Solutions, Inc. (OTSI).

As President of and principal author for Online Press, she developed the *Quick Course* series of computer training books for beginning and intermediate adult learners. She was also the first managing editor of Microsoft Press, an editor for Sybex, and an editor for the University of California.

Joan Preppernau

Joan has worked in the training and certification industry for 13 years. As President of OTSI, Joan is responsible for guiding the translation of technical information and requirements into useful, relevant, and measurable training and certification tools.

Joan is a Microsoft Office Master (MOM), a Microsoft Certified Application Specialist (MCAS), a Microsoft Certified Technology Specialist (MCTS), a Microsoft Certified Trainer (MCT), and the author of more than two dozen books about Windows and Office (for Windows and Mac).

Curtis Frye

Curtis Frye is a writer, speaker, and performer living in Portland, Oregon. He is the sole or lead author of more than 20 books, including *Microsoft Excel 2010 Plain & Simple*, *Microsoft Access 2010 Plain & Simple*, and *Excel 2007 Pocket Guide*. In addition to his writing, Curt presents keynote addresses on Excel and motivational topics.

The Team

This book would not exist without the support of these hard-working members of the OTSI publishing team:

- Kathleen Atkins
- Jan Bednarczuk
- Jenny Moss Benson
- Rob Carr
- Susie Carr
- Jeanne Craver
- Patty Gardner
- Elizabeth Hansford
- Kathy Krause
- Marlene Lambert
- Patty Masserman
- Brianna Morgan
- Jaime Odell
- Jean Trenary
- Liv Trenary
- Elisabeth Van Every

We are especially thankful to the support staff at home who make it possible for our team members to devote their time and attention to these projects.

Devon Musgrave provided invaluable support on behalf of Microsoft Learning.

Online Training Solutions, Inc. (OTSI)

OTSI specializes in the design, creation, and production of Office and Windows training products for information workers and home computer users. For more information about OTSI, visit:

www.otsi.com

How To Download Your eBook

Thank you for purchasing this Microsoft Press® title. Your companion PDF eBook is ready to download from O'Reilly Media, official distributor of Microsoft Press titles.

To download your eBook, go to

http://go.microsoft.com/FWLink/?Linkid=224345

and follow the instructions.

Please note: You will be asked to create a free online account and enter the access code below.

Your access code:

PGJPJZN

Microsoft® Office Home & Student 2010
Step by Step

Your PDF eBook allows you to:

- Search the full text
- Print
- Copy and paste

Best yet, you will be notified about free updates to your eBook.

If you ever lose your eBook file, you can download it again just by logging in to your account.

Need help? Please contact:
mspbooksupport@oreilly.com
or call 800-889-8969.